Frank Holl

Emerging from the Shadows

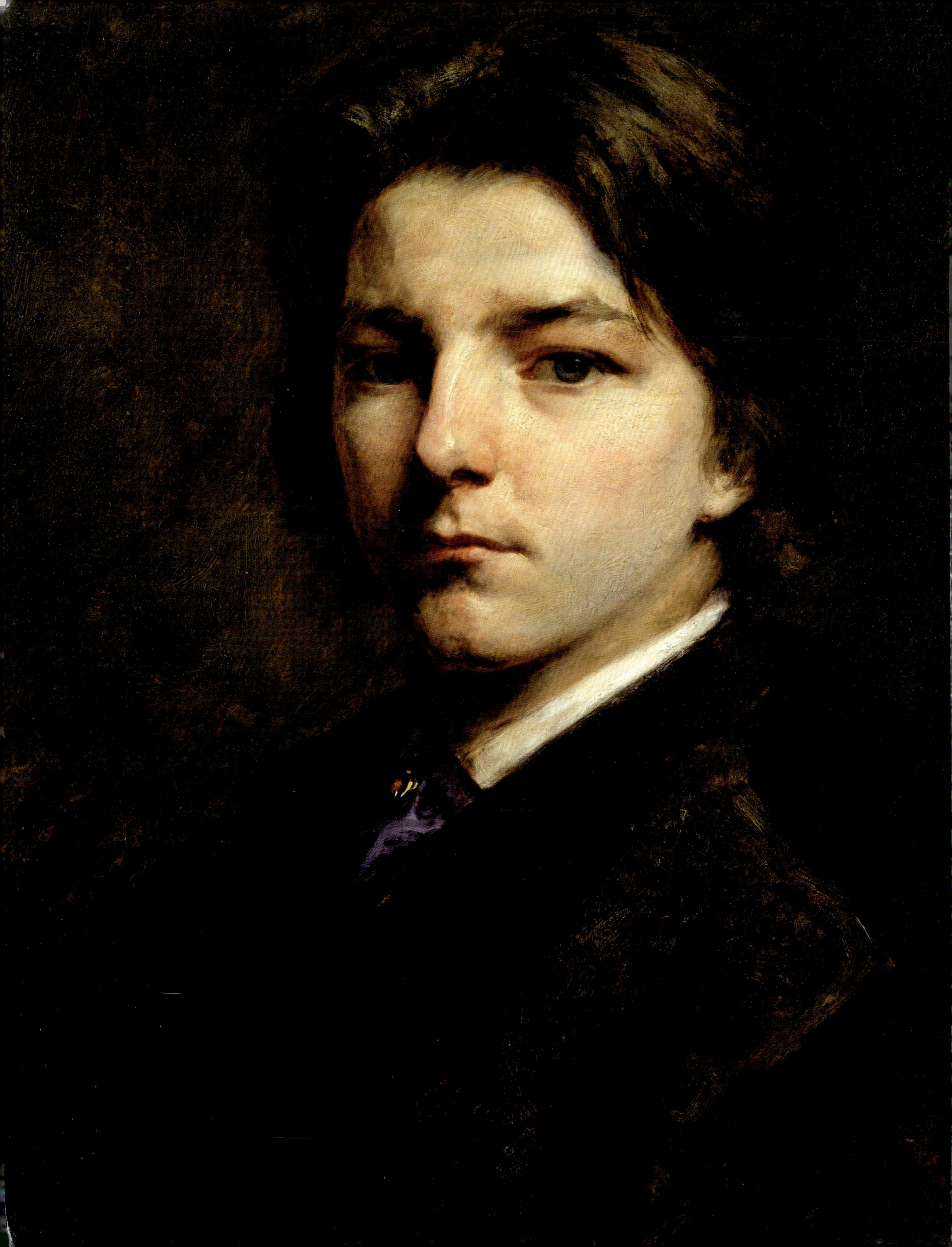

Frank Holl
Emerging from the Shadows

Mark Bills

with contributions by
Peter Funnell
Barbara Bryant
Jane Sellars
Sophie Gilmartin
Philip McEvansoneya
Mary McMahon
Carol Blackett-Ord

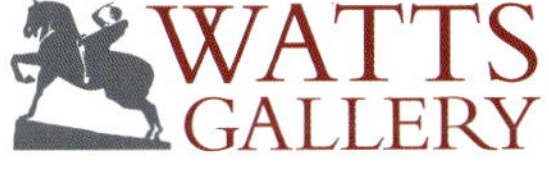

PWP

First published by Philip Wilson Publishers in association with Watts Gallery on the occasion of the exhibition Frank Holl: Emerging from the Shadows, Watts Gallery, 18 June – 3 November 2013 Mercer Art Gallery, Harrogate: 23 Nov 2013 – 30 March 2014

Philip Wilson Publishers
an imprint of I.B.Tauris & Co Ltd
6 Salem Road
London W2 4BU
www.philip-wilson.co.uk

ISBN 978-1-78130-016-9

Distributed in the United States and Canada exclusively by Palgrave Macmillan
175 Fifth Avenue, New York NY 10010

Copy edited by Colin Grant

Designed by Ian Ross www.ianrossdesigner.com
Printed in Italy by Printer Trento

Watts Gallery Registered Charity No. 313612

Frontispiece: Frank Holl, *Self-Portrait*, 1863, oil on canvas.
© National Portrait Gallery, London

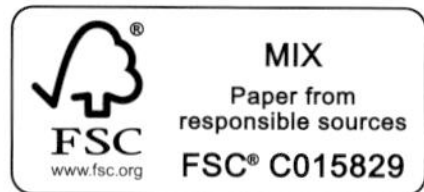

Contents

Acknowledgements

The Watts Gallery is most grateful to all those who have contributed to the publication and exhibition *Frank Holl: Emerging from the Shadows*.

Mark Bills
Barbara Bryant
Peter Funnell
Sophie Gilmartin
Jane Sellars
Carol Blackett-Ord
Colin Grant
Dr Philip McEvansoneya
Staff at Philip Wilson Publishers
David Hawkins
Anne Jackson
Mary McMahon
Jennifer Roberts
Desna Greenhow
Staff at Watts Gallery
Trustees of the Watts Gallery
National Portrait Gallery
Sandy Nairne
Tarnya Cooper
Tim Moreton
David McNeff
Robin Francis and his colleagues in the Heinz Archive and Library
Mercer Art Gallery
Crown Fine Art
Dr Julia Winterson
Andrew Saint
Christopher Marsden
Julius Bryant
Valerie Johnson, The National Archives
Pat Hardy, Museum of London
Philippa Martin, Government Art Collection
Emma Shepley and Laura Sleath, Royal College of Physicians

Foreword

Watts Gallery seeks to present jewel-like exhibitions which focus on an aspect of nineteenth-century art, bringing new insight into the period and exploring the context of the Watts collection. This exhibition of Frank Holl is a poignant retrospective of another leading portraitist of the nineteenth century. It demonstrates why, in Christopher Wood's words, 'Holl was one of the most popular, and one of the best of all Victorian portrait painters'. It is a tragedy that Holl died so young at the age of forty-three, as with a longer life his reputation and legacy would be far greater. Once again, through both the exhibition and the catalogue, Watts Gallery will shine a light on a little-known artist to offer visitors and scholars an opportunity to revise their views.

Holl was Watts's preferred choice of artist for the portrait commissions that he was unable to undertake himself. In a letter held in the National Art Library at the V&A, Watts wrote to Holl's widow saying 'I beg you to believe that no-one had greater admiration for your husband's genius and no-one can sympathise more truly with you in your domestic bereavement'. It will be fascinating for visitors to Watts Gallery to view Holl through the eyes of Watts and discover whether they sympathise with the huge reverence and admiration felt towards this artist by his contemporaries. This exhibition will also provide a contextual insight into Watts's beliefs on portraiture and the subject of social need. The essays in this catalogue draw together compelling new research by the authors, who each bring significant insight and expertise to the subject of this important artist. Furthermore, this new research is brought together for the first time in celebration of the first retrospective of Holl's life and work since the Royal Academy exhibition on his death.

This is the final exhibition which has been curated, researched and produced by Watts Gallery's fifth Curator, Mark Bills. During his seven-year tenure at Watts Gallery he has restored the national interest in Watts through his innovative and exploratory exhibitions. The Trustees of Watts Gallery are most grateful for his considerable contribution to the understanding and appreciation of G.F. Watts in the context of the nineteenth century.

Watts Gallery is very appreciative of the support and assistance of the National Portrait Gallery in mounting this exhibition and it is an honour that the Director, Sandy Nairne CBE, has agreed to open it.

Perdita Hunt
Director of Watts Gallery

Preface

The Watts Gallery in Compton, Surrey, and the Mercer Art Gallery in Harrogate, North Yorkshire, may at first sight seem unlikely partners, but over the last seven years we have worked together on a number of exhibitions. What unites us is a focus on nineteenth century art, and a desire to curate exhibitions that bring new insights into the great British artists of the period.

We got to know curator Mark Bills in his pre-Watts days in 2007, when we worked together, with Vivien Knight, on the book and exhibition *William Powell Frith: Painting the Victorian Age*. This was the first show for over fifty years of Frith, a Yorkshire-born exact contemporary of Watts. We followed this up in 2008 by taking the Watts Gallery touring show, *Victorian Artists in Photographs: The World of G.F. Watts*, which we hung alongside some of the Victorian masterpieces in our own collection. Then in 2009 we played host to *G.F. Watts: Victorian Visionary*, the wonderful exhibition of a large part of the Watts Gallery collection which showed only in London and Harrogate when the Watts Gallery was closed for restoration.

I have admired Frank Holl's paintings ever since I worked at the Walker Art Gallery in Liverpool which has in its collection Holl's *The Fisherman's Home*. Julian Treuherz's exhibition of Victorian social-realist art, *Hard Times*, at Manchester City Art Gallery in 1987, told us more about Holl than we had ever known before, but it is not until now, thanks to Mark Bills, that Holl has become the sole subject of an exhibition and catalogue that also look at the portraits he painted in the latter part of his career. The Mercer Art Gallery's visitors will enjoy the opportunity to discover the work of an artist who is so little known today, but who in his lifetime was revered by both gallery goers and his fellow artists.

Jane Sellars
Curator of Art
The Mercer Art Gallery
Harrogate Borough Council

Lenders, Sponsors and Donors

Lenders
Ashmolean Museum, University of Oxford
Geffrye Museum, London
Government Art Collection
Guildhall Art Gallery, City of London
The McManus, Dundee Art Galleries and Museum
Museum of London
National Portrait Gallery, London
The New Art Gallery Walsall
Royal Albert Memorial Museum, Exeter
Royal Collection
Royal College of Physicians
Royal Holloway, University of London
Museums Sheffield
Southampton City Art Gallery
Tate, London
Victoria and Albert Museum
Walker Art Gallery, National Museums Liverpool

Exhibition and Catalogue Sponsors
The Deborah Loeb Brice Foundation
The Paul Mellon Centre for Studies in British Art
The Marc Fitch Fund
Robert Freidus and Ellie Packer

Watts Gallery is deeply grateful to all its donors. These benefactors have provided particularly generous support
Art Fund
David Pike
The de Laszlo Foundation
Guildford Borough Council
The Robert Gavron Charitable Trust
Hamish Dewar Ltd
Peter Harrison Foundation
The John Ellerman Foundation
The Finnis Scott Foundation
James and Clare Kirkman
The Restoration Fund
The Wolfson Foundation
The Mercers' Company
KPMG Foundation
The Pilgrim Trust
Miklos and Sally Salamon
Surrey Hills LEADER
The Hazelhurst Trust
The Anson Charitable Trust
The Billmeir Charitable Trust
The Monument Trust
Surrey County Council
Man Charitable Trust
The Henry Moore Foundation
John Lewis OBE
Wates Foundation
John Beale
The Michael Marks Charitable Trust
The Rothschild Foundation
Oxford Exhibition Services
The Michael Varah Memorial Fund
Spencer Wills Trust
And those who wish to remain anonymous

Watts Gallery Trust also acknowledges the generous support of all its Patrons, Friends and Volunteers.

Chronology

1845 Francis Montague Holl born on 4 July at 7 St James's Terrace, Camden Town, London, second child and eldest son of the engraver Francis Holl (1815–1884) and Alicia, née Dixon (1820–1899); grandson of William Holl the elder, engraver (1771–1838); and nephew of William Holl the younger, engraver (1807–1871)

1854–8 Attends Mr Rae's school, Hampstead

1858–60 Attends University College School, wins prizes for Latin, geography and mathematics, and receives his first painting commissions

1860 Becomes a 'Probationer in the Royal Academy, where, at the next term being admitted as a Student, he soon won silver and gold medals and a scholarship' (*Athenaeum*, 4 August 1888, p. 168)

1862 Wins the R.A. silver medal for drawing from the antique

c.1862–3 Produces his first oil painting, *Mother and Child*, which is exhibited in a London gallery and sold for £40

1863 R.A. silver medal for drawing from life and gold medal for the historical painting, *Abraham about to Sacrifice Isaac*, for which he receives £50 over two years

Travels to Barmouth, the first of many visits to Wales

1864 First showing at the R.A. Summer Exhibition, where he exhibits every year, except 1875, until his death

Visits Betws-y-Coed

R.A.: *Turned out of Church* (526); *A Portrait* (145)

1865 British Institution: *Turned out of Church* (147), 75 gns; *The Mountain Child* (219), 15 gns

Society of British Artists: *Knitting* (343), £36 15s

R.A.: *A Fern Gatherer* (612), bought for 50 gns by the Art Union

1866 Visits Italy with Frank Topham

Society of British Artists: *'Is it a Purse or a Coffin?'* (112), £26 5s; *A Boulogne Fish Child* (241), £47 5s

R.A.: *The Ordeal* (421)

1867 May: Married Annie Laura Davidson (1842–1931), daughter of Charles Davidson (1824–1902), the landscape painter

They spend six months on honeymoon at Beddgelert, Wales, before moving to 30 Gloucester Road, London

R.A.: *Convalescent* (232); *Faces in the Fire* (519)

1868 July: Visit to Whitby

10 December: awarded the R.A. two years' Travelling Studentship in Painting for his work, *'The Lord gave and the Lord hath taken away, Blessed be the Name of the Lord'*

Society of British Artists: *'There's Many a Slip'* (154), £57 15s

R.A.: *Francis Holl, Esq.* (767)

1869 Daughter Ada Mabel, author of Holl's biography, born (d. 1965)

*c.*May: Begins his travel scholarship and visits Paris. Sees the Louvre and Versailles and makes colour sketches of Titian's *Entombment* (*c.*1520). Travels through Basel and Lucerne on his way to Italy, then through Milan to Venice, where he resigns the scholarship. Returns home via Verona, Munich, Mayence and Cologne. His final stopping place is Antwerp, where he sees the glories of Northern painting, including Rubens's *The Descent from the Cross* (1612–14) in Antwerp Cathedral

August: Arrives in London at St Katherine's dock

R.A.: *'The Lord gave and the Lord hath taken away, Blessed be the Name of the Lord'* (210)

1870 June: Visits Cullercoats, Northumberland, and begins *No Tidings from the Sea* for Queen Victoria

R.A.: *'Better is a dinner of herbs where love is than a stalled ox and hatred therewith'* (42)

Society of British Artists Winter Exhibition: *Up a Court at Whitby* (a sketch, 241), £31 10s

1871 Daughter Olive Gertrude born (d. 1930)

R.A.: *No Tidings from the Sea* (595); *Winter* (1086)

1872 Begins contributions to *The Graphic* illustrated paper with 'At a Railway Station – A Study', 10 February 1872

R.A.: *A Milkmaid* (435); *I am the Resurrection and the Life* (954)

1873 R.A.: *Leaving Home* (611)

1874 Illustrates Trollope's *Phineas Redux* in *The Graphic*

Daughter Madoline (Nina) born (d. 1964)

Discusses turning to portraiture with Henry Weigall, the portrait painter

At Oban in Scotland with John Pettie, Tom Graham and C.E. Johnson

R.A.: *Deserted* (487)

1875 Spends year mainly on black and white work, apart from painting replicas, and does not exhibit anything at the Royal Academy

1876 At the American Centennial Exhibition *'The Lord gave …'* won a medal

Visits Wales with Weedon Grossmith

R.A.: *Her Firstborn* (286)

1877 March: Moves to 4 Camden Square, London

R.A.: *Going Home: 'Some of these return no more; others again return and find all things strange'* (585)

Tooth's Winter Exhibition: *Gone*

1878 Exhibits a commissioned portrait for the first time 19 June: Elected an Associate of the Royal Academy

R.A.: *Newgate, Committed for Trial* (423); *A Portrait* (599)

1879 Exhibits portrait of Samuel Cousins to great acclaim Travels to Wales, meeting up with Benjamin Williams Leader, the landscape artist, and others

13 April: A son born but dies at birth

R.A.: *The Gifts of the Fairies* (160); *Samuel Cousins, Esq., R.A.* (189); *Signor Piatti* (579); *The Daughter of the House* (950); *Absconded* (1385)

1880 Begins exhibiting portraits at the Grosvenor Gallery

R.A.: *S. Adams Beck, Esq.* (123); *Major George Graham, Registrar-General of England, 1842–1879. Presentation Portrait, etc.* (302); *Ordered to the Front* (366); *Rev. C.W. Payne Crawford* (413); *Rupert Alfred Kettle, Esq., Judge of the County Courts of Worcestershire. Presentation Portrait* (583)

Grosvenor Gallery: *Portrait of H.J. Bushey Esq.* (134)

1881 Autumn: Visits Holland and Belgium with the Pawle family

Commissions Richard Norman Shaw to design and build a studio in the fashionable artist area of Hampstead at 6 Fitzjohn's Avenue, a few doors away from his friend John Pettie

R.A.: *Major General Sir Henry Rawlinson, K.C.B., Late Envoy and Minister to the Court of Persia* (82); *The Rev. Edward Hartopp Cradock, D.D., Principal of Brasenose College, Oxford. Presentation Portrait* (253); *'Home again!'* (401); *Stephen G. Holland, Esq.* (451); *Lord de Tabley, Rt. Worshipful Provincial Grand Master of Cheshire. Presentation Portrait* (458)

Grosvenor Gallery: *T.H. Farre, Esq., Secretary to the Board of Trade* (77); *Viscount Holmesdale, M.P.* (150)

1882 Becomes a founder-member of the Society of Painter-Etchers, but only ever exhibits one etching, a portrait of Heywood Hardy, in the same year

Now at the height of his career, producing 24 portraits and 5 subject works this year.

May: Daughter Phyllis born (d. 1956)

October: Moves into his new house, The Three Gables, at 6 Fitzjohn's Avenue (demolished *c.*1965)

R.A.: *Robert Few, Esq. Painted for Marlborough College* (150); *Lieut. General Sir Frederick Sleigh Roberts, Bart., V.C., G.C.B., C.L.E. Painted for Her Majesty the Queen* (223); *The Late Captain Alexander Mitchell Sim. Painted for the Surrey Commercial Dock Company, etc.* (260); *Vice-Chancellor Sir James Bacon* (269); *Rt. Hon. Sir Arthur Hobhouse, Q.C., K.C., S.L.* (466); *Viscount Cranbrook, G.C.S.L.* (1456); *Sir Charles John Herries, K.C.B. Presentation Portrait, etc.* (1470)

Grosvenor Gallery: *J. Jones Esq., M.P.* (7); *Miss Tonks* (87); *E.H. Pember Esq., Q.C.* (125)

1883 26 March: Elected an Associate of the Society for the Painters of Watercolours (Old Watercolour Society)

29 March: Meeting of the R.A., elected Royal Academician

Paints HRH The Duke of Cambridge, his first royal portrait commission

Old Watercolour Society: *Leaving Home* (the only work he exhibited at the society)

Munich International Art Exhibition: *Das letzte Kleinod (The Last Gem)* (910)

R.A.: *General Lord Wolseley, G.C.B., G.C.M.G.* (240); *H.R.H. The Duke of Cambridge, K.G., etc.* (250); *Rt. Hon. John Bright, M.P. Presentation Portrait, etc.* (278); *Owen Roberts, Esq., M.A., F.S.A., Clerk to the Worshipful Company of Clothworkers* (396); *Rev. T.T. Carter, M.A., Hon. Canon of Christchurch, Oxford, etc. Presentation Portrait* (442); *Lord Winmarleigh. Painted for the Board Room, Royal Albert Asylum, Lancaster* (514); *General Sir Lintorn A. Simmons, G.C.B., Colonel Commandant Royal Engineers. Painted for the Royal Engineers* (885); *William Agnew, Esq., M.P.* (1433)

Grosvenor Gallery: *R. Jasper More, Esq.* (11); *John Tenniel, Esq.* (89); *J. Mullholland, Esq., M.P.* (170); *Ernest Hart, Esq.* (180)

1884 Visits Italy again, meeting up with Topham, John MacWhirter and Colin Hunter; invited to contribute a self-portrait to the Uffizi collection of artists' self-portraits, but dies before it is produced

R.A.: *'Did you ever kill anybody, Father?'* (67); *E.H. Corbutt, Esq., M.P.* (155); *Rev. W. Haig Brown, LL.D., Head Master of Charterhouse School* (285); *H.R.H. the Prince of Wales, K.G., Master of the Bench of the Hon. Society of the Middle Temple* (298); *George Rae, Esq.* (415); *Viscount Cranbrook* (560); *The Late Francis Holl, A.R.A.* (659); *George Fenwick, Esq.* (1656)

Grosvenor Gallery: *James Spicer, Esq., J.P.* (33); *Portrait of W. Weldon, Esq., FRS* (67)

1885 His country retreat at Burrows Cross, Surrey, built by Norman Shaw

R.A.: *General Sir Arthur Lawrence* (25); *Rev. Henry Latham, Fellow and Tutor of Trinity Hall, Cambridge* (125); *Mr. Wilson Barrett as Hamlet* (203); *The Earl of Dufferin* (211); *Viscount Hampton as Speaker of the House of Commons. Presentation Portrait* (213); *S. Weir Mitchell, Esq., M.D. of Philadelphia* (219); *The Bishop of Peterborough (William Connor Magee)* (1141); *Evan C. Sutherland, Esq.* (1143)

Grosvenor Gallery: *Portrait of William I. Palmer, Esq., J.P., of Reading* (28); *The Late Lord Overstone* (33); *Portrait of Henry Drake, Esq.* (333)

1886 It is rumoured that Holl will paint Queen Victoria

R.A.: *The Late Earl of Chichester* (28); *Lord Carrington* (203); *The Duke of Cleveland, K.G.* (210); *The Rt. Hon. J. Chamberlain, M.P.* (274); *The Rev. the President of St John's College, Oxford* (335); *Sir John E. Millais, Bart., R.A., Diploma Work* (401)

Grosvenor Gallery: *Portrait of W. Nicholson, Esq.* (30); *Portrait of the Rev. E. Warre, D.D., Head Master of Eton College* (63)

1887 R.A.: *Sir George O. Trevelyan, Bart. Presentation Portrait* (36); *Baron Henry de Worms, M.P.* (154);

Junius S. Morgan, Esq. (222); *W.S. Gilbert, Esq.* (300); *Edward Waters, Esq., M.D.* (457); *Rt. Hon. David Plunkett, Q.C., M.P.* (623); *The Earl of Yarborough* (658); *Lord Richard Grosvenor, now Lord Stalbridge. Presentation Portrait* (989)

Grosvenor Gallery: *Portrait of Lord Harlech* (54); *Portrait of Alexandra Binnie, Esq.* (69); *Portrait of Archdeacon Hornby* (132)

1888 Work exhibited for the only time at the New Gallery

Put forward for a baronetcy

April: Visits Spain briefly with A.C. Gow

31 July: Dies at home after a short bout of a recurrent illness; his death is widely attributed to overwork

7 August: Funeral service at St Peter's Church, Belsize Park, and buried at Highgate Cemetery

31 August: His will leaves a personal estate of £36,180 14s 6d

December: Retrospective exhibition at the Royal Academy, A Special Selection from the Works of Frank Holl, R.A., R.A. Winter Exhibition; selected by William Powell Frith (1819–1909), it includes 23 subject paintings and 31 portraits

R.A.: *Sir Andrew Clark, Bart., M.D., F.R.S., LL.D., President of the Royal College of Physicians* (22); *The Attorney-General, Sir Richard Everard Webster, Q.C., M.P.* (28); *H.R.H. the Prince of Wales, K.G., as an Elder Brother of the Trinity House (Painted for the Corporation)* (179); *Earl Spencer, K.G.* (221); *Sir William Jenner, Bart., M.D., K.C.G., Physician in Ordinary to H.M. the Queen, and H.R.H. the Prince of Wales. President, 1881–1888, of the Royal College of Physicians (Subscription Portrait)* (228); *The Rt. Hon. W.E. Gladstone, M.P.* (499); *The Hon. Baron Huddleston* (506); *John L. Townsend, Esq., of New York* (742)

Grosvenor Gallery: *Lord Brassey, KCB (18); Sir George Stephen, Bt. (29); Rt Hon. Sir John Rose, Bt, Q.C., M.P.* (33); *The Late W.R. Gilmore, Esq.* (73)

1889 January: The Frank Holl Memorial Fund set up with Mr William Agnew as secretary for a memorial in St Paul's Cathedral

25 May: The sale of the late Henry Hill (d.1882) of Brighton, one of Holl's main patrons, includes 16 works by Holl, which fetch high prices

June: Subscriptions to the fund end and make a disappointing £600, not enough to buy a work for the National Gallery of British Art, nor place a monument in St Paul's, due in part to the large fees levied by the cathedral

Memorial to Holl by Alfred Gilbert and Joseph Edgar Boehm paid for by subscribers, which is positioned in the crypt at St Paul's

1901 Glasgow International Exhibition: *The Wayside Rest* (174); *The Seamstresses* (181A); *'Better is a dinner of herbs where love is than a stalled ox and hatred therewith'* (Proverbs 15: 17) (186)

1987 *Hard Times* exhibition at Manchester Art Gallery explores the social-realist movement in Victorian art, including a section on Frank Holl

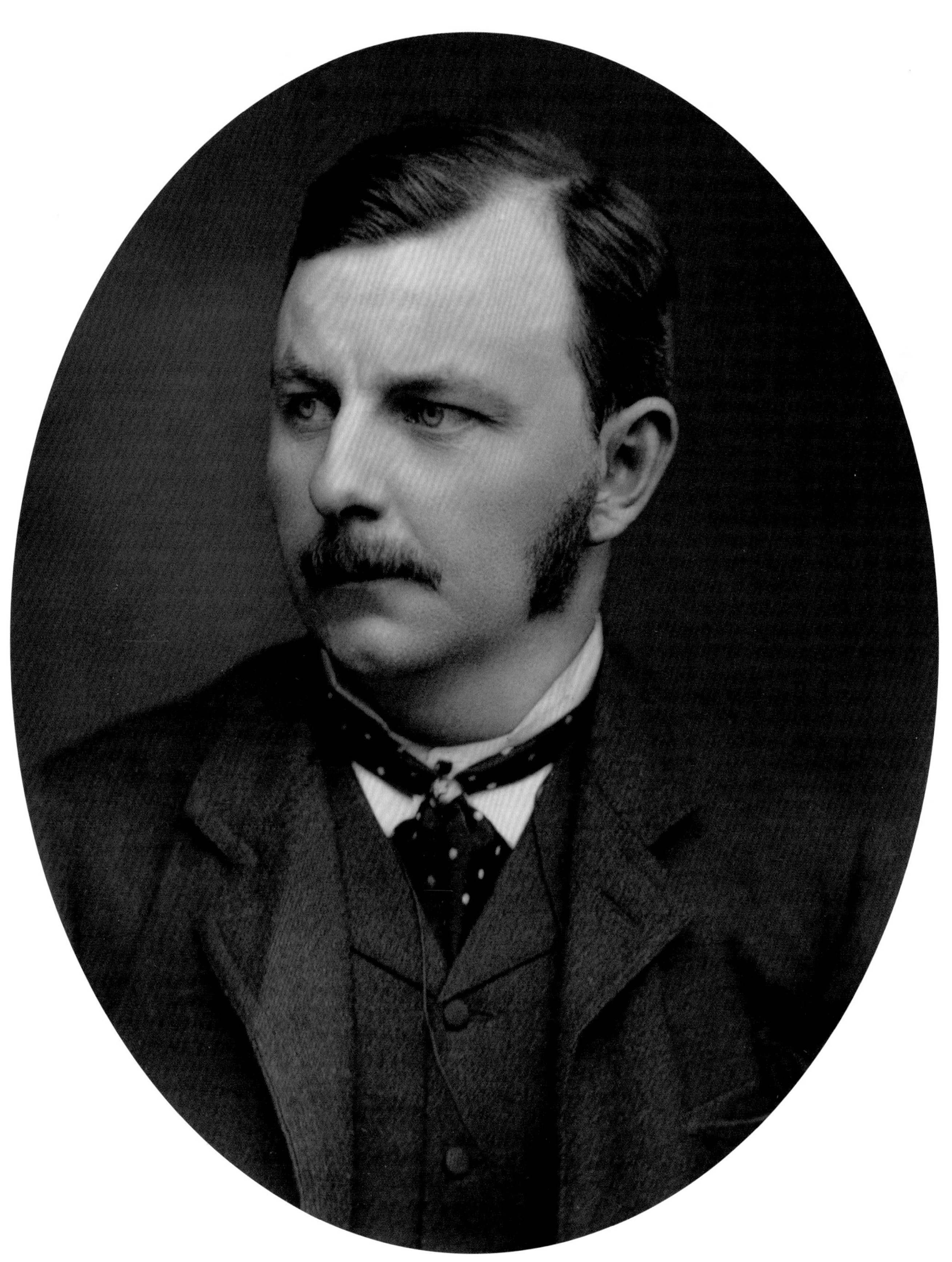

'Death and absence differ but in name': The Subject Paintings of Frank Holl

Mark Bills

At the 1889 annual Royal Academy Winter Exhibition 'of works by the old masters and deceased masters of the British school' at Burlington House, galleries four and five were set aside for a painter who had died tragically young the previous year (figs. 1, 2). The exhibition, advertised as 'A Special Selection from the Works of Frank Holl, R.A.', was a tribute to an artist and leading Royal Academician who had achieved a staggering reputation by the time of his death at just forty-three. William Powell Frith (1819–1909), who selected the paintings for the exhibition, noted that, such was the support for Holl, all the loans requested for the exhibition were easily obtained from the owners, who included the Queen, William Agnew, Henry Tate and numerous private collectors.[1]

From his prizes at the Royal Academy and his first exhibition at the Royal Academy Summer Exhibition of 1864, critics and fellow painters alike noted the worth of Holl. The lithographer Thomas Way (1837–1915) wrote to J.A.M. Whistler (1834–1903) on 1 May 1880 about the Grosvenor Gallery exhibition where Holl was showing for the first time: 'The best work is a portrait by Frank Holl who beats Millais in strength & bottles up poor Gregory [painter and illustrator] entirely.'[2]

Holl did not begin his career as a portraitist but as a painter of subject pictures, often traumatic depictions of the poor. Indeed, he is considered a central figure in what is deemed Victorian art's social-realist movement, which emerged in the late 1860s and 1870s.[3] Like other artists of this movement, he abandoned subject painting in the 1880s in favour of portraiture. The celebrations of Holl's life's work at the Royal Academy of 1889 included both genres, even though tastes were changing and social paintings were increasingly viewed as inimical to the emergent aestheticism, particularly embodied in the Grosvenor Gallery. By 1912, when Holl's eldest daughter, Ada Mabel Reynolds (1869–1965), published the biography of her father, tastes had completely changed. She wrote:

> His lasting fame as an artist will rest on his portraits alone ... His subject pictures are inclined to have that undue balance of literary or rather anecdotal interest characteristic of so much Victorian painting ... The mind of our time is turned, and justly turned, obstinately against this tradition.[4]

It seems unjust that such an opinion was expressed by the artist's own daughter and testifies to the power of bias against narrative painting at this time. At the beginning of his career his subject paintings were celebrated: indeed, his work, *'The Lord gave and the Lord hath taken away, Blessed be the Name of the Lord'*, won him the prestigious Royal Academy two-year Travelling Studentship in Painting, awarded on 10 December 1868. His social-realist drawings, which became wood engravings for *The Graphic*, were equally celebrated and Vincent van Gogh (1853–1890) collected them. Writing to Anthon van Rappard in 1883, he said: 'Nonetheless, I can't resist mentioning a few prints

Fig. 1. Lock & Whitfield, *Frank Holl*, date unknown, photograph. Rob Dickins Collection, Watts Gallery Archive

EXHIBITION

OF WORKS BY

THE OLD MASTERS,

AND BY

Deceased Masters of the British School;

INCLUDING

A SPECIAL SELECTION FROM THE WORKS OF

FRANK HOLL, R.A.,

AND A

Collection of Water-Colour Drawings by

JOSEPH M. W. TURNER, R.A.

WINTER EXHIBITION.

TWENTIETH YEAR.

MDCCCLXXXIX.

LONDON:

PRINTED BY WM. CLOWES AND SONS, LIMITED, 14, CHARING CROSS,

PRINTERS TO THE ROYAL ACADEMY.

Fig. 2. *Royal Academy Winter Exhibition Catalogue*, 1889. Watts Gallery Archive

that are absolutely matchless. For example, *The foundling* by *Frank Holl* ... Then there's a funeral, also by him, several people going into a churchyard, beautiful in sentiment. He calls that print: I am the Resurrection and the Life.'[5]

Since Holl's death he has become a lesser-known figure, something that began shortly after his death and was evident in the Frank Holl Memorial Fund set up in January 1889 with the intention of buying a major work for the national collections and erecting a large monument in St Paul's Cathedral. The subscriptions closed in June with much disappointment at the £600 raised. 'The smallness of the fund', reported a paper, 'will not allow the committee to carry out the original plan of buying one of his pictures for the National Gallery.'[6] His early death, at a point when the art world was rapidly changing, has to a great extent robbed Holl of his rightful position as a leading portraitist alongside Millais and Watts, and also as the most convincing Victorian painter of social realism. The 1987 exhibition *Hard Times* began to reveal Holl as an artist, and the aim of this book is to allow a much needed reassessment so that he can emerge from the shadows. This chapter specifically explores his subject paintings, which are distinguished from those of his contemporaries in several ways: the close engagement with the tragedy that unfolds in the work, the almost masochistic submersion in the emotions of the scenes, and the authenticity of depiction, achieved through his masterly use of light and shade, where the poor are portrayed as human beings with whom their audience could empathize.

The search for a subject

his peculiar and distinctive choice of subjects[7]

According to the available accounts, mainly those of his eldest daughter Ada Mabel, Holl emerged from an essentially happy but occasionally austere home. His father and grandfather were engravers of some note, raising the bar in their often neglected profession. The life of an engraver was very different to that of an artist – they were afforded a much lower status, epitomized by the Royal Academy not allowing engravers among its members, despite growing objections, including those of Charles Dickens. For the most part it also involved making images without colour, largely black and white, and copying rather than original drawing. This made an impact on the young Holl, who very early on learnt the ethic of industry and the power of black and white, light and shade, although throughout his career he was often criticized for his subdued palette. William Powell Frith famously commented on his first painting exhibited at the Royal Academy, *Turned out of Church*: 'Yes, Holl, it is very clever, but – he will never be a colourist.'[8]

Aware of the higher status of painters above engravers, Holl aspired to be a painter in oils. His daughter recalled:

Many an hour he spent in the old studio in company with father and his assistant, and some fine old picture which was in the course of being engraved. Here, as a child of six or seven years old, he would sit and meditate in his grave, old-fashioned way, and say to himself, 'I, too, will be a great painter some day, and paint big pictures like that.'[9]

This ambition led him to apply to the Royal Academy Schools, and his natural ability ensured that he was accepted as a probationer in 1860. His transition to a full student seems to have been smooth as he was accepted to that position the following term. His ability was rewarded with several medals, silver for drawing from the antique in 1862 and drawing from life in 1863, and a gold medal in 1863 for a historical painting, *Abraham about to Sacrifice Isaac*, which also won him £25 a year for two years. He had begun his first painting in the previous year, and interestingly it was his first attempt at one of his characteristic themes: 'an attempt to bring home, in forcible language, the wretchedness of the poor', as Reynolds expressed it.[10] He had drawn the subject from his observation of the world around him, depicting a scene at the now demolished 'old Hanover Chapel', where he saw a flower seller and her sickly child finding shelter, 'a beggar woman with a child in her arms, seated on the steps of a church ... Misery and hunger are stamped upon the face of the cowering woman, who shelters in her bosom her starving infant from the driving rain – a cold, comfortless world, a dreary waste!'[11] The painting was completed in January 1863 and found a northern buyer through its exhibition at a small commercial gallery in London.[12]

Although very clearly and naturally drawn to such subjects, Holl was young and ambitious and the subjects and style of his paintings were yet to be fully formed. He was persuaded by the august Royal Academy and by his fellow artists to depict historic and literary themes, the preoccupations of a serious artist. His gold-medal-winning painting of 1863 appears to be his first attempt at such a subject. The dramatic climax of the biblical narrative of Abraham and Isaac, 'The Trial of Abraham's Faith', a subject that had long been popular with artists, was the choice set for students by the council of the R.A.[13] According to Reynolds, the subject 'was not particularly congenial to him', nor did he judge the painting a particular success.[14] He had some interest in it but was much more attracted by the contemporary relevance of the Scriptures than archaic biblical scenes.[15]

The drama of the theme no doubt engaged Holl more than the popular costumed literary and poetic subjects favoured by many of his artist friends, and there is a record of his abandoning such works. In 1865 a painting based on Longfellow's *Evangeline* was left unfinished.[16] Two years later, in 1867, he

> commenced his first and only attempt at historical painting. Being to a certain extent associated with the Scottish set of young painters settled in London just about this time, he had come a good deal under the influence of John Pettie and W.Q. Orchardson, and it was partly due to the suggestion of the former that my father directed his ideas into a fresh channel, but one in which it must be honestly confessed he had but little sympathy. He started on a large picture, the subject being that of Othello where he describes his adventures to Desdemona: 'She loved him for the dangers he had passed, and he loved her that she did pity him.' The composition was somewhat stiffly conceived, but carried out with considerable power and great beauty of colour. But his heart was not really in it, and the figure of Othello, the principal and central idea, was never satisfactory, and would not come right, so that, in a sudden fit of anger and disgust at being unable to get what he wanted, he painted out the figure of Othello two days before sending-in day for the Royal Academy, leaving himself with no picture to represent him at that year's exhibition ... He determined henceforth upon two things: first, never again to attempt historical subjects, or indeed any subject which was not absolutely 'felt' by him, and secondly, to fight through with whatever subject he did decide upon.[17]

His first two paintings exhibited at the 1864 Royal Academy Summer Exhibition comprised a genre subject, *Turned out of Church* (526), which depicted a young miscreant being ejected from a service, and a remarkable self-portrait (145; fig. 3, cat. 3) showing the penetration, power and earnestness that were the hallmarks of Holl's work. The latter also reflected the two paths his paintings were to take, even though portraiture went into the background until later in his career and his genre painting developed a far more tragic aspect.

By this time Holl had already begun visiting Wales as both a leisure destination and a place for his work. His interest in the depiction of peasant life was sparked by these visits and the influence of European painting, as can be seen in his exhibits at the Royal Academy, British Institution and the Society of British Artists, including *The Mountain Child* (British Institution 1865: 219), *A Fern Gatherer* (R.A. 1865: 612) and *A Boulogne Fish Child* (Society of British Artists 1866: 241). In addition, the paintings show the influence of the circle of artists with whom Holl associated at this time, such as Frank Topham, R.I. (1838–1924), John Burr (1834–1893), Thomas Graham (1840–1906), William Quiller Orchardson (1932–1910) and John Pettie (1839–1893); he visited Italy with Topham in 1866.

Fig. 3. Frank Holl, *Self-Portrait*, 1863, oil on canvas. © National Portrait Gallery, London

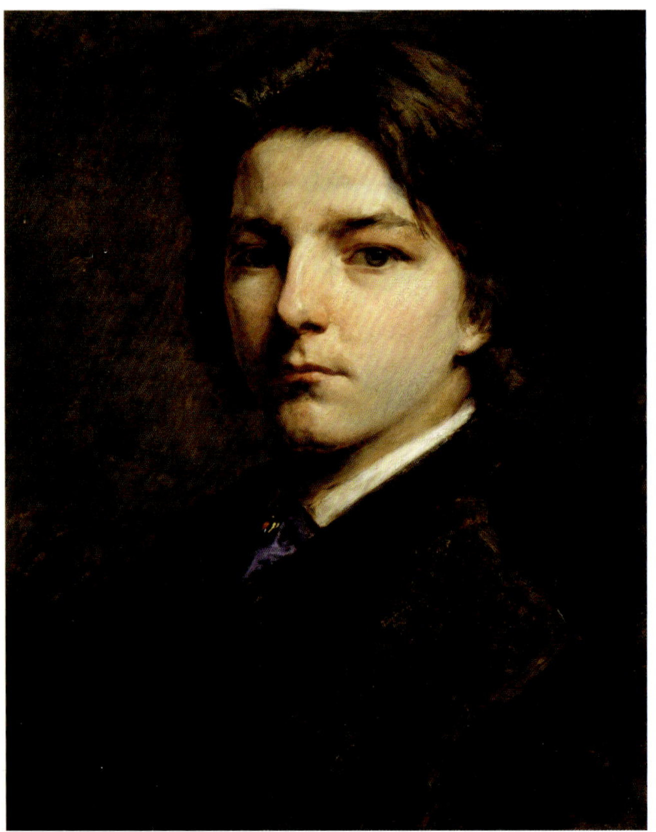

In July 1868 Holl and his new wife Annie Laura, whom he had married the previous year, visited the fishing town of Whitby on Yorkshire's east coast. While there, he received a letter from the artist Claude Calthrop (1845–1893) alerting him to the travelling scholarship on offer at the Royal Academy.[18] The prize was awarded in a competition of works submitted by students, and given the limited time for entry, Holl decided to enter a painting he had already begun, *'The Lord gave and the Lord hath taken away, Blessed be the Name of the Lord'* (cat. 5), whose subject was drawn from the popular novel *The Head of the Family* (1852) by Dinah Maria Craik, née Mulock (1826–1887). It depicts the bleak scene in chapter 1 of a family in mourning around the dinner table, where the elder brother, who is a curate, assumes the duties of the head of the family.[19] With its emotive subject and depiction of darkness in the black mourning dress and the room descending into gloom, it is a masterly piece of painting. The preoccupation with death, or rather with the effects of death on the living, was to be a powerful theme in his painting and this is his first great piece on the subject.

The travelling prize was awarded annually to a painter, architect and sculptor in turn, so for a painter was only available once every three years. It was 'Mr. Frith', Reynolds writes, 'who whispered to my father that he gained the Scholarship, so he was fully prepared for the surprise when the envelope containing the passport was placed in his hands.'[20] The prizes were announced on 10 December 1868, and Holl's friend Calthorp won the gold medal for historical composition with his *Last Song of the Girondists*, but Holl took the main prize, the funds that allowed him to travel around Europe and study the masters of painting who could be seen there.[21]

The painting received great acclaim in the R.A. exhibition of 1869 and Holl waited until after the opening of the exhibition in May before going to

Europe. 'Though painful in subject,' wrote a critic, *'The Lord gave …'* is 'rendered with great delicacy and pathos. The expression of sorrow which pervades the figures, and fills the place where death has left a void as with an atmosphere oppressively sad, is wrought out with great power and truth.'[22] The terms of the travelling scholarship required that the student spend a year of the two years in Italy, so Holl set off there, stopping first in Paris where he spent time at the Louvre and Versailles. He made a couple of colour copies from masterworks, including Titian's *Entombment* (*c.*1520), with its dramatically grieving figures. Travelling through Basel and Lucerne, he stayed for some time in Milan before going to Venice where he had arranged to meet artist friends, including Mr and Mrs Deane who had an apartment in an 'Old palace on the Giudecca'.[23] In La Serenissima, despite the appealing beauty of its artistic heritage, 'the present wearied him' and Italy was, according to his daughter, a 'closed book'.[24] The south did not appeal to Holl, who had 'an unconscious preference for the graver, greyer aspect of life'.[25] His artistic sensibilities were for northern painting, not for the exuberant colour and design, but for simplicity of manner and life depicted; he was at heart a northern artist in sentiment and character, something that the travelling scholarship had made most apparent to him. He longed 'to portray the simple, somewhat rugged home-life of the English people … With a simple decision and directness characteristic of him he sent in his resignation letter to the Academy.'[26]

Looking at Holl's career, it becomes clear that his character, which was unusually earnest in nature and uncompromising in its commitment to the development of his art, led to some decisive turning points. His later rejection of history painting and his abandoning of subject paintings were key events, but in his search for his subject and in the understanding of his own art, arguably the most significant moment was the abandonment of his travelling scholarship. To put aside such a hard-earned honour and opportunity, only offered every three years, must have been a big decision for Holl. What the scholarship had in effect allowed him to do was discover the kind of painting to which he aspired and how important the subject was for his work. Many artists, indeed many of his friends, painted the exotic scenes of a sunny south with its costumes and colour. For Holl this indicated lack of a real and deep understanding and empathy of what they portrayed. As Wilfred Meynell (1852–1948) expressed it, 'He had also formed the intention, fulfilled in all his later work, of avoiding the conventionalities into which an artist must fall who sets himself to paint a life, and customs, and manners with which he is not in familiar and intimate sympathy.'[27]

Having declined his scholarship, he set off back home via Verona, Munich, Mayence and Cologne. His final stopping place, Antwerp, was perhaps the most significant for him. Here in the cathedral Holl saw Rubens's masterpiece *The Descent from the Cross* (1612–14). It was also where he first felt the full force of the Dutch and Flemish paintings found in all the city's picture galleries. His wife recalled their subsequent return visits to the Low Countries to see 'their wonderful pictures, their quaint scenery and picturesque towns, and lovable and unspoilt simplicity of ways and life'.[28] Dutch painting in particular had a profound influence on Holl, and the directness and simplicity of its subject matter appealed to him as much as the painterly techniques. Both subject and treatment in the paintings of the contemporary Dutch painter Jozef Israëls (1824–1911) had a significant impact, but it is not certain that Holl saw his work in Antwerp in 1869. However, Israëls exhibited in London from the early 1860s and at the Royal Academy throughout the 1870s, and his output was widely available in print. In 1872 a review noted: 'Holl, the most talented of recent gold medallists, seems determined to earn the appellation of the English Israëls.'[29] On a later visit to Holland and Belgium with his patron, the eminent collector Frederick Charles Pawle, JP (*c.*1828–1915),[30] and his family in 1881, he saw Rembrandt's work, which had an enormous influence on his portraiture.

Picturing nature as simple, tragic existence

> *He chooses Nature in her striking moments, but it is always to Nature that he goes; we do not want him indulging himself with an arbitrary effectiveness.*[31]

As a boy of around fourteen, Holl was commissioned to make watercolours of ten farms owned by a Mr Clarke, which were dotted on the northern outskirts of London.[32] With the £10 he received on completion of the works

> he went down into Devonshire with a friend, one of the very few companions of his own age he had made. Lodged in a fisherman's cottage, taking their meals at the common board with the family, the two boys were sublimely happy. The wholesome simple food, the outdoor life, the long rambles over the hills and moors ...[33]

Reynolds gives us a picture of a boyhood paradise amid the idyllic simplicity of rural coastal life, something that Holl was continually drawn to, even though his mature paintings of rural life became the backdrop for human tragedy. Holl was attracted by picturesque fishing communities. Whether Hope and Clovelly in Devon, Whitby and Cullercoats on the English east coast, or Barmouth and Criccieth in Wales, these were the places where he holidayed and which became the backdrops to his paintings. Reynolds writes that her father chose 'North Wales as the scene of so many of his pictures ... I see by his diary that he must have made ... his first visit to Wales in 1863.'[34] Such locations were already popular with artists, although in the 1860s they were mainly attracting landscape painters. These regular visits offered him a subject for his work that he had failed to find in Italy. Here he could immerse himself in the more familiar life and customs of communities, which allowed him to engage in a deeper and more authentic way.

When Queen Victoria attended the 1869 Royal Academy exhibition, she was impressed by Holl's *'The Lord gave ...'* and wished to buy the painting. But Fred Pawle, who had already bought the work, was reluctant to sell, and instead the Queen commissioned Holl to paint her a subject of his choosing. After that the artist went to Europe on his travel scholarship and was, as a result, tardy in addressing this prestigious invitation.[35] Holl finally tackled it in 1870, deciding to paint a fishing community on the north-east coast. The choice of Cullercoats over North Wales was made in the hope of finding a more dramatic subject. It was known as a wild part of the coast with its dangerous seas: 'many were the tales', wrote Reynolds, 'of the terrors of life up there on that rocky coast, and of the risk each man took when he put out to sea, a risk even unusually great, since the dangers of that particular coast are more than ordinarily perilous.'[36] The danger was well known, as was the heroism of those who fished and manned the lifeboats. In February 1870, for example, *The Graphic* published a wood engraving of a 'Life Brigade Man' (fig. 4) with accompanying text that describes the scene of a shipwreck:

> The whole population of Cullercoats are out on the shore watching that ghastly sight. The women are screaming, the frightened children are clinging to their mothers' sides. The sympathy felt is such as only those can feel who have fathers and husbands and lovers away at sea, and liable to the same danger. Many of those staring so wildly seaward have lost sons and husbands and brothers off the same and off other coasts.[37]

Holl must have been drawn by the dramatic beauty of the coastline as well as the opportunity of witnessing human tragedy played out. In the four months he stayed there, he took some lodgings near the village and its beach in order to be close to the fishing community. His immersion in the life of the villagers was driven by the impetus, learnt during his travelling scholarship, to be true to nature, not only in his depiction of material objects but also on a human and empathetic level. 'My father lived much amongst the village folk,' Reynolds recalled, 'going freely in and out of their cottages (his genial, sympathetic manner attracting them much), studying their ways and customs, and sketching incessantly.[38]

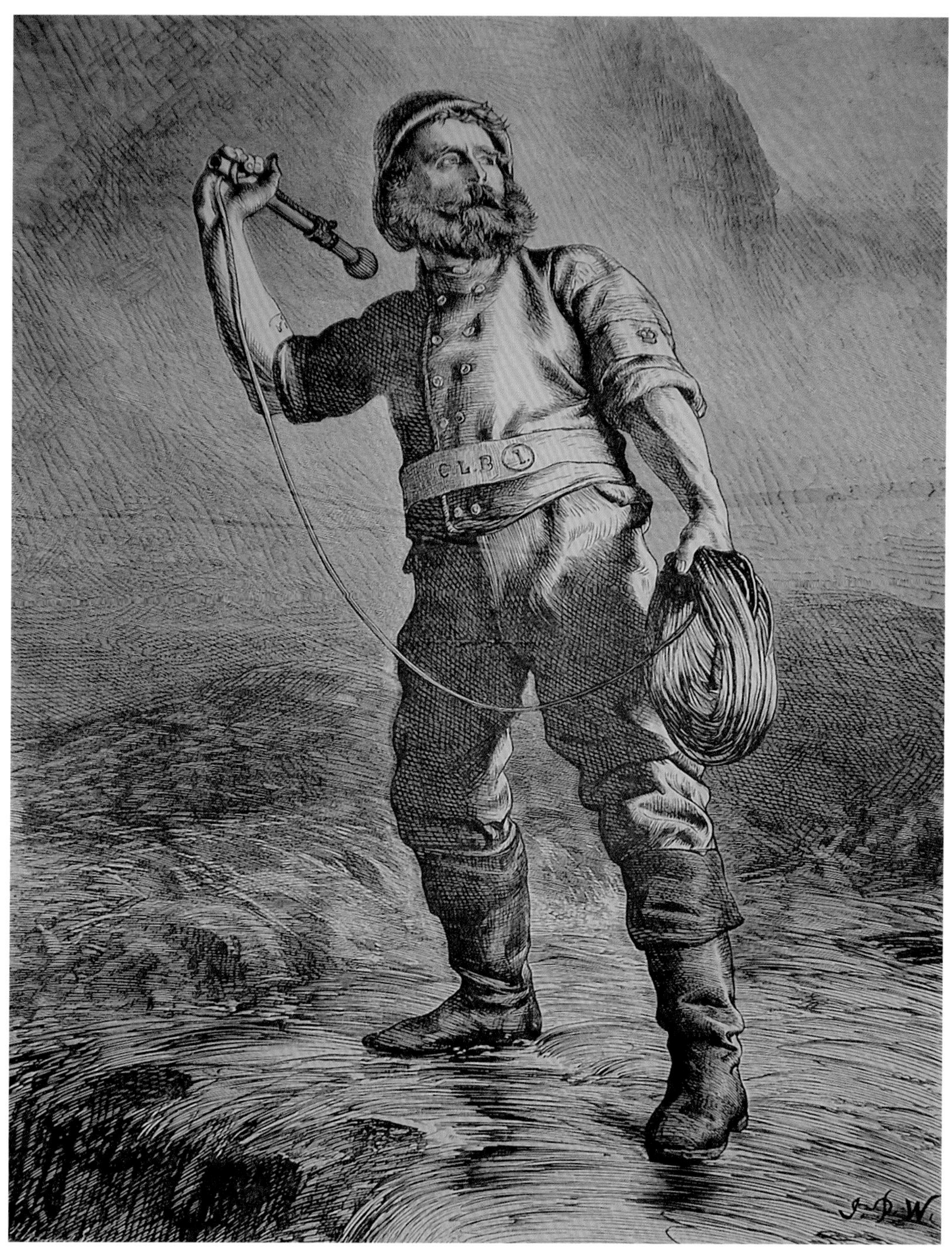

Fig. 4. Frank Holl, 'Life Brigade Man', *The Graphic*, 19 February 1870, wood engraving. Private collection

Holl had visited the east coast in July 1868 on a visit to Whitby, where he painted a 'sketch' of a poor child entitled *Up a Court at Whitby*, which he exhibited at the Winter Exhibition of the Society of British Artists in 1870. Highlighted as one of

> very few of the more prominent pictures. Mr. F. Holl's *Up a Court at Whitby* is an unfinished portrait of 'a gutter child,' of swarthy complexion and uncomely feature, clothed almost in rags. The work is impressive from its life-like look, breadth of treatment and vigorous execution, the colour being subdued to sombreness in tone. The artist deserves credit for his decisive rating of truthfulness above merely conventional attractiveness.[39]

It is interesting that Holl had sought out the subject and undertaken its direct depiction on his visit to Whitby. At Cullercoats he tried to instil the same 'truthfulness' in his work and while there, as Reynolds notes, he was 'more than once an unwilling spectator of domestic calamity'.[40] Such tragedy, common in fishing villages, became the subject of his royal commission. Whether Holl was an 'unwilling spectator' is debatable, as he was never attracted to the merely picturesque and his large finished paintings of everyday life invariably draw from a central drama.

Fig. 5. Frank Holl, *No Tidings from the Sea*, 1870, oil on canvas. Royal Collection Trust, © HM Queen Elizabeth II 2012

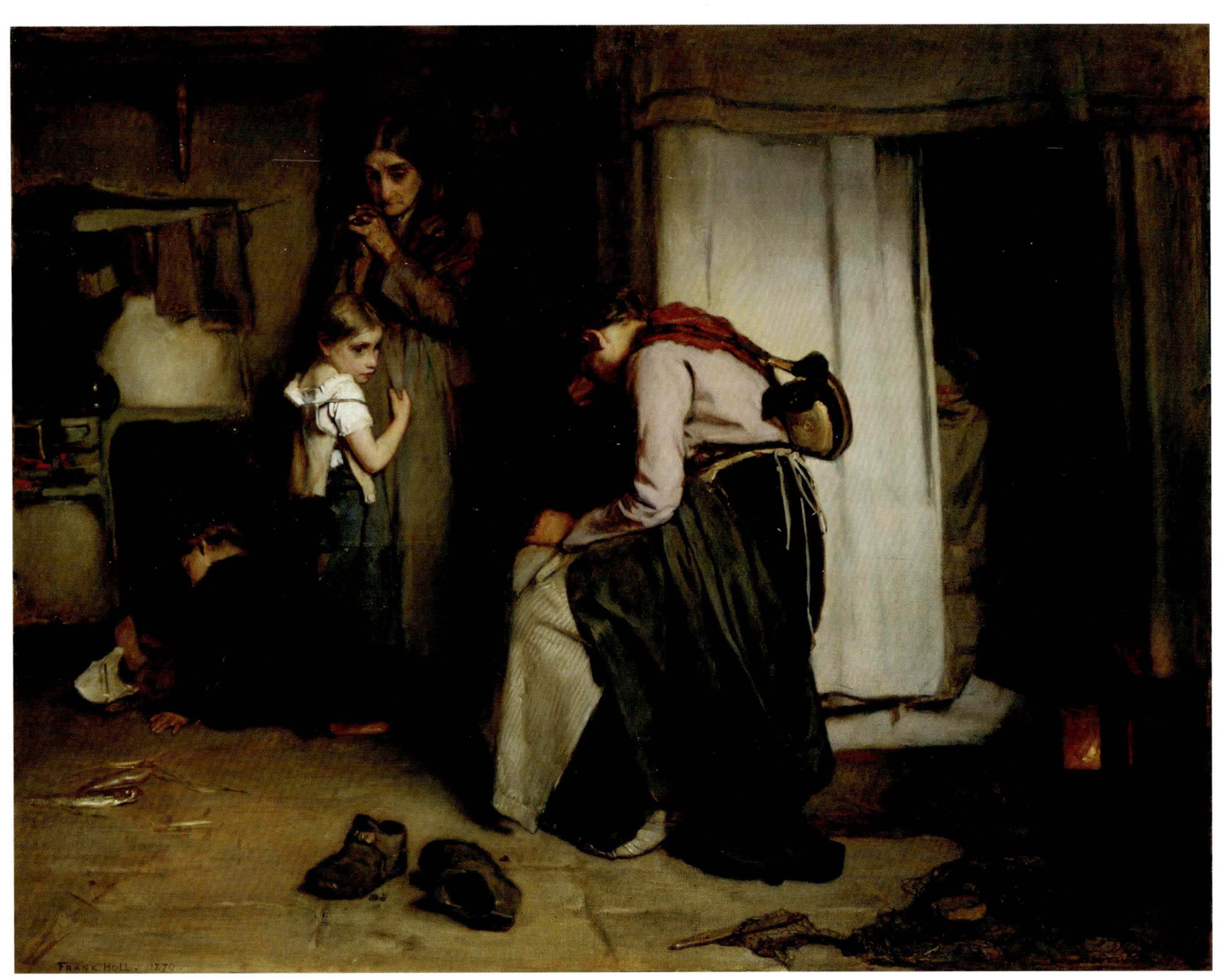

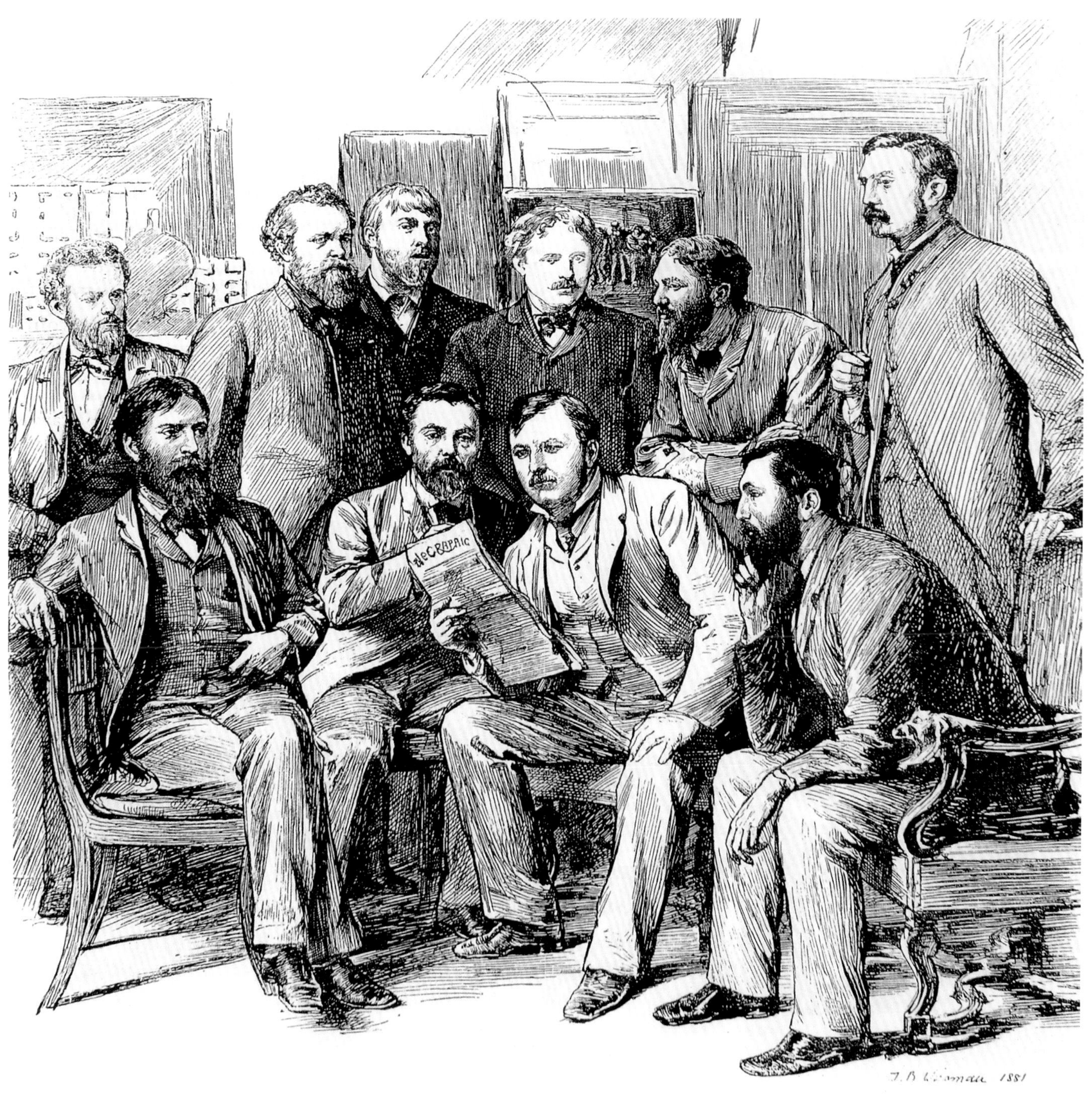

Fig. 6. T. Blake Wirgman, 'The Graphic Artists,' *The Graphic*, 1881, later printed in *The Magazine of Art*, 1890, wood engraving. Watts Gallery Archive

Reynolds is very vivid in her description of events in Cullercoats, even though she was barely two at the time. Her account of the inspiration of *No Tidings from the Sea* (fig. 5, cat. 6) is as dramatic as her father's finished work. She describes him painting in a fisherman's cottage when the door was flung open by a woman 'half mad with suspense and misery'.[41] This was shortly followed by the dripping corpse of her husband being brought into the cottage. At the sight of her dead partner the agonized woman called for her own death. 'My father', Reynolds writes, 'was greatly moved and upset at the sight of her grief, terribly primitive in its intensity, which haunted him for days, finally resolving itself into a conception for a picture which he eventually painted, calling it "No tidings from the sea."'[42]

The painting depicts the interior of a fisherman's cottage with the grief stricken woman being fearfully observed by her own daughter clinging to the skirts of an old woman, 'the old mother of one of the neighbours'.[43] The mourning woman's young son is seated on the floor oblivious to the unfolding events. Holl developed a 'truth to nature' in terms of emotion as well as observation of physical objects. Whether these include fish, teapot or bread knife, the simple and homely still lifes set within the thick-walled fishermen's cottages are truthfully observed, and we know Holl painted inside these houses. The human drama and emotion, the outward signs of grief, were similarly witnessed at first hand. The artist believed that this observation was necessary in order to make a convincing portrayal, and critics often praised the veracity of the scenes that he depicted, not showy or overtly sentimental, but real in their tragedy. In Meynell's assessment of the artist written in the *Magazine of Art* in 1880 he made clear this distinction:

> The one thing that is needful is that sadness in painting should be a sincerity – that it should be real in feeling, and not caught at the end of the pencil, or produced as a cheap and almost ready-made effectiveness ... The difference between the sham and the true in melancholy art of all kinds is always utterly unmistakable – too subtle to define, yet clear to the apprehension.[44]

The plain interiors that Holl adopts in his cottages were the stage for tragic incidents. From a painterly perspective this allowed him to use light most effectively: small rooms with deep-walled recessed windows as the main source of light heightened the sense of drama, the light penetrating the gloom to illuminate grief. Areas of light and dark, of shadow and delineation of form, showed the skill of his use of chiaroscuro, something praised by contemporary critics. In darkness colour is subdued, and the lighting of faces and forms emerging from shadows presents humanity as light against the dark background of material reality, emphasized by the penury of the people depicted.

When it came to the models for the figures in his paintings, Holl was occasionally able to use the villagers. Such veracity was consistent with the approach that he would go on to take with portraiture, a later critic noting: 'Mr. Holl himself once told me that unless he felt that he had dipped his soul into his sitter's character and painted with that, the conviction always came upon him that he had failed.'[45] Things were slightly more complex in his subject paintings of course, and such modelling was not always possible or appropriate. We know, however, that in his painting *'The Lord gave ...'* Holl used his own family as models, although the picture was based on fiction. As in a portrait, he wanted to show particular features and reactions, even though to his audience they were generic accounts of humanity rather than specific named individuals that required a recognizable likeness. Some of the villagers whom Holl used as models were not the actual people who had suffered the tragedy that had inspired his paintings, and there is a fascinating account of a model he discovered on his many visits to Criccieth in North Wales: 'The woman had scarcely any English, but her magnificent build and presence at once inspired my father with the idea of a large composition. She was of a massive and almost savage type, living quite alone with her children, and seeing no one for weeks together.'[46] This model appears in a number of Holl's interiors including *Waiting*, his first painting of her.[47] She represented for Holl the strength, beauty and simplicity of the people whom he wished to portray, in particular the nobility of facing the adversity of a life making a living from the sea.

Holl continued to paint fishing communities and it seems clear that he had an influence on a slightly younger generation of artists such as Walter Langley (1852–1922) and Percy Craft (1856–1934). Within subject painting Holl had found an approach of sincerity and fidelity, linked with the inspiration of Dutch painting. He would also apply this method to metropolitan subjects, which began in earnest with his association with *The Graphic* illustrated magazine.

The Graphic and the depiction of urban life

> *Some of the most remarkable black-and-white drawings that ever were seen in the course of illustrated journalism.*[48]

The Graphic illustrated weekly began as a rival to the *Illustrated London News*. Its first edition appeared in December 1869. In format it was similar to its rival, mixing journalism with a large quantity of good-quality wood engravings, its principal attraction being its illustrations. The novelty of *The Graphic* was that its editor, William Luson Thomas (1830–1900), wanted to encourage the highest quality of illustration and to this end he commissioned not only the staple engravers and illustrators but also new fine artists (rather than hack illustrators) who would explore subjects with a fresh eye.[49] Notably, for its first issue Luke Fildes (1843–1927) drew 'Houseless and Hungry', which subsequently became the celebrated Academy picture *Applicants for Admission to the Casual Ward* (1874). What distinguished *The Graphic* from other illustrated newspapers was its ability to evoke through its prints an empathy and humanity often devoid from more journalistic black and white images. *The Graphic* became particularly good at highlighting the poor of London, most particularly in the East End, and Holl followed this precedent in many of his drawings for the paper.

Fig. 7. Frank Holl, 'At a Railway Station – A Study', *The Graphic*, 10 February 1872, wood engraving. © National Portrait Gallery, London

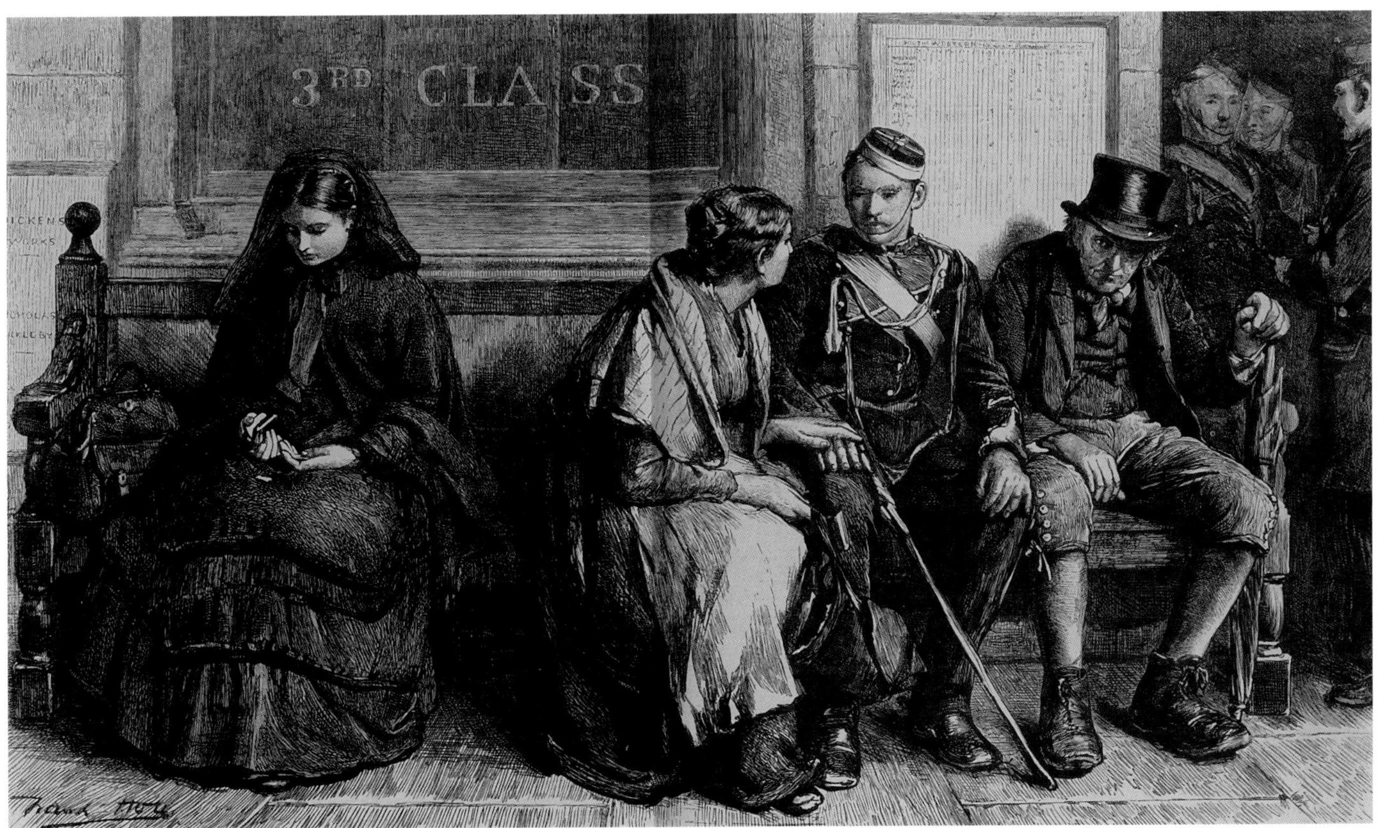

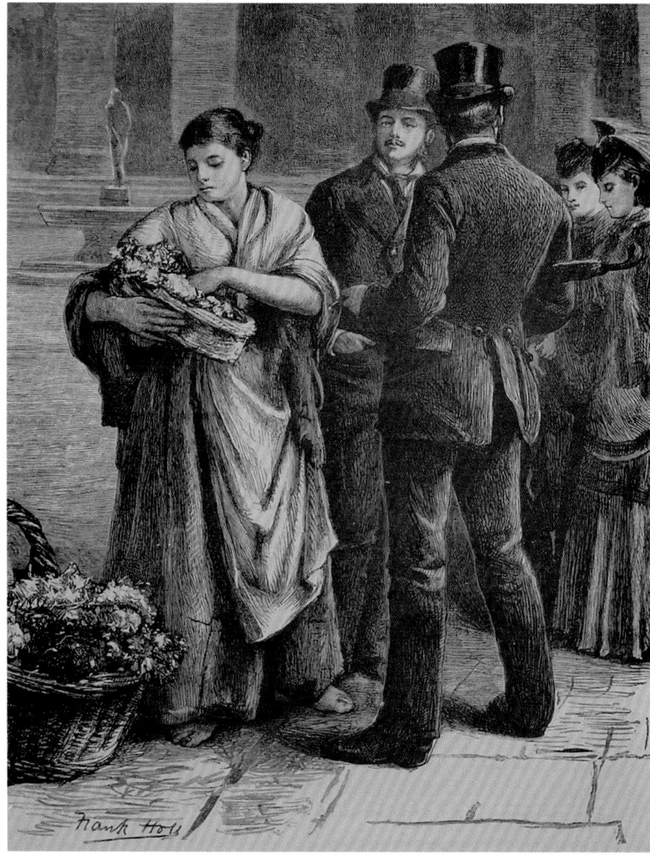

Fig. 8. Frank Holl, 'Sketches in London – A Flower Girl', *The Graphic*, 22 June 1872, wood engraving. Private collection

In December 1871, two years after the first issue of *The Graphic*, James Dromgole Linton (1840–1916) from the paper contacted Holl, still only in his mid-twenties, and asked him to submit a drawing. The work, 'At a Railway Station – A Study', was approved the following year by Thomas and the artist received 30 guineas for it (fig. 7).

It is uncertain how far *The Graphic* determined the subject matter of the pieces Holl submitted. In some cases he clearly had a specific brief, while in others he had complete freedom. He was acknowledged as being 'on the staff' and was furnished with regular work for over a decade (fig. 7).[50] This included the illustration of news stories, such as 'Pope Pius IX hearing mass at the Sistine Chapel, Rome' and 'From the Press Gallery of Queen Victoria's visit to St. Paul's at the thanksgiving on the recovery of the Prince of Wales from a dangerous illness',[51] but his best contributions were the one-off full-page and double-page illustrations that were so admired by Vincent van Gogh. These were presented with an accompanying explanatory text. In some cases images such as 'Sketches in London – A Flower Girl' (fig. 8) were part of a series of metropolitan scenes that included works by other artists, such as 'Sketches in London – Before the Bar' by Arthur Boyd Houghton (1836–1875).[52] The texts that accompanied these often provided generic social commentary on the places and characters of metropolitan life chosen for the drawings.

There is little doubt that *The Graphic* was instrumental in turning Holl to urban subjects for his art. Up until the early 1870s Holl's subject painting had focused on the lives of the poor at the most elemental and tragic that he had found in and around rural communities. He had not until his work for *The Graphic* chosen to depict the scenes of poverty that were visible around him in London. Marion Harry Spielmann (1858–1948) made some interesting observations about this in the paper shortly before Holl's death: 'The curious leaning towards the miserable was entirely wholesome in its character, the result, as I have said, of deep sympathy with misfortune, and from a naturally thoughtful disposition, as well as from a honest desire, by impressing the public, to assist in solving the problem of London life.'[53] Holl had always been driven by acute sympathy for the plight of the poor, but in his work for *The Graphic* he was instilled with a greater sense of social purpose.

What remained consistent within Holl's art was the depiction of the poor with tragic narratives. Holl always claimed, and his daughter reiterated this in her biography, that *The Graphic* had a wide-reaching and positive influence on the art of her father.

> My father found that he benefited enormously by this new branch of Art, for not only did he find the work in itself fascinating and engrossing to a degree, but it served as a corrective to a tendency which he shared in company with many another, that of a proneness to be uncertain of himself – a lack of self-confidence – a tendency to hesitate, to be dissatisfied with a design, to worry at it, pull it about, until staleness, disillusion, and a dislike for the subject would take the place of the first enthusiasm for the idea, and

> the design would be thrown aside, for another to take its place, only to follow the same fate; in fact, the wood-drawing came to him, just at the right moment; artistically and morally it helped him; to steady his aim, to concentrate his forces, fix his purpose, and enable him to *finish and carry right through that which he began* ... It also gave him, indirectly, stability, self-confidence, courage and concentration – invaluable and essential assets. This discipline was the making of the man, and laid the foundation of those characteristics of his work in later life which marked him out above most of his contemporaries.[54]

The discipline of illustrated journalism clearly benefited Holl, helping him develop his subject matter and his art. 'In order, therefore to cultivate confidence and self-restraint in painting, as well as practice in drawing and schooling in punctuality,' Spielmann wrote, 'he joined the staff of this journal, for the purpose of contributing at stated intervals pictures of life and character in black-and-white.'[55] The need to respond quickly to pictorial decisions and attempt to capture the scene depicted imbued his work with a freshness and boldness in his contemporary life that he had hitherto not achieved. This is particularly important when one considers the number of his *Graphic* illustrations that became the basis of paintings, such as *At a Railway Station, Deserted – A Foundling, Gone* (cat. 14) and *Summoned for Active Service*.

An essential element of Holl's fisher subjects had been his immersion in their lives, not only to understand them at first hand but to build an empathetic relationship that he would express in his bleak narratives. He clearly felt the need to experience the London poor in the same way, and he achieved this not through living in a poor community as he did on the coast but rather through trips into the heart of poverty in the city. Although, as Booth's *Descriptive Map of London Poverty* (1889) makes very clear, the wealthy and poor were never that far apart, the East End was a particular labyrinth of poverty. In this often dangerous area, the surroundings reflected tragedy for many. Here Charles Dickens and Gustave Doré had trekked, exposing themselves of the underbelly of the city, and here Holl sought the subjects for both his *Graphic* work and his metropolitan paintings that 'occupied his brush, not so much, however, because he was morbidly inclined as because he desired to bring home to the mind and heart of Mayfair the "crime of poverty and temptation to which the poor are for ever subject."'[56]

In the early 1870s when Holl joined *The Graphic* he was living at 30 Gloucester Road, a street where many artists had settled. A couple of doors away at 35 Gloucester Road lived an artist friend Charles Edward Johnson, R.I. (1832–1913), who became Holl's regular companion on his visits to the East End.[57] Reynolds recalls of this period:

> My father was now at work upon a large drawing for *The Graphic*, the subject of which had suggested itself to him on one of his prowls about the East End. He was very fond of doing this, in company generally with Mr Johnson, and the two men would very often go down east in search for material for a picture or its accessories. The docks and their vicinity were a very favourite hunting-ground with my father, and it was there that he found many a suggestion for a picture.[58]

Reynolds also relates the regularity of the visits and that it was common for her father to go walking at dusk: 'Sometimes he would take a long walk instead, going over Hampstead and Highgate, or, again, he would make a tramp of it with Mr Johnson.'[59] Holl and Johnson became known to the police in the neighbourhood, who knew 'both their faces well, and helped them considerably in their search for "local colour"'.[60] The 'tramps' to the East End were an important part of the development of Holl's art, enabling him to experience the worst of London's poverty up close:

> These ramblings in the very poorest quarters of London brought my father face to face with many terrible scenes of misery and poverty, and even crime. It was scarcely a morbid attraction for the seamy side which led him forth upon these unsavoury peregrinations, but rather, I take it, a latent idea that by depicting them forcibly and poignantly in his own work, he might bring home to the

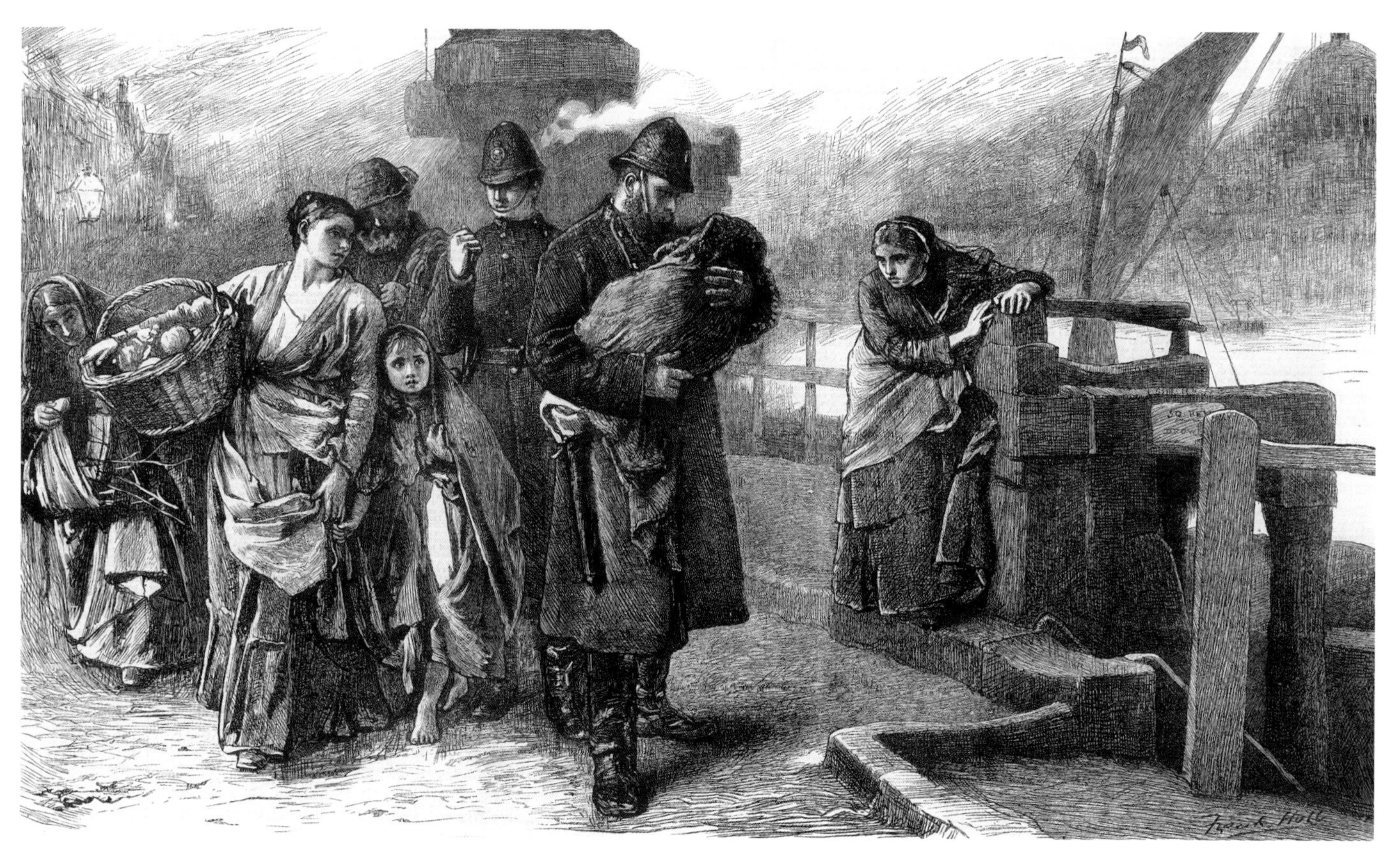

Fig. 9. Frank Holl, 'London Sketches – The Foundling', *The Graphic*, 26 April 1873, wood engraving. Watts Gallery Archive

indifferent eyes and hearts of the public the wretched and iniquitous state of affairs which lies close to our own doors. This may have been the reason he so nearly always took for his subjects some story of poverty, of sorrow, or of crime.[61]

His search for authenticity did not just concern the experience itself but also the details that would be contained in his works, and there are several accounts of his visits being a search for props for his paintings:

> My father used to find most of his accessory material, in the shape of old clothes, old sailors' and soldiers' uniforms, children's rags, and various other 'properties' of use to the painter, down in these filthy alleys or in some old rag-and-bone shop; pawnbrokers', rag-pickers', haunts of the remotest and most unsavoury were ransacked for useful material ... [He] always made a point of getting material for his pictures, in the shape of backgrounds, furniture, and even the very clothes themselves direct and never made use of homely makeshifts, which cannot have the same impress of character or suggestion in them: even the very dirt, the very creases and fold of the rags gave the necessary touch which home-manufactured 'rags' could.[62]

Such lengths emphatically reflect Holl's belief in the veracity of the image and the importance of the process in the work's creation. Holl's London paintings and *Graphic* drawings show the real costumes of the poor and real characters, giving a rare glimpse into that world. They are also important in historical terms, for so few outfits worn by the poor have survived in historic clothing collections. Worn and second-hand cast-offs, which were recycled until unusable, were not collected as fashionable garments were. Similarly, most paintings and prints of the poor are often a generic abbreviation, whereas Holl shows us rare detail and observation.

If Holl's fishing cottage interiors are quite generic in their settings, his metropolitan subjects in contrast often take specific recognizable locations. Holl depicts Euston Station, Newgate Prison and the Docks, places where tragic dramas are daily played out, whether an abandoned child, the splitting of a family or the tragic consequences of the judicial system. There is within these works a journalistic element reinforced by the accompanying text that provides the social context. They also presented a more generic truth, but one that arose from the powerful image of specific people with whom their audience could empathize, a graphic illustration of a social ill, as the paper finds in one of Holl's drawings: 'This picture represents one of the scenes in a tragical drama which is being perpetually performed by a continuous succession of hapless actors.' The work to which it referred was 'The Foundling' (fig. 9), part of the London Sketches series, whose background was described in the paper: 'Year after year, hundreds of innocent girls, though they have heard and read of the treachery and inconstancy of lovers when once their passions are satiated, yet believe that their own sweethearts must be true.'[63] The scene is brilliantly handled by Holl, with the human drama and setting merging into a stunningly convincing contemporary account. Van Gogh was particularly taken with this work, the image of the city remaining with him, as he recalled to Anthon van Rappard:

> Nonetheless, I can't resist mentioning a few prints that are absolutely matchless.
>
> For example, *The foundling* by Frank Holl. This shows several policemen in waterproof capes who have taken up a child left as a foundling between the beams and planks of a quay beside the Thames. Some curious onlookers watch, and through the fog one sees the grey silhouette of the city in the background.[64]

Although *The Graphic* commissions drew Holl to explore a metropolitan background for his human dramas, his greatest urban masterpieces came from another source, a visit to an infamous London institution: Newgate Prison (fig. 10, cat. 15). Like all his major works, it was inspired by a real incident, and Holl had for some time 'conceived the idea of painting a picture, typifying some stirring, dramatic incident, into which he could throw his whole being'.[65] Newgate had long been a much-visited place and Dickens had famously written about it. Holl's opportunity for a visit came through his friendship with the Governor of Newgate Prison, Mr Sidney Robert Smith, and sometime in the mid-1870s he went to see it. The painting emerged a few years later, when he recalled the part of Newgate Prison known as 'the cage' where visits were allowed. Holl was struck by the variety of people brought together in the prison and clearly illustrates this in the picture. 'I shall never forget the impression it made upon me,' he wrote. 'It is particularly impressive for scenes of such pathos & agony of mind on both sides took place.'[66] Holl believed the strength of his work was its acute observation. Like many Victorian artists, he had a great admiration for the work of William Hogarth, who was seen as one of the greatest observers of human life, rich in narrative and showing the lives of everyday people. Holl wrote of Hogarth's art: 'You turn at last from them with the feeling that you have known the career of the unfortunate beings represented from their early life to their miserable end – all observation.'[67] *Newgate* was a huge success, securing his Associateship to the Royal Academy and selling in auction in 1882 for £808 10s.

The rejection of subject painting

Holl's solid reputation was built on his subject paintings, which accounted for his early success at the Royal Academy and his growing popular acclaim. Most of his key subject works were bought by important

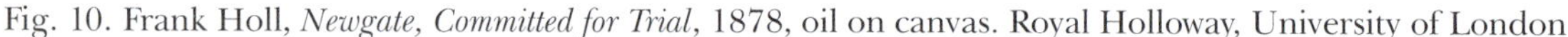

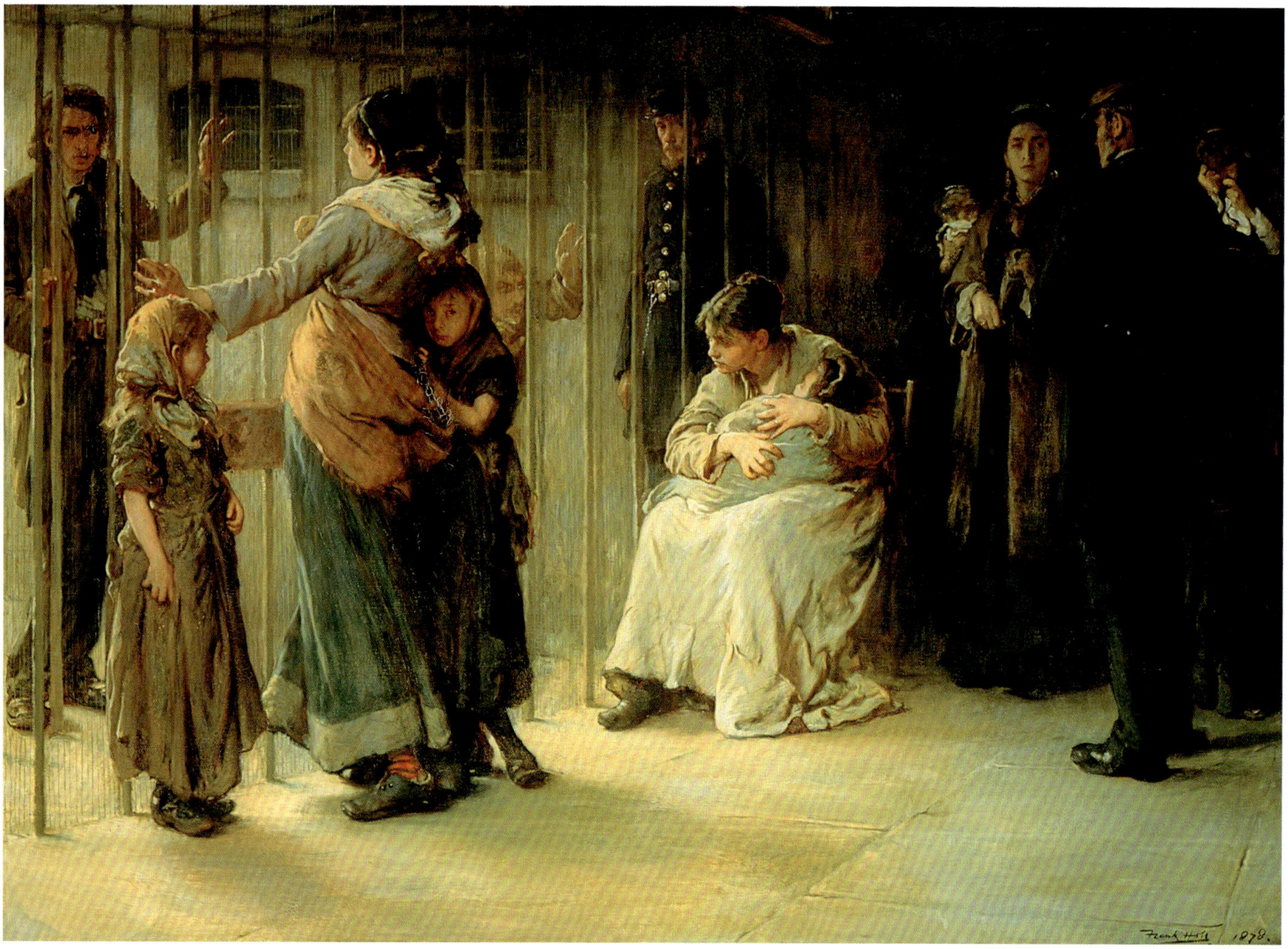

Fig. 10. Frank Holl, *Newgate, Committed for Trial*, 1878, oil on canvas. Royal Holloway, University of London

patrons, who included the Queen. Despite this, in the early 1880s Holl underwent a dramatic volte-face and he stopped exhibiting and, eventually, painting subject pictures.[68] 'The modes of Victorian genre lost their hold on him,' Reynolds notes, 'and save under some external compulsion he did not again paint a subject with a narrative intention.'[69] Up until this point subject painting had seemed the very character of his work, so it is worth considering the reasons for such a dramatic rejection of the genre that had been the basis of his success.

Undoubtedly, critical and popular opinion had changed, something very apparent in the memorials to Holl that emerged just after his untimely death. A popular magazine writing of the Frank Holl Memorial Fund noted: 'There would have been even more cause for regret if in a national collection he were represented by one of his morbid sentimental pictures, instead of one of his really fine portraits.'[70] Although many of Holl's supporters lamented his move from subject painting, particularly Harry Quilter,[71] by the late 1880s it seems clear that such subjects were seen as excessively sentimental, something that Reynolds echoes in her biography of her father. Indeed, other social-realist artists associated with *The Graphic*, including Luke Fildes and Hubert von Herkomer (1849–1914), similarly abandoned such depictions in favour of portraiture. In its obituary of Holl *The Times* declared that he had moved away from subject painting because of critical opinion, claiming that such criticism was not exclusive to the 1880s but something that had dogged him throughout his career: 'It is interesting to note that his chief reason for taking to portraiture was disgust at the treatment which his subject pictures had received from the hands of the critics.'[72] There is further evidence of this in a letter written by Holl in 1887: 'I painted a head portrait, which I exhibited at the same time as the Newgate picture ... I felt almost a little regret that it seemed to gain me more praise.'[73]

With Holl there were undoubtedly other factors, and the dramatic break seems to have come at a time when financial pressures played an important role in the direction of his art. His own modest roots, with their strong work ethic,[74] had given him a particular sympathy for the poor, but also seemed to lead him to want to exhibit material signs of his artistic success. In 1881 he purchased a plot of land near his friend John Pettie, R.A., in the artist area of Fitzjohn's Avenue in Hampstead, and employed the fashionable architect Richard Norman Shaw (1831–1912) to design and build quite an extravagant studio house, which he named 'The Three Gables'. The house was completed in 1882, with all the expense that entailed, and he also commissioned a further house from Shaw in 1885 at Shere in Surrey. The impact on his practice in order to fund his lifestyle is immediately apparent, occurring at the same time as his portraiture eclipsed subject painting. The year 1882 is important in the move away from subject paintings, and the majority of them produced at this time were commissioned replicas and repeats of familiar themes rather than new works.[75] And there is a dramatic change in his exhibition practice, seemingly also instigated by new financial pressures. Between 1879 and 1881 his average submission to the major annual exhibitions was six paintings, but in 1882 it increased to sixteen works and remained in double figures until his death in 1888. Reynolds, who was working from Holl's diary and papers, relates that 1882 was the most prolific year for her father, when he produced twenty-four portraits and five subject paintings.[76]

Holl's move to portraiture appears to be driven by more than one factor, and even though portraits were extremely lucrative and his prolific work rate had an effect on his health, it cannot be seen as a purely financial decision. It should be remembered that his subject pictures also continued to command a value. *Leaving Home* was based on a 30-guinea commission from *The Graphic*, 'At a Railway Station – A Study' (10 February 1872), and became an oil on canvas sold to Henry Hill in 1873 for 220 guineas. In Christie's posthumous sale of the great Brighton collector's effects on 25 May 1889, the same picture (lot 130) sold for 530 guineas. Holl responded to commissions of replication of subject pictures, and although he stopped sending subject paintings to the Royal Academy, they were still shown at dealers' exhibitions, such as those of Arthur Tooth, for example, where a replica of *No Tidings* appeared in a spring exhibition of 1883. One thing is certain: his work and exhibition rate dramatically increased in 1882 with the change in his lifestyle, which coincided with his move away from subject painting. Success also proved a further burden for Holl.

Death, sentiment and tragedy

The whole question of sentiment in Victorian painting has often been oversimplified, a simplification that began with the increasing rejection of genre and narrative content in painting by artists and critics throughout the late nineteenth century. Such wholesale dismissal failed to account for the breadth of subject painting in Victorian art, nor did it make a clear distinction between powerfully tragic and indulgently emotional sentiment. Undoubtedly, Holl did produce sentimental paintings with a narrative element, such as the child portraits that include *'Did you ever kill anybody, Father?'* (1883, R.A. 1884), but these must be distinguished from his poignant and tragic paintings of loss. To view the depiction of a girl petting a rabbit as having the same emotional content as the painting of a funeral of a child is to stretch the idea of sentiment too far, and a distinction should be made between sentiment and tragedy evoked by genre and narrative painting, with both subject and treatment being considered.

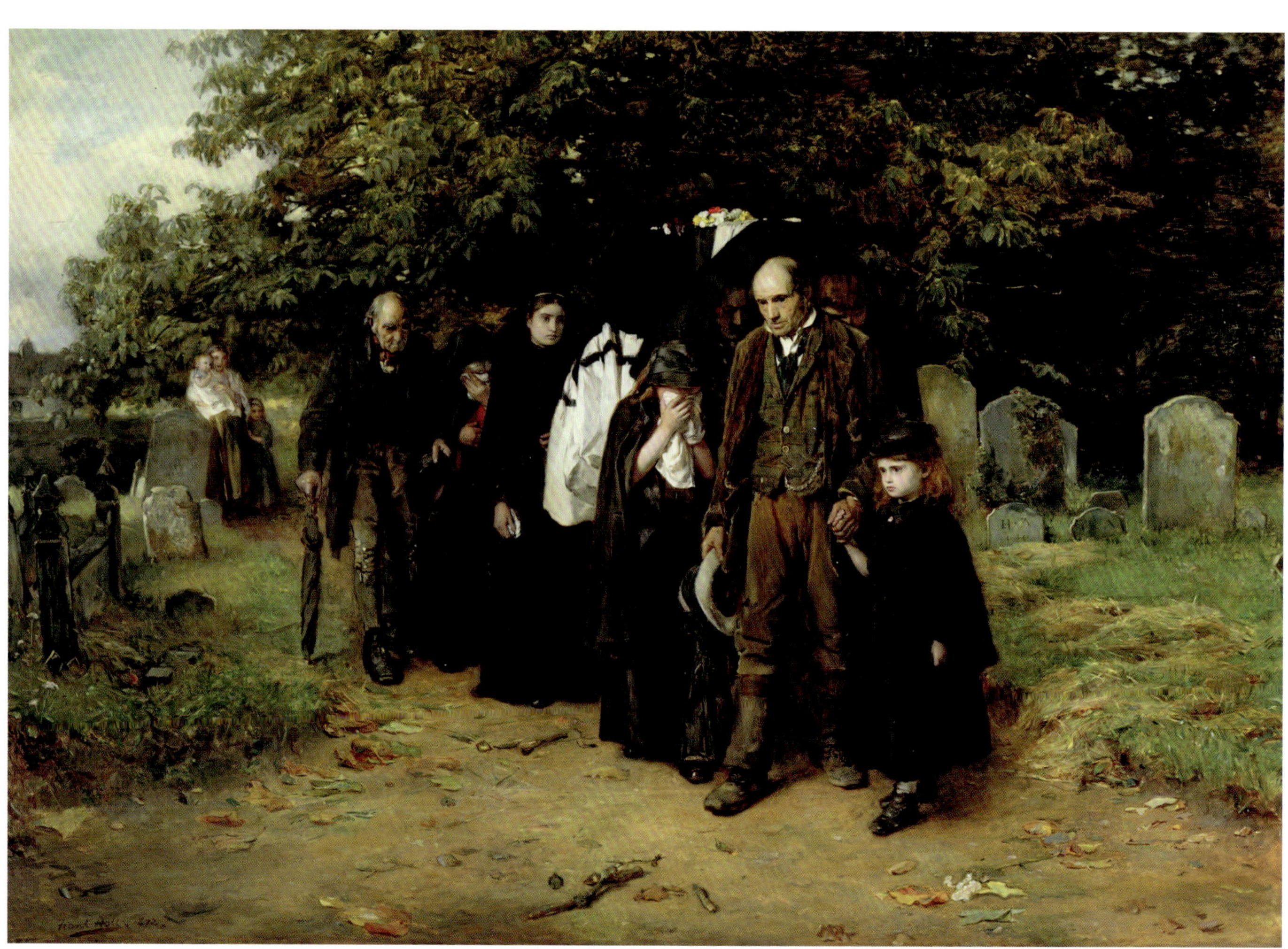

Fig. 11. Frank Holl, *I am the Resurrection and the Life (The Village Funeral)*, 1872, oil on canvas.
Leeds Museum and Galleries (Leeds Art Gallery)

A distinguishing factor between sentimental and tragically emotive painting is that sentiment plays to an audience rather than seeks to express a more poignant truth. Sentiment is excessively indulgent and sweetens the portrayal of its subject, whereas tragedy has an authenticity that does not arouse sham emotion. Holl's daughter expressed this forcefully: 'It would be a deep injustice to class him with the genre-mongers of the late Victorian academies.'[77] Contemporary critics and viewers recognized this distinction and found within Holl's great subject paintings a profounder expression of humanity than mere sentiment. According to Spielmann, he was 'pathetic or tragic in his work, but never morbid; tender, but never maudlin; religious, earnest, and serious, but never bigoted or ascetic'.[78]

Where Holl did indulge in sentiment was in paintings of middle-class children, but they never became the main focus of his art. For his subject painting he chose a different class at the bottom end of society, where events and tragedy are more apparent and openly displayed. His central theme was the grief of loss through death or parting in difficult and unfortunate circumstances. While his direct treatment of such subjects struck a chord with the contemporary audience, they were often seen as excessively 'gloomy' subjects redeemed by Holl's painting ability. 'While we condemn the choice of the subject,' wrote Professor Weir, 'we cannot but admire the consummate skill of the artist.'[79]

Grief is a universal theme and the loss of children was an experience sadly familiar to virtually all families at this time. Holl's directness of treatment, avoiding the overtly sentimental, was often hard for his audience even though it found favour with important patrons. So why did the artist choose such a relentless exploration of tragic themes? Contemporary critics often speculated about this question, and Holl's character and personal experiences were considered a contributing factor. This was vigorously denied by his daughter who wrote: 'Some mistaken idea seems to have existed that my father had in early days a great struggle for existence, and that his choice of subjects of such a dismal and melancholy nature was due in part to his own immediate surroundings.'[80] Although she was able to defend this viewpoint, she did hint that Holl's personal understanding of difficulty gave him a greater empathy with the subjects of his paintings: 'Therefore the child early learnt to know the grey and seamy side of life, and one can scarcely wonder at his choice of subjects in after life, nor marvel when to him existence seemed to be cast in a mould of somewhat narrow proportions.'[81]

Holl's direct experience of death and child mortality was fortunately relatively small, all his four daughters living into old age. He did suffer the anguish of the loss of a child in 1879, as *The Times* reported on Sunday 13 April, when 'the wife of Frank Holl, Esq. A.R.A.,' gave birth to 'a son, stillborn'.[82] Holl was able to empathize with the events that he observed, and it seems that such keen and sympathetic observation, rather than direct experience, influenced his choice of subjects. He painted the issues that deeply touched and 'haunted him'. He did not seek to embellish them, but to depict them in such a way as to elicit a similar response in the viewer of the painting. 'An artist,' Holl wrote, 'if he does not study life, will have no thoughts of his own', and that observation 'is the secret of all original and impressive work'.[83] As such, his pictures served as powerful memento moris, reminding viewers, through others' misfortunes, of the brevity of their own place in the world. These scenes of simple lives openly and graphically displayed the human tragedy of all existence. Such a fascination was expressed by Reynolds who realized that 'it appeals almost at once to the onlooker, bringing him almost literally face to face with death itself'.[84]

If these paintings appealed to the common experience and misfortune that everyone comes across in life, they also powerfully illuminated an underclass that suffered even greater tragedies. Indeed, the empathetic approach of Holl did much to humanize the poor in society and highlight their plight. They had long been illustrated in black and white in papers like the *Illustrated News*, but were almost always reduced to a type, closer to the scientific depiction of a genus rather than human beings with particular feelings and concerns. *The Graphic* had been instrumental in the process of encouraging serious artists to paint the poor and sick, and its editor noted that 'the same kindly feeling to the poor and lowly was displayed

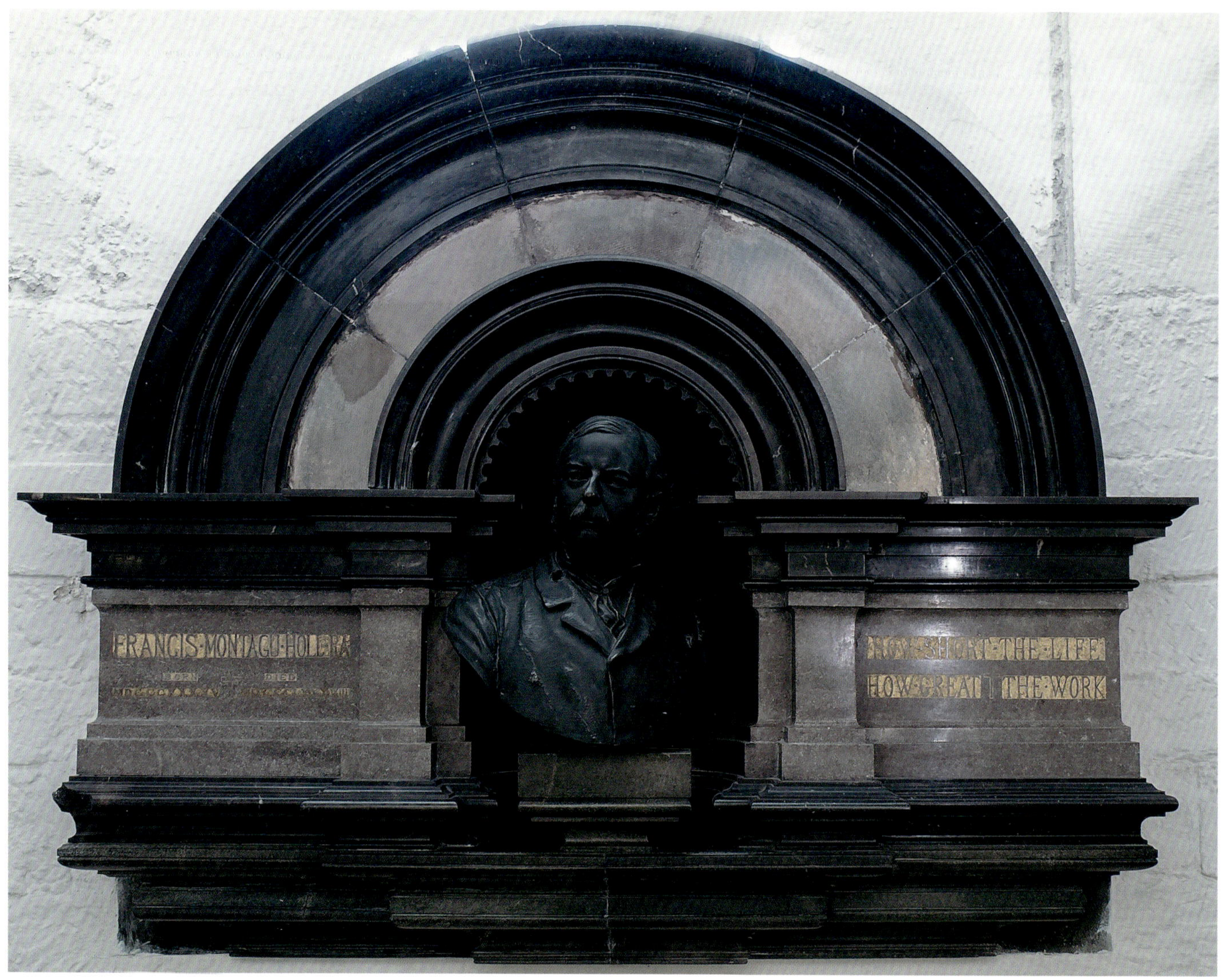

Fig. 12. Joseph Edgar Boehm and Alfred Gilbert, *Monument to Francis Montague Holl*, *c.*1889, bronze and sculpted marble. St Paul's Cathedral

with more dramatic force in numerous drawings by Frank Holl'.[85] Holl had shown in the universal appeal of his subjects that the more fortunate could at once relate to the tragedies he depicted and, in so doing, empathize with the poor who were the unfortunate actors in the dramas.

Holl's work also emanated a religious sensibility, something puritan in approach that echoed his love of Dutch painting. Although there is no specific account of his religion, we know that he was a Protestant whose funeral was held in an Anglican Church. How important religion was in his early life cannot be certain, but he was instinctively ethical in his approach to painting.[86] It is also of note that the titles of several of his early works were biblical quotations applied to the experience of modern life: *'The Lord gave and the Lord hath taken away, Blessed be the Name of the Lord'*, *'Better is a dinner of herbs where love is than a stalled ox and hatred therewith'* and *I am the Resurrection and the Life* (fig. 11). All illustrated faith and stoicism in the face of tragedy and indicated the comfort found in religion.

It is clear that Holl's paintings appealed to a diverse body of people in Victorian society (fig. 12).

There was the commission from the Queen, and Holl had two loyal patrons in Captain Henry Hill of Brighton and Fred Pawle of Reigate. Many dealers, too, including William Agnew and Arthur Tooth, regularly commissioned and sold Holl's works. In his portraits he presented a broad range of society, even if they were almost exclusively male. In terms of a wider public audience, his paintings found their way into numerous public galleries, including the collection of Henry Tate, but, perhaps above all, into the full-size illustrations and supplements for *The Graphic* and occasionally the *Illustrated London News*.[87] These were often framed in poorer households or retained in collections, most notably by Vincent van Gogh, who recalled:

> If the painters were to close ranks to ensure that their work (which, after all, is made for the people, in my view – at least I believe that is the highest, noblest vocation for any artist) could also come into the hands of the people and was put within everyone's reach, that would be something that would produce the same results as were produced in the first years of *The Graphic*.[88]

The universalism of the works and their highlighting of the plight of the poor, painted with dignity and empathy, ensured a wide audience. Despite this, as artistic expressions, they were considered outmoded by the end of the nineteenth century. And Holl's premature death has to a certain extent robbed him of his true significance. Had he lived, he would have received a baronetcy, which was to have been conferred in the 1888 birthday lists, but he 'died just two months before it was ratified'.[89] Enthusiasm for Holl evaporated quite quickly in the 1890s and the fact that he was no longer present meant a leading subject and portrait painter became overlooked. In the twentieth century's rejection of Victorian art he was one of many Academicians in that category, not badly thought of, but simply one of many.

In the 1980s the exhibition *Hard Times* did much to rediscover Holl as a leading figure in social realism,[90] and the National Portrait Gallery has shown his importance as a portraitist in their permanent displays. Holl has a relevance today: beyond the politics and changing *fin de siècle* artistic tastes he appears as a consummate artist, a great painter with a singular vision driven by his belief in truth and observation. His fidelity to these precepts steers him away from unctuous sentiment, and his love of the great Dutch painters shows his understanding of an art that can reveal universal truths. As such, we do not need to see him purely as a painter of social ills that are specific to late-nineteenth-century Britain. He has emerged from the shadows as one of Victorian art's most significant painters.

Notes

[1] 'As you know the selection of the Holl pictures has been left to me, we have something like 50 promised – not a single refusal – from the Queen downwards. I think he could scarcely be better represented. I fancy from what I hear we shall have a fine winter show' (William Powell Frith to M.H. Spielmann, 17 November 1888, John Rylands Library, Manchester University).

[2] Thomas Way to Whistler, 1 May 1880, MS Whistler W79, Glasgow University; the portrait referred to is *J. Bushby, Esq.* (134).

[3] See Treuherz 1987 (ch. 9 'Frank Holl: "the graver, greyer aspect of life"').

[4] Reynolds, p. 311.

[5] Vincent van Gogh, Letter 304, 'To Anthon van Rappard. The Hague, on or about Thursday, 25 January 1883'. Three works by Holl preserved in Van Gogh's estate all came from *The Graphic* (1872–3).

[6] *The Penny Illustrated Paper and Illustrated Times*, 27 July 1889, p. 139.

[7] Meynell 1880, p. 188.

[8] Frith quoted in Reynolds, p. 24.

[9] Reynolds, pp. 11–12.

[10] Reynolds, p. 20.

[11] Ibid.

[12] The painting entitled *A Mother and Child* (private collection) was exhibited at a small gallery in London and sold for £40 to a Mr Schofield of Rochdale, 1863. For an image see McEvansoneya 1998, p. 9.

[13] R.A. Council Minutes, 23 January 1863, R.A. Archive.

[14] Reynolds, p. 21.

[15] Shown, for example, in works like '*The Lord gave and the Lord hath taken away; blessed be the name of the Lord*' (cat. 5), '*Better is a dinner of herbs where love is than a stalled ox and hatred therewith*' and '*I am the Resurrection and the Life*' (fig. 11).

[16] 'He [Holl] says that in April (1865) he "commenced a picture from Longfellow's 'Evangeline' and left it unfinished. Took a dislike to it"' (Reynolds, p. 26).

[17] Reynolds, pp. 43–4.

[18] Calthrop was the same age as Holl and his works, though historical and less successful than Holl's, show a similarity and affinity of approach.

[19] The biblical text, however, appears later in the novel (vol. 2, pp. 227–8): 'Of his own words, what could he say? So he only uttered those consecrated of old by the deepest affliction, and balm to all other affliction since: "The Lord gave and the Lord hath taken away: blessed be the name of the Lord!"'

[20] Reynolds, p. 40.

[21] 'To Frank Holl, the two years' Travelling Studentship in Painting', the annual distribution of prizes 10 December 1868, *Art Journal*, 1868, p. 29.

[22] Professor Weir quoted in Meynell 1880, p. 190.

[23] Reynolds, p. 58: probably the artist Dennis Wood Deane (*c.*1822–1900) and his wife.

[24] Reynolds, p. 62.

[25] Reynolds, p. 59.

[26] Reynolds, p. 62.

[27] Meynell 1880, p. 187.

[28] Annie Laura Holl (1842–1931), quoted in Reynolds, p. 71.

[29] Leeds Mercury, Thursday, 23 May 1872, p. 6.

[30] Frederick Charles Pawle, a stockbroker living at Northcote, Reigate, had a long-standing friendship with Holl and his family. He was a keen collector of modern paintings and was an active promoter of cultural activities in Surrey. He owned a number of other works by Holl including '*The Lord gave and the Lord hath taken away…*' (1868), which he bequeathed to the Guildhall Art Gallery in 1916, and *Hush!* and *Hushed* (both 1877).

[31] Meynell 1880, p. 191.

[32] Reynolds, pp. 16–17.

[33] Reynolds, p. 17.

[34] Reynolds, p. 23; sadly, the diary to which she refers is unlocated.

[35] See Millar 1992, pp. 122–3.

[36] Reynolds, p. 83

[37] 'Life Brigade Man', *Graphic,* 19 February 1870.

[38] Reynolds, pp. 83–4.

[39] 'Winter Exhibition of the Society of British Artists', *Graphic*, 10 December 1870.

[40] Reynolds, p. 84

[41] Ibid.

[42] Ibid.

[43] Reynolds, p. 85.

[44] Meynell 1880, p. 190.

[45] Anon. 1888a, p. 8.

[46] Reynolds, p. 133.

[47] 'My father went back to Criccieth full of enthusiasm for his idea, and next day took along materials, and started a picture which, when completed he called "Waiting" – also a rather large canvas, "L'Ennemi" … Both canvases were painted in September [1876]' (Reynolds, pp. 133–4).

[48] M.H. Spielmann on Holl's drawings for *The Graphic* in Spielmann 1888a, p. 693.

[49] For an account of wood engraving in pictorial weeklies see Mark Bills, '"A distinctive character to the Illustration of News": Sir John Gilbert and the Pictorial Press', in Spike Bucklow and Sally Woodcock, ed., *Sir John Gilbert Art and Imagination in the Victorian Age*, Farnham 2011.

[50] According to Spielmann, he was 'on the staff' for only

three years, although contributions by or after his work continued into the 1880s: Spielmann 1888a, p. 693. His drawings for *The Graphic* include: 'At a Railway Station – A Study', 10 February 1872, pp. 128–9; 'Sight seeing – A study from nature at Mortlake', 20 April 1872, pp. 368–9; 'A drawing done for the Shoemaking Department at the Philanthropic Society's Farm School at Redhill', 18 May 1872, p. 448 (text, p. 455); 'Sketches in London – A Flower Girl', 22 June 1872, p. 573; 'I am the resurrection and the life', 17 August 1872, pp. 148–9; 'London Sketches – The Foundling', 26 April 1873, pp. 392–3; 'London Sketches – the Deserter', 25 September 1875, pp. 312–13; 'Gone – Euston Station. Departure of emigrants, 9.15 p.m. Train for Liverpool, September, 1875', 19 February 1876, pp. 180–1; 'The school board elections – A board school' 2 December 1876, pp. 544–5; 'The Gifts of the Fairies', 25 December 1878, supplement; 'Summoned for Active Service', 11 January 1879, pp. 32–3; 'Discipline and Dissipation', 22 April 1879, pp. 416–17; 'Bereaved', 29 April 1882, supplement (with the following verse, 'By hope unsoothed, by comfort unbeguiled, / The widowed mother mourneth o'er her child, / Talk not of joys the world may yet confer, / That tiny baby was all the world to her'); 'Alone', 10 February 1883, supplement.

[51] Reynolds, pp. 99–100.

[52] Frank Holl, 'Sketches in London – A Flower Girl', *Graphic*, 22 June 1872, p. 573, and A.B. Houghton, 'Sketches in London – Before the Bar', 11 May 1872, p. 440.

[53] Spielmann 1888a, p. 693.

[54] Reynolds, pp. 97–8.

[55] Ibid.

[56] Anon. 1888a.

[57] 'The C.E. Johnsons were, of course, my parents' nearest neighbours then, living, as they did, next door but one to us' (Reynolds, p. 119).

[58] Reynolds, p. 107.

[59] Reynolds, p. 139.

[60] Reynolds, p. 109.

[61] Reynolds, pp. 108–9.

[62] Reynolds, pp. 109, 110.

[63] 'London Sketches – The Foundling', *Graphic*, 26 April 1873, pp. 392–3.

[64] Vincent van Gogh, Letter 304, 'To Anthon van Rappard. The Hague, on or about Thursday, 25 January 1883'.

[65] Reynolds, p. 144.

[66] Holl to Carey, 1 September 1887, Royal Holloway Archive, quoted in Chapel 1982, p. 96.

[67] Frank Holl, Presidential Address, delivered Sutton Coldfield, 14 January 1888, in Reynolds, p. 330.

[68] His subject work virtually came to a halt in the early 1880s and his last subject painting appears to be *One of the Six Hundred* (1885).

[69] Reynolds, p. 198.

[70] *Penny Illustrated Paper and Illustrated Times*, 27 July 1889, p. 139.

[71] Quilter 1888.

[72] Obituary, *The Times*, 1 August 1888, p. 10.

[73] Letter to A.M. Broadley, 30 November 1887, Pierpoint Library, New York, quoted in Chapel 1982, p. 97. At the R.A. summer exhibition of 1878 Holl exhibited two paintings: Newgate, Committed for Trial (423) and A Portrait (599).

[74] 'The household expenditure was truly of the most meagre description, and the children were taught to look upon their father as a poor and hard-working man, and, in the case of little Frank, so soon as he should be old enough, not only must he not look to them for maintenance, but in turn must do his utmost to help his father, and thus save the eyes and hands of the toiling bread-winner of the home' (Reynolds, pp. 10–11).

[75] Take, for example, 'At a Railway Station – A Study', *Graphic*, 10 February 1872, which became *Leaving Home* (R.A. 1873) and was then copied three times on commission as a replica made for the engraving, an oil on panel, and a watercolour exhibited at the Old Watercolour Society in 1883.

[76] Reynolds, p. 213.

[77] Reynolds, p. 316.

[78] Spielmann 1888b, p. 412.

[79] Professor Weir quoted in Meynell 1880, p. 190.

[80] Reynolds, p. 27.

[81] Reynolds, p. 11.

[82] *The Times*, 16 April 1879, p. 1.

[83] Frank Holl, Presidential Address, delivered Sutton Coldfield, 14 Jan. 1888, in Reynolds, pp. 330–1.

[84] Reynolds, p. 85.

[85] William Luson Thomas, 'Graphic Artists', *Graphic*, 6 December 1890, p. 634.

[86] Reynolds (p. 234) notes that 'it often came to working, when time pressed, through the whole of Sunday, although he was always loath to do this'.

[87] These include: 'Home again', *The Illustrated London News*, 3 Sept. 1881, extra supplement, pp. 236–7, and 'Ordered Off', *The Illustrated London News*, 13 Sept. 1884, supplement, pp. 264–5.

[88] Vincent van Gogh, Letter 278, 'To Theo van Gogh. The Hague, Wednesday, 1 November 1882'.

[89] Reynolds, p. 264.

[90] Treuherz 1987, ch. 9.

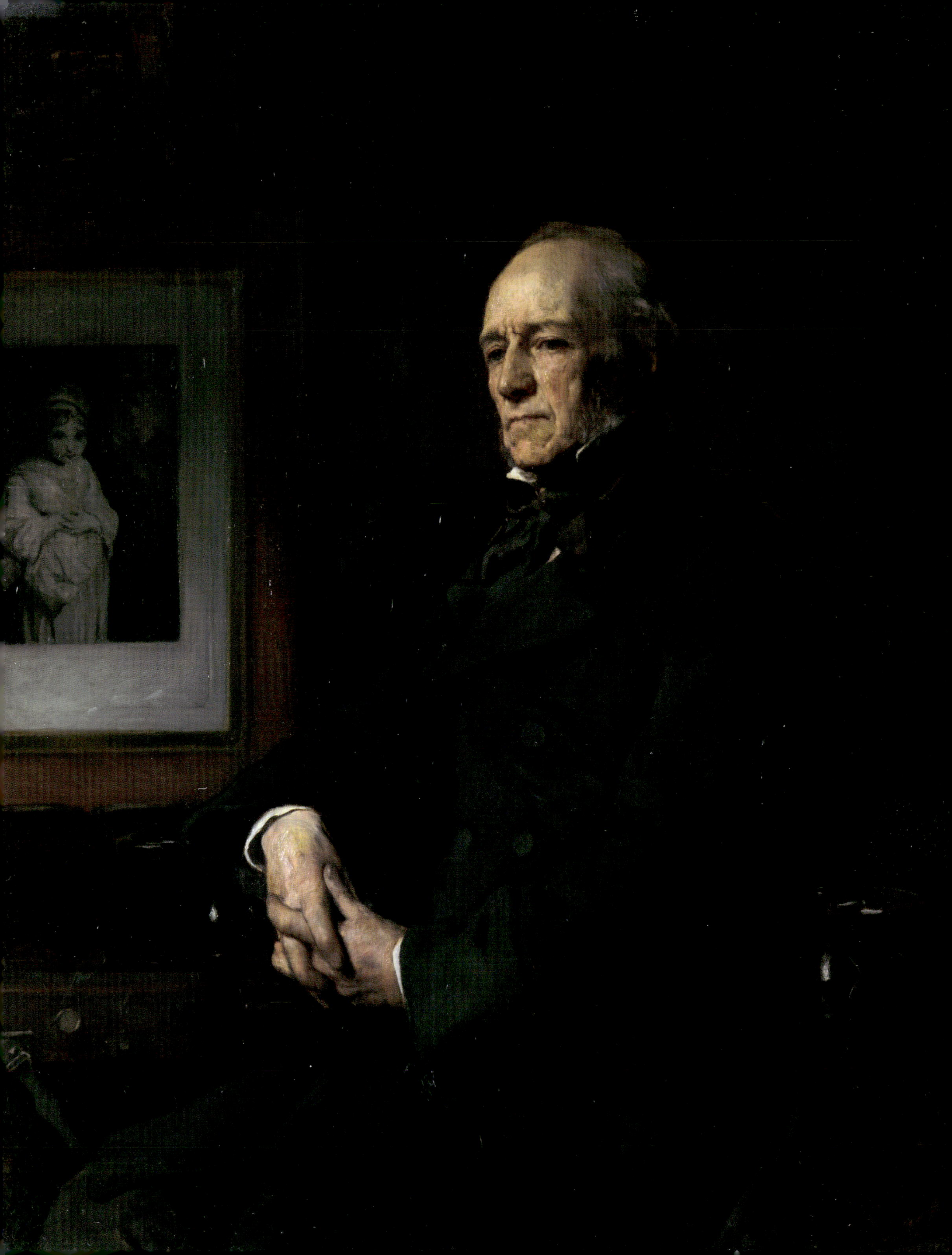

Frank Holl: Portraits and the 'Modern Englishman'

Peter Funnell

Holl's portrait practice

Holl's professional practice as a portrait painter began in 1879. He had exhibited a little-noticed 'head' in the previous year's Royal Academy exhibition, and had painted or drawn family portraits, but two portraits exhibited in the 1879 Academy, of the cellist Alfredo Piatti and of the engraver Samuel Cousins (fig. 13, cat. 17), are generally regarded as establishing Holl as primarily a portraitist for the remainder of his career. The Cousins portrait in particular was considered by contemporaries to be the key marker in this shift in direction. According to the writer on art Marion Harry Spielmann, Holl's move into portrait painting had been encouraged by his father, the engraver Francis Holl, and the choice of Cousins as a subject suggested by the senior Academician, John Prescott Knight.[1] The portrait was widely admired when exhibited – if not by Cousins himself apparently – and became seen as quintessential of the portraiture in which Holl was to specialize and be most identified with in the following eight years or so. Although recent scholarship on Holl has focused on his subject pictures – and they of course receive equal weight in this exhibition – for his contemporaries Holl's greatest success was to be seen in his portraits. Virtually all his obituarists and the reviewers of his posthumous exhibition at the 1889 Winter Academy regarded his most distinctive achievement as having been in portraiture with works such as that of Cousins.

Fig. 13. Frank Holl, *Samuel Cousins*, 1879, oil on canvas. Tate

Holl painted very few portraits of women and children. His portrait oeuvre consists almost entirely of paintings of men and it was on these that he was judged. According to Gertrude E. Campbell, reviewing the Winter Academy for the *Art Journal*, 'from 1879 may be said to date Holl's greatest successes, for in that year he revealed himself as the greatest portrait-painter of men of his time'. And later she asserts that 'he yet stands, as a portrait-painter of men, ahead of most if not all of his contemporaries, and it may be many a long day before anyone arises in this country capable of taking his place'.[2] The nature of Holl's male portraiture, and how it exemplifies a particular type of masculinity of the period, will be the main subject of this essay. But first it will be helpful to consider Holl's practice as a portrait painter and aspects of portrait production, exhibition and reception from 1879 until his early death in 1888.

Holl's output as a portraitist during this period was considerable. It has been estimated that he painted approximately 200 portraits in these years, a figure roughly confirmed by the annual reckonings of his daughter A.M. Reynolds in her biography of her father: she records that he painted twenty-four portraits and five subject pictures in 1882 and twenty-three portraits in 1885, for instance.[3] Hard work and the toll this took on Holl's health are a recurrent theme in Reynolds's *Life*. Writing of his daily routine in 1885, she says that portraiture 'took up all his time, and more, for it encroached even upon that which ought to have been the necessary allowance of leisure', and that his was 'not an easy life, one may well conceive –

in fact, it was pretty nigh slavery'.[4] As I shall suggest, this account feeds into a broader narrative of work and fortitude. Nonetheless, the words of Holl's fellow portrait painter and friend, John Everett Millais (1829–1896), in a letter to him shortly before Holl's death seem real enough. 'Portrait-painting', Millais writes, 'is *killing work* to an artist who is sensitive, and he must be so to be successful, and I well understand that you are prostrated by it.'[5]

We have accounts of Holl's approach to painting a portrait from both Spielmann and Reynolds. According to Spielmann, Holl would begin by taking 'mental notes' of his sitter's characteristics, the first sitting often consisting mainly of conversation and observation. In Reynolds these mental notes are translated into 'jotting down in pen and pencil on any scrap of paper a few rough lines' suggestive of a sitter's actions.[6] This approach is perhaps confirmed by Holl himself when he spoke in an address to students of correcting his portraits in subsequent sittings by referring to a drawing to recall a 'first sight' impression of a sitter.[7] A 'fresh eye' is Holl's emphasis here, and a directness of approach is a theme in Spielmann's account of his method. He would always paint on a white ground, he tells us, as opposed to coloured grounds favoured, for example, by G.F. Watts, and would apply paint directly without underdrawing: 'What Mr. Holl wishes to avoid is that "underdone" look, so "low in tone," that we often see in portraits, with the loss of freshness.'[8] And Spielmann's admiration of Holl's style, his 'accustomed breadth and firmness', carries through into his Academy reviews in the 1880s.[9] Spielmann was notable for being sympathetic to artists and throughout these reviews is keen to champion what he saw as the triumph of British portraiture during this period. He was, as Ford Madox Brown commented, 'the kindest of critics'.[10]

Holl's portrait style received less favourable treatment from other exhibition reviewers. The influential and mainstream *Art Journal* was generally very favourable though in 1884 noted a 'trick of manner' in his more recent work, while the critic who had the most reservations was Frederic George Stephens (1828–1907) writing in *The Athenaeum*. One of the founding members of the Pre-Raphaelite Brotherhood, Stephens's artistic preferences are said to have broadened in this period. But, with his Pre-Raphaelite and Aesthetic movement sympathies, it is understandable that he would have found it difficult to admire Holl's style.[11] Although Stephens is far from being entirely critical, there is always a sense in which he found Holl's style antipathetic, and what for some seemed a fluid and vigorous approach to painting could seem to Stephens unrefined. Holl's portrait of John Bright, for instance, is criticized for 'its empty forms, want of fusion in the tones, and lack of softness in the tints of the flesh', while in 1885 Holl's portraits are disparaged for being modelled '*en bloc*, more like a mosaic than a finished piece of painting ... (a swift and easy-going method for a deft painter), and in such a manner as to suggest that the artist is very much mistaken if he thinks he is working in the style of Rembrandt'.[12] If this barbed comment wasn't enough, Stephens became increasingly hostile in the following year when he observed that Holl 'takes less pains than ever', attacks his 'coarse technique' and finds a portrait of the Duke of Cleveland that others greatly admired 'flashy and crude' and the Duke's expression 'exaggerated to moroseness'. 'We marvel', Stephens continues, 'that so able an artist as Mr Holl ventures to defy Fortune so openly as he has done this year. Close at his heals tread not-only half a dozen portrait-painting Academicians, but half a score competent outsiders.' And he concludes that 'the mode of painting Mr. Holl has pursued till probably he cannot avoid its snares has brought disaster upon him just where his critics felt sure it would'.[13] For Stephens Holl was to some extent redeemed in the following year when he noted 'a return to a more thorough mode of painting' and, while he still found room for improvement, thought it 'creditable to an artist who is overwhelmed with orders that he should have recognized the necessity of greater care'.[14]

Stephens's comments on Holl should be seen as part of a more widely held anxiety as to the highly competitive and commercial practice of portrait painting in the mid-1880s. As Stephens's remarks about competitors suggest, Holl was not alone in having turned to portraiture in the late 1870s and to have made it a principal part of his practice in the 1880s. For those like Spielmann the boom in portrait painting in this decade was cause for celebration. Likewise

Wilfred Meynell (1852–1948), in a *Magazine of Art* profile of Holl in 1880, identified him with a broader revival in portraiture. Noting the great eighteenth-century heritage of portrait painting in British art, Meynell asserts that, with a few exceptional artists, it had in recent decades 'sunk among us to the least intelligent branch of art'. So it was 'with real pleasure, with renewed hope and confidence do we find our foremost artists ... turning their powers to the worthy work of portraiture.'[15] Undoubtedly, one cause for the phenomenon was that a successful portrait practice at this time was potentially very lucrative. Holl's rise in wealth and status is, for example, indicated by the building of sizable new houses for his family in London and Surrey within a few years of his turning to portrait painting. A prime example of the profitability of portrait painting was Millais, the unquestioned leader in the field, who could charge the highest prices: he sold his 1881 portrait of Disraeli, for example, with copyright to the Fine Art Society for the considerable sum of 1,400 guineas. And nowhere is this more blatantly stated than by Hubert von Herkomer (1849–1914), an artist who like Holl had moved from social-realist painting to portraiture. 'Here comes in an astonishing item,' Herkomer wrote to his father in July 1882, 'the extraordinary rapidity with which one can make money' and he goes on to calculate how in the past two and a half months he earned from thirteen portraits 'six thousand six hundred and fourteen pounds sterling'.[16]

But the price of this was stiff competition. To the senior Academicians noted as Holl's competitors by Stephens, such as Millais or Watts, could be added portrait specialists such as the dependable Walter William Ouless, and artists who continued to paint subject pictures like Edwin Long, William Blake Richmond, William Quiller Orchardson and Holl's Hampstead neighbour, John Pettie, but for whom portrait painting was an important staple. Then there were up and coming artists like John Collier whose practice benefited from the scientific connections he made through his marriage into the family of Thomas Henry Huxley. There were foreign competitors exhibiting at the Academy: Carolus-Duran showed there during these years and the decade also saw the emergence in England of his most famous pupil, John Singer Sargent. Although, as I shall argue in the case of Holl, there was an element of specialization in the types of clients a portraitist painted, some of the most famous individuals of the day sat to a number of portrait painters. Their portraits could occasionally be exhibited at the same time, fuelling eager comparison on the part of the critics. Thus Stephens notes with some relish that Holl was 'brought into direct rivalry with Mr. Ouless when the Queen commissioned him to paint Sir F.S. Roberts, as in No. 223, and two works (see No. 23) were produced which may be compared here'.[17] And in the following year he adds to his criticism of Holl's portrait of John Bright by saying how it unwisely challenged comparison with a portrait of the politician by Stephens's old friend, Millais. It is hardly surprising that Holl was elated several years later when in 1887 he was able to report of the reception of his portrait of Gladstone, one of his greatest challenges, that 'the general impression is that I have beaten the Millais' (see fig. 19).[18]

The competitive nature of the annual Academy exhibition had of course been a phenomenon since the eighteenth century. But the increase in exhibition venues in the later Victorian period – Holl showed portraits at the Grosvenor Gallery and regional exhibitions as well as the R.A. – and a burgeoning art press reinforced a sense of artists vying with each other in public. We have seen how Stephens blamed the prolific nature of Holl's practice for a decline in standards, saying that he was 'overwhelmed by orders' in his telling phrase with its hint of trade and commercialism. Holl was also a principal, if not the sole, focus of a campaign in the mid-1880s against portrait painters exhibiting too many works. Stephens took up the cause in his 1887 review, noting that Holl had submitted eight portraits, the full allowance traditionally given to Academicians, and that this was another sign of his over-productivity: 'Would they were fewer, and the same amount of study expended on them as the eight.' But it was the *Art Journal* that had most consistently led the charge. It noted in 1883 that Holl had sent in his full eight portraits and asked whether the French system of limiting artists to two works should be adopted. The *Journal*'s suspicions of artists' motives are confirmed when it goes on to lament that, as soon as they have attained success, 'they turn aside towards the pecuniary rewards held out to portrait painting, and Mr Alma-Tadema, Mr Long and Mr Herkomer are amongst the most recent followers of the road so successfully travelled over by Mr Millais and Mr Watts'.[19] And, again focusing on Holl's contribution to the 1885 Academy, the *Art Journal* makes explicit the link between numbers exhibited and money. 'It is impossible to conceive that any benefit – except a commercial one to the artist – can be gained from the display of eight portraits by Mr Frank Holl, or half a dozen each by Mr Sant, Mr Sidney Cooper, Mr W. Ouless or Mr Edwin Long.'[20]

Indeed, 1885 seems to have marked the highpoint of critical objections to the commercial boom in portrait painting, with Stephens's attacks on Holl as a portrait painter at their most intense. But Stephens also sees this as part of a general decline in the genre in Britain: 'Our artists, spoiled by flattery and big prices, have, it seems, forgotten that for two thousand francs a sitter can get in Paris a better head than all but the very best of the pictures we have criticized, the prices of which may range from 400*l* to 800*l*.'[21] As one might expect it was Spielmann, again, who came to Holl and his fellow portraitists' defence when he ended his 1888 profile of Holl by assuring his readers that 'the persistent rumour of the fabulous sums earned by

Fig. 14. Frank Holl, *Sir William Schwenck Gilbert*, 1886, oil on canvas. © National Portrait Gallery, London

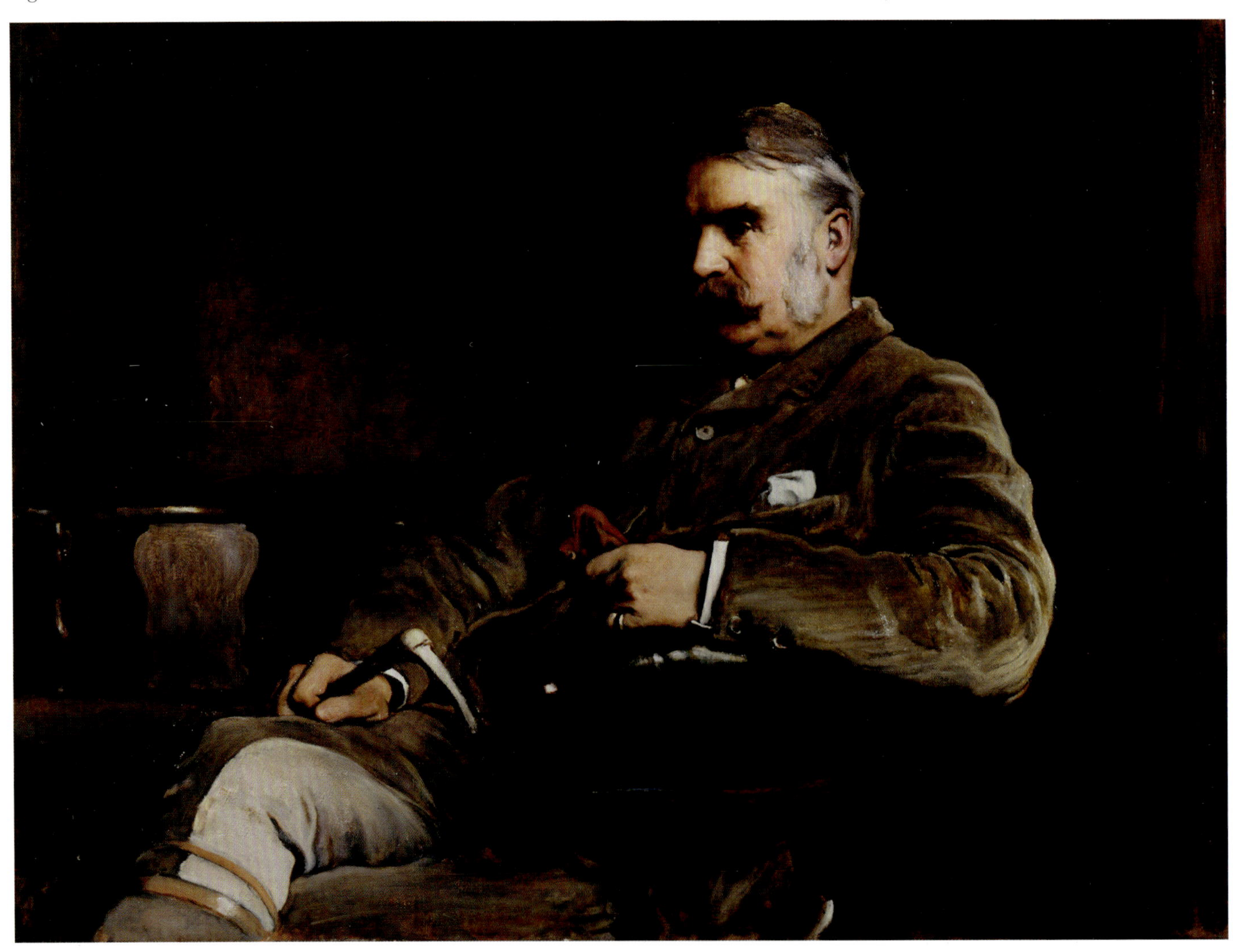

portraitists is not to be believed'. 'I make no doubt but that Mr Holl succeeds in making both ends meet;' he concludes, 'but the tall talk of gigantic prices is, I know, only the pleasant conjuring up of a wonder-loving public'.[22]

In spite of this, we know that in 1887 W.S. Gilbert paid Holl £525 for his portrait (fig. 14, cat. 26). And Gilbert's correspondence with Holl, commissioning the portrait in early November 1886 and arranging sittings in late November and December, suggests the efficiency and dispatch with which Holl could complete a three-quarter-length portrait. And, while not matching Millais's prices, even a rough calculation based on Holl's annual output indicates that his income from portraiture alone placed him among those who, I shall now argue, formed his principal clientele.

The 'modern Englishman'

Echoing other commentators, the *Art Journal*'s obituary of Holl recorded that he 'was the painter of the modern Englishman'.[23] The remainder of this essay will explore what is meant by the phrase 'modern Englishman' both in terms of the type of men he portrayed and the values he shared with them. In determining the nature of Holl's clientele, an examination sitter by sitter is revealing. He certainly painted members of the landed aristocracy such as Lord Spencer (1888) or the diplomat, the Marquess of Dufferin and Ava (1885). Likewise politicians made up a portion of his practice. But the list of Holl's sitters is striking for the preponderance of what could be called 'professional men'. Historians of the phenomenon of 'professionalization' in the later nineteenth and early twentieth centuries have urged caution about the term. It can too readily lead to teleological expectations of 'a direct path of development' or idea that there was a distinct 'professional consciousness' across the wide range of occupations that could be called the professions.[24] Nonetheless it can clearly be argued that professionalization was a feature of British society in the period when Holl's subjects were making their mark in their careers and having their portraits painted.

Later-Victorian professions can be loosely, yet helpfully, divided between those that were traditional and non-industrial – religion, law, medicine, education, the civil service and the military – as opposed to occupations connected to the post-industrial world such as accounting or civil and mechanical engineering. As T.R. Gourvish has argued, however imprecise definitions of the professions are, it is clear that 'existing professional occupations cemented their position in late Victorian society, and at the same time others coalesced to form new, distinct, professional groups'.[25] Evidence that this was the case ranges from the sheer increase in numbers of those pursuing particular occupations, through legal reforms such as the Medical Act of 1858 that controlled medical registration, to the development of professional associations that sought to 'formalize training, systematize knowledge and control entry' into a given occupation.[26]

Examples of many of these types can be given from the eight or nine years of Holl's practice as a portrait painter. Of the older professions there are Archbishops or Bishops of York, Dublin and Gloucester. There are Lord Mayors of London and mayors of the newer industrial cities such as Leeds and Birmingham. Military figures include national heroes such as Lord Roberts (1881) and Lord Wolseley (R.A. 1883). The law constitutes a significant group, with jurists including Sir James Bacon (1881), Sir Arthur Hobhouse (1882) and Lord Justice Fry (1883). Indeed, Reynolds records Holl's ambition, unfulfilled at his death, 'of painting a trial scene in which should be included portraits of a number of the most celebrated judges of the day'. Education is another important occupation to be included in the list of Holl's sitters with Heads of Oxbridge Colleges, such as Edward Hartopp Cradock (1880) and James Bellamy (1886), and the Headmasters of Charterhouse, Eton and Marlborough. Medicine is represented by portraits of the medical journalist Ernest Hart (1883) and the physicians Sir George Johnson (*c.*1887), Sir Andrew Clark (1888; fig. 15; cat. 28) and Sir William Jenner (1888). The fact that Holl's death was noted in *The Lancet* is perhaps testimony to his role in painting portraits of some of the leading figures in this profession.[27] That, even at this date, medicine was an

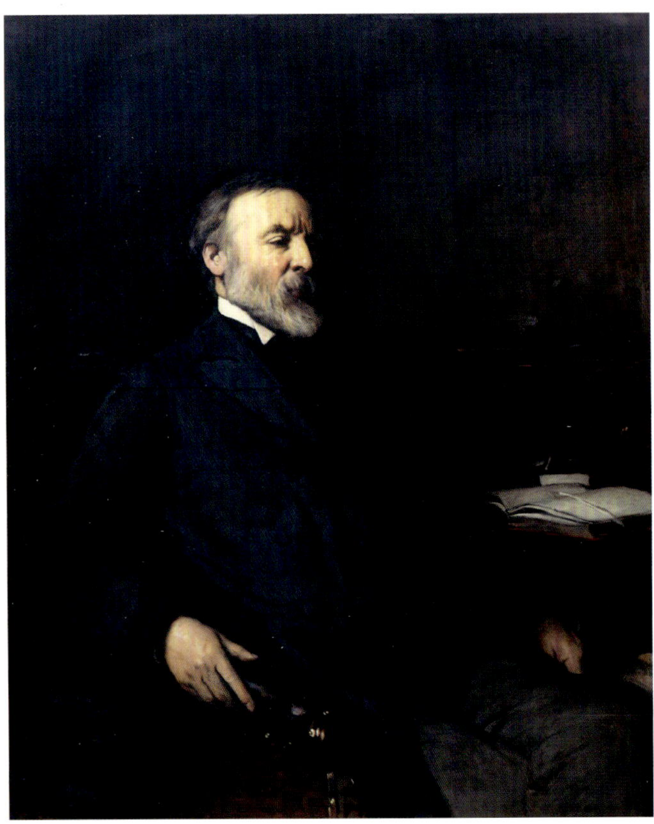

Fig. 15. Frank Holl, *Sir Andrew Clark, Bt.*, 1888, oil on canvas. Royal College of Physicians

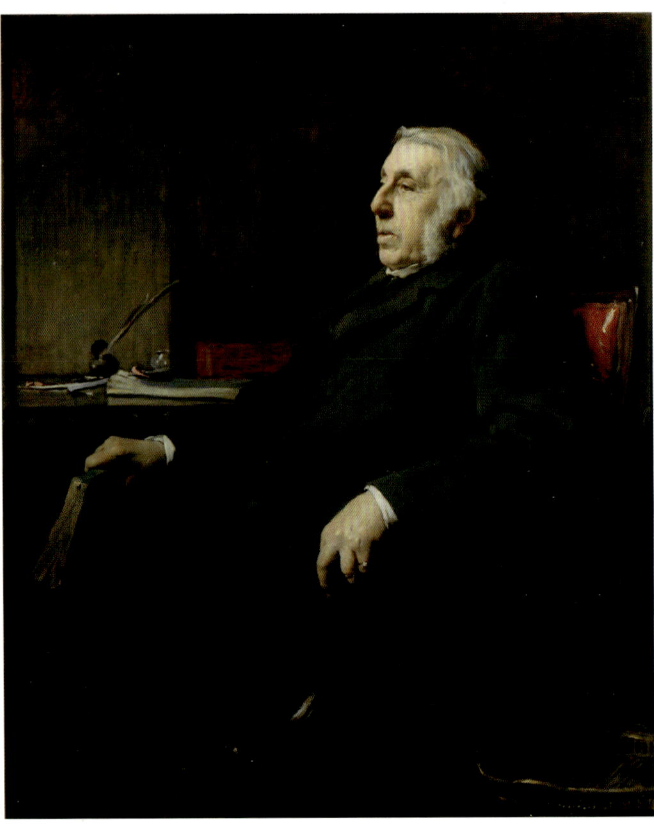

Fig. 16. Frank Holl, *Major George Graham*, 1880, oil on canvas. Government Art Collection

occupation whose professional standing could still be at issue will be discussed shortly.

As we look at the less traditional occupations among Holl's sitters, individual case histories show how resistant to strict categorization some of their occupations were or reveal individuals pursuing occupations that were effectively new. Thus there are figures such as Simon Adams Beck (1880) or Sir Thomas Paine (1883) who both started off as lawyers but who pursued City careers that were deeply influenced by emergent industries. Beck, whose position was ostensibly that of clerk and solicitor of the Ironmongers' Company, where Holl's portrait of him still hangs, was closely involved in London's gas production companies. Likewise Paine's City law practice grew prosperous through acting for railway companies and breweries, investment trusts and, in the 1880s, the London and Lancashire Life Assurance Company, of which he was a director. City patronage was significant for Holl, with the bankers (and both notable art collectors) Lord Overstone (1881) and George Rae (1883 and 1885) sitting to him. The civil service provided subjects such as the chairman of the Inland Revenue, Sir Charles Herries (1882); the Registrar General, George Graham (1880; fig. 16; cat. 18); and Thomas Henry Farrer (1881), who sat to Holl the year before his brother-in-law, the judge Sir Arthur Hobhouse, indicated the networks of clients on whom Holl's practice prospered. Both Graham and Farrer worked at a time when an expanded government effectively gave rise to new professions within the civil service. Graham was the second Registrar General in the newly formed General Register Office, assembling and interpreting critical population data including the decennial censuses from 1851 to 1871, while Farrer presided over a Board of Trade that grew from a staff of forty-eight in 1850 to 362 in 1886 and, again, regulated industries and businesses that reflected Britain's expanding economy.

Finally, there were those who contributed more directly to this phenomenon and whose occupational identity is distinct from, but closely connected to, other professions already noted: industrialists and entrepreneurs. They are again prominent among Holl's sitters and can also be seen to constitute a new or 'modern' type of sitter. They include figures who made their mark in technological industries, such as the industrial chemist, Walter Weldon (1884), the engineer Sir Frederick Bramwell (1887), and Nathaniel Clayton and Joseph Shuttleworth, who both sat to Holl in 1882 and who, as Clayton and Shuttleworth, ran a successful engineering firm building steam engines and agricultural machinery. Then there are those who remain household names: the Belfast shipbuilder Edward Harland (1884) of Harland and Wolff, and William Isaac Palmer (1885) of Huntley and Palmers, the biscuit manufacturers.

Two portraits and their sitters in this exhibition help elucidate what the portrayal of these professional types means. That of Sir Andrew Clark reveals concerns over professional status, while Holl's portrait of George Graham shows him facing the challenge of portraying a civil servant whose accustomed habitat was the office. By the time Holl painted him in 1888, Clark's social standing was by all accounts very settled. Physician to leading figures in later Victorian society, most notably W.E. Gladstone, Clark conducted his practice from his house and consulting room in Cavendish Square, bought a country house near Hatfield in later life, was made a baronet in 1883 and became President of the Royal College of Physicians in 1888, the year his family commissioned Holl's portrait. Yet *The Lancet's* account of Clark's grand and elaborate funeral in Westminster Abbey makes us aware of the fairly recent recognition of medicine as a profession of high status – within Clark's own lifetime – and its relative fragility even in the 1880s. It was an event for which there was 'no precedent', *The Lancet* says and in its lengthy description returns repeatedly to the point that it was not only a tribute to Clark himself but an important marker of the status of the medical profession. 'The poet – in prose and in verse, the statesman, the soldier, the divine, the scholar and the judge have had a like homage justly paid to them.' Now similar 'respect has been rendered to a representative of the medical profession' showing that 'appreciation of the medical profession is increasing'.[28] And it goes on to quote from an 1876 address by Clark himself on the subject when he spoke of the need for physicians to 'take our just place beside the other professions in Society and in the State'.[29]

To have an oil portrait painted is of course an affirmation of social status much in the way that the other trappings of success are, whether wealth and gentrification, national honours, or recognition among one's occupational peers. Holl's portraits of such men were frequently made for presentation purposes and are recorded as such in the Royal Academy catalogues. They are therefore bound up with their subjects' professional standing and are themselves confirmation of their success, perhaps created by and for the professional associations of which they were among the most distinguished members, or produced at a critical point in their subjects' careers such as retirement. One such is the engaging portrait of the Registrar General, George Graham, which was made for presentation to him 'on his retirement from office by the Central and Local Officers of the Registration Department, as a token of their respect and esteem'. It records his distinguished career in the GRO, which had seen Graham administer and interpret not only the nationwide registration of births, marriages and deaths but three rounds of the ever more sophisticated census in 1851, 1861 and 1871, and is also a study of modern office life. The GRO engaged in activities that were enormously paper intensive and this is wittily reflected in Holl's portrait, with the pen and inkstand prominent on Graham's work table, the two 'Blue Books', or Annual Reports, one of which Graham grips in his right hand, and in the lower right corner a wastepaper basket. As in the Clark portrait, there is also an air of repose, as if to give a sense of a life well and productively lived. As Spielmann noted in his 1888 *Graphic* profile, it was 'one of Mr. Holl's theories of portraiture, that repose is necessary'.[30] Yet in Graham's portrait this amounts almost to a sense of weariness as if he is finally succumbing to the sheer quantity of work that he has undertaken in his long career. This is intensified by the profile pose of Graham's heavy body and the superb characterization of his face with its slightly parted lips and the watery eyes of an old man. In fact it has been said that Graham's retirement at the end of 1879 aged seventy-eight may have been because he felt too old to organize his fourth census in 1881.

Graham was one of many sitters with whom Holl appears to have developed a close empathy, his subjects often remaining as acquaintances after the portrait was completed. Sociability was of course a necessary part of being a successful portrait painter. Herkomer made it

> a rule to talk with my sitters incessantly ... Once you have a fidgetty old lady, the next hour a political person, or a clergyman, or a great musician, or a man of law or business ... so my fiddle must be quickly tuned to play to all these varied conditions.[31]

But with Holl there is also a sense of shared professional identity, especially with the newer and more emergent professions as evidenced by his clientele as a whole as well as by individual sitters. A meritocratic element is apparent in his subjects, and he himself wrote of how portraiture had brought him 'into contact with many men who are of much interest in the history of the day', while his daughter records the 'distinguished and clever men who sat to him'. That Holl should be drawn to such men is unsurprising given his own background, which was itself enmeshed in issues of emergent professionalization. The son and grandson of engravers, with three uncles who also practised printmaking, Holl was brought up among those working in the most notoriously 'outsider' profession in the art world. Engravers repeatedly suffered from institutional marginalization at the hands of the Royal Academy and Holl would have grown up among those who strove to achieve professional status for what they did. In this sense the portrait of Samuel Cousins is of further significance. Not only was it Holl's breakthrough portrait, it also showed a man who was the unquestioned head of the engraving profession and who had the distinction of having been one of only two engravers to be elected full Royal Academician in 1855. Holl's own father, in spite of his success as an engraver, had to wait until 1883 to be admitted to the R.A. and then in the somewhat concessionary category of Associate Engraver. Holl himself in the meantime had been made an Associate in 1878 and was made full R.A. in the same year of 1883. Indeed, as I have noted, Holl's own professional success, with all the trappings that came with it, put him in a similar social position to many of those who came to sit to him and could be thought a further source of the synergies between the artist and his subjects.

We can, then, identify a particular aspect of Victorian society in the 1880s that Holl was noted for portraying. But are there other characteristics of his clientele? Notably, there is the age of his sitters. As determined by their professional nature, Holl's sitters were painted when they had reached a particular stage in their lives and careers and were therefore often advanced in years. Indeed, male old age becomes a recognizable subset in Holl's output that contemporaries commented on. Thus the *Art Journal* wrote of Holl's portrait of the Earl of Chichester, exhibited at the 1886 Academy, that it was 'one of those portraits of old men in which the artist excels' and of the Duke of Cleveland in the same exhibition that it was 'a masterpiece; it would be impossible to render old age with more truth and character'.[32] The portrait of Cleveland, born in 1803, and that of Captain Alexander Sim (fig. 17, cat. 22), well into his nineties when he sat to Holl, are most frequently cited – and admired – as showing Holl's skill in painting very old men. Frederick Wedmore, reviewing Holl's memorial exhibition, writes of both that 'an unconscious pathos ... heightened to the very last the interest of his pourtrayal [sic] of the effort of the very old still to live'.[33] Yet the notion of pathos, or of struggling to live, was contrary to how most reacted to these portraits or of how such individuals were more generally perceived. Pat Thane, writing of how the elderly in the wealthy and the powerful classes in this period saw themselves and were regarded by others, has identified a strong tendency to emphasize the defiance of the effects of old age. Drawing on a series of case studies, Thane concludes that they

> demonstrate the different ways in which people with wealth, status, or power could be recognized

as old yet still command, and know themselves to command, authority, within the family and/or in public life ... They provided highly visible models of what old age could be, most of them offering challenges to easy stereotypes of its characteristics.[34]

Sim is certainly represented in this way. Recalling his visits for sittings, Reynolds presents us with the image of him as 'hale and hearty, with a cheery laugh and a twinkling eye' and in spite of his 'great age, with a step as light and an eye almost as clear as any young man in his twenties'.[35] And she contrasts Sim's response to old age, his 'boyishness which made him the wonder and delight of all who knew him', to that of another of Holl's sitters, Lord Overstone. Overstone, whom Holl portrayed in his wheelchair, was 'a mass almost of inert flesh ... utterly powerless to move his huge body, which was partly paralysed'.[36] Yet Reynolds's unsympathetic account of Overstone's disability also entailed a view of his personality and of his unwillingness to overcome his failings: 'He was a man of morose and surly disposition, with a forbidding manner, ill-calculated to set his companion at ease.' On the contrary, critical responses to Sim's portrait revolved around his defiance of old age and Holl's success in capturing this. Campbell, in her review of Holl's memorial exhibition, cites it as one of his greatest achievements. 'It would indeed be hard to find', she wrote, 'a truer or more unexaggerated rendering of a stately old gentleman', and she went on to praise the manner in which Holl has suggested Sim's challenge to his years through his upright bearing and the telling way in which 'he clutches the crutch-handled stick which has helped the old sea-dog so long to stand as erect as of yore'.[37]

Another portrait in which these perceptions of male old age are central, and for which we have Holl's own reflections on the subject, is that of Gladstone (fig. 18, cat. 27). As Thane and others have argued, Gladstone was the prime example of a man defying old age: the quintessential 'Grand Old Man'. Prime Minister for the fourth time in 1892 at the age of eighty-two and a prolific author, Gladstone was a byword for physical and mental endurance, noting of himself on his eightieth birthday that 'my physical conservation is indeed noteworthy' and continuing his well-known pastime of tree-felling at his Hawarden estate until 1891.[38] Very alert to the image he presented, Gladstone engaged in 'a calculated attempt to keep age at bay'.[39] An article on 'Mr Gladstone and His Portraits' in the January 1889 issue of the *Magazine of Art* noted how painting Gladstone was almost like receiving a professional diploma for a contemporary portraitist and pointed to age as being the chief issue. The changeability of his expression, not just 'from hour to hour, almost, one might say, from moment to moment', presented immense difficulties and was the result of Gladstone's elderly physical frame belying his youthful vigour. For although 'he presents a picture of extreme old age', in 'an instant all is changed. The eyes flash forth the fires of youth, the head is raised as though in defiance, not merely of the crowded benches opposite, but of Time himself.'[40]

Holl, who travelled to Hawarden in late October 1887 to paint Gladstone and kept a journal of his stay there, formed a similar idea of him and wrote of how this informed his approach to his portrait. We have seen how in the portraits of Graham and Clark (who as Gladstone's physician can take some credit for his enduring health) a frequent strategy of Holl's was to place his subjects in a position of repose. But he quickly determined that this would not be so in the case of Gladstone. Describing the first sitting on 31 October 1887, Holl writes that 'at once I decided that it should be standing; to sit is to be at ease, and not the character of the at once wonderful and extraordinary life he has led'.[41] And in a passage in his journal he reflects on old age and the 'restless life' he detects in Gladstone:

> Still retaining all the ambitions of youth, even, I should think, more than youthful restlessness, as it is the restlessness of waiting still more ... and his age – now, I think, about seventy-six – not giving him the natural chances of many years, either to obtain or hold it.

While for many old age results in contentment, Holl writes, there is 'something very painful' in Gladstone's condition since 'his consciousness of not many more years must make a restless impatience that must be almost unendurable'.[42] It was these reflections, Holl

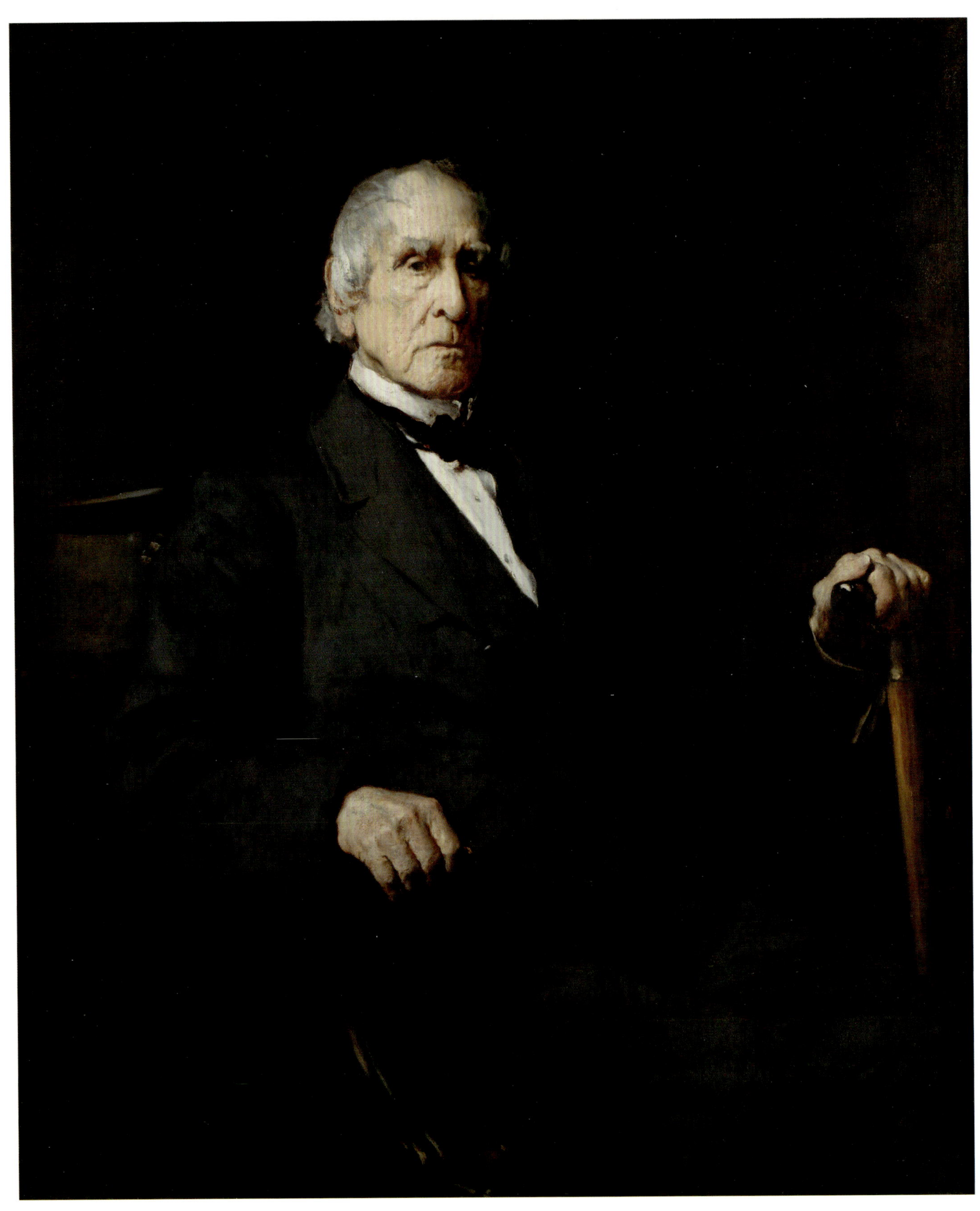

explains, that determined the standing pose and 'to attempt the expression and idea of firm determination in a cause'. Again the critical reception of the portrait shows how contemporaries identified with Holl's intentions, Stephens noting in *The Athenaeum* how the 'force' of Gladstone's features 'is enhanced by the characteristic grip of the hands on the book, and other indications of an excess of nerve-power', even though, as might be expected, he thought Holl had taken it a little too far.[43]

Teutonism, character and manliness

If Holl became identified with painting a particular type of man, is it also possible to discern a set of values that are associated with him and that were, perhaps, shared with his sitters and expressed in his portraits of them? In her conclusion to her life of her father, Reynolds asserts that Holl's move away from subject painting to portraiture, his abandonment of what she sees as the outdated conventions of Victorian narrative painting, had made his art more enduring than that of many of his contemporaries. It stemmed, she says, from an awakening that

> life itself [is] the only true textbook. The Cousins portrait and that of Piatti bespeak his first complete realisation of this.

And in a revealing passage she continues:

> Uninfluenced by any breath of Pre-Raphaelitism, untouched by any light from modern France, my father's art, in no less a degree than that of his greatest contemporaries, Burne-Jones, Watts, or Rossetti, shows the strength of hereditary or racial influences. Just as the art of Burne-Jones is Celtic, just as that of Rossetti is Latin, so, in its preference for strong character, its almost religious realism, that of Holl is Teutonic.[44]

Fig. 17. Frank Holl, *Captain Alexander Mitchell Sim*, 1881, oil on canvas. Commercial Dock Company, Port of London Authority

Holl's preference for Northern Europe over Italy is a recurrent theme in Reynolds's biography of her father, a key moment for her being his abandonment of his Royal Academy travelling scholarship in 1869. Two months in Venice 'slipped by, but before this my father had begun to suspect that he was not in sympathy with Italian life'.[45] The journey back to England, on the other hand, with a stay in Antwerp and the Netherlands, is recorded with enthusiasm by Holl's wife: 'In fact all of Holland and the Netherlands have ever been most dear to us both.'[46] Reynolds is keen to emphasize the hereditary nature of this preference, tracing the Holl name and lineage back to the Netherlands, and of course to identify her father's artistic inheritance in Dutch painting, whether from Rembrandt (notwithstanding Stephens's puncturing of this association) or contemporaries such as Jozef Israëls. Holl's lack of ease in Italy – 'it is curious and not agreeable, my sensation in Italy', he wrote to his wife on a second Venice visit – is also noted by contemporaries.[47] Wilfrid Meynell in his 1880 *Magazine of Art* profile of Holl also emphasizes the significance of Holl's cutting short his travelling scholarship.

Holl's 'Teutonism' should, however, be seen in much broader terms than purely personal preference. Teutonism, or 'Teutomania' as Matthew Arnold called it, was a dominant way of thinking about England's history in the mid- to later-Victorian period, amounting to a cast of mind and wider view of the world and England's place in it. It took many forms but at its heart was a belief that England's institutions owed most to its Anglo-Saxon heritage. This in turn, as Peter Mandler has described, informed a powerful vision of the English national character and of the proper conduct of those men who contributed to it.[48] As a historical and intellectual construct, Teutonism was at its height in the late 1860s and 1870s when Holl was a young man and many of his sitters were cementing their professional careers. But as Reynolds's use of the term suggests, its popular impact was long lived. The racialist – some would say racist – ideas of one of its key proponents, the historian E.A. Freeman, for instance, remained influential in the United States and Australia well into the early twentieth century.[49] The racially determinist aspect

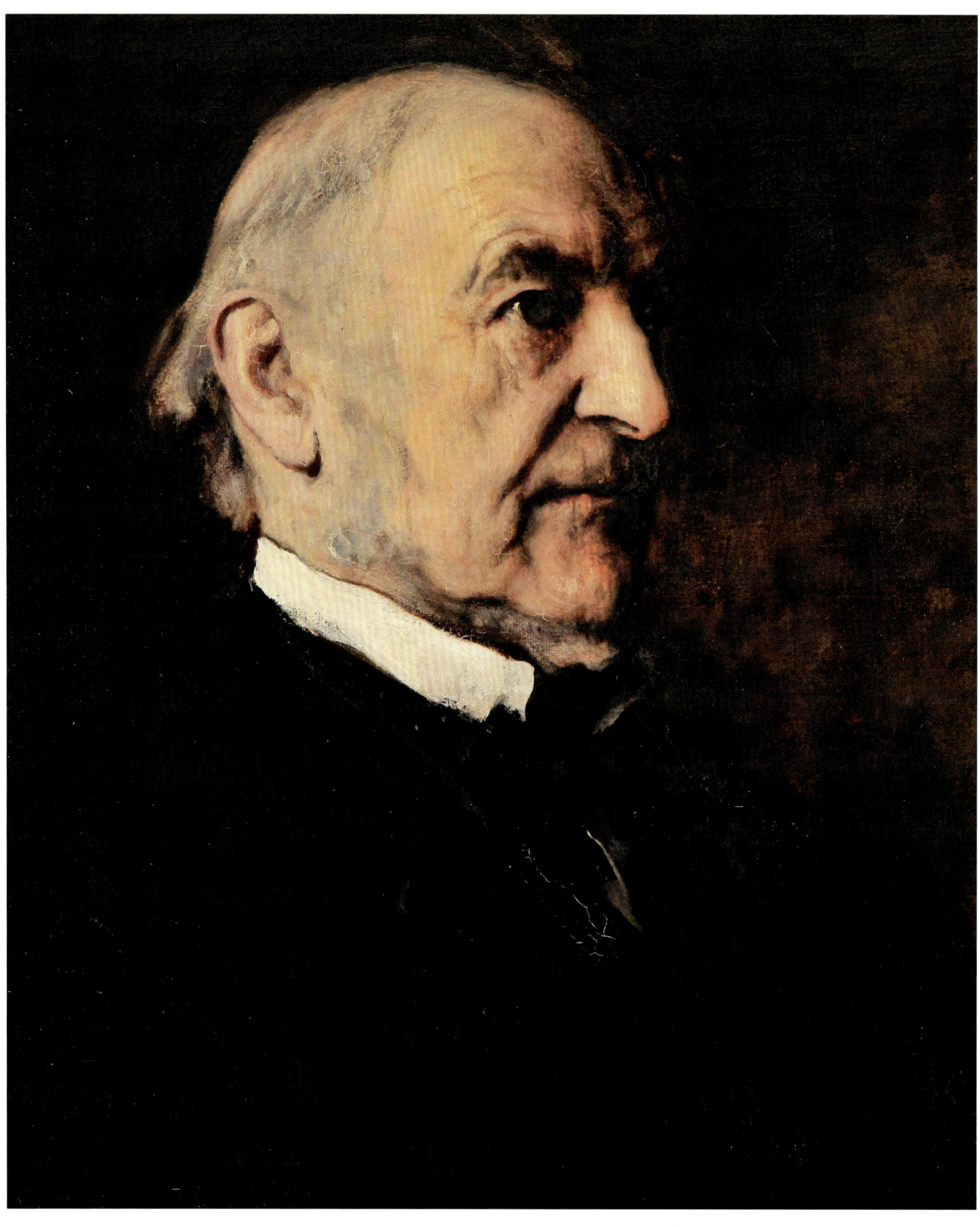

of Teutonism is very evident in Reynolds's account of her father. Holl's dislike of Italy is construed in national stereotyping and she writes of her father's impatience with 'the easier, less strenuous ways of life' that he encountered in Italy. And again Holl's own letter to his wife from Venice is cited to demonstrate his inability to satisfy his need to work hard in Italy. 'Although I know I work very hard,' he writes, 'yet not to work is harder work still to me ... *hunger for work is always on me, and it is when I cannot satisfy this hunger that I get so worn out*.' This Reynolds interprets as 'a truthful expression of his point of view about the Continent and his mistrust of its easy-going ways'.[50]

The values associated with Teutonism can give insights into how Holl was perceived both as a man and as an artist, and much of this revolves around ideas of dedication and hard work. As Mandler has described, the Victorian notions of character and manliness are imbued with a particular set of qualities according to Teutonic discourse, central to which is 'the capacity for self government'. '"Self-reliance" was the mid-century byword', suggesting 'a well-balanced person, responsible, dignified, "self-possessed", "self-respecting", and, where necessary, "self-denying"'. And 'most important of all to English "manliness" or "self-reliance" was work'.[51] Work is of course the key to the telling of Holl's life: his extraordinary capacity for hard work both as he himself reflected and as was so clearly evidenced by his output as a portrait painter. But work is also held to contribute to his undoing and his early death. There are other qualities identified in Holl that contribute to the Teutonic account of him. He possessed, Reynolds says, an 'instinct to overcome', and later in her biography this is reinforced by an anecdote of one of his sitters, the financier Lord Mount Stephen, who spoke of his successful completion of the Canadian Pacific Railway and drew the conclusion that 'many times when things appear impossible, when the obstacles to success appear insurmountable, the carrying out is, comparatively speaking easy'. 'This was his philosophy', Reynolds observes, 'and this, I take it, was the philosophy, unspoken indeed, and possibly an unconscious one, of my father.'[52]

Fig. 18. Frank Holl, *William Ewart Gladstone*, 1887–8, detail of cat. 27 (p. 154)

Yet it wasn't just Reynolds who constructed this image of Holl. Rather her book can be read as an extension of a view of him already established in his lifetime or by those later recalling him, who found in Holl the traits of an ideal type of English manliness. Spielmann noted that 'the distinguishing feature of Mr Holl's character was his straightforward vigour and persistence, his consistency of purpose and his determination to carry his object through'.[53] George Otto Trevelyan spoke of Holl as 'the example of a brave, honest, straightforward, manly life'. And Sir Johnston Forbes-Robertson also recorded that Holl's 'capacity for work was enormous' and noted his 'singular charm and simplicity of manner, very modest and retiring', those 'self-possessed' aspects of self-reliance.[54] Hard work, simplicity and an open and honest straightforwardness are the characteristics constantly identified in Holl. In a way that often occurs in the 'artist at home' literature of the period, these qualities are read into Holl's domestic circumstances, Helen Zimmern noting in the *Magazine of Art* that Holl's Hampstead house was 'furnished without artistic or aesthetic affectation'. She further recorded that Holl was 'pre-eminently tidy' with 'a pronounced dislike to that species of litter which has to some persons got to be synonymous with art'.[55] His extreme tidiness and orderliness represented, perhaps, another facet of Holl's commitment to self-reliance.

Most of all, of course, the traits of Holl's English manliness are to be found in the portraits that he painted. Reading an artist's character into their works was a commonplace of the period, stimulated perhaps by the rise of art journalism and the elevation of artists into celebrities. Millais was accorded a bluff and hearty type of masculinity not dissimilar to Holl's, which in turn was registered as a manly physicality and decisiveness in the act of painting as evidenced in his portraits.[56] In the case of Holl, the critical language applied to his portraits also resonated with the image of the artist himself. Spielmann, for example, found the portraits of the elderly Lord Chichester and the

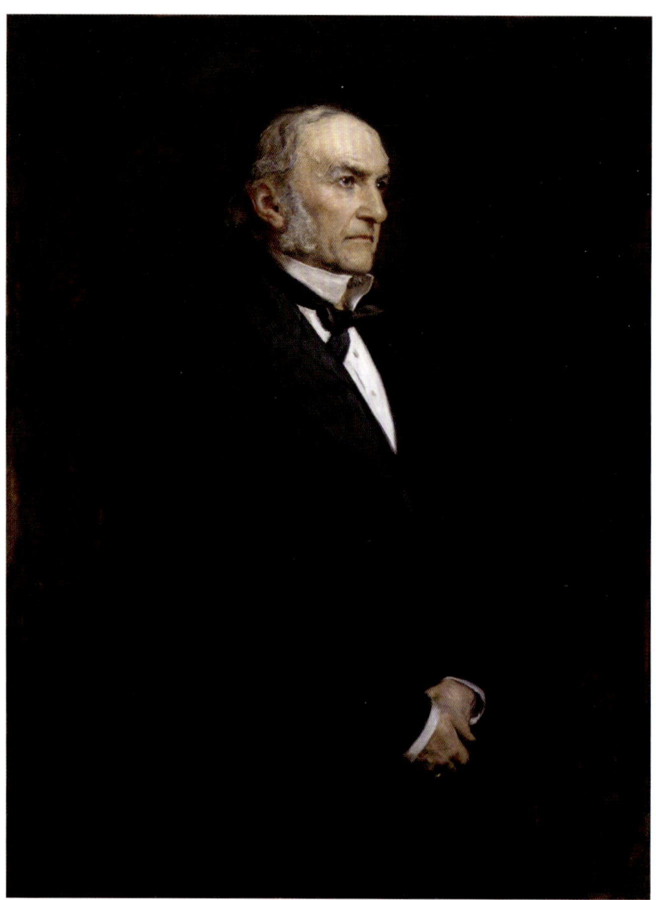

Fig. 19. Sir John Everett Millais, *William Ewart Gladstone*, 1879, oil on canvas. © National Portrait Gallery, London

Duke of Cleveland, to be 'examples of simple, dignified, manly portraiture', while the *Art Journal*'s obituary characterized his portraiture in the following terms:

> He excelled in the presentation of his sitters under a striking pictorial aspect – an aspect, that is, which, if it commonly wanted beauty, was never lacking in conspicuousness and force; and so vigorous was his brushwork, so complete – within certain limits – his command of material, and so forthright and direct his insight into character that, as a painter of men, he stepped at once to the head of his profession.[57]

And of course this vigorous and forceful approach, with its emphasis on the personalities he painted, was seen as appropriate precisely because Holl was predominantly a painter of men and an artist whom many saw as excelling in portraits of what Reynolds describes as 'rugged types' such as Samuel Cousins.[58] In this sense accounts of Holl's portraits are further gendered. Wedmore, for example, noted how 'habitually Holl's triumph was obtained in fixing on the canvas the features of the strongly marked. Beauty had no temptation for him; smoothness repelled him.'[59] Likewise, Holl's *Times* obituary, in pointing to the lack of female sitters in Holl's output, commented that 'his almost over-masculine art might have found it difficult to adapt itself to smooth texture and soft outline'.[60]

Holl's subjects, Spielmann wrote shortly before the artist's death, were 'men ... eminent in every walk of life, and all of them men of character'.[61] The empathy that appeared to have existed between Holl and many of his sitters has already been noted, and it is not unreasonable to think that, in spite of the frequent generational difference, these men of character shared many of the manly values attributed to Holl. It was also, for some, in Holl's change from subject painting to portraiture that he had redeemed his own masculinity. Was there in his subject pictures a morbidity that would have been considered decidedly unmanly? There is a hint of this in Spielmann's defence of Holl's 'curious leaning to the miserable' in his subject pictures as being 'entirely healthy and wholesome in its character'.[62] And it is made more explicit elsewhere when the *Art Journal*, reviewing Holl's *Newgate* (cat. 15) in 1878, pondered 'how an artist, personally so healthy, bright, and manly, can year after year give way to this melancholy habit of mind and brush is beyond our comprehension'.[63] The decisive move to portrait painting in the following year was likewise considered by Campbell in terms of the artist gaining in masculinity. 'In portrait-painting', Campbell wrote, 'Holl seemed to discover within himself a strength, one might almost say a virility, which is, with one or two exceptions, totally wanting in his subject pictures.'[64]

Notes

[1] *The Graphic*, 30 June 1888, p. 693.
[2] *Art Journal*, 1889, pp. 57, 59.
[3] Lee MacCormick Edwards in her *Oxford Dictionary of National Biography* entry on Holl calculates that he painted 197 portraits after that of Cousins; Reynolds, pp. 213, 252.
[4] Reynolds, pp. 251–2.
[5] Reynolds, p. 301.
[6] *The Graphic*, 30 June 1888, p. 694; Reynolds, p. 203.
[7] Reynolds, p. 335.
[8] *The Graphic*, 30 June 1888, p. 694.
[9] *The Graphic*, 12 May 1883, p. 486.
[10] Cited in Julie F. Codell, 'The artist's Cause at Heart: Marion Harry Spielmann and the Late Victorian Art World', *Bulletin of the John Rylands Library*, Spring 1989, p. 141.
[11] On Stephens's critical tastes see Dianne Sachko Macleod, 'F.G. Stephens, Pre-Raphaelite critic and art historian', *Burlington Magazine*, 128, June 1986, pp. 398–406.
[12] *Athenaeum*, 16 June 1883, p. 770, and 27 June 1885, p. 828.
[13] *Athenaeum*, 12 June 1886, pp. 785–6.
[14] *Athenaeum*, 11 June 1887, p. 772.
[15] Meynell 1880, p. 190.
[16] See Funnell and Warner 1999, p. 29, citing J. Saxon Mills, *Life and Letters of Sir Hubert Herkomer: A Study in Struggle and Success*, London 1923, p. 130.
[17] *Athenaeum*, 3 June 1882, p. 705.
[18] *Reynolds*, p. 290.
[19] *Art Journal*, 1883, p. 201.
[20] *Art Journal*, 1885, p. 189.
[21] *Athenaeum*, 27 June 1885, p. 828.
[22] *The Graphic*, 30 June 1888, p. 694.
[23] Art Journal, 1888, p. 287.
[24] Stefan Collini, Public Moralists: *Political Thought and Intellectual Life in Britain 1850–1930*, Oxford 1991, p. 203, and Garrard and Parrott.
[25] T.R. Gourvish, 'The Rise of the Professions', in T.R. Gourvish and Alan O'Day, eds, *Later Victorian Britain, 1867–1900*, Basingstoke 1988, p. 18.
[26] Garrard and Parrott, p. 151.
[27] *Lancet*, 4 August 1888, p. 226.
[28] *Lancet*, 18 November 1893, p 1261.
[29] *Lancet*, 18 November 1893, p. 1262.
[30] *The Graphic*, 30 June 1888, p. 694.
[31] J. Saxon Mills, *Life and Letters of Sir Hubert Herkomer C.V.O., R.A.: A Study in Struggle and Success*, London 1923, p. 130.
[32] *Art Journal*, 1886, pp. 185, 210.
[33] *Magazine of Art*, 1889, p. 168.
[34] Thane 2000, p. 270.
[35] Reynolds, pp. 193–4.
[36] Reynolds, p. 210.
[37] *Art Journal*, 1889, p. 58.
[38] Thane 2000, p. 268, citing Matthew 1994, p. 258, and on the image he presented through this activity see Ruth Clayton Windscheffel, 'Politics, Portraiture and Power: Reassessing the Public Image of William Ewart Gladstone', in Matthew McCormack, ed., *Public Men: Masculinity and Politics in Modern Britain*, Basingstoke 2007.
[39] Thane citing Matthew 1994, p. 279.
[40] T. Wemyss Reid, 'Mr. Gladstone and His Portraits', *Magazine of Art*, 1889, p. 83.
[41] Reynolds, p. 279.
[42] Reynolds, p. 279.
[43] *Athenaeum*, 23 June 1888, p. 800.
[44] Reynolds, p. 312.
[45] Reynolds, p. 59.
[46] Reynolds, p. 71.
[47] Reynolds, p. 313.
[48] Mandler 2006, p. 106 (citing Mandell Creighton); Mandler's ch. 3 contains an extensive discussion of Teutomania.
[49] Freeman's colonial influence is discussed in Marilyn Lake, '"Essentially Teutonic": E.A. Freeman, liberal race historian. A transnational perspective', in Catherine Hall and Keith McClelland, eds, *Race, Nation and Empire: Making Histories, 1750 to the Present*, Manchester and New York 2010, pp. 56–73.
[50] Reynolds, p. 314.
[51] Mandler 2006, pp. 101, 103.
[52] Reynolds, pp. 268–9.
[53] Anon. 1888a.
[54] Sir Johnston Forbes-Robertson, *A Player Under Three Reigns*, London 1925, p. 57.
[55] Helen Zimmern, 'Artists' Homes. Mr. Frank Holl's, in Fitzjohn's Avenue', *Magazine of Art*, 1885, pp. 144–180, esp. 146 and 150.
[56] I have discussed this in Peter Funnell, 'Millais's Reputation and the Practice of Portraiture' in Funnell and Warner 1999, pp. 11–35, esp. 31–2.
[57] *The Graphic*, 1886, p. 554; *Art Journal*, 1888, p. 287.
[58] Reynolds, p. 191.
[59] *Magazine of Art*, 1889, p. 168.
[60] *The Times*, 1 August 1888.
[61] *The Graphic*, 30 June 1888, p. 693.
[62] Ibid.
[63] *Art Journal*, 1878, p. 168.
[64] *Art Journal*, 1889, p. 58.

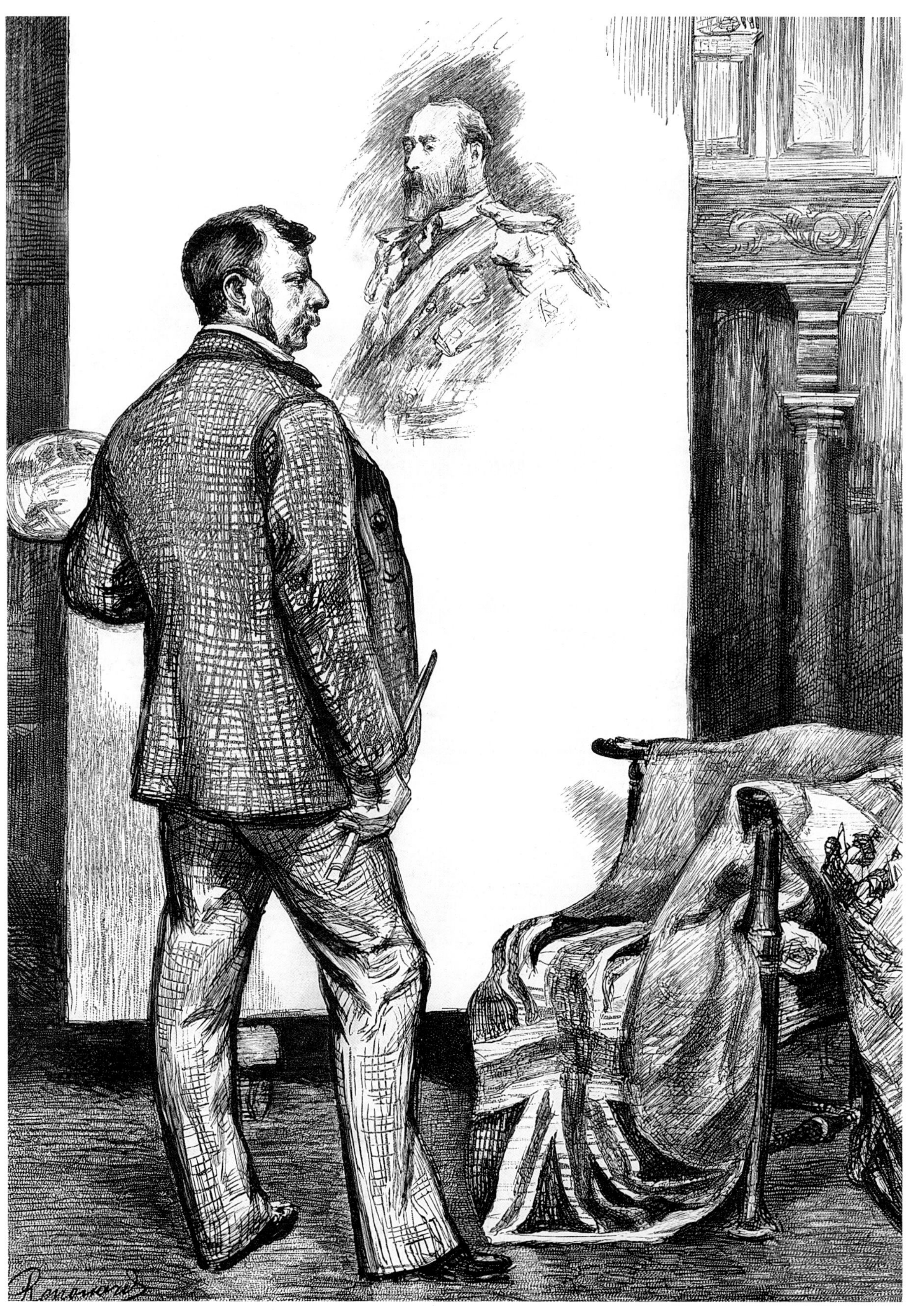

The Private and Public Life of Frank Holl: The Journey from Camden Town to Hampstead and Surrey

Barbara Bryant

The upward progress of Frank Holl's career can be mirrored by his search for a home and studio that did justice to his vision of himself as a successful artist (fig. 20). The impetus for this progress depends on understanding his early life, as he endeavoured to escape from his modest beginnings as the son of a hard-working engraver in Camden Town, north London. Holl drove himself to improve his social standing and professional status with a series of residences, each of which served one stage in his career. He would always take cues from other artists in his circle. For the artist in Victorian London a residence served several inter-linked roles: domicile, place of work and manifestation of status. This essay will consider where Holl lived and worked, and how and why he adapted, and later created, environments suited to his art practice.

Camden Town and Gloucester Road, Regent's Park, 1845–77

Holl's choices in life seemed almost predetermined. His paternal forebears were engravers going back to the eighteenth century. William Holl (1771–1838) specialized in the 'chalk manner' and three of his four sons including Frank Holl's father, Francis (1815–84), followed in his footsteps. The family were based in Camden Town, a mile or so north of central London's outer perimeter, as it was in the mid-nineteenth century. Due to cheaper properties, this area attracted middle-ranking artists and especially engravers;[1] nearby lived George Cruikshank, the Dalziels (engravers) and the Goodalls (see below). In 1845, the year of Frank's birth, the family lived at 7 St James's Terrace, one in a row of recently built terraced houses on the southern stretches of Kentish Town Road, in the centre of Camden Town and near the junction of two main thoroughfares.[2] It was not far from Bayham Street where Holl senior had been born.[3]

Fig. 20. Charles-Paul Renouard, 'Frank Holl', *The Graphic*, 30 June 1888, wood engraving. Watts Gallery Archive

Despite the impressive-sounding name of Francis Montague Holl, young Frank grew up knowing the 'grey and seamy side of life'. His poor health and weak lungs forecast serious conditions as an adult. He recalled a childhood where money was in short supply, and amusements were few, although he became an excellent musician and recalled the amateur theatricals among the artistic community in Camden Town. His father had steady employment, but the work was grindingly difficult, not highly paid and not well regarded by the premier art institution, the Royal Academy of Arts, with engravers only able to become full Academicians in 1855. His greatest achievement was his print after William Powell Frith's popular painting, *The Railway Station* (1862). Yet it always seemed that engravers laboured in the shadows of the illustrious fine artists whose works they reproduced. For the young Holl this was a path to be avoided. Instead, encouraged by his budding talents as a draughtsman, he set his heart on becoming a painter. An abiding memory was spending time in his father's studio and seeing 'some fine old picture which was in the course of being arranged … I, too, will be a great painter some day, and paint a big picture like that.'[4]

By the 1850s, thanks to constant hard work and a growing reputation, Holl senior had moved his family from the small terraced house in Camden Town to a street of new semi-detached ones in Gloucester Road, NW1 (now Gloucester Avenue), just a short way from Regent's Park (figs. 21, 22). The actual house no longer stands, but others in the street do, and these are comfortable residences. The Holls were at no. 30, near the Regent's Canal, situated on the side of the road that backs onto the railway tracks running up from Euston Station. The upper floors looked out over the tracks, and various goods yards and warehouses, including the vast premises of Pickford and Co. The considerable noise (still evident today) and attendant dirt were a drawback, but Holl senior had clearly made a step up in the world and, importantly, he could conduct his work in his own engraving studio. Later this house would come to Frank.

Holl senior had aspirations for his son to do better than follow in his footsteps and sent him to school in Hampstead and then University College School. But the lad loved to draw and had talent, so he soon left formal education to join the Royal Academy Schools at the young age of fifteen in 1860. Here he learned from older, successful artists such as local family friend, Frederick Goodall (1822–1904). When Goodall took his turn as a Visitor in the Schools, Holl joined him for the walk northwards from the Royal Academy in Trafalgar Square to Camden Town and confided how he aimed 'to illustrate modern society'. Holl also took particular note of the older artist's house and studio in Camden Square, which Goodall had tailored for his artistic practice. Goodall recalled: 'It was his ambition to have a similar one.'[5] And, as it turned out, Holl eventually moved into these very premises some fifteen years later.

Fig. 21. Map showing Holl's birthplace at St. James's Terrace (centre), and residences on Gloucester Road (to left) and Camden Square (to right) circled. Reproduced from map of 1913 with the kind permission of the Ordnance Survey

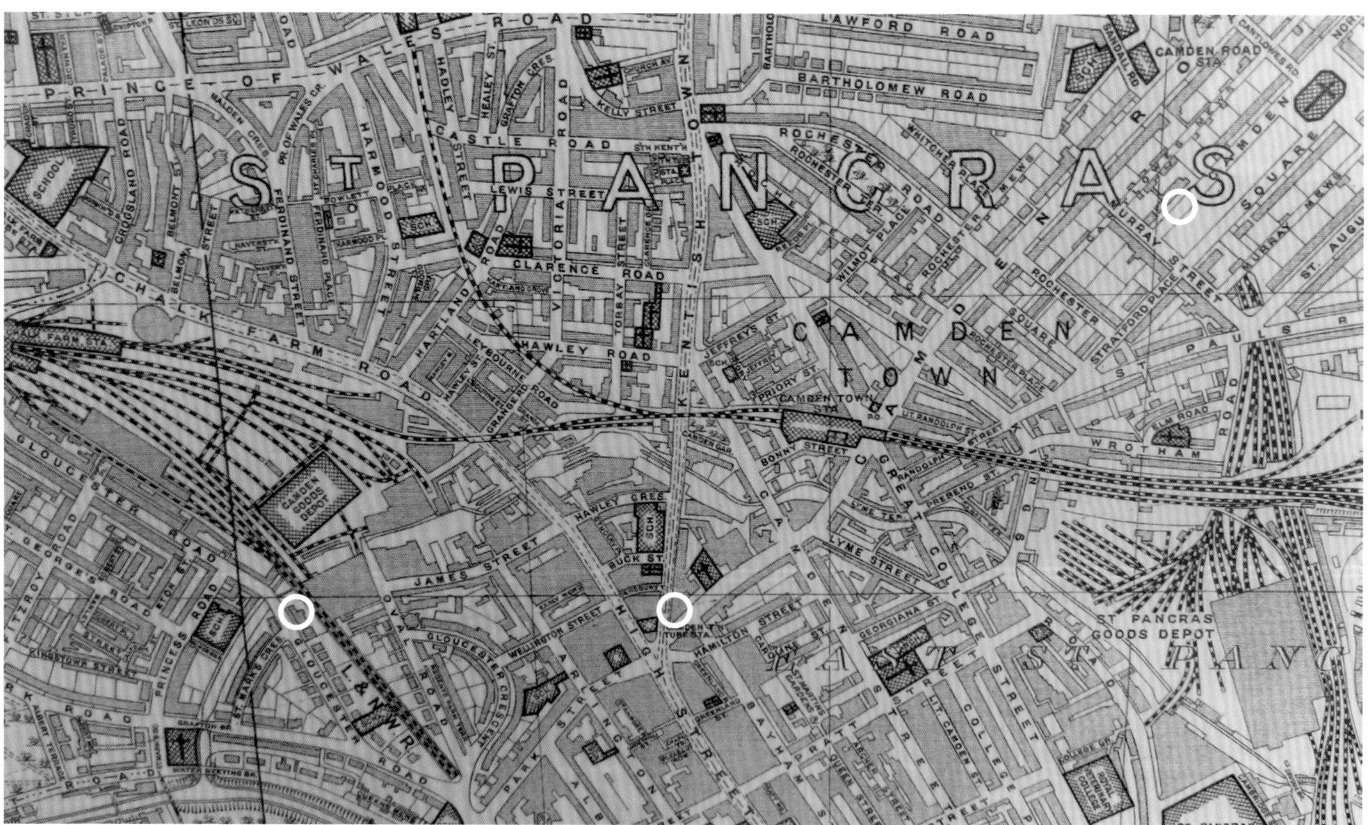

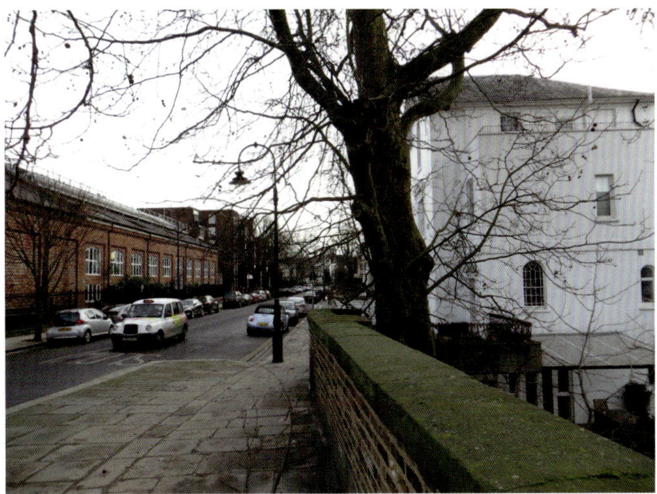

Fig. 22. Gloucester Road today showing the view from the bridge over Regent's Canal with the site of Holl's residence on the left

Frank Holl's burgeoning career progressed with awards for his drawings and the gold medal for historical painting in 1863. He earned his own money with commissions for landscape views in watercolour and sales of oil paintings. Right from the beginning Holl worked for art dealers in London such as Leggatt's, Arthur Tooth and Ernest Gambart. His small-scale genre studies, often focusing on children, found a ready market among middle-class patrons. In 1864, aged eighteen, he had a painting exhibited at the annual Academy exhibition. Since this was sent from no. 40 Gloucester Road, it seems he had a room to use as a studio apart from his parents' residence. But these were hard years when he had 'to battle with poverty'.[6] An idea of his early life appears in *A Difference of Position* (1866),[7] in which a young artist (almost certainly a self-portrait) paints from a child model in a cluttered room filled with studio paraphernalia. Seeking to move on from this kind of messy environment, at around this time he used some of his earnings to build a new studio at no. 30, an early indication of his desire to shape his working environment. In May 1867, aged twenty-one, he married Annie Davidson, the daughter of Surrey watercolour painter, Charles Davidson, and from that point onwards he had new responsibilities.

In 1868 Holl's painting '*The Lord gave and the Lord hath taken away* ...' (cat. 5) earned him a travelling studentship from the Royal Academy. This prestigious award provided a young artist with the opportunity to go on an artistic 'grand tour' for two years to study the antique and Old Master paintings. Holl set off in spring 1869 with his wife, travelling via Paris, Switzerland and Venice where he met up with artist friends F.W. Warwick Topham and William Wood Deane. But Italy did not impress him: he did not like the Italians and missed 'the rugged home life of the English peoples'.[8] 'Give me a grey day', Holl commented, whereupon he resigned the studentship and headed home via Germany and Belgium. His father despaired: 'Frank, you will never be an Academician now. They will never forgive you for this.'[9]

Back in England Holl retreated to Surrey, where his wife's family resided and where his father had now obtained an additional home, a country place called The Hermitage, in the picturesque village of Elstead. Frank Holl loved this environment. Apart from his sketching tours, he had never had the experience of living in the country. Camden Town and its environs were his home, but he always had a keen sense of nature and enjoyed walking around Hampstead Heath. He viewed Surrey as beautiful, pure environment, filled with fresh air and tranquillity, a contrast to the dirt, smoke and soot of dingy London.[10] The villages of Elstead, Godalming, Boxhill, Abinger, Shere, Albury and Gomshall became his favourite resorts from the stresses of urban life, and later on he often rented cottages for the summer or managed the occasional weekend break. It also helped that there was a thriving community of fellow artist refugees from north London in the area, including Paul Falconer Poole (cat. 16), E.W. Cooke, John Linnell and James Clarke Hook.

With Holl's rejection of the Academy's travelling studentship and the assumptions that Old Master traditions reigned supreme, he turned decisively to his own brand of subject matter. Not for him history painting, nor indeed popular historical genre or literary scenes; instead, he portrayed modern life, unvarnished and unromanticized, in a series of exhibition pictures on themes of death, loss, abandonment and misery. Success came in the form of buoyant sales, even if the critics in the press perennially requested happier subjects. In 1871 the Queen commissioned him to do a work of his own choice (cat. 6), a great coup for a young artist. Holl embarked on illustrative work for *The Graphic* in the 1870s, which brought in additional income for his growing family (three daughters were born in the space of five years – Ada in 1869, Olive in 1872 and Madoline in 1874). His black and white work gave him additional confidence, as well as opening up a new range of realist subjects for his exhibited paintings. Even so, as a personality, Holl had an anxious temperament, exacerbated by increasing heart trouble.[11] Traces of this anxiety can be read in some portraits and photographs of him (fig. 23).

Fortunately for Holl, when his father retired to Surrey (Elm Lodge in Milford), the house on Gloucester Road came to him, so he then had his own place. Immediately, he embarked on adapting and rebuilding no. 30, while he lived with his wife and children in a rented cottage in Frognal, Hampstead. The time he spent in this semi-rural enclave had a crucial impact on him. Long walks over the heath gave him an intimate knowledge and affection for this area, so that, much later when his circumstances allowed a move, 'Hampstead was almost as a matter of course the chosen neighbourhood'.[12]

Once complete, the Camden residence, no. 30 Gloucester Road, proved an agreeable working environment. The artist earned ample money from his paintings, which were sought after by collectors such as Captain Hill of Brighton. Some fetched as much as 800 guineas, with most going for between £250 and £400. His prices escalated with constant demands from London's dealers to produce replicas, which, by all accounts, took up 'fully half his time'. Gloucester Road had its drawbacks with the street enveloped in smoke and the corrosive grime invading the interiors.[13] Holl's daughter recalled her mother's vain attempts to create a garden in the small green area that abutted the railway tracks at the back of the house. But Holl himself worked well there; the expansive view of the sky, when not clouded with smoke, and the open area behind the house brought light in. When he added a billiard room, something his father could never afford, it indicated his increased status, as well as the convivial socializing that went on with his artist neighbours. Nearby in Gloucester Road were the transplanted Scots, John Pettie (1839–1893), who became a lifelong friend, and the landscape painter Charles Edward Johnson (1832–1913). The years in this location saw Holl begin to create his reputation. He exhibited at the Royal Academy and elsewhere, sold well and enjoyed the company of his colleagues, but as his circumstances improved, he left the house he had grown up in and looked to the future.

Camden Square, 1877–82

In 1877 Holl moved less than a mile east to no. 4 Camden Square where he took over the house, which still stands (fig. 24),[14] and studio of his older friend, Frederick Goodall, a specialist in paintings of the East. A new development in the mid-1840s, known as Camden New Town, this square was almost a self-contained community, situated to the east of the busy Camden Town junction and set behind Camden Road.[15] Reputedly the longest square in London, it had as its centrepiece the handsome church of St Paul's. Some of the spacious villas that extended around the four sides of the square aspired to grandeur, with applied pilasters and Corinthian capitals. In 1849 Goodall moved into one of the new villas and resided there until 1872/3,[16] when he relocated to his own country residence in Harrow, Graeme's Dyke (1870–2), built for him by R. Norman Shaw (1831–1912). Camden Square had a gathering of fellow professionals including the engraver Samuel Cousins and the sculptor Henry Armstead. Although a Midland Railway tunnel ran under part of it, for the most part this was a quiet place with a beautiful leafy garden within the square.

When the opportunity came for Holl to acquire no. 4, he must have jumped at the chance to get away from the perennial soot and noise of Gloucester Road. He could bring his family to a larger, more comfortable home with its own extensive back garden. The bonus was that Goodall had already tailored the premises to suit his work as a painter of

Fig. 23. Elliott & Fry, *Frank Holl*, *c.*1880, photograph. Rob Dickins Collection, Watts Gallery Archive

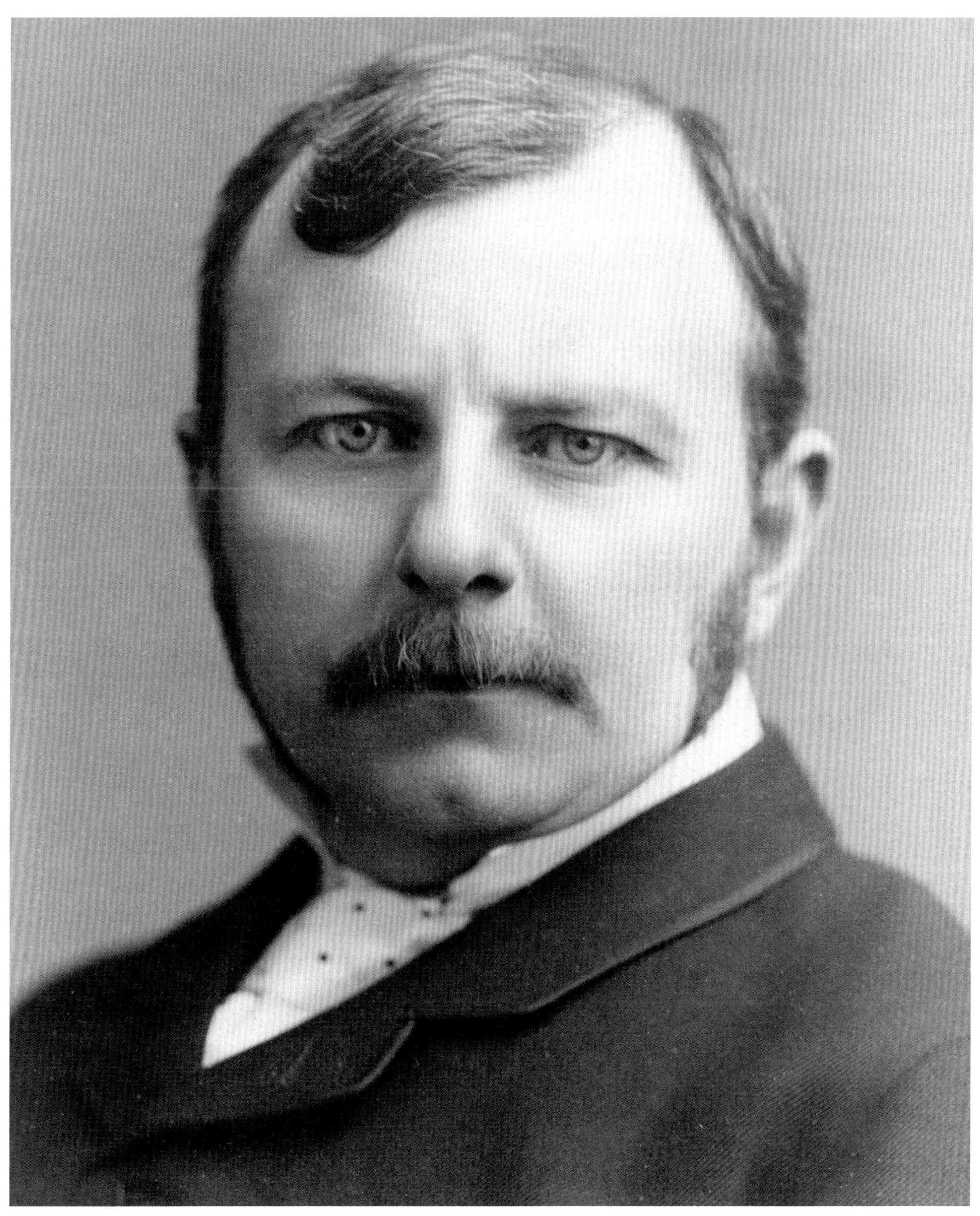

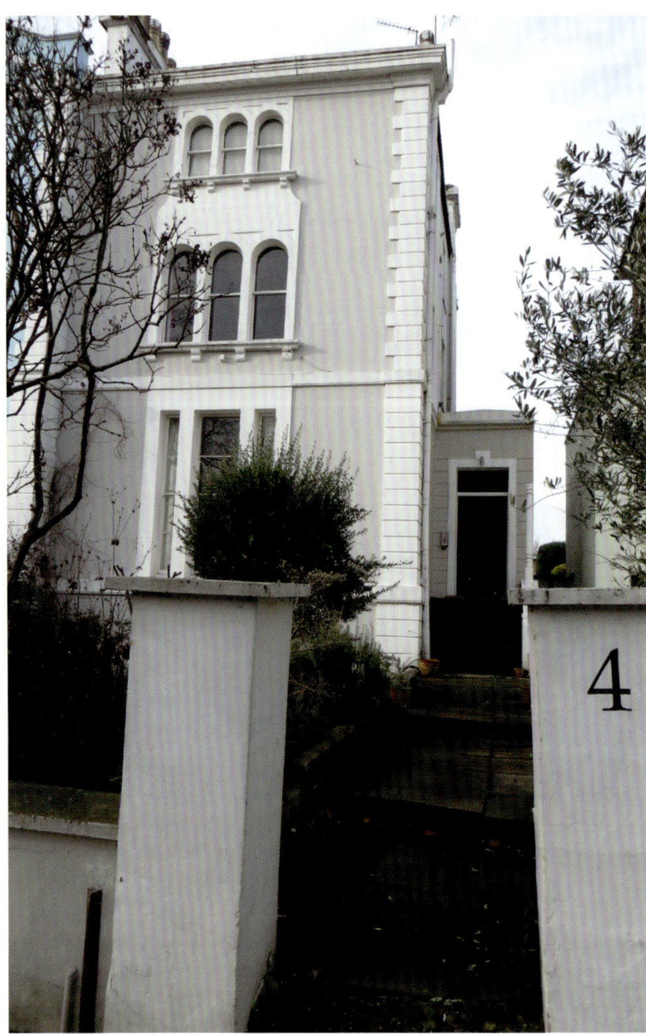

Fig. 24. The Camden Square house today

large subject pictures. He had built a studio at the end of the garden, away from the house itself and backed by a quiet mews behind. Holl considered that this spacious studio was one of the finest in London.[17] Connecting it to the main house was a long glass corridor, like a conservatory, with vines growing in it and a fountain at one end sporting gold fish and decorated with mosaics. With his family happily ensconced in the house, he was busy in what he called 'the workshop'. These years at Camden Square saw his career accelerate, and his ambitions and confidence as an artist grew. In 1878 he exhibited *Newgate, Committed for Trial* (cat. 15), some 7 feet across. The sensation of the year at the Royal Academy exhibition, it sold for 1,000 guineas, a remarkable sum for an artist still in his early thirties. Thanks to the more spacious studio at Camden Square, he had the right environment to tackle large-scale works. On the strength of *Newgate*, the Academy elected him an Associate, a professional accolade his father feared he might never achieve.

At the same exhibition Holl also showed a portrait that he had done for a family friend. It attracted considerable praise, so much so that some family members and friends advised him to branch out into portraiture. His father, commenting 'Stick to heads, Frank! Stick to heads!',[18] suggested he paint another one, as did the influential and recently retired Secretary of the Royal Academy, John Prescott Knight, and other Academicians. Holl reluctantly implemented this idea even though, without a specific commission, it occupied valuable time. Samuel Cousins (1801–87), the elderly and eminent engraver, a friend of Holl senior, lived in Camden Square, and so Frank Holl took up his brushes and produced a portrait that determined the rest of his career (cat. 17). Although this portrayal of Cousins dissatisfied 'the old bear', it delighted everyone else and Holl's career changed course as the commissions rolled in. The critics had provided another stimulus with their constant carping on the gloominess of his subject paintings. Holl was ready for a change and seemingly found the work congenial, with sitters coming to the studio for a limited number of sessions. His assertive technique of applying the paint straight onto the canvas's white prepared ground made progress rapid. His output increased dramatically, averaging twelve works a year exhibited at both the R.A. and the Grosvenor Gallery. The workload and stress also increased, taking their toll on the artist's health. The five years the artist lived at Camden Square marked a key transition in his career, but a career has to move forward. As Holl gained a second royal commission and observed his fellow artists going up in the world, he must have realized it was time for another move.[19]

Fitzjohn's Avenue, Hampstead, 1882–8

One of Holl's closest friends, John Pettie, who had left Gloucester Road in 1869 for St John's Wood, bought a plot of land on the new Fitzjohn's Avenue, which ran from Swiss Cottage northwards to Hampstead village. Pettie commissioned a new house, The Lothians, at no. 2, designed by an architect friend William Wallace (and his partner William Flockhart). Alerting Holl to this area, Pettie urged him to buy a similar plot two doors down at no. 6 and Holl did just that, with a view to commissioning a new studio house of his own. This house no longer stands (fig. 25), but through drawings, archival photographs and descriptions in the contemporary press it can be recreated (figs. 26-30).

Artists' houses proliferated in the outer sections of London from the 1870s, with Chelsea, Kensington and Hampstead as the favoured areas. Purpose-built to feature large studios for work, these houses also offered an outward show of prosperity and achievement; indeed, by this time such structures were all but essential to the upwardly-mobile professional artist.

Fig. 25. The Three Gables, 6 Fitzjohn's Avenue, Hampstead. Photograph published in Hermann Muthesius's *Die Englische Baukunst der Gegenwart*, Leipzig 1900, pl. 87 (RIBA Library Photographs Collection)

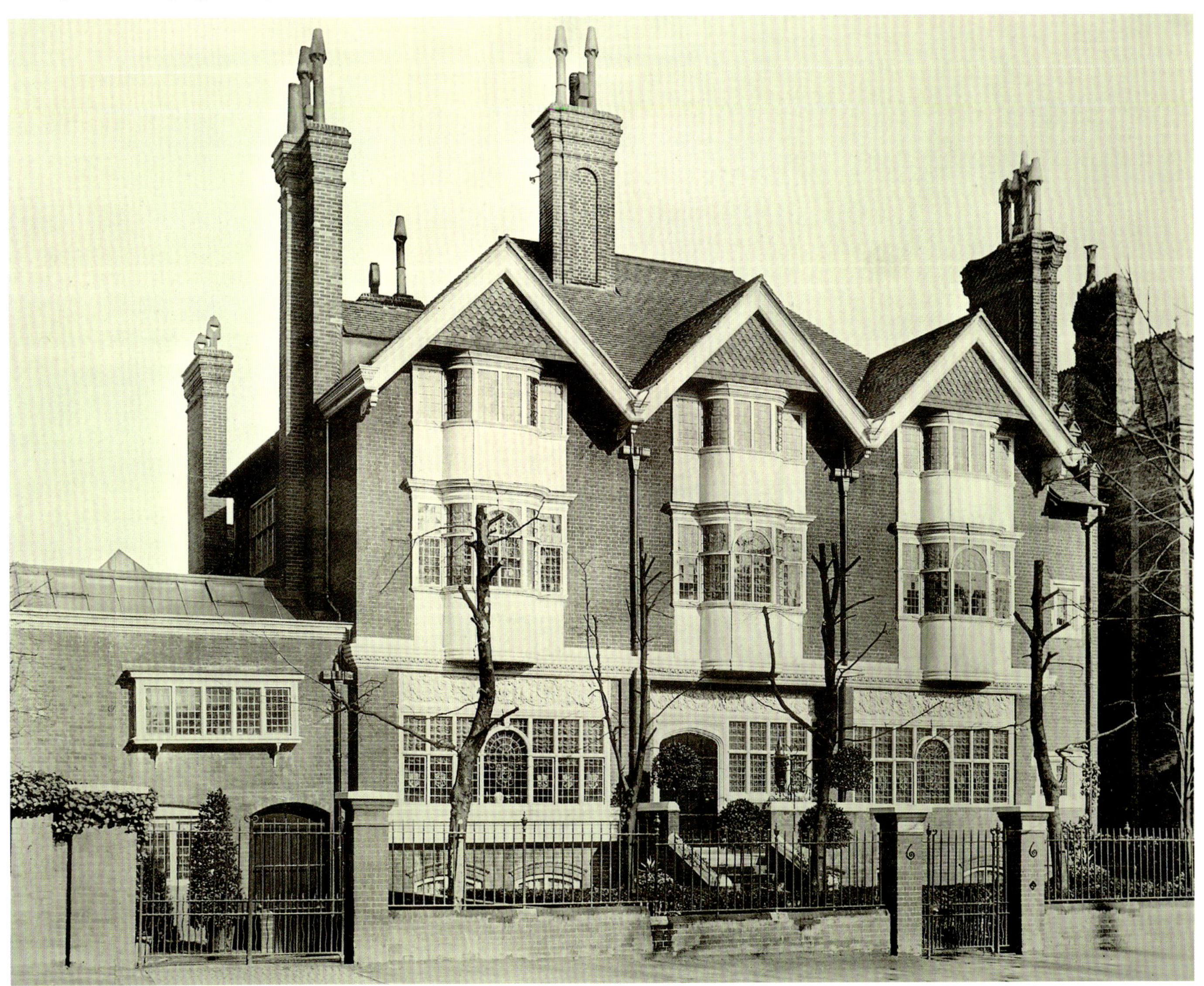

In 1878 John Everett Millais had a virtual palace built near Kensington Gardens.[20] Frederic Leighton, President of the Royal Academy from 1878, led the way in Holland Park, Kensington, in 1865, with its expansions culminating in the addition of the showpiece Arab Hall (1877–81).[21] G.F. Watts commissioned New Little Holland House in Melbury Road, Kensington, in 1874, adding a picture gallery in 1881, which he opened to the public to display his art.[22] Certain architects, such as R. Norman Shaw and George Aitchison, came to specialize in this type of commission, usually due to friendships at the Royal Academy. In the mid-1870s excitement surrounded the construction of Shaw's elegant houses for young Academy aspirants, Marcus Stone and Luke Fildes, on Melbury Road and one nearby for George Henry Boughton.

The Holland Park circle were all in place by the 1870s; in Hampstead the creation of Fitzjohn's Avenue from 1876 opened up a new area for artistic colonization. This part of north London had always had traditional associations with the British school as the residence or occasional resort of John Constable, Clarkson Stanfield and Ford Madox Brown. More recently, Shaw had created houses for himself on Ellerdale Road (1874–6) and for artist Edwin Long (designed 1876–7, built from 1878).[23] Holl looked to older family friends who had already built new houses towards Hampstead village on what became the upper reaches of Fitzjohn's Avenue: recently deceased Paul Falconer Poole at Uplands (1869) in 'elephantine Gothic'[24] and F.W. Topham (the elder) at no. 4 Arkwright Road (1873), both by T.K. Green. The development of Fitzjohn's Avenue proceeded, as Sir Spencer Maryon Wilson, whose family were lords of the manor in Hampstead, came closer to realizing his goal of this broad stately boulevard lined with trees and substantial dwellings running up from Swiss Cottage.[25] Contracts for sales of land stipulated that houses must be valued at more than £3,000,[26] thereby ensuring spacious homes for affluent clients. For a while the area looked like a building site. One

Fig. 26 (left). R. Norman Shaw, The Three Gables, as illustrated in Maurice Adams, *Artists' Homes*, London, 1883 (photograph courtesy Cambridge University Library, S402.bb.88.2). Fig. 26a (right). Detail of the ground plan for The Three Gables

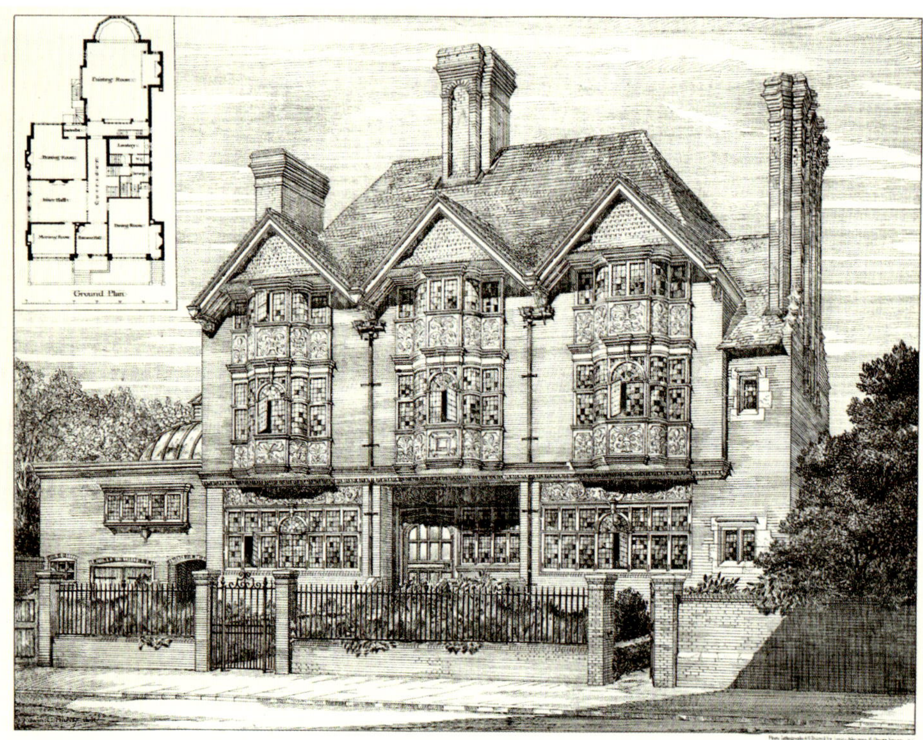

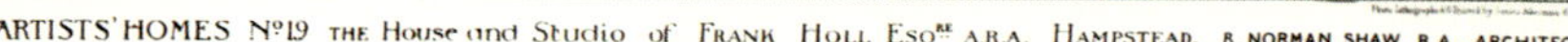

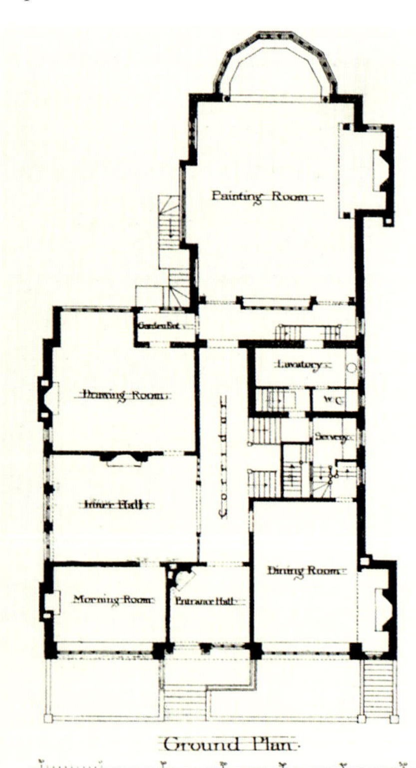

contemporary observed: 'It is not a countrified spot, but rather a wilderness of brickfields being converted into houses more or less aping the 'Queen Anne' style.'[27]

Holl opted for Shaw as his architect, no doubt bearing in mind the precedents of Glen Andred in Surrey for the older Academician E.W. Cooke and Graeme's (later named Grim's) Dyke in Harrow for his friend Goodall, as well as the nearby Kelston, Shaw's first house for Long.[28] As Andrew Saint has observed, 'Shaw had become the natural choice as the wealthy painter's architect'.[29] Initially, Holl believed that his forthcoming commissioned house 'of course ... will be beautiful inside, but probably like a brick on end outside', an assessment of Shaw's architecture based on Kelston with its four-square solidity and plain exterior.[30] But as the building evolved, its exterior ornament contributed greatly to its visual appeal.

Holl's project for a studio house signalled his ambitions and aspirations. For someone without benefit of family money and only thirty-five years old, it was also a costly risk. But with copious portrait commissions at this point in 1880, he had every reason to foresee an uninterrupted path to the top of his profession. Key to that ascent was a 'statement residence' in the newly fashionable part of London represented by Fitzjohn's Avenue. So certain was he of this decision that he bought the land without even consulting his wife.[31] The building progressed rapidly after the architect produced the first designs in spring 1881 with the building firm of William Tongue of Plumstead on board. Shaw lived nearby so could supervise progress. On Sundays Holl and his daughters walked up to inspect their new home. Unlike Pettie and Long, who named their houses after areas of England with which they had familial associations, Holl selected a more descriptive appellation, The Three Gables.

In early 1881 Shaw drew plans, exterior and interior views, with a further seventeen drawings (now in the Royal Academy) dating from the following year and showing more detailed aspects of the interior.[32] He addressed all elements of the design. His attention to the interior woodwork and details of decoration comes across in the drawings, particularly in his choice of coloured washes, such as the pale turquoise for the staircase hall. In 1882 Shaw exhibited two drawings for a 'House at Hampstead', which brought Holl's project to public and critical notice. The elaborate perspective drawing shows the three gables rising up from the ground-level entrance in a revised version (see fig. 26) of the original idea in the contract drawing, which had a more formal-looking doorway.[33] Holl seems to have preferred a simpler, low entrance. Each gable featured projecting double oriel windows, their panels filled with ornamental swirls and arabesques (although this was simplified in the finished building). Tile-hanging in the upper part of the gables lent texture to the surface. Adjoining to the right (northern) side of the building was a low-lying coach house, but other than this the frontage was symmetrical with its horizontality emphasized by decorative plaster panels, also known as pargeting, running along

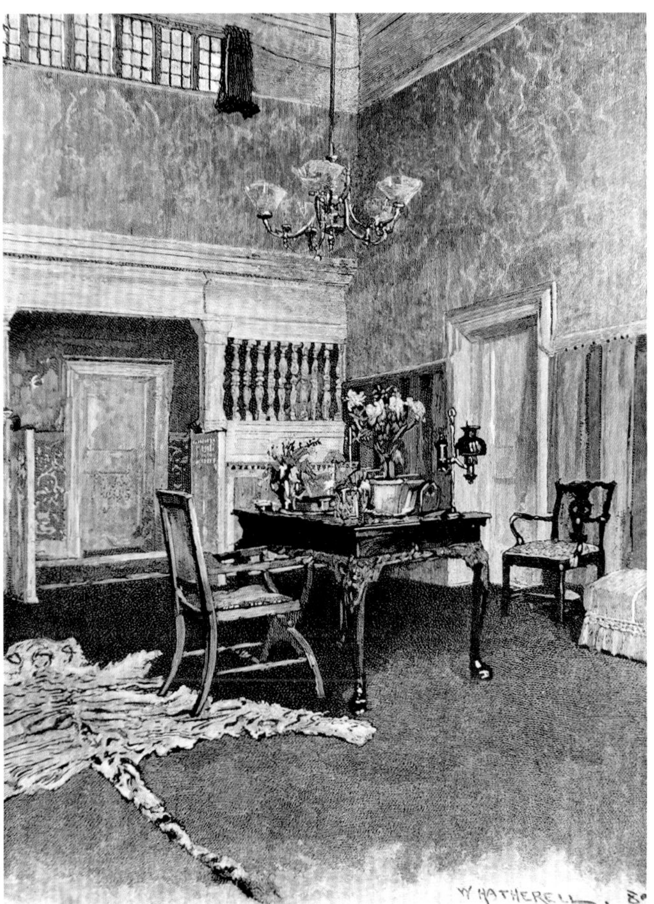

Fig. 27. 'The Inner Hall, The Three Gables', *Magazine of Art*, 1885. Watts Gallery Archive

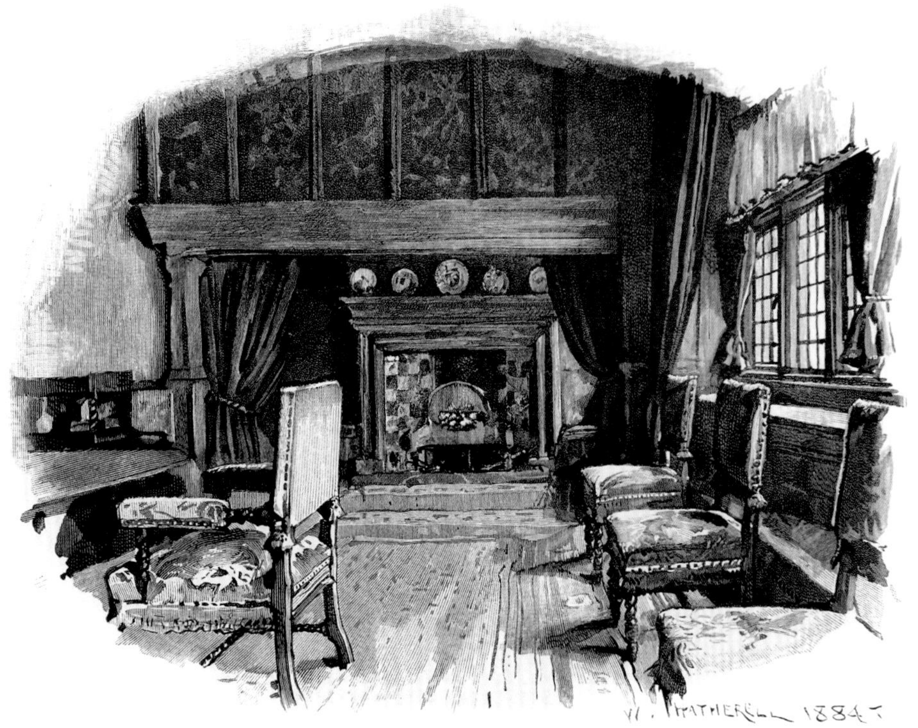

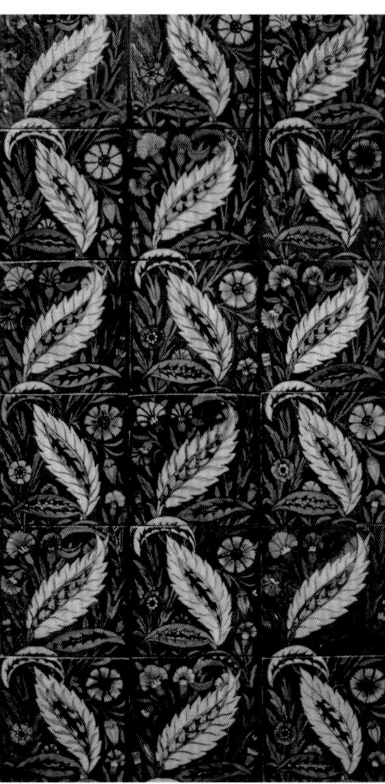

Fig. 28 (left). 'Dining Room, The Three Gables', *Magazine of Art*, 1885. Watts Gallery Archive. Fig. 29 (right). William de Morgan, tiles from a fireplace at The Three Gables. Victoria and Albert Museum, Circ. 35-1970

the top of the ground-floor windows. On Shaw's drawing of the exterior elevation he noted 'plaster frieze will be provided', which eventually took the form of a wide panel of high- relief, chunky, swag-like arabesques. The irregularity of the chimneys and the picturesque roof line, tile-hung gables and white woodwork linked the building with the Queen Anne style of the 1870s, although it also displayed features associated with 'Old English' architecture, such as the Tudor windows.[34]

Shaw's pen and ink perspective of The Three Gables is a stunning example of his famed architectural draughtsmanship.[35] The precise inked lines do not just convey information but create a satisfying image of a dwelling situated in a leafy environment, using schematized leaf patterns for the trees and Shaw's characteristic cross-hatching in the shadows. The style of drawing indicates its readiness for line engraving. Photolithographic reproductions in the periodical press of such ink drawings, virtually in facsimile, had progressed to such an extent that new architecture was immediately in the public domain through publications like *The Building News*, where the engraving of The Three Gables appeared on 8 September 1882 (fig. 26). As attractive as Shaw's drawing is, it does not convey the warmth of the red brick or the Brosely tiles (famous for their range of strawberry-toned reds) in combination with the cream-white-painted woodwork.

Shaw's designs for The Three Gables reveal a perfectly simple and clear solution to the creation of an artist's studio house. He had by this time plenty of practice in this particular architectural genre. What Holl required was ample studio space for his painting (now largely portraiture) and spacious accommodation for his wife Annie and four daughters. On the first and second floors were bedrooms, and the basement had the addition of a schoolroom for the younger children,[36] as well as the usual below-stairs practicalities. The plan shows the ground-floor layout (fig. 26a): after the entrance hall a long corridor led directly back to the studio, or one could linger in the double-height inner hall off the corridor to the left, with walls stencilled in amber and gold (fig. 27). A further turn to the left led into the morning room at the front of the house or, to the right, a drawing room at the back with light yellow wallpaper by Morris and Co. Off the central corridor, to the right, was a large dining room with an inglenook fireplace, a classic trait of Shaw's cosy domestic interiors (fig. 28). Enclosed by terracotta-coloured velvet curtains, the inglenook was lined with Spanish leather and dominated by the reddish-marble fireplace. Tiles by William de Morgan featured here and elsewhere in the house, as in the Persian-inspired tiles with a dramatic pattern of sinuously flowing leaves and flowers on a deep blue background (fig. 29). Given Shaw's interest in the design of the interiors, he must have suggested De Morgan, as he had for other commissions. Indeed, there was an Aesthetic-movement taste to the interiors with their pale colours and some 'Japanesy' elements. This clean and uncluttered environment suited the artist's personal taste. When Holl initially commented on how beautiful the interior would be, we need to recall that he was fastidiously tidy by his own daughter's and press accounts: 'Mr Holl admits that he is no devotee of the fashionable dinginess. He likes this fresh-looking white paint.' [37] Mess and disorder he associated with his early, poorer days; now he had attained a new lifestyle.

The studio, the *raison d'être* of the structure, took precedence over everything else (fig. 30). Discreetly positioned at the back of the building, projecting into the garden, the 'Painting Room' (as it was called on the plan) provided a large open area approximately 40 by 20 feet. A separate outdoor entrance could be

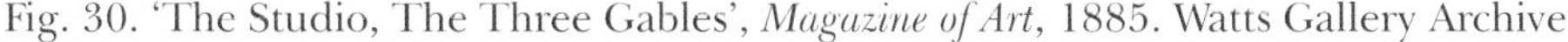

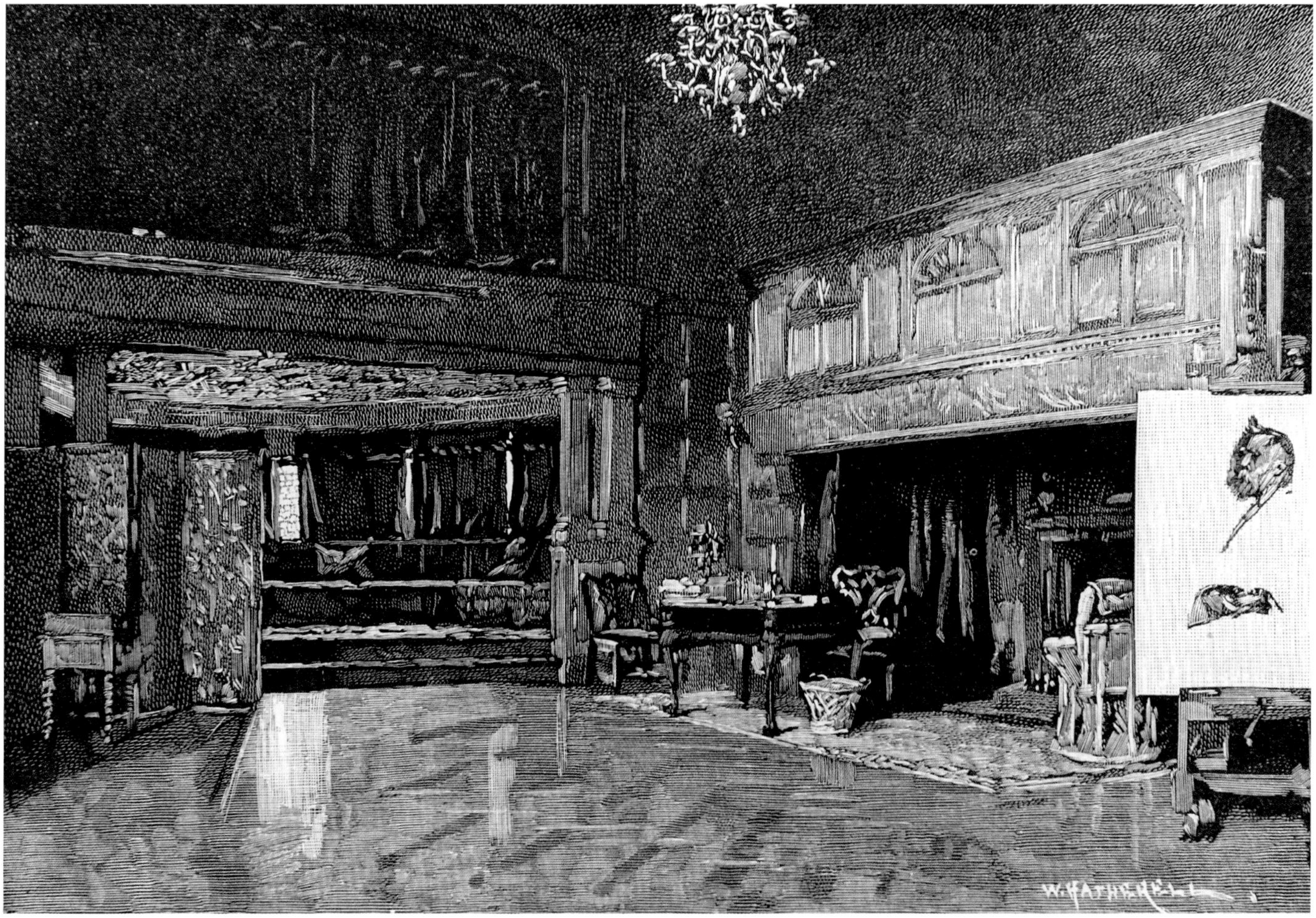

Fig. 30. 'The Studio, The Three Gables', *Magazine of Art*, 1885. Watts Gallery Archive

used for models (Holl used stand-in models for his eminent sitters), and stairs led down to the painting-room store on the lower-ground floor. At the far end of the studio stood a raised apsidal dais, encircled by a window. Above this was another large window, usually covered with curtains. Generally, sitters took up their position on the 'throne', an unusual corner chair of a type often used in libraries, which the artist placed near the fireplace. With Holl's sitters now including an increasing number of prominent members of society (generals, peers of the realm and royalty), the artist required a space that was both functional and imposing. A massive inglenook fireplace, supported on marble columns, stood to the side of the room. This impressive, almost baronial feature lent gravitas to the space. Peacock-blue curtains could be pulled to enclose it. Although the artist insisted on white woodwork throughout the living areas of the house, a darker atmosphere prevailed in the studio, a choice that related directly to his art. As Andrew Saint has pointed out, Holl's portrait work required gradations of light, not the overall brightness sought by painters of large subject pictures.[38] Some of Holl's later portraits show sitters set against a mainly dark background, with just one shaft of light breaking through, as he absorbed the lessons of his key portrait exemplars, Rembrandt and Velázquez. The evocative darkness of the studio is clearly evident in the pen and ink view (now in the Victoria and Albert Museum) by his friend, the artist-turned-actor Weedon Grossmith (1854–1919), showing how Holl could control illumination by moving one section of curtain to let a restricted amount of sunlight in. No studio bric-a-brac cluttered his environment: he needed a direct encounter with his sitter with, as he said, 'nothing getting into his eye' and distracting his attention.

Shaw's Three Gables served Holl's every need. He now had a studio worthy of the clientele he sought to attract. The budget for a house of this sort was in the thousands of pounds. Reportedly, Shaw commented of one client, probably Holl, when he complained about an extra cost: 'Oh, he can paint another nose.'[39] Indeed, the artist's lucrative portrait work enabled him to finance this venture. One friend, the editor of the *Daily News*, noted the artist told him that 'he paid the purchase money out of a single year's earnings, and houses of Norman Shaw architecture in Fitzjohn's Avenue are not cheap'.[40] The risk had paid off: when Holl commissioned it, he was an Associate Academician, but less than a year later he was elected a full member of the Academy.[41]

Holl in Surrey, 1885–8

The artist and his family had spent summers in Surrey for some years. Once they moved into The Three Gables late in 1882 and Holl settled into his new home, his thoughts turned to the idea of another building project – a modest country residence. He bought some land on the hills above Gomshall in Surrey, commissioning Shaw to build 'just a little place to run down to',[42] which he named Burrow's Cross. The contract was signed in February 1885.

The plans (now in the Royal Academy) show a low, wide-ranging brick building in a style that might be best described as 'Surrey vernacular', featuring tile-hanging and sober detailing. The studio again took up the most space on the floor plan, jutting out and giving light from both sides. This was to be a retreat from the stresses and strains of producing twenty or more portraits a year; in a way it was the artist's reward to himself. But of course this was an additional expense to shoulder. Even when he did visit, portraiture preoccupied him. He sounded optimistic when he wrote in 1886 that he looked forward to welcoming a local sitter as the first in his 'delightful studio'. Holl struck a happy pose in the doorway of the new house (fig. 31), but in the end he did not have much time to go there. Immediately after his death another artist, Benjamin Williams Leader (1831–1923), bought Burrow's Cross, employing Shaw to make changes to the building.[43] Leader painted the area often and the house can be seen in some of his landscapes.[44]

The celebrity artist at home

With the completion of The Three Gables, Holl had created a stage on which to enact his life as an artist. Now he could entertain properly. One of the key reasons for building a studio house was to provide a setting for the phenomenon of 'Show Sunday'. Towards the end of April Royal Academicians opened their residences to invited guests, including journalists, to view their submissions prior to the annual exhibition at Burlington House. Artists' lifestyles had become a topic of consuming interest in popular journals since the later 1870s. As new artists' houses were built, publicity fuelled a sense of competition among these professionals: a beautiful house and sense of exclusive access would attract purchasers for the works of art as well as place the artists in an elevated sector of society.

After the publication of Shaw's drawing in 1882, accounts of Holl's new house appear regularly. In 1883 Maurice Adams of the *Building News* included The Three Gables in *Artists' Homes: A Portfolio of Drawings including the Houses and Studios of Several Eminent Painters, Sculptors and Architects*. In April 1883 the syndicated 'Our Ladies' Column' commented that 'Artists' houses are now as attractive and beautiful as their pictures'. The author toured the artists' residences of Fitzjohn's Avenue. At The Three Gables she commented on the impressive 'gallery of portraits', before turning her attention to details of the house's decor.[45] The *Art Journal* of 1884 featured two sketches in 'Recent Building in London',[46] but it was artists' lifestyles that really captured the public mood. In 1885 the *Magazine of Art* commissioned no less than five drawings showing the interiors of The Three Gables (figs. 27, 28, 30), which provide much useful information. Although Holl did not have a Zulu native answering the door, as Long did, nor an array of arms and armour like his friend Pettie, his perfectly neat and pristine interior did present one or two surprises, such as the tiger skin rug in the inner hall and a bear skin in the drawing room. He greatly prized an original proof engraving of J.H. Ramberg's *Exhibition of the Royal Academy, 1787*, with Joshua Reynolds and the Prince of Wales in the Great Room at Somerset House. This possession speaks of Holl's pride at belonging to the Academy.

Frank Holl, like other successful Academicians, attracted public attention, especially once he had the setting to match his reputation. More than that, the image of the artist himself entered general circulation. J.P. Mayall produced a series of photographs published as photographic engravings with biographies.[47] Issued in parts throughout 1883 and then as a book, *Artists at Home*, in 1884, the project ran out of steam before all the photographs appeared. Although some now well-known images of Watts and Leighton were included, the two photographs of Holl were not published in his lifetime. One seems to be unknown and is reproduced here for the first time (fig. 32). The other is more conventional, though it does show the arrangement of unfinished canvases turned to the wall. The former presents Holl in his new studio, seated informally (and somewhat uncomfortably) on an upturned basket, before the massive inglenook fireplace. At work, he sits before the easel, holding his palette.

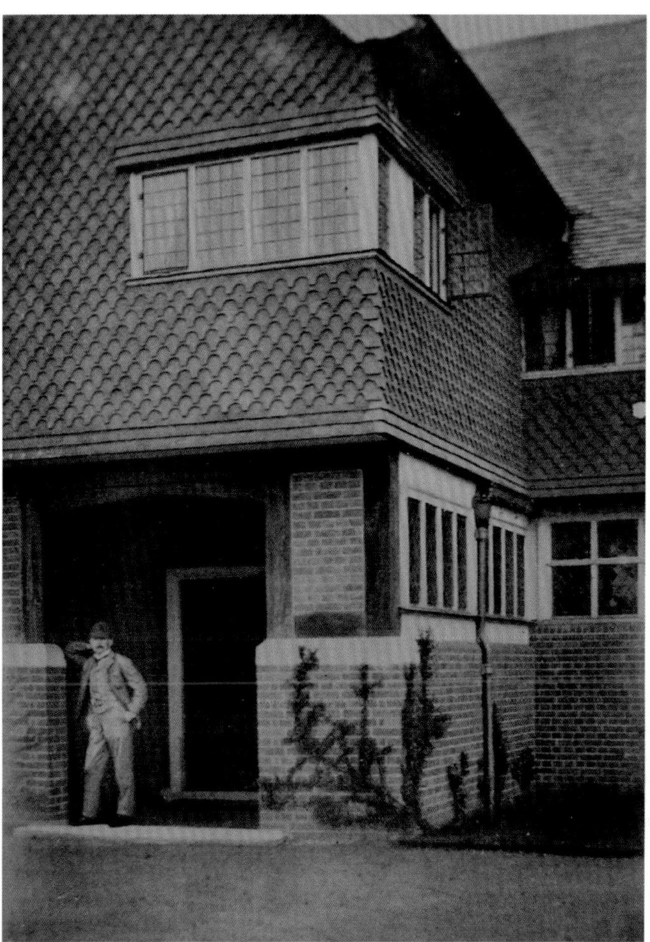
Fig. 31. 'Frank Holl in "The Porch" at Burrow's Cross, Gomshall, Surrey', from Reynolds, *The Life and Work of Frank Holl*, London 1912. Watts Gallery Archive

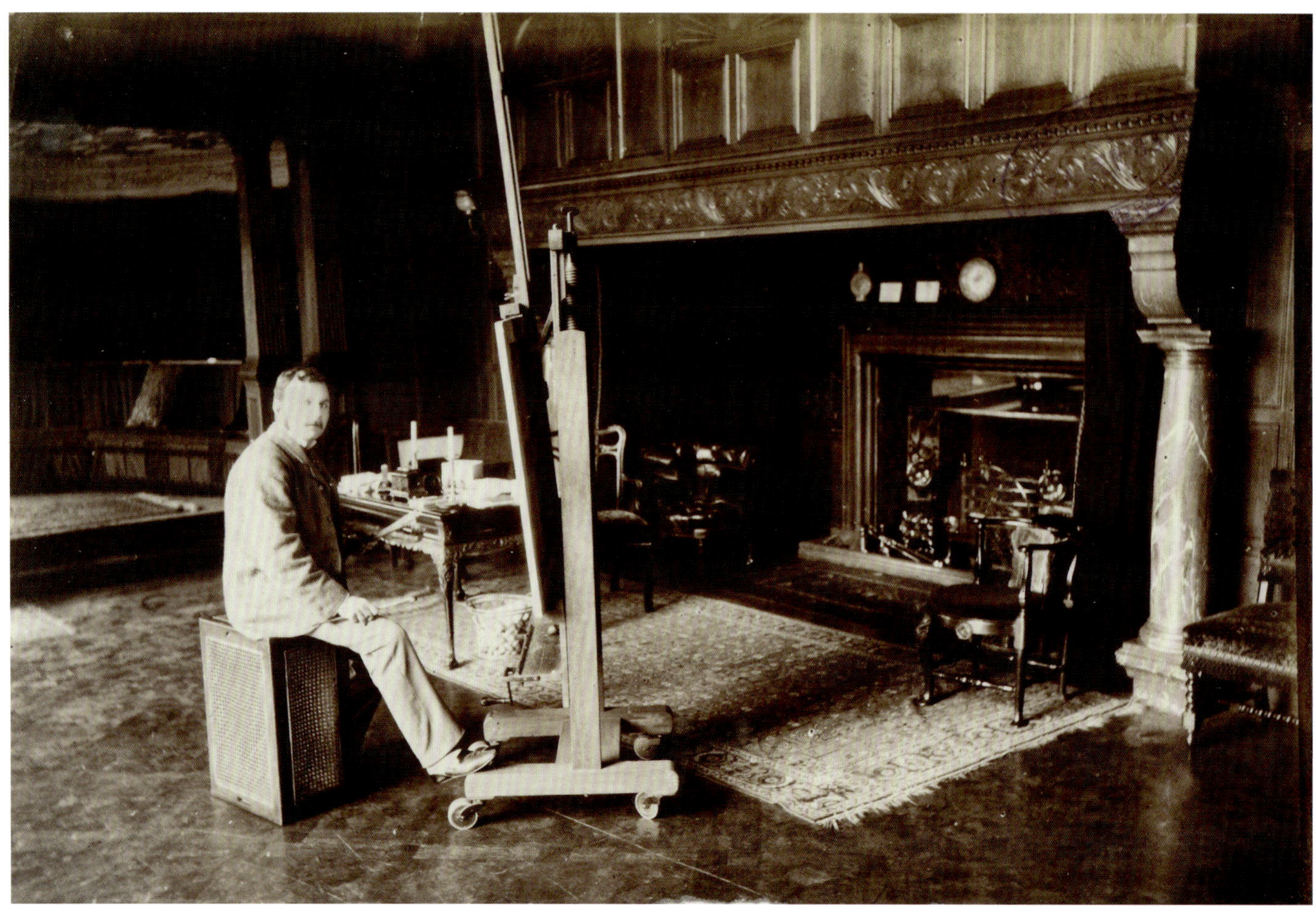

Fig. 32. Frank Dudman, *Frank Holl*, photograph, copyright registered by J.P. Mayall, September 1883, (National Archives)

He stares straight out, his gaze so direct that it makes an unusual challenge to the observer (perhaps the reason why it was never published). The sitters' chair, or 'throne', familiar from many of his portraits, is visible to the side of the fireplace. But the setting might well be a study, with the desk filled with paperwork and the tidy environment showing none of the evidence of mixing paints. This is how Holl preferred to be viewed: the gentleman artist, not slaving away in a garret but a prince in his own domestic palace.

Another series of illustrations appeared in *The Graphic*, feeding the public craving for information about the increasingly familiar figure of the successful professional artist. In June 1888 Holl appeared as the fourth in the series, 'Painters in their Studios', each accompanied by a full-length drawing from life by the French artist, Charles-Paul Renouard (1845–1924; fig. 20) and an article by Marion Harry Spielmann, the noted art critic who was on friendly terms with most artists in later-Victorian London. Renouard's lively image of Holl, a large illustration, shows the artist wearing his distinctive check suit, striking a vigorous pose. It celebrates the prestigious commission for a second portrait of the Prince of Wales. Holl had inherited the commission for the first portrait, for the Middle Temple, from G.F. Watts, who had tried and failed to produce a convincing full-length of this royal sitter,[48] and Holl's version proved to be a coup once it appeared at the Royal Academy in 1884. Later, Trinity House required the artist to paint a full-length of the Prince as an Elder Brother of the company. This is what we see in Renouard's illustration. Holl is just beginning work on a fresh canvas using virtually the same pose as his first portrait, although here the Prince wears military uniform. The sitters' chair is covered with the vivid pattern of the British standard flag, a new element in the composition. This image of Holl presents him at the peak of his profession, filled with the confidence of a royal commission in hand.

There is a certain gossipy content to many of the press accounts, a sense that the writer is relaying details of the private lives of artists. Several mention distinguished visitors arriving for their sittings, such as the Prince of Wales and William Ewart Gladstone. Holl entertained journalists eager to tell of 'celebrities at home'. One first-hand account gave a vivid description: 'If you chance to call before four o'clock in the afternoon a neat maidservant who opens the door ... will inevitably tell you with an ominous smile that Mr. Holl *is* at home, but *cannot* be spoken to for any earthly consideration.' A visit later in the day permits entry to the studio, 'where he is busily engaged in putting away his palette and carefully turning his unfinished canvases to the wall'. With his palette cleaned, he receives the journalist. His collie dog Tweed makes an appearance as well. When at work, Holl, we learn, 'generally wears a suit of check tweed',[49] resorting to his pipe when puzzled or in doubt. His business-like attitude to his art belied the chronic workaholic who had three sitters a day and churned out twenty portraits a year. Even though Holl was very serious about his art, it comes as a relief to learn from one popular article that the studio's polished oak flooring made it the perfect venue for dancing parties, which, as the father of four daughters, he permitted.

Fig. 33. Frank Holl, *The Sketching Club in Holl's Studio*, with John Pettie (centre) and others, watercolour on paper, 23.3 x 32.3 cm, 1883, British Museum. © Trustees of the British Museum

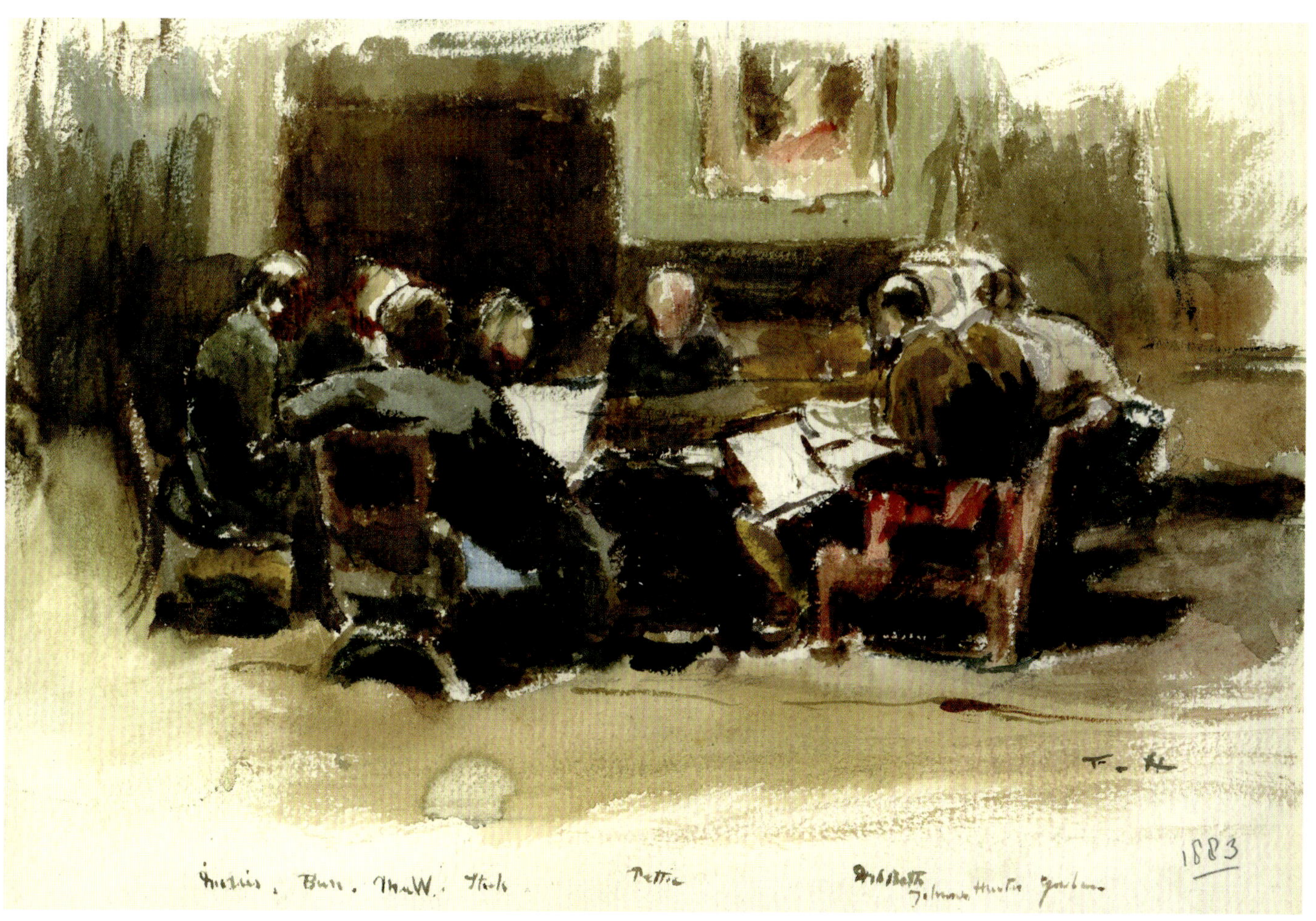

The studio functioned as a social space for the artist himself. Holl banished clutter to the lower painting store since he felt that 'a studio should be as much as possible a living-room, in which the evidences of work can be put aside'.[50] Here in the evenings, with the workday complete and after his daily constitutional over Hampstead Heath, he hosted the Sketching Club, a gathering of artist friends, some from the old days in Gloucester Road. Holl, their 'energetic secretary',[51] delighted in having this group to his new studio (fig. 33). A recollection of one meeting survives in Holl's watercolour sketch, which gives an intimate glimpse of the artists, including Pettie, Hook and John MacWhirter, busily sketching in the darkened, almost Rembrandtesque interior of the studio.

In January 1887 noted American journalist, James Gordon Bennett of the *New York Herald*, visited The Three Gables to ascertain Holl's plans for an imminent trip to America. Having portrayed several eminent American sitters, Holl planned to break into the market across the Atlantic, although he told Bennett, 'my principal object in going there is to get the ocean trip, change of air and recreation'.[52] The newspaperman assured him of 'a warm welcome whenever he reached New York'. Indeed, Holl still had huge ambitions for himself and for his art on the international stage. He desperately wanted to paint the 'magnificent head' of Otto von Bismarck, so he could 'cross swords or brushes' with Franz von Lenbach (1836–1904), the celebrated German portrait painter.[53]

Holl enjoyed the celebrity status he attracted, yet he constantly strove to push himself beyond his physical limits. His nervous energy would not let him rest. No one could tell from photographs and carefully staged images of him that this was a man with a serious heart condition prone to incessant breathlessness and even fainting. Harry Quilter, the polemical art critic and magazine editor, who knew Holl well, saw through this carapace of celebrity, recording his observations after the artist's death:

> We do strange things with our artists in England: we are desperately afraid lest they should not be respectable and successful; we judge their art by the dwelling-place of its master in a fashionable locality, by the amount of material dollars he gains per annum ... The artist once drawn into this vortex of expense and popularity is no longer master of himself. He *must* live to some extent as his patrons live; he *must* be ready at all hours to force his art to work to order; he must produce a certain quantity to meet that huge expense into which he has almost insensibly been drawn.[54]

This was Holl's dilemma. He had to maintain the position. Overwork took its toll on his declining health; despite this, he maintained a punishing schedule of portrait work. Then an ill-advised trip to Spain, in the hope that seeing the works of Velázquez would help his recovery, instead wore him down further. His illness was national news. Holl died in July 1888 just weeks after his forty-third birthday. Unfulfilled honours included an expected baronetcy (such as Millais and Leighton had received) and a portrait of himself for the gallery of artists' self-portraits at the Uffizi in Florence, not to mention his projected American sojourn, which would have sealed his international reputation.

Holl's life played out in chapters, each closely allied to his immediate environment and the places where he lived. These locations had their impact on how he viewed and presented himself. By the end of his life his main residence had never been more than about two miles from the place of his birth – from the centre of Camden Town to the slopes of lower Hampstead to his gravesite at Highgate Cemetery – but this had been a journey of greater magnitude than mere distance and one that was cut off in full flow with the artist's sudden and premature death.

Epilogue

Holl's family left The Three Gables after his death. Built as an artist's house, it did not suit his wife and four daughters, who relocated to the home of Holl's late father and mother in Milford, Surrey. Both Burrow's Cross and the Three Gables were sold. The latter was a landmark building and its sale for £11,000 in December 1894 was reported in the *British Architect*.[55] Edward Ledger (d. 1921), as the proprietor of *The Era*, a well-known weekly journal of the theatre world, appreciated the publicity value of owning such a house, with the studio space perfect for displaying his collection of furniture and armour. As an example of Shaw's architecture, it also attracted fame, appearing with full-page photographs (fig. 27) and illustrations in Hermann Muthesius's important publication, *Die Englische Baukunst der Gegenwart* (1900; fig. 25).

The Second World War did not kill off The Three Gables, but bombing nearby on Fitzjohn's Avenue (including Pettie's Lothians) meant that the house passed into the ownership of the National Health Service as a nurses' home and annex of the Marie Curie Hospital. By the early 1960s the government of the day and Ministry of Health promised the North-West Metropolitan Regional Hospital Board premises for the Tavistock Clinic, and the land on which Holl's house stood was part of a sizeable plot intended for a new building. Rumours of the potential loss of The Three Gables spread. Fortunately curators at the Victoria and Albert Museum's Circulation Department, under the leadership of Victorian-design advocate, Peter Floud, examined no. 6 Fitzjohn's Avenue and saved some twenty-three tiles by De Morgan that surrounded one of the fireplaces at the house (fig. 29).[56] These can now be seen on display in the Ceramics Galleries of the museum, a lucky survival of the famously attractive interiors of Holl's residence.

News of the planned demolition also reached the Victorian Society and the Hampstead Heath and Old Hampstead Protection Society. No less a figure than Professor Nikolaus Pevsner, himself a Hampstead resident and a great admirer of R. Norman Shaw's work, lent weight to a campaign to save The Three Gables. At a time when Victorian architecture had to fight its corner, Pevsner believed the house's international reputation gave it special status, plus it was one of Shaw's best in London and several others had already been lost.[57] But due to an administrative anomaly in the planning regulations, the house was a Crown property and not subject to the usual historical buildings' regulations. The protests were to no avail: the house went under the bulldozers in February 1965. The *Hampstead and Highgate Express* reported 'The End of Holl's House',[58] illustrating a pile of rubble, all that was left. A better fate awaited the Surrey house, Burrow's Cross. This remains, much changed, but still part of the landscape in the beautiful hills around Milford and Godalming, the chief remaining link with the private life of Frank Holl.

Notes

For assistance and discussions regarding R. Norman Shaw's work for Holl, I would particularly like to thank Andrew Saint; I am also grateful to Nick Savage at the Royal Academy of Arts. Christopher Marsden helped in assessing the role of the Victoria and Albert Museum in 1965 at the time Holl's house was demolished.

[1] As noted in Francis Holl's obituary in the *Athenaeum*, 19 January 1884, p. 96.

[2] Although most sources relate that Holl was born in Kentish Town, this is not correct. His birthplace was at the section of Kentish Town Road that begins in Camden Town and leads to Kentish Town, a mile up the road and in the 1840s a separate area. St James's Terrace was situated between Regent's Canal and the point where Kentish Town Road joins with Camden Road. Today it is on the same spot as the row of shops opposite the easternmost entrance to Camden Town Underground Station and the bus stops.

[3] As late as the 1920s, descendants named Holl still lived at 22 Bayham Street NW1.

[4] Reynolds, p. 11.

[5] Goodall 1902, p. 168.

[6] Henry William Lucy, *Sixty Years in the Wilderness: Nearing Jordan*, vol. 3, London, 1916, p. 376.

[7] Illustrated in the sale catalogue, Sotheby's, 11 June 1986, no. 201.

[8] Reynolds, pp. 60–1.

[9] Weedon Grossmith, *From Studio to Stage*, London 1913, p. 34.

[10] Reynolds, p. 76.

[11] In 1880, at the age of only thirty-five, this condition hampered his activities. During a visit to Wales while ascending Moel Siabod, Holl had to turn back a quarter of the way up; see Temple 1918, p. 86.

[12] Reynolds, p. 112.

[13] Still the situation into the 1950s, according to one resident, John Richardson, as noted in his *Camden Town and Primrose Hill Past: A Visual History of Camden Town and Primrose Hill*, London, 1991, p. 47.

[14] The front of the house is much the same as it was in Holl's time some 140 years ago. The extensive back garden has, however, been built on and the entire mews is now lined with infill housing from the 1960s. Long associated with creative artists, Camden Square has been home to Royal Academicians Tess Jaray and William Turnbull, and also to singer Amy Winehouse.

[15] On Camden Square see Valerie Hart et al., *Camden Town, 1791–1991: A Pictorial Record*, London 1991, pp. 98ff.

[16] Apart from the time he was abroad in Italy (1857) or Egypt (1858–59). He also rented no. 4 to Lawrence Alma-Tadema in 1871.

[17] Reynolds, p. 136.

[18] Reynolds, p. 155.

[19] Apparently one of his daughters was prone to diphtheria and this was another reason he wanted to relocate, as noted by Goodall 1902, p. 169.

[20] The topic of artists' houses and their uses has been discussed in the art-historical and architectural literature, as in Paula Gillett, *The Victorian Painter's World*, New Brunswick, NJ and Gloucester, UK, 1990; Walkley 1994; and Caroline Dakers, *The Holland Park Circle: Artists and Victorian Society*, New Haven and London 1999.

[21] For the most recent assessment of Leighton's working environment, see essays by Charlotte Gere, Anne Anderson and Barbara Bryant in Daniel Robbins, ed., *Closer to Home: The Restoration of Leighton House*, London 2010.

[22] Barbara Bryant, *G.F. Watts in Kensington: Little Holland House and Gallery*, Compton 2009.

[23] See Saint 2010.

[24] Bridget Cherry and Nikolaus Pevsner, *The Buildings of England: London 4 North*, London 1998, p. 237.

[25] For further information see 'Hampstead: Frognal and the Central Demesne', in T.F.T. Baker, ed., *A History of the County of Middlesex: Vol. 9 Hampstead and Paddington Parishes*, Oxford 1989, pp. 33–42; also www.british-history.ac.uk.

[26] Christopher Wade, *The Streets of Belsize*, 2nd edn, London 2003, p. 57.

[27] Zimmern 1885, p. 144.

[28] See Bills 1998, pp. 14–23, and in the same volume Juliet Kinchin, 'Mr. Long has the Finest Studio in London …', pp. 31–43.

[29] On Shaw's artists' houses see Saint 2010, pp. 175ff.

[30] See illustration in Bills 1998, p. 35.

[31] Reynolds, p. 207, although his daughter says the purchase took place in autumn 1881, this must be an error for 1880.

[32] Two are included in the online catalogue of architectural drawings in the Royal Academy's collection; some of the

contract drawings bear the signature of William R. Lethaby, Shaw's assistant, but this does not necessarily mean the drawings are by him, just that he was present when the builder, Tongue, signed.

[33] Original idea illustrated in Saint 2010, p. 180.

[34] For more detailed descriptions of the architecture see Saint 2010, p. 180, and Walkley 1994, pp. 109–11.

[35] The original drawing is illustrated in the Royal Academy's online collections (03/2601).

[36] The older children were sent to boarding school in Brighton.

[37] Zimmern 1885, p. 146.

[38] Saint 2010, p. 180.

[39] My thanks to Andrew Saint for telling me about this remark, which has been recounted by John Betjeman, among others. It seems to originate in W.R. Lethaby's discussion of Shaw in *Philip Webb and his Work*, London 1935, p. 75.

[40] Henry William Lucy, Sixty Years in the Wilderness: Nearing Jordan, vol. 3, London 1916, p. 375.

[41] Ironically, his engraver father was only elected an Associate Academician in January 1883, when he was aged sixty-seven; this was a matter of months before Frank became an R.A.

[42] Reynolds, p. 233.

[43] Shaw's drawings for extensions and changes to Burrow's Cross undertaken for Leader, dating from 1889, are in the collections of the Royal Academy of Arts. Photographs appear in the *Art Journal: Art Annual*, London 1901, pp. 25–30.

[44] A view of the house appears in *Burrows Cross, Surrey*, sold 25–6 January 2012, Christie's, Paris.

[45] 'Penelope', 'Our Ladies' Column by one of themselves', syndicated in, among other papers, the *Leicester Chronicle, Wrexham Advocate and Nottinghamshire Guardian*, 21 April 1883.

[46] *Art Journal*, 1884, pp. 17, 20.

[47] National Portrait Gallery online catalogue of Later Victorian Portraits lists (but does not illustrate) these images as by Frank Dudman. Mayall registered them for copyright.

[48] See Barbara Bryant, *G.F. Watts Portraits: Fame & Beauty in Victorian Society*, London 2004, p. 34.

[49] Quotations in this paragraph from 'Celebrities at Home. Mr. Frank Holl ...', *The World*, 21 December 1887, p. 6.

[50] Zimmern 1885, p. 150.

[51] Martin Hardie, John Pettie, *R.A., H.R.S.A.*, London 1908, p. 48.

[52] James Gordon Bennett, jun., 'Frank Holl Coming: A Well Known English Portrait Painter to Visit the United States', *New York Herald*, 23 January 1887.

[53] 'Reminiscences of Frank Holl', *Pall Mall Gazette*, 2 August 1888.

[54] Quilter 1888, pp. 487–8.

[55] *The British Architect*, 41 (1894), p. 56.

[56] Barbara Morris, a curator in the V&A's Circulation Department, inspected the house before demolition and managed to secure the tiles that surrounded one of the fireplaces. These entered the museum in 1965 but were not accessioned until 1970 (CIRC.35-1970).

[57] Pevsner included it in *The Buildings of England: London* in 1952; in later editions he regretted the loss of this outstanding building.

[58] *Hampstead and Highgate Express*, 19 February 1965, p. 1.

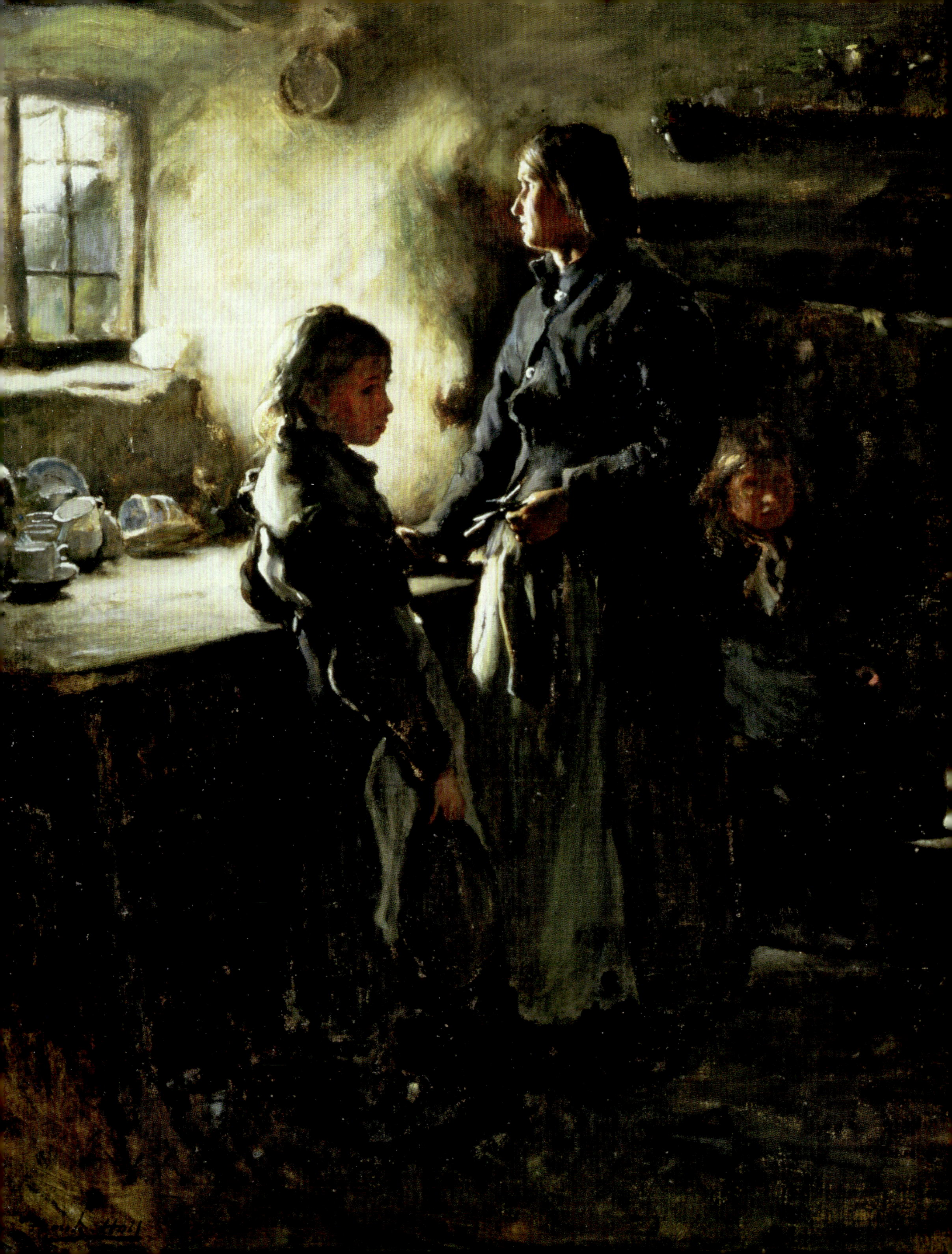

A Daughter's Story: Frank Holl and Women

Jane Sellars

Women play a significant part in the art of Frank Holl. They are the central figures in his subject pictures, which deal almost exclusively with aspects of women's suffering in Victorian society. Furthermore, it is to a woman writer that we turn for the most [illegible] source of information about his life. Holl's [illegible] Ada Mabel Holl, became the writer [illegible] lds, who in 1912, twenty-four years [illegible] death, published *The Life and Work* [illegible] ly twenty years old when her father [illegible] ook, which she published in her early [illegible] t exactly the same age as her father was at his death, she produces plenty of detailed information. She tells us much about the Holls' family life and her father's business and social life that conveys a strong sense of his affection and admiration for women. After all, he lived in a household dominated by women, with his wife Annie née Davidson, whom he married in May 1867, and four daughters, Ada born 1869, Olive born 1871, Madoline – or Nina – born 1874 and Phyllis born 1882. As she wrote, Ada had to hand a wealth of Frank Holl's personal papers, including his diary and letters from clients. For instance, describing her father's punishing work schedule as a fashionable portrait painter with illustrious sitters clamouring for his attention, she quotes 'in its entirety my father's own diary, which he kept of the Hawarden visit [where he was staying to paint Mr Gladstone's portrait in 1887], the only diary, I may add, that he ever kept'.[1] Ada must also have had his studio record books, because she scrupulously lists the dates and specific details of his subject pictures and portrait commissions, as in 1882:

> Following the Bright portrait were two subject pictures, 'Pets' and 'No Tidings' – both of them painted for Arthur Tooth. Then followed two women's portraits, Mrs Taylor and Mrs Ireland. After these that of J. Lyon Bristowe, Esq., head of the great engineering firm of Clayton and Shuttleworth, and a replica of the same, a head only, and John Foster Esq.

As the oldest daughter, Ada must have appointed herself as the keeper of her father's archives. She also had resort to her mother's diary of the Holls' visit to Italy in 1869,[2] and her mother's memories of early married life.

Ada's biography of her father is written very much in the style of the time and is to some extent hagiographical in her attitude to the artist. She writes a lot about when she and her siblings were very young, conjuring up images of an idyllic childhood with summers spent in the countryside in Surrey or in Wales: 'Happy days of sunshine, of the singing of birds, of the pungent scent of may-blossom, of hedges covered with wild rose, and, later still, the air sweet with the smell of new-mown hay.'[3] Yet at the same time she tells us a great deal about the reality of living with an artist who, despite his success, constantly doubted his own abilities and overworked to such an extent that

Fig. 34. Frank Holl, *Hope*, 1883, detail of cat. 23 (p. 147)

he brought unending anxiety to his family and his own premature death. She often quotes her mother, Annie Laura Holl (1842–1931), on the strain of the situation:

> She really used to dread the summons to the studio, immediately on the departure of the sitter, to give her opinion on the day's work – she says it seemed scarcely necessary for her to speak, so exactly did he read approval or the reverse in her eyes, in her very attitude before she spoke. And frequently an adverse remark on her part had undone an entire morning's work ... She, therefore, learnt to keep a very careful guard over herself and her feelings with regard to his work, and hardly dared venture on any disparaging remark.[4]

Many Victorian family biographers of famous artists tend to dwell more on the father's (or mother's) domestic life than on his professional one. Elaine Phillips, daughter of the painter John Atkinson Grimshaw, left an unpublished memoir of her father that gives the reader much general and, it has to be said, extraordinarily revealing information about family life, but less so about his professional practice.[5] Ada, however, does not disappoint us in this area. From her we learn about Holl's female models for the subject paintings, his methods of working, the evolution of his subject pictures and his personal opinions of his sitters.

Models were essential to Holl's work, as they were to all Victorian artists, some more than others. William Powell Frith (1819–1909), bastion of the art establishment and Holl's near contemporary, created a vogue for modern-life subjects with his crowded panoramas of *Life at the Seaside (Ramsgate Sands)*, *Derby Day* and *The Railway Station*, which demanded numerous models. Frith relied on professional models, people he met on the street, and his own family, friends and servants to populate his paintings.[6] The women Frith depicted were predominantly middle class, whereas Holl in his subject pictures portrayed the poor. His paintings of course had far fewer figures, and Holl was very specific about the female models he sought for works such as *I am the Resurrection and the Life* (fig 11, page 32), *Hush!* (cat. 12), *Hushed* (cat. 13) and *Newgate, Committed for Trial* (cat. 15). Like Frith, he used professionals, family and women whom he encountered by chance and identified as a particular character for a painting. At the beginning of his career Holl, like Frith, was compelled to call on his nearest and dearest to model for him. In late 1867, shortly after returning from their honeymoon, Annie Holl was required to model for *'The Lord gave and the Lord hath taken away ...'* (fig. 35, cat. 5) a scene taken from Mrs Craik's novel *The Head of the Family* (1852), which depicts the family bereaved of their father and the oldest son taking his place to say grace at table:

> My mother sat for one of the persons in the picture, a seated figure of a woman in black, her head drooping forward, the arm hanging listlessly by her side. My uncle also sat for one of the figures ... A difficulty arose as to the providing of a long-trained black dress which must be the garb for the woman in the picture, and it was only by dint of the utmost economy that my mother was able to get together enough spare cash to buy the dress, which she made herself.[7]

Poor Annie's despondent look in the painting is admirable, no doubt helped by the fact that she was probably in the early stages of pregnancy at the time.

Although Ada claims that her father wrote only one diary in his lifetime, it is hard to believe that he did not himself write about the events of his days and his ideas for paintings when reading the intensely detailed passages in her book, where she recalls episodes in Holl's life from over forty years earlier. Indeed, she describes his daily routine in 1885 thus:

> [Portraiture] took up all of his time, and more, for it encroached even upon that which ought to have been the necessary allowance of leisure... although... he never allowed anything to interfere with his daily walk of one hour. Between 6 and 7 was his usual time, then back to dinner, and afterwards to sit at his desk writing, writing, writing, until all hours of the night.[8]

Maybe he was writing his own memoir, so providing Ada with the material for her biography.

A passage of Ada's describes a tragedy Holl witnessed when staying at the artists' haunt, the Northumberland fishing village of Cullercoats, in June 1870, when she was a babe in arms:

> He was painting in one of the cottages where the inmates were discussing the chances of those who had not yet come home, when the door was flung wide, and a woman with hair dishevelled, and wild eyes, tottered in muttering and moaning distractedly, wandering from door to window, from window to door, half mad with suspense and misery. Even whilst thus she wandered, a shadow darkened the doorway, and a dripping burden was carried into the cottage, all that remained of the young fisherman, her husband, whose body had just been found. The poor woman gave a great gasp of agony and horror, and fell prone upon the lifeless body of her mate, calling to him in vain, with agonized sobs of entreaty to God 'to take her too.' My father was greatly moved and upset at the sight of her grief, terribly primitive in its intensity, which haunted him for days, finally resolving itself into a conception for a picture which he eventually painted, calling it 'No tidings from the sea' [fig. 36, cat. 6].[9]

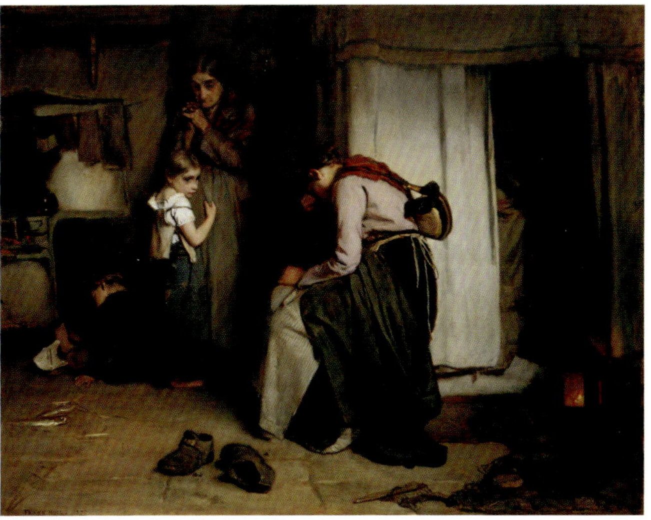

Fig. 35. Frank Holl, *No Tidings from the Sea*, 1870, oil on canvas. Royal Collection Trust, © HM Queen Elizabeth II 2012

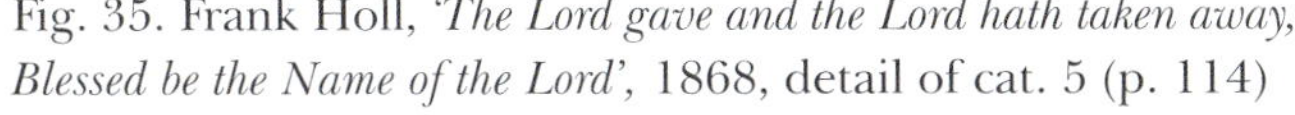

Fig. 35. Frank Holl, *'The Lord gave and the Lord hath taken away, Blessed be the Name of the Lord'*, 1868, detail of cat. 5 (p. 114)

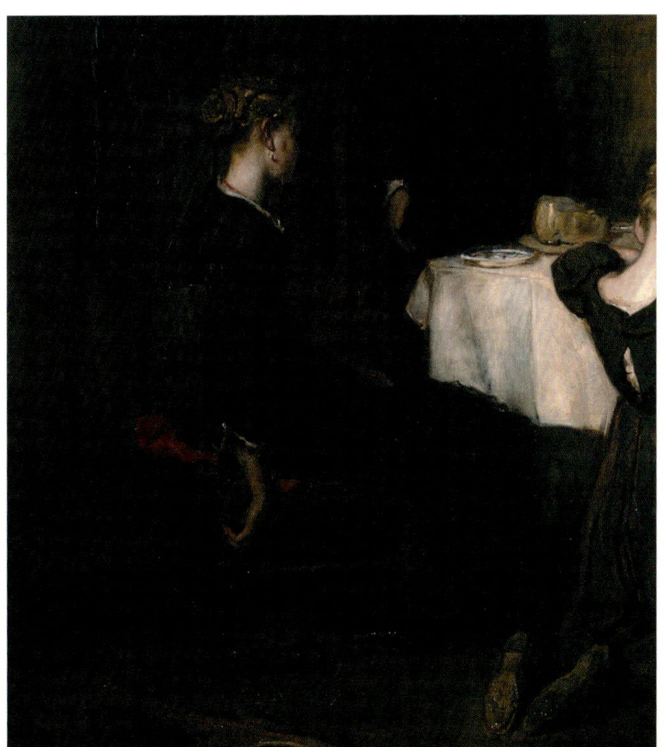

The scene Ada describes is not the one in the painting but it is written with such detail and passion that it might have come from a primary written source. Maybe the stories Holl told of the inspirations for his paintings were well known in his immediate circle and were often retold. It is quite likely that Ada's mother passed on these stories to her children as memories of their father, whom they had lost when they were all quite young. On the other hand, the impact of the story could be put down to Ada's skills as a writer.

Holl's painting *I am the Resurrection and the Life* (1872) had its genesis in another scene that the artist witnessed, this time in the Surrey countryside, where the family had gone to Gomshall on holiday in May 1871. Ada was then about three years old and her mother was expecting sister Olive. Walking through Albury Park on what later became the Duke of Northumberland's estate, he witnessed the funeral procession for the wife of an old gamekeeper.[10] Touched by the incident, Holl decided to make a painting and started with sketches of the old church and of the gamekeeper and his granddaughter. The progress of the picture was immediately interrupted by the need to return home for Annie's confinement.

Olive was born 1 September 1871 and Annie became dangerously ill as a consequence of the birth. Frank Holl took his wife to Elstead in Surrey to convalesce while he went back to Gomshall to carry on with preparation for his painting, making detailed studies of the gamekeeper. Ada describes this model, rather patronizingly: 'The other figures he could easily replace, but the old man himself was unique, as a specimen of the type to which he belonged.' Back in London, Holl had to find a model for the little girl. One of his regular models, Mrs Doe, recommended her four-year-old niece, Connie, and brought her to the studio for her very first sitting.

> The child was an exquisite little creature, winning and docile in manners, and wonderfully intelligent ... a wonderful little model she proved and a standby to my father for many years ... She seemed to embody in her small self the very spirit of the picture, and really seemed to become the actual person she represented.[11]

This perfect model turned out to be Miss Constance MacDonald Gilchrist (1865–1946), whose history was the stuff of Victorian romance (figs. 36, 37). From an early age Connie also modelled for Frederick Lord Leighton, culminating in a whole procession of dancing girls for his painting *The Daphnephoria* (1876). She posed for Whistler as *The Gold Girl* (1873) and then *The Blue Girl* (1879). At the age of twelve Connie made her debut at the Gaiety Theatre in London as a skipping-rope dancer, which developed into a successful career as a dancer and actress in comedy and vaudeville, a career that was cut short in the late 1880s when she married and became the Countess of Orkney.

Ada writes at some length about Connie, with great sympathy for the hard-working life she led as a child model contending with a harsh mother:

> Once father went down to try and get Connie for a sitting the following day, and found the poor child in tears after a beating at the hands of her mother, because she refused to have her hair washed after eleven o'clock at night. The child was simply dead beat and utterly exhausted after a long day's sitting and the hard work at the theatre.[12]

She tells how she and Olive loved Connie and played with her in the nursery, and how their parents took them to see Connie perform as a skipping fairy in a pantomime. Although Ada recalls that Connie modelled for her father frequently, it is possible to identify her in just a few paintings other than *I am the Resurrection and the Life*. These include *A Deserter* (1874; fig. 39), in which Connie is the beautiful child regarding the soldier deserter with great interest, and possibly *Faces in the Fire* (1867; fig. 40, cat. 4). However, once Holl began to work for *The Graphic* at the end of 1871, he was constantly in need of models to work to tight deadlines for his drawings for the newspaper and Connie certainly sat for these (fig. 41).[13]

Both William Powell Frith and Atkinson Grimshaw used their children as models in their work, but Holl rarely did so. Ada does not mention sitting for her father herself, but he did paint Nina, the third of his four daughters. In fact, Ada tells us more about Nina than she does about her other two sisters, Olive and Phyllis. In 1879 Holl painted two pictures of little girls: one, *The Gifts of the Fairies*, of two poor children who have hopefully left their shoes by the fireplace on Christmas Eve awaiting Santa Claus; the other, *The Daughter of the House* (fig. 42), 'in which a little girl is just recovering from a severe illness, and who sits up in bed, supported by pillows, and surrounded by picture-books, toys and flowers, together with a favourite parrot, bestowed upon her by her parents, whose idol she is'. Nina suffered from poor health, which Ada mentions several times, and when this subject was painted, she had recently recovered from a severe illness: in Ada's words, 'doubtless the child's expression inspired my father to paint the picture'.[14] It is also likely that Holl feared he might lose his child and therefore painted her portrait to remember her by.

There is another portrait of Nina, clearly painted at the same time as *The Daughter of the House*, in which she is wearing the same white frilled dress and blue necklace, this time sitting in the garden with a pet rabbit on her lap. The child in a further work, *Convalescent* (*c.*1879), showing her lying in bed with primroses scattered on the bedcover, would also appear to be Nina. In 1883 Holl was painting a portrait of Field Marshal Lord Wolseley, who posed in uniform with his ceremonial sword. Ada writes:

> [Nina] had one day wandered into the studio after one of Lord Wolseley's sittings (she was always rather a privileged young person and had a way of ingratiating herself with people, and wriggling her way into places that we, or rather I, would never have ventured), and had calmly mounted the throne and taken up Lord Wolseley's sword, which happened to be lying across the chair. She contemplated it gravely for a few moments, and then suddenly looking up, said, 'Did Lord Wolseley ever kill anybody with this, father?' – a sufficiently gruesome suggestion for a child her age.[15]

This inspired a portrait of Nina with the sword, originally intended as Holl's diploma work for full membership of the Royal Academy and entitled

Fig. 37. Frank Holl, *I am the Resurrection and the Life (The Village Funeral)*, 1872, detail of fig. 11 (p. 32) showing Connie Gilchrist

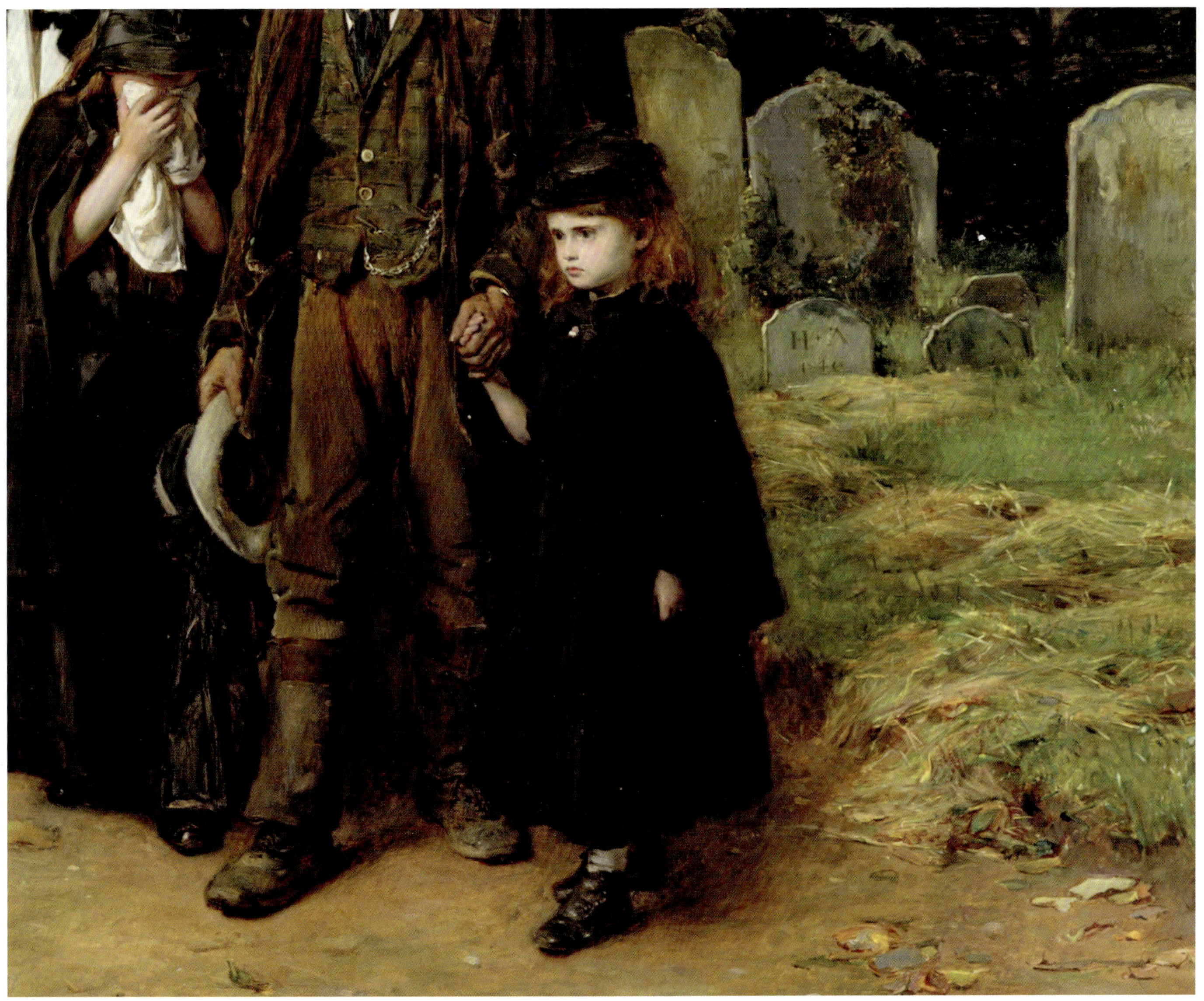

'Did you ever kill anybody, Father?' (1883; fig. 43). In the event, Holl gave it to his wife, who later sold it to their loyal patrons Mr and Mrs Tonks of Sutton Coldfield, on condition that she could buy it back if she wished, although she never did. In 1884 Holl painted a companion picture for this one, again of Nina, *The First Violin*, also acquired by Mr Tonks.

It would certainly appear that Nina was the favourite child, or perhaps just the most obliging model of the four daughters. There is evidence that Holl did also make a portrait of Phyllis, the youngest child. Ada writes about her father's sensitivity to criticism, 'even of the feeblest folk', and describes how he once made an oil study of five-year-old Phyllis: 'This small person, who, by the way, rather ruled the roost generally, when shown the sketch, turned up her nose, saying, "*That's* not like me at all, it's not pretty enough!" My father tweaked her hair and called her a conceited little monkey, but he altered it nonetheless!'[16]

The most compelling of Holl's representations of women are those that appear in his subject pictures, of women in poverty suffering grief, loss and abandonment. Ada – describing her father's prowls around London's East End to observe and sketch poverty at close quarters and bring home old clothes and props for his paintings – is protective of her father's reputation for this aspect of his art, as Mark Bills records above (see pp. 27–28). One of Holl's best-known images 'London Sketches – The Foundling', made for *The Graphic* in 1873, was prompted by an incident he witnessed in Dockland, when an abandoned baby had been found under an archway and was carried away tenderly by a policeman, followed by 'a sympathetic, murmuring crowd'. For his drawing for *The Graphic* Holl added the figure of the stricken mother, the fallen woman who has been compelled to leave her child, gazing in despair as the baby is taken away. The subject of the fallen woman was one that few artists were attempting then. The most memorable works predate Holl by about twenty years, such as Augustus Egg's *Past and Present* (1858), G.F. Watts's *Found Drowned* (*c.*1848–50) and William Holman Hunt's *The Awakening Conscience* (1853). Perhaps not surprisingly, Ada makes no comment anywhere in the book on the sexual exploitation of women that was at the root of so much female poverty in the world that her father depicted. There was one particular review of her father's work that Ada quotes at length, so fully did she approve of it, in which the critic writes: 'Mr Holl has a penchant for dipping his pencil "in the gloom of earthquakes and eclipse", but in so doing he never harrows the feelings or offends against the canons of good taste.'[17]

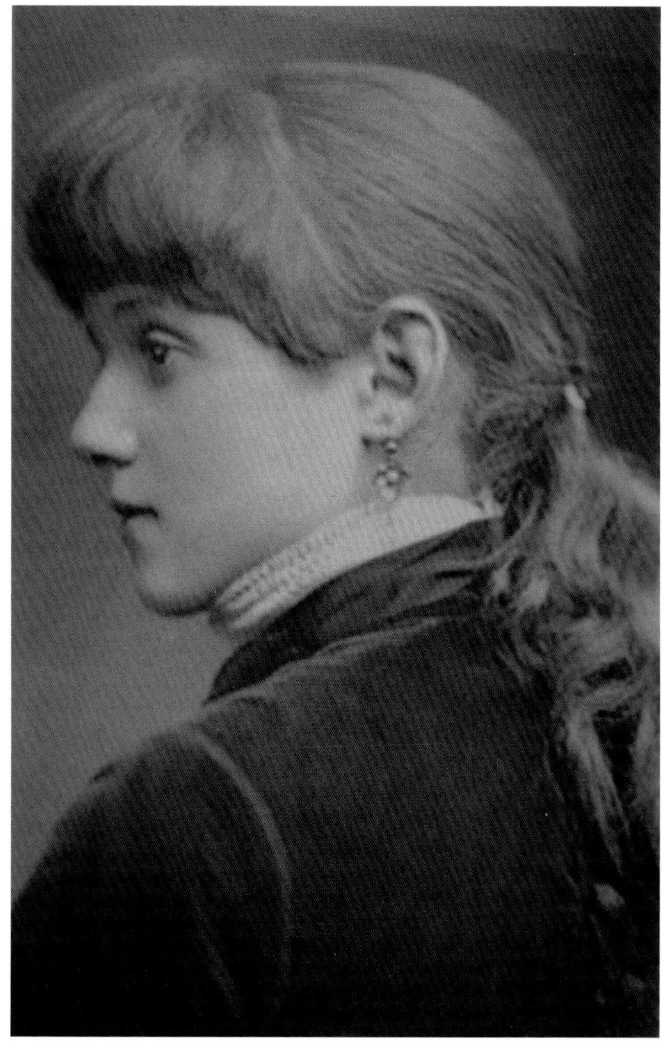

Fig. 38. *Connie Gilchrist*, date unknown, photograph. Rob Dickins Collection, Watts Gallery Archive

Holl and his family spent their summers together away from London, selecting places where the artist could find time and inspiration for his work. Many of his paintings of women's suffering are set in the dark, shadowy interiors of humble cottages, with the light filtering in through one small window to create his

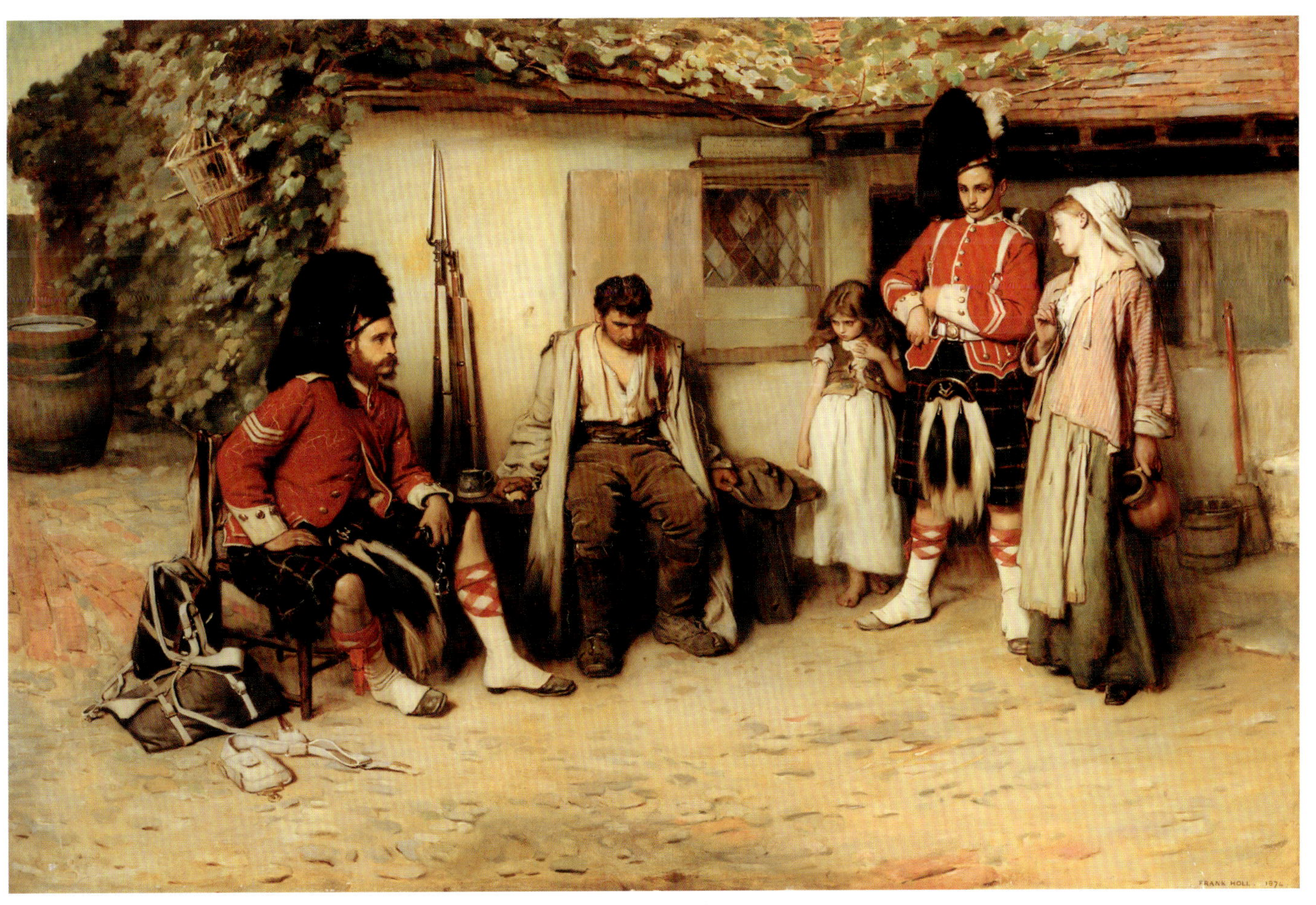

Fig. 39. Frank Holl, *A Deserter*, date unknown, oil on canvas.
© Christie's Images

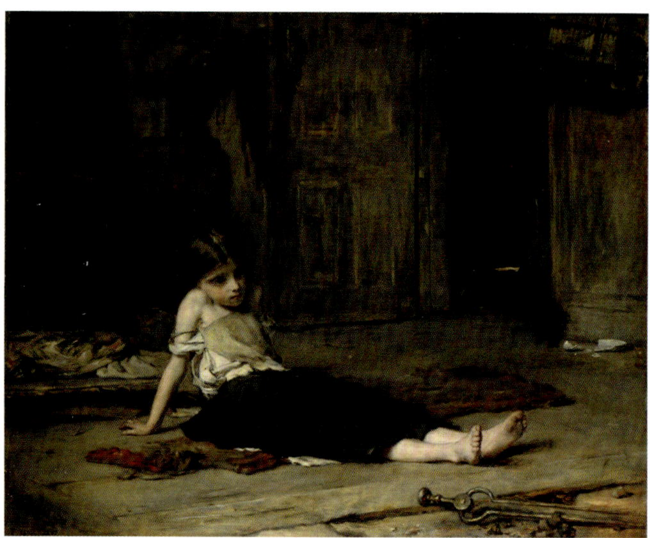

Fig. 40. Frank Holl, *Faces in the Fire*, 1867, oil on canvas. Ashmolean Museum, University of Oxford

favoured chiaoscuro effects. In 1876 the Holls went to Criccieth in Wales, where Frank Holl found a most inspiring model:

> Wandering one day over the sandy dunes to the right of the village, he took shelter from the rain in a little cottage, scarcely more than a hut, on the banks of a stream ... This hut was tenanted by a widow with two young children, one quite a baby, the other some five or six years old. The woman had scarcely any English, but her magnificent build and presence at once inspired my father with the idea of a large composition. She was of a massive almost savage type, living quite alone with her children, and seeing no one for weeks together.[18]

This woman became the model for *Waiting* and *L'Ennemi* (both 1876) and many other works later. The oil study *Head of a Welsh Fishergirl* (*c.*1870s; fig. 45, cat. 9) is one of Holl's Criccieth studies of this same striking woman.

In 1877 they returned to Criccieth so that Holl could again paint the woman in her home, this time producing the pair of works *Hush!* and *Hushed*, a tragedy in two parts. In *Hush!* the mother leans forward in anguish over her sick baby in the cradle, with her other child intensely watching her face. In *Hushed* the cradle is empty and the woman collapses into an attitude of despair. Holl creates these heartbreaking scenes without melodrama or sentimentality. In neither picture do we see the woman's face, but we read her agony in her pose and in the bewildered expression of the little child who watches her. In the Welsh woman, living her independent life, he truly found an outstanding model. In 1879 they were back in Criccieth again, with Holl painting four or five pictures. This time he took the children to visit his 'wonderful fisherwoman', as Ada calls her. 'She welcomed us most heartily, expressing her welcome most admirably and convincingly in much gesture, facial play, and voluble Welsh, none of which we could understand.'[19]

The Welsh cottage pictures provided Holl with a steady source of income, and he continued to paint the 'wonderful fisherwoman' for some years and in the same setting. On this subject Ada feels the need to defend her father's paintings of the woman in her cottage, acting out the roles of bereaved mother, widow and protector of her children, from those who might accuse her father of being prone to enquire too closely into the seamy side of life. 'True it was that he saw life – so far, at least, as the painter in him was concerned – through dun-coloured spectacles, but that he was thoroughly sincere in everything he undertook, I feel convinced.'[20]

Holl turned his attention to criminality in what is probably his best-known picture, *Newgate, Committed for Trial* (1878; fig. 46, cat. 15). Strikingly, this painting has much to say about the plight of women: one of them a battered wife, the other a woman whose previously respectable husband has been found guilty of embezzlement. Ada tells us that *Newgate* was the result of her father conceiving 'the idea of a picture, typifying some stirring, dramatic incident, into which he could throw his whole being, and which should prove to be the complete expression of all the best that was in him'. A visit to the old prison as the guest of the governor meant that he witnessed the incident that forms part of the story in the work:

> A young wife was seeing for the first time her husband, a young man of good family, and who had filled the trusted position in one of the largest and most important banking houses. Falling amongst evil companions he had been tempted to misappropriate

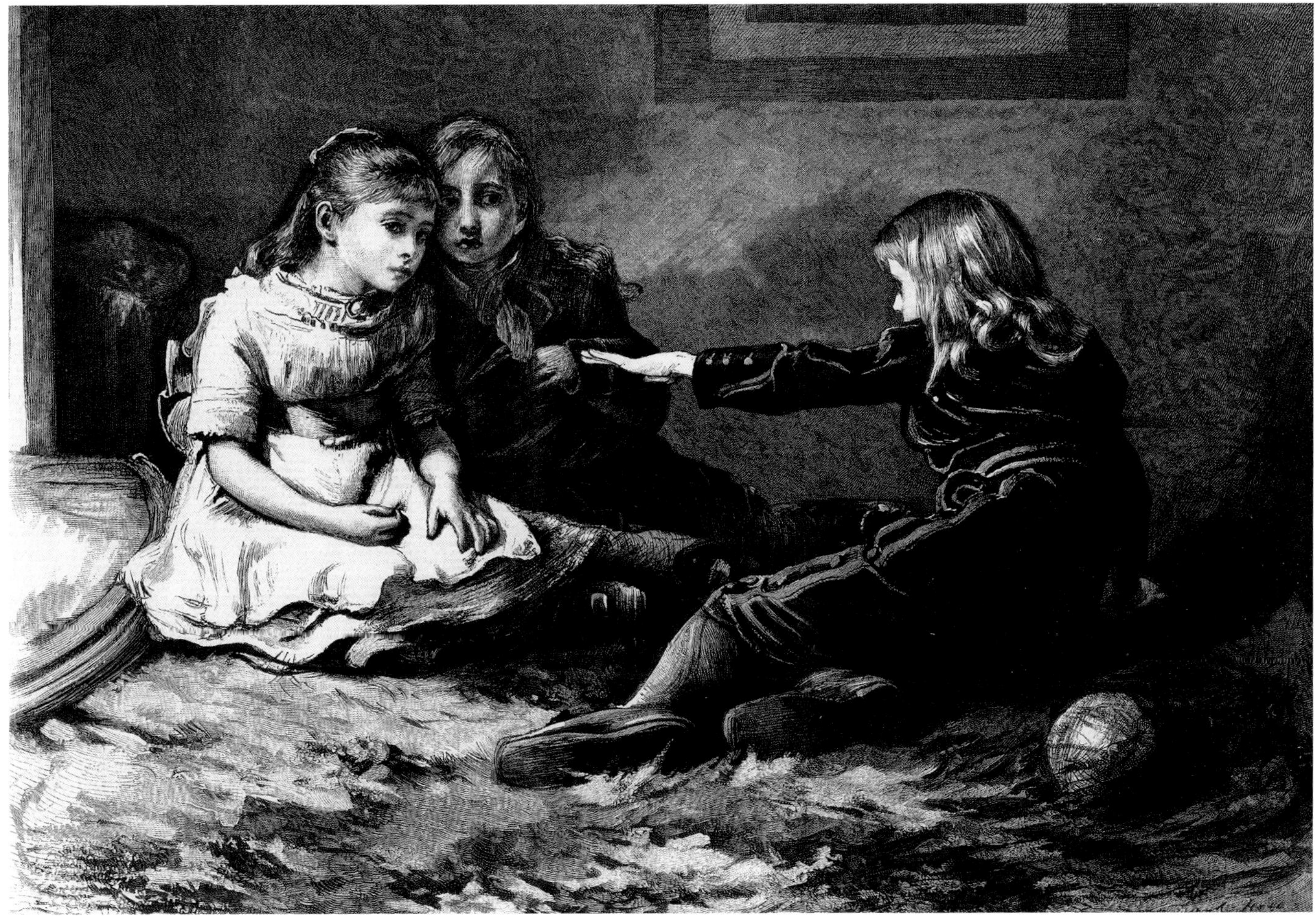

Fig. 41. Frank Holl, 'Little Mim', *The Graphic*, 25 December 1876, wood engraving. Private collection

a very large sum of money ... He was arrested, tried and sent to five years penal servitude.[21]

However, instead of using this scene as the focus of the painting, he made the principal group a cowering woman with her baby. The man who glowers at her through the bars of the cell is her violent husband, whose imprisonment for her assault has brought her a merciful release. The model's poses are particularly telling in this work. On one side the standing woman holds out her hands beseechingly, mirroring that of her guilty husband. One of her children hides her face in her mother's skirts, while the other stares at the pitiful figure of the battered wife, thus linking the two groups together.

Holl painted very few formal portraits of women. Ada reports:

[Holl] had a curious distaste for the painting of women's portraits. As he has said, 'Well you know if anything goes wrong I can't fling my brush at my sitter's head, nor indulge in any strong language to ease my mind a bit!' Whatever the real reason was, it must be admitted that his rather harsh, stern characterization was unfitted to the rendering of the more graceful types of womanhood, so that such successes as he has had with women's portraits were in those cases where the sitter met him half way, and was of pronounced and strongly marked features.[22]

One senses here that Ada perceives her father's paintings of working-class women as a type of 'stern characterization' appropriate to their social class and one that is inappropriate to the depiction of middle- and upper-class women. Although Frank Holl did not

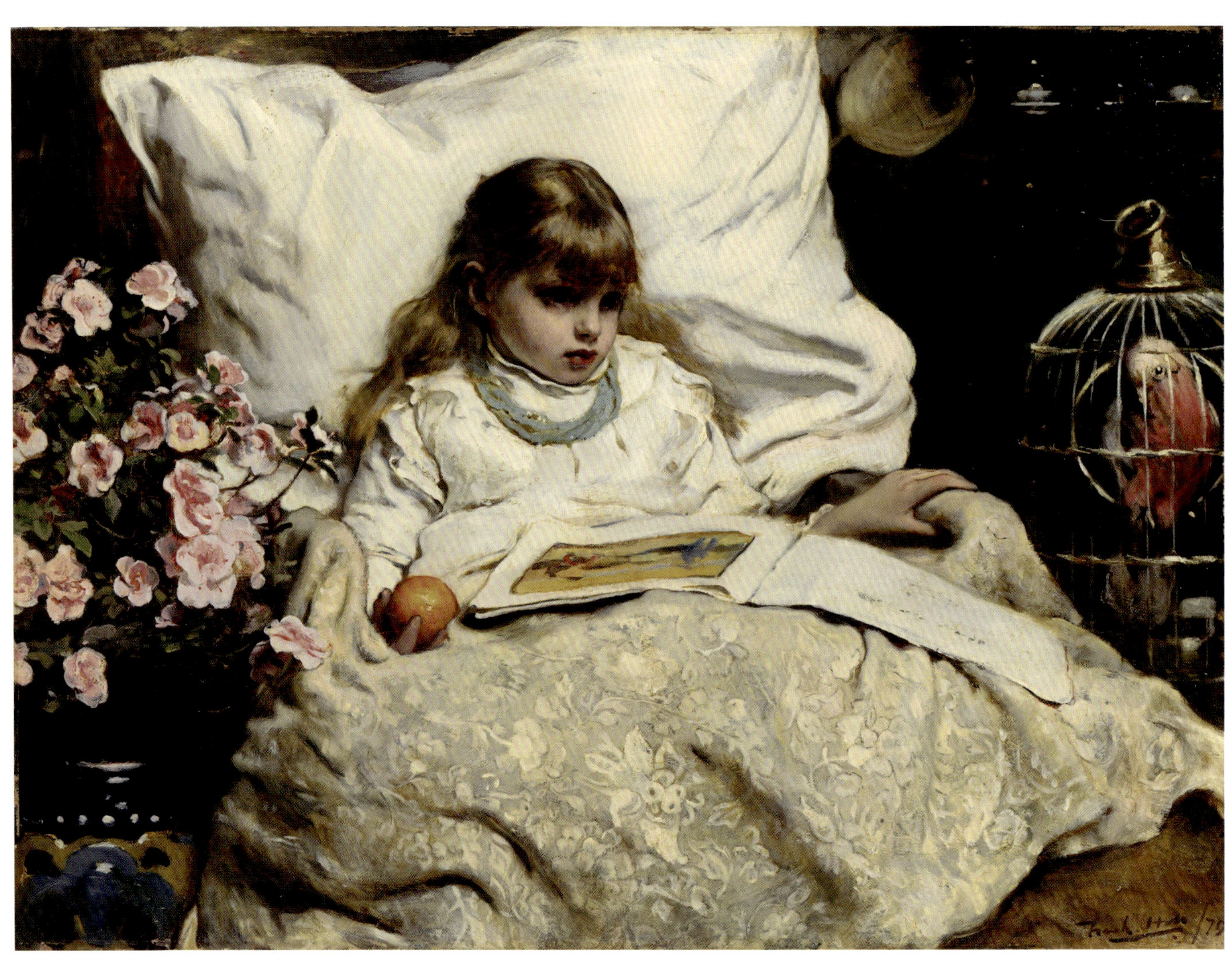

Fig. 42. Frank Holl, *The Daughter of the House*, 1879, oil on canvas. National Gallery of Victoria, Melbourne, Australia

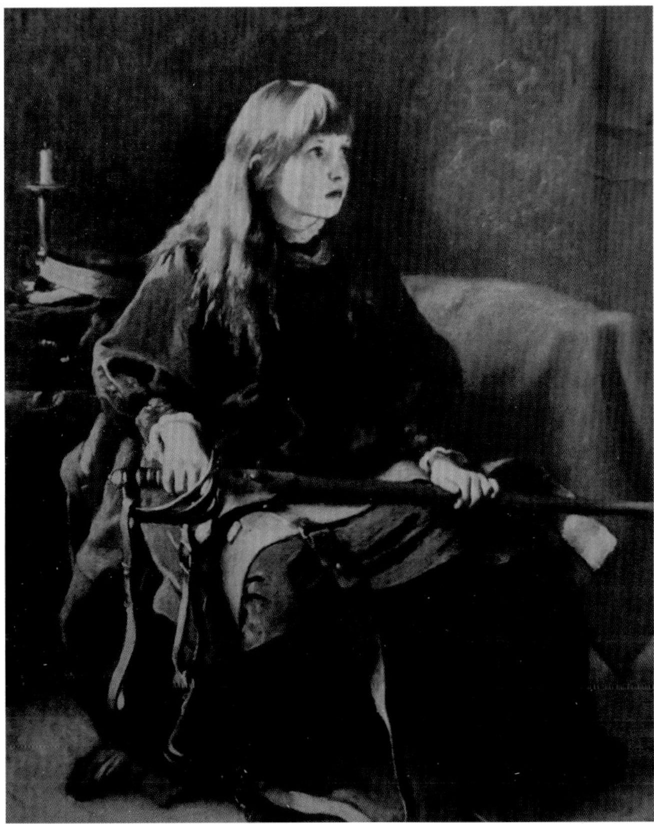

Fig. 43. Frank Holl, *'Did you ever kill anybody father?'*, From Reynolds, *The Life and Work of Frank Holl*, London, 1912. Watts Gallery Archive

like painting women's portraits, he clearly felt a deep sympathy for women who were trapped in poverty. He came from a socialist background and in the first part of his career he dedicated his skills and energy to creating emotive pictures that moved his audience to pity for the tragic female world he depicted.

In 1877 Holl painted his first portrait, of Mr Richardson of Reigate, an old friend of his wife's family. This first step eventually led Holl to concentrate on portraiture as his main source of income. In her book Ada lists an astonishing 160 portraits by Holl, yet only 8 of them are of women: Mrs Lee (1878), Mrs Tonks (1881), Miss Tonks (1882), Mrs Taylor (1882), Mrs [Clayfield-]Ireland (1882), Miss Annie Tonks (1883), Mrs Hart (1883) and Miss Harvey (1883).[23] The portrait of Mrs Letitia Clayfield-Ireland depicts the comfortable-looking figure of the wife of a Somerset landowner, dressed in black with white-lace collar and fichu showing off her jet mourning jewellery (fig. 47). The image of Mrs Clayfield-Ireland is a far cry from Holl's Welsh fisherwomen. Ada tells us much about the personalities of Holl's male sitters, with stories of their visits to the studio, but she says little about the female sitters. Mr Tonks was one of Holl's greatest patrons, so it would have seemed churlish of him to refuse to paint his wife and daughters. Indeed, Ada comments that Mrs Tonks's strong features made the commission more palatable to him.

Frank Holl died of heart failure on 31 July 1888 when he was only forty-three. His obituaries glowed with praise for his achievements and regretted the premature loss of such a significant artist. In 1889 a retrospective exhibition of his work was held at the Burlington Galleries in London. However, even this short time after his death, he was not so admired, certainly not in the review of the show in the *Art Journal* written by Gertrude E. Campbell that year.[24] Although not wholly dismissive of Holl's work, Campbell opens her review by declaring that 'he appealed for many years of his life to the love of cheap sentimentality which is so notoriously characteristic of the inhabitants of the British Isles'. These words clearly stung young Ada Holl and stayed with her for nearly twenty-five years until 1912 when her book was published. In her writing she repeatedly returns to a defence of her father against the accusation of 'sentimentality'. Why did Ada choose to write a life of her father and why did she wait nearly a quarter of a century to do so? This might also be considered particularly questionable at a time when modernism was getting its grip on art and Victorian painting was entering the period of its greatest unpopularity, which was not to end until the late 1950s. It is worth taking a look at Ada's own life to find the answers to these questions.

Ada Mabel Holl was born at the beginning of 1869 in Hampstead and was baptized at St Saviour, Hampstead, on 19 March 1869. She was not the Holls' first child; records show that their first baby was a son who was stillborn. A mere month after Ada's baptism, her parents set off on their travels to Italy, funded by the scholarship that Holl had won at the Royal Academy to study the Italian old masters. Ada was left in the care of her grandparents and was not to see her mother

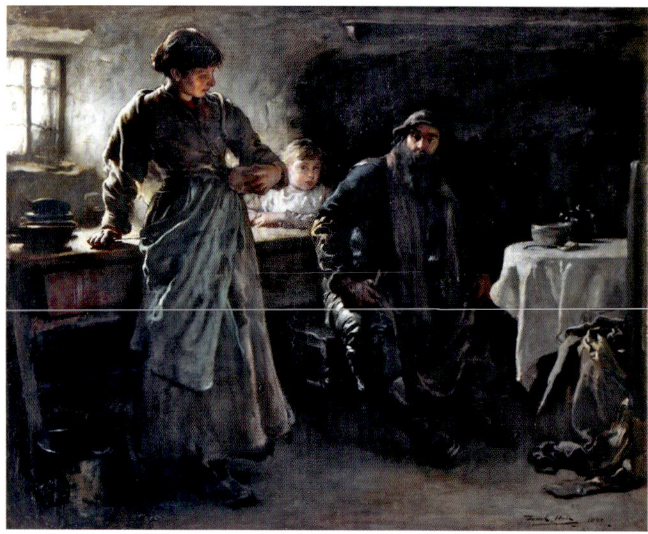

Fig. 44. Frank Holl, *A Fisherman's Home*, 1881, oil on canvas. Courtesy National Museums Liverpool

and father again until five months later in August 1869. The abandonment of a newborn baby by the parents would be frowned on now, but in the Holls' class and times it was more common. Nonetheless, one cannot help but feel that it left its mark on Ada. Two years later Olive was born, followed by Nina in 1874 and then a late child, Phyllis, in 1882. It is likely that Mrs Holl lost other babies in those intervening eight years. The family moved several times, into ever more desirable homes. When Ada was less than twelve months old, they moved from Eaton Terrace in Hampstead to 30 Gloucester Road, Regents Park, then in 1877 to 4 Camden Square, culminating in 1882 – when Holl's financial success as an artist allowed – with a new house in Fitzjohn's Avenue, Hampstead, designed for them by Norman Shaw. After her father died, the 1891 census records mother and daughters Ada (twenty-two), Olive (nineteen), Nina (seventeen) and Phyllis (eight) living in Milford in Surrey.

In her biography Ada tells us nothing of her own ambitions and interest in art. But, in a circuitous way, we discover that she did have ambitions to be an artist herself. This is in a newspaper report of her divorce from Mr Charles McRae, an actor, who had obtained a decree nisi because of the adultery of his wife Ada, maiden name Holl, with Mr Victor Eustace Reynolds, an artist, in 1901. The report goes on to say: 'The [McRae] marriage took place in 1900, at which time the respondent was connected with the theatrical profession. Soon after the marriage the respondent refused to go on tour with her husband, saying she desired to study art at Venice, and subsequently she lived with the correspondent.'[25] So in 1911 we find Ada living with Victor Eustace Reynolds at 4 Haarlem Road, Hammersmith, both of them giving their occupation as 'painter/artist'. Victor, who was ten years younger than Ada, was the son of a Cheshire farmer who taught art at Haberdashers School, Cricklewood, and life-drawing classes at Lambeth School of Art, which is probably where he and Ada met. The 1911 census records that Ada and Victor were married and had been for six years. One living child is also listed, but not in residence at the time. However, Ada and Victor did not actually marry each other until the summer of 1914, at the outbreak of the First World War. Soon after, Victor left for the battlefront as a captain in the Prince of Wales's Own West Yorkshire Regiment. Victor Reynolds, like so many others, was never to return, reported killed in action 4 May 1916.[26]

Ada's biography was published in 1912 by Methuen and Co. Ltd. At that time she was six years divorced and living with her artist lover. There is some suggestion in her book that she had spent time,

Fig. 45. Frank Holl, *Head of a Welsh Fishergirl*, Undated [mid-1870s], oil on millboard. Victoria and Albert Museum

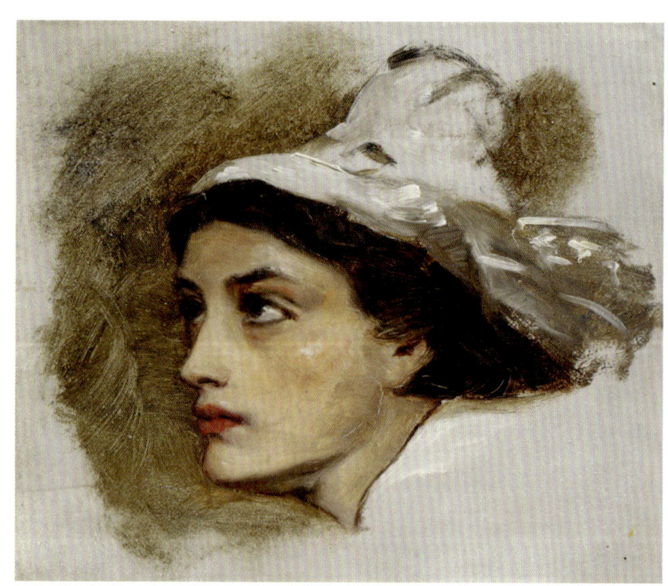

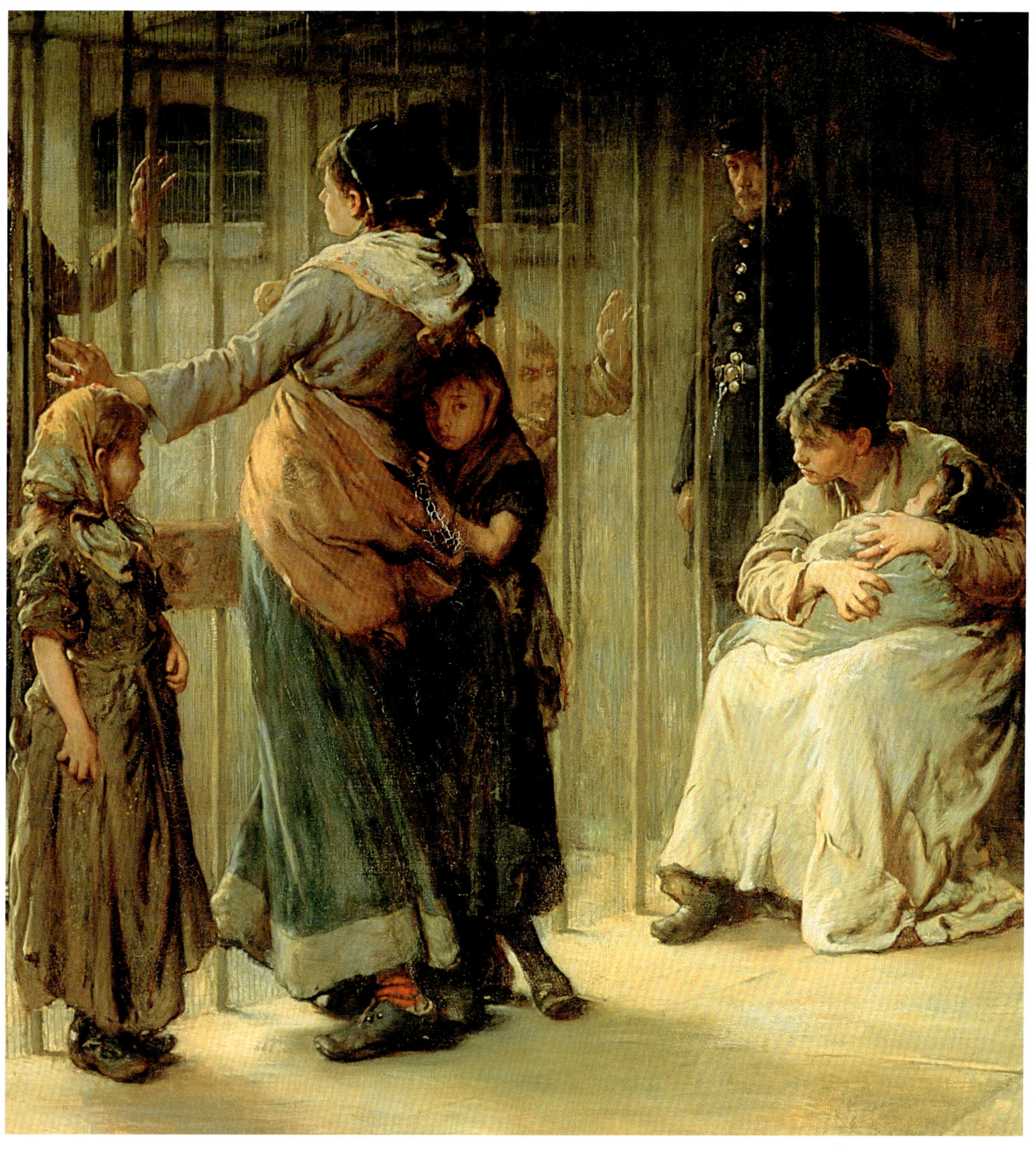

Fig. 46. Frank Holl, *Newgate, Committed for Trial*, 1878, detail of cat. 15 (p. 131)

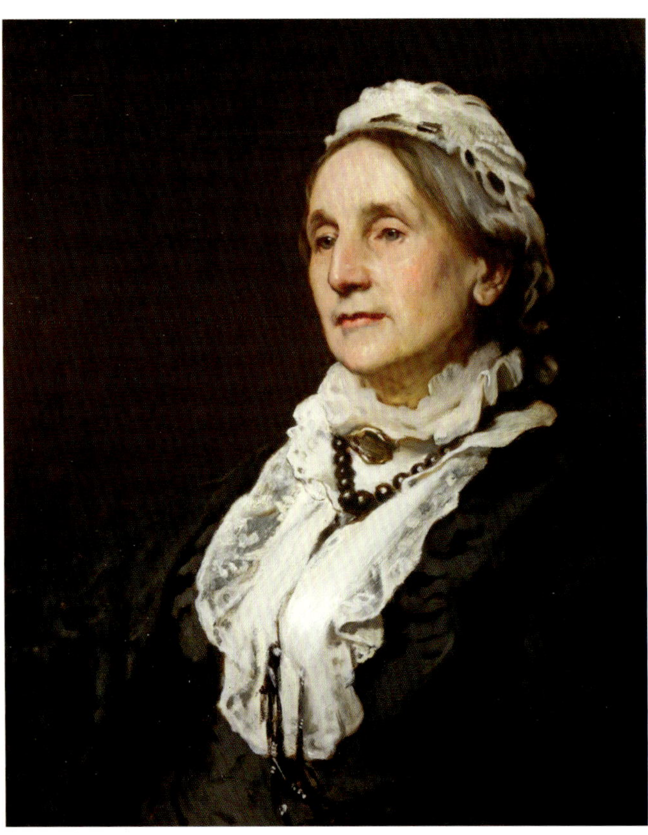

Fig. 47. Frank Holl, *Mrs Letitia Clayfield-Ireland*, 1882, oil on canvas. Bristol Library, Bristol City Council

presumably with Victor Reynolds, in Paris and in Venice, as she writes with apparent first-hand knowledge of these particular places when describing her father's European travels. In 1912 her mother and three sisters were all still alive, so assuming that family relations were still maintained, she could have reminisced with her family about her late father. However, given that she had been 'connected with the theatrical profession', was divorced and living with a man who was not her husband, her situation was not exactly respectable, so maybe that was not the case. In fact, there is a hint in the book that her family may well have not approved of her, if mother and sisters had shared her father's opinions on how one should lead one's life. In one of the many passages in which she refutes the accusation that Holl was a 'sentimentalist', Ada goes on to say that he was 'too much opposed in his own character to sentimentalism or decadence, which he loathed as heartily as he did anything which savoured of Bohemianism'.[27]

Ada gives the impression that she had a long-held desire to write about her father and in 1912 at last found herself in a situation where she could do this. She was fortunate also in the existence of the publishers Methuen, founded in 1889 by Algernon Methuen Marshall Steadman (1856–1924), a teacher and headmaster who believed in books that were educational and published mostly non-fiction academic works. Steadman was also a great supporter of women writers. Indeed, the first book he published was a novel by Edna Lyall, a campaigner for women's emancipation and other progressive causes. Ada's other impetus for writing her book was most likely that she needed to earn some money. When Victor died four years later, he left his wife just £78 17s 9d. Ada's mother lived until 1931, and although Ada was the only one of her daughters living alone on what must have been a restricted income – the other three all made successful marriages – Mrs Holl left the considerable sum of £12,251 11s 2d to two of her grandsons.

Ada herself lived a long life, possibly not an entirely happy one, dying at the age of ninety-five in a Brighton nursing home in 1965. The true key to her reasons for writing her immensely engaging and informative life of her father Frank Holl is, I think, found in these words: 'My love for him was deep and intense, with an admiration which was almost an obsession, but which curiously enough took the form of making me intensely reserved and shy of him, so that neither he nor I ever rightly understood the other.'[28]

Notes

[1] Reynolds, p. 272.
[2] Reynolds, pp. 48–71.
[3] Reynolds, p. 89.
[4] Reynolds, p. 205.
[5] Jane Sellars, ed., *Atkinson Grimshaw: Painter of Moonlight*, Harrogate and London 2011, pp. 49–69.
[6] Mark Bills and Vivien Knight, eds, *William Powell Frith: Painting the Victorian Age*, New Haven and London 2006, pp. 131–44.
[7] Reynolds, p. 46.
[8] Reynolds, p. 252.
[9] Reynolds, p. 84.
[10] Reynolds, p. 91.
[11] Reynolds, p. 93.
[12] Reynolds, p. 96.
[13] Reynolds, p. 94: Connie sits for five hours for an illustration to 'Little Mim', a story by W.S. Gilbert, illustrated in *The Graphic*, 1876.
[14] Reynolds, p. 167.
[15] Reynolds, pp. 228–9.
[16] Reynolds, p. 205.
[17] Reynolds, p. 171.
[18] Reynolds, p. 133.
[19] Reynolds, pp. 169–70.
[20] Reynolds, p. 187.
[21] Reynolds, p. 144.
[22] Reynolds, p. 192.
[23] Reynolds, pp. 341–3.
[24] Irish-born Gertrude E. Campbell was also Lady Colin Campbell, a scandalous figure in Victorian society, known for the trial in 1886 at which she was refused a divorce from Lord Campbell, even though he had knowingly infected her with syphilis.
[25] *Dundee Courier*, 1 May 1906.
[26] *Manchester Evening News*, 15 May 1916.
[27] Reynolds, p. 129.
[28] Reynolds, pp. 184–5.

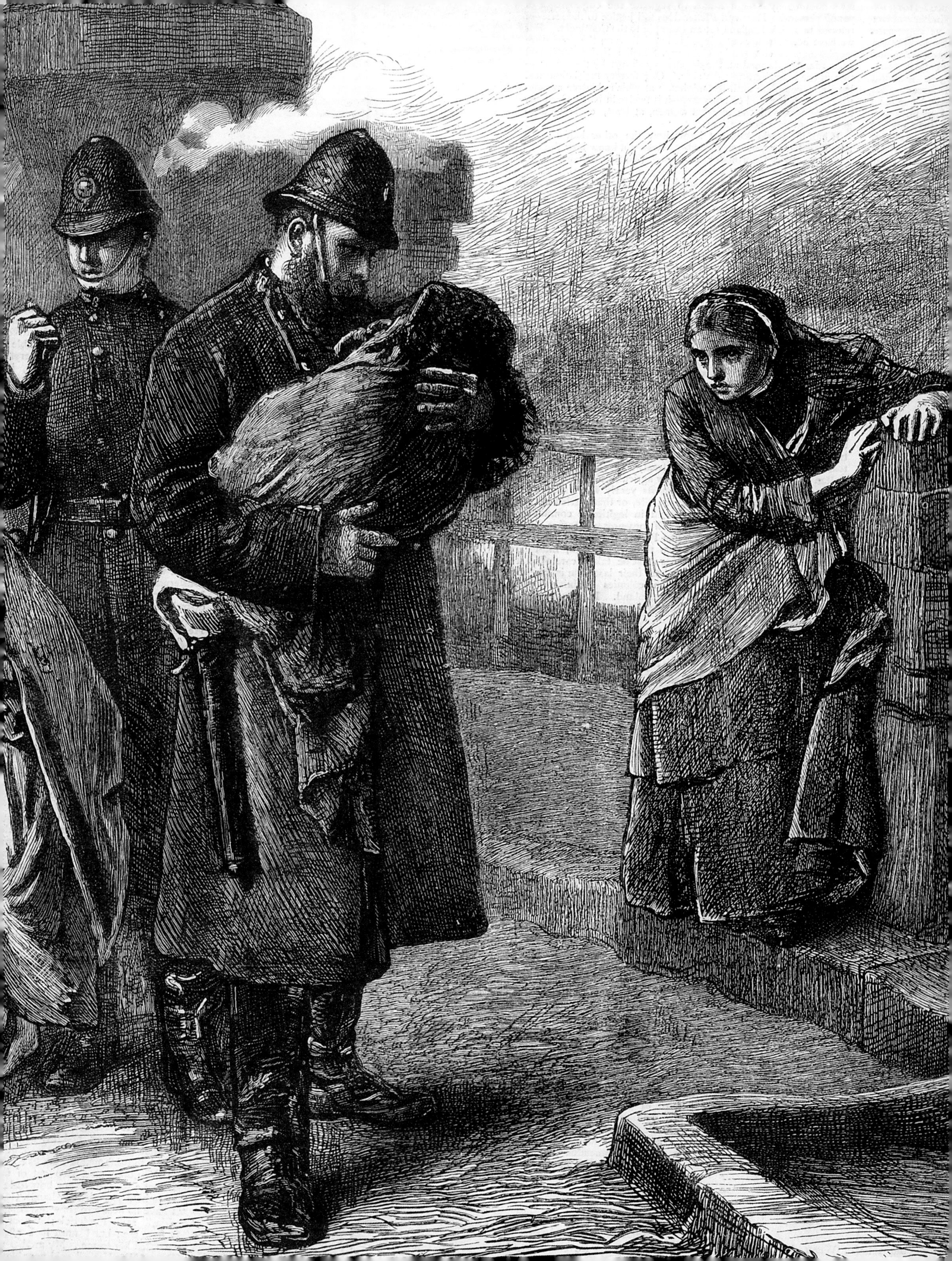

Frank Holl and *The Graphic*: Sketching London's Labour in Light and Dark

Sophie Gilmartin

From Venice Frank Holl wrote to his wife in London that he could not rest and relax as he was supposed to do. He had gone to Venice under doctor's orders from that most eminent of Victorian physicians, Sir William Jenner, as he was febrile and ill from overwork. Holl, however, complained to his wife:

> It's all very well and very good of you to be anxious for me not to work, although I know I work very hard, yet not to work is harder work still to me (and yet I waste so much time at times) – *hunger for work is always on me, and it is when I cannot satisfy this hunger that I get so worn out.*[1]

Something of Holl's anxiety is apparent in the fact that he mentions the word 'work' five times in this rather feverish run-on sentence. But his preoccupation marks him out as a man of his time, fully invested in a Victorian work ethic that was championed by so many: in Thomas Carlyle's writings, in Ford Madox Brown's painting *Work* (1852/65) and in the words of George Eliot's Caleb Garth in *Middlemarch* (1871/2):

> You must have a pride in your own work and in learning to do it well, and not always be saying, There's this and there's that – if I had this or that to do, I might make something of it. No matter what a man is – I wouldn't give twopence for him ... whether he was the prime minister or the rick-thatcher, if he didn't do well what he undertook to do.[2]

Holl's daughter, Ada Reynolds, wrote in her 1912 biography of the artist that 'hard work' was 'the true saviour of manliness'. Yet a few pages later she also wrote of her father's early death at the age of forty-three: 'By the very excess of his energies he wore his vitality away. It is not too much to say that my father threw his life away by his utter inability to rest from work.'[3]

While the crushing pace of his portraiture work seems to have exacerbated his illness (and Millais had written to Holl that 'portrait-painting is *killing work* to an artist who is sensitive'[4]), his illustrations for the new periodical, *The Graphic*, trained and honed his work habits. Previously a hesitancy, a 'worrying-over' and lack of confidence in his work would result in his becoming disillusioned or abandoning a design altogether. But his daughter wrote that the deadlines and discipline, 'of having to have the block ready to the moment when the "Graphic" messenger presented himself at the studio door gave him the necessary impetus ... This discipline was the making of the man.' His daughter's words echo those of Caleb Garth; to her mind *The Graphic* work 'fix[ed] his purpose, and enable[d] him to *finish and carry right through that which he began*'.[5] It may also be that these everyday work habits gave him an investment in and a sympathy with those around him who worked, whether shoemaker, street seller, fisherman or policeman, all of whom he depicts as dignifying work in his genre pictures and illustrations.

Fig. 48. Frank Holl, 'London Sketches – The Foundling', *The Graphic*, 26 April 1873, detail of fig. 51 (p. 96)

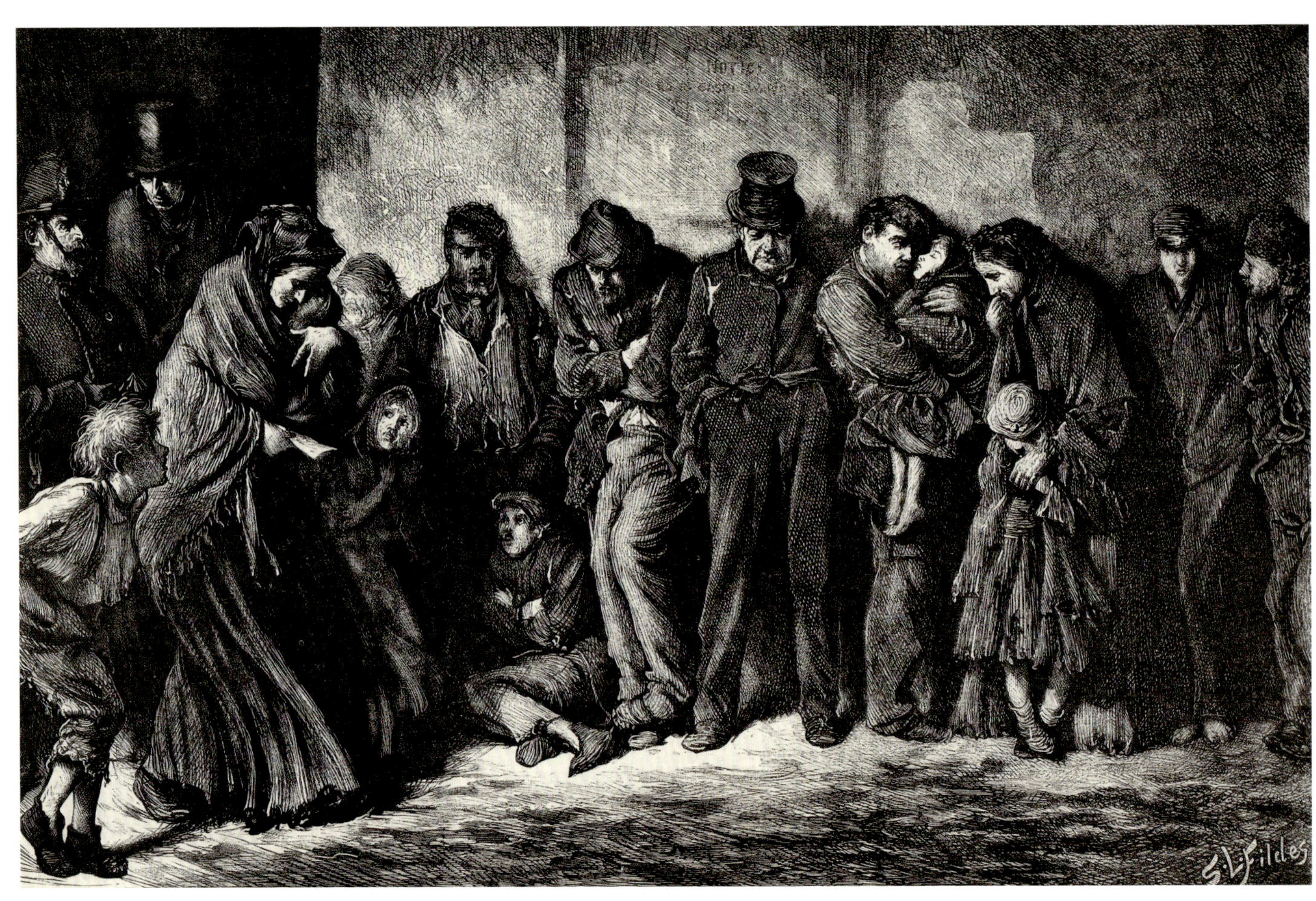

Fig. 49. Luke Fildes, 'Houseless and Hungry', *The Graphic*, 4 December 1869, wood engraving. Private collection

Holl was twenty-six and the father of a young family when it was first suggested to him to try drawing on a wood block for submission of pictures to *The Graphic*. This illustrated periodical first appeared on 4 December 1869, joining the ranks of other illustrated periodicals and newspapers such as the *Illustrated London News*, *Punch* and *Good Words*. It was a market that had burgeoned since the 1840s, but *The Graphic* set itself apart from these and especially from its main competitor, the *Illustrated London News (ILN)*. *The Graphic*'s founder, William Luson Thomas (1830–1900), was a publisher, skilled engraver and illustrator. Previously he had worked for the *ILN*, and there he had been deeply frustrated by the second-class treatment of the artists in their employ, and the resulting second-rate illustrations produced through cheap and shoddy engraving. In addition to his many parts, Thomas was also a fine watercolourist and a social reformer. He wanted what was due to good artists, and also to include illustrations that addressed social problems and injustice. The illustrators for the *ILN* were for the most part draughtsmen on wood blocks rather than fine artists. Engravers for the *ILN* cut corners by recycling backgrounds on the wood blocks and dividing the blocks between different engravers to save time, obviating the artistic coherence of the image, and even its physical coherence when the joins showed.[6]

Thomas wanted to bring together in his new magazine 'the best writers, artists, engravers and printers'.[7] His first commission was to the illustrator Luke Fildes. Fildes's 'Houseless and Hungry' depicted a queue of homeless men, women and children waiting outside a police station on a freezing, snowy night for an admission ticket to a night shelter, a 'casual ward' of the dreaded workhouse (fig. 49). There are few touches of sentimentality in this powerful image, which appeared as a full-page illustration in the first issue of *The Graphic*. While some of the other magazines had depicted the poor and street life in their illustrations, Fildes's work in many ways set the tone for a less sentimental and 'grittier' art that the artists insisted came from direct observation on the streets. *The Graphic* began to gather to it social-realist artists who felt that their best efforts should communicate to a wide circulation the poverty, misery and obscurity of the Victorian underclasses. Hubert von Herkomer, Luke Fildes, William Small, Frank Holl and others illustrated what they saw in the streets, on London's bridges, in train stations, slum housing, prisons and workhouses.

This was not the first time that a newspaper had emphasized the documentary aspects of its work. Henry Mayhew's articles for the *Morning Chronicle* in the 1840s set out to categorize the thousands of street workers in London: he described their work, where they lived, their family and social groups, and what their days were like on the streets. He also interviewed them, and through him we hear the voices of London's costermongers, flower girls, mudlarks, fruit sellers, street photographers and rat-catchers, among a myriad of other occupations. Mayhew's monumental work was published in three volumes in 1851. His accounts of the working poor differ from those of his contemporary Charles Dickens in that they aim to be empirical and unsentimental (although the sentiment is at times there, as much from Mayhew's material as from any influence he may have exerted on his interviewees). Both Mayhew's and Dickens's writings whetted public appetite to know more of what happened in places like St Giles and the Tom-All-Alone's slum housing of Dickens's *Bleak House*. In addition then to his interest in social reform, Luson Thomas knew that there was a market for the social realism of his artists that could contribute to the profitability of his paper. Indeed, this public appetite was a factor in the brilliant success of some *Graphic* artists: Fildes produced a large oil painting based on 'Houseless and Hungry', his *Applicants for Admission to a Casual Ward*, which was such a sensation at the 1874 Royal Academy show that it required a rail in front of it to keep back the over-eager crowds. Frank Holl also produced oils and watercolours derived from some of his *Graphic* illustrations; notably, 'At a Railway Station – A Study' (fig. 50) became *A Seat in a Railway Station – Third Class* (R.A. 1873), and 'London Sketches – The Foundling' (26 April 1873) became *Deserted – A Foundling* (R.A. 1874).

Stressing the documentary aspects of his illustration 'Houseless and Hungry', Fildes wrote: 'When I first came to London, I was very fond of wandering

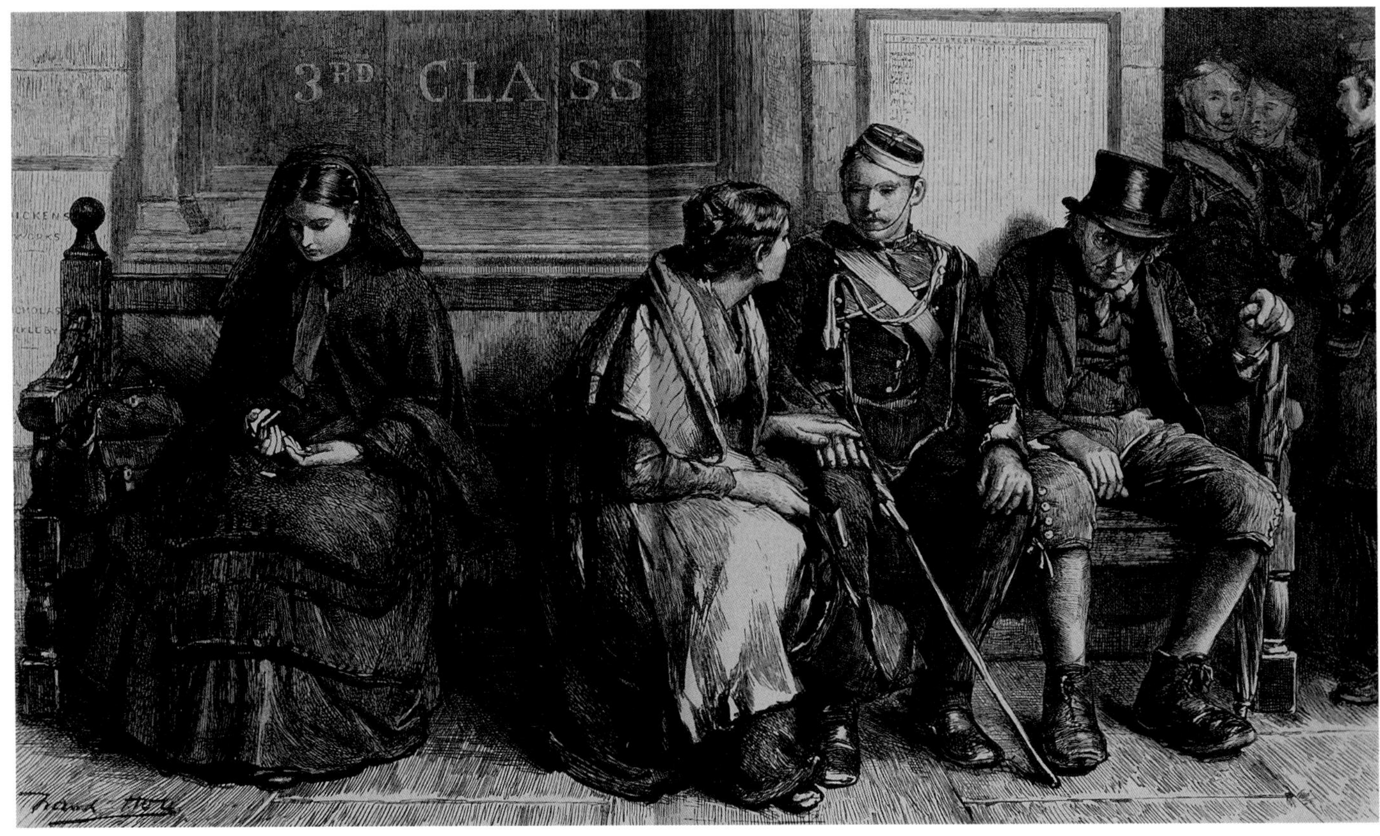

Fig. 50. Frank Holl, 'At a Railway Station – A Study', *The Graphic*, 10 February 1872, wood engraving. © National Portrait Gallery, London

about, and never shall I forget one snowy winter's night the applicants for admission to a casual ward.'[8] Frank Holl's daughter wrote of her father's 'prowls' in the East End, as he looked for material with his friend and neighbour, the artist C.E. Johnson:

> These rambles in the very poorest quarters of London brought my father face to face with many terrible scenes of misery and poverty, and even crime. It was scarcely a morbid attraction for the seamy side which led him forth on these unsavoury peregrinations, but rather, I take it, a latent idea that, by depicting them forcibly and poignantly in his own work, he might bring home to the indifferent eyes and hearts of the public the wretched and iniquitous state of affairs which lies close to our own doors.[9]

Holl's large illustration, '"Gone" – Euston Station', filled two pages of *The Graphic* for 19 February 1876 (fig. 51). It depicts a small group of women seeing off the train to Liverpool that carries relatives and husbands off to ships for emigration. Holl impresses on the viewer that this scene is witnessed and socially 'real' by subtitling the illustration, 'Departure of Emigrants 9:15 Train for Liverpool, September 1875'. It means to be the caught moment, exactly timed, and in the painted version the dispersing steam over the track and around the women tells us the train has just gone (cat. 14). In the illustration the caught moment is evoked by the women comforting each other and the central woman's bonnet hanging down her back in her hurry to be seen from the train at the last moment. Holl wants to 'bring home' to the viewer the sadness and the sacrifices made by those poor who must leave home; with his exact timing of '9:15' he underlines to his

Fig. 51. Frank Holl, '"Gone" – Euston Station,' *The Graphic*, 19 February 1876, wood engraving. © National Portrait Gallery, London

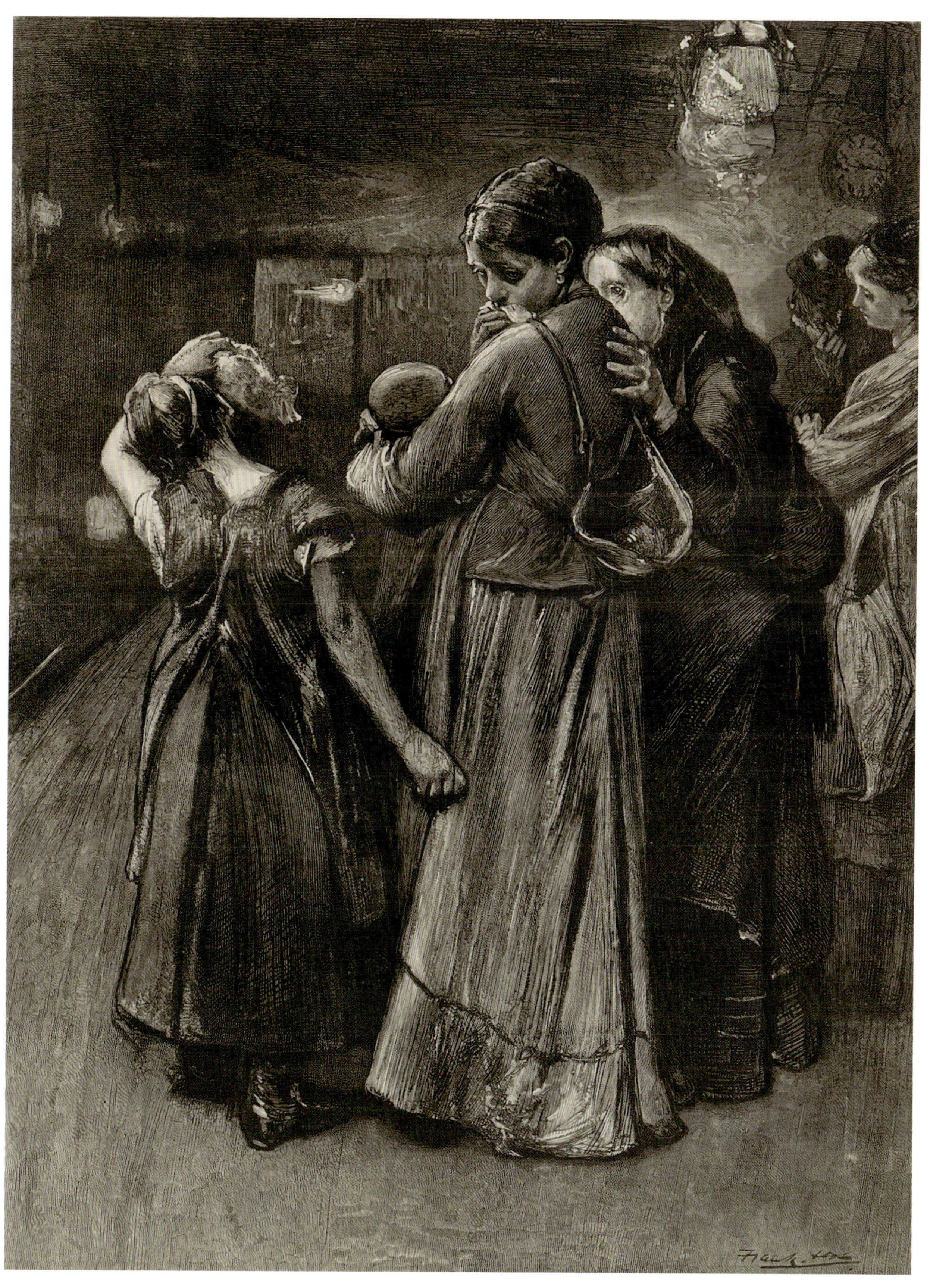

contemporary viewers that these moments are urgently with them, happening in the present, if they would care to see.

Ada Reynolds stressed that it was not 'a morbid attraction for the seamy side' that led her father to explore the slums of Whitechapel and the docks.[10] She was defending her father from the accusation that he was simply another 'slum tourist'. This type of tourism, coined as 'slumming' at some point in the early 1880s,[11] had begun with investigative and philanthropic intentions: the middle and upper classes visited the slums to be shocked and horrified by the conditions there, but also ostensibly to do something about them. However, a fashion developed in London (soon spreading to New York City and Boston) to tour the slums for more hidden and perhaps barely self-acknowledged reasons: a desire for the sensational or for a brush with danger and excitement, the latter sometimes of a sexual, prurient nature. But Frank Holl was no slum voyeur. His social realism, evident in so many of his illustrations for *The Graphic*, is not overly sentimental or sensational. While he emphasizes that his pictures capture a moment of street life, he does of course choose his moments, rendering them artistically, so that without sensationalism or gore they are dramatic; without a cloying sentimentality, they are still affecting.

This is evident in his illustration for the magazine, 'London Sketches – The Foundling' of April 1873 (fig. 52). The picture's scene was witnessed by Holl when walking by the Thames: a baby had been found, 'under an archway, and ... my father and Mr Johnson met the little procession headed by a stalwart policeman carrying the baby, followed by a sympathetic, murmuring crowd'.[12] However, in his picture Holl moves away from the documentary, discovered event into the realms of the theatrical by adding the figure of the baby's mother, half crouching and hiding herself, but eager to see the fate of her child. Pat Hardy locates the depiction of this woman within a nineteenth-century literary and artistic

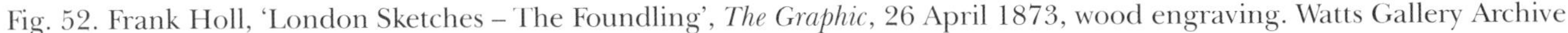

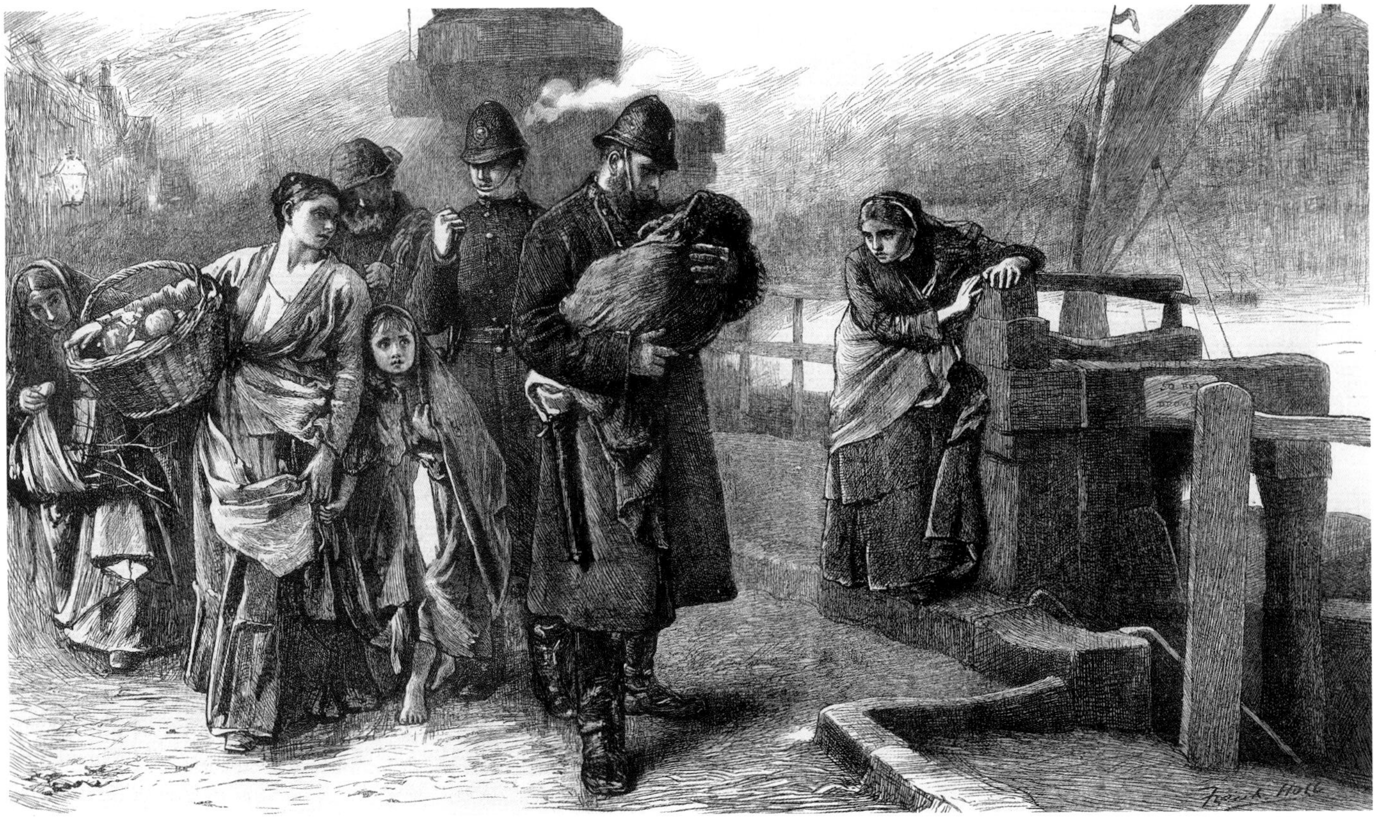

Fig. 52. Frank Holl, 'London Sketches – The Foundling', *The Graphic*, 26 April 1873, wood engraving. Watts Gallery Archive

tradition that associated the fallen woman with the Thames and its bridges, places where she could end her troubles through suicide.[13] This tradition was influenced, if not begun, by Thomas Hood's 1844 poem 'The Bridge of Sighs', and Hardy looks at paintings such as Augustus Egg's triptych *Past and Present* (1858) and G.F. Watts's *Found Drowned* (1848–50). To this could be added many other literary and visual examples: George Cruikshank's last plate of eight for his series *The Drunkard's Children*, depicting the 'gin-mad' and desperate daughter flinging herself into the Thames (1848; fig. 54), or the prostitute Nancy's premonitions of death as she walks over London Bridge in Dickens's *Oliver Twist* (1837). But Hardy argues that Holl's approach to the fallen woman/Thames theme is different from these earlier treatments in that the emphasis is on the fate of the abandoned child rather than the woman. Certainly, this view is corroborated by the fact that the eyes of all but one (the second policeman) are focused on the baby, swaddled from our view, in the foremost policeman's arms. The baby's head is literally the central focus of the picture, both spatially and dramatically.

According to Hardy, 'Holl's other main adaptation of the fallen woman theme lies in the river which is practically obliterated from the canvas'.[14] However, here I would argue that Holl's brilliant and much-noted handling of chiaroscuro and his division of the picture provide for a multiple, if not multiplot, narrative. In *The Graphic* illustration the river is a bright backdrop of reflected light, and the theme of fallen woman and fateful river is thrown into relief by the looming presence of St Paul's Cathedral in the top right. St Paul's was often a component in pictures of desperate women by the Thames, as for example in Gustave Doré's 1871 title-page illustration to Hood's poetical works (fig. 52), Phiz's 1849 illustration of Martha by the river in *David Copperfield* (fig. 55) and G.F. Watts's *Under a Dry Arch* (*c.*1848–50; fig. 56).

On the left-hand side of the picture Holl draws a crowded scene: there are houses, lamp light, an old man and woman with firewood, the second policeman and an attractive street seller with her basket of wares, holding the clutching fingers of a pretty, barefoot child. On this side of the picture, then, there is community,

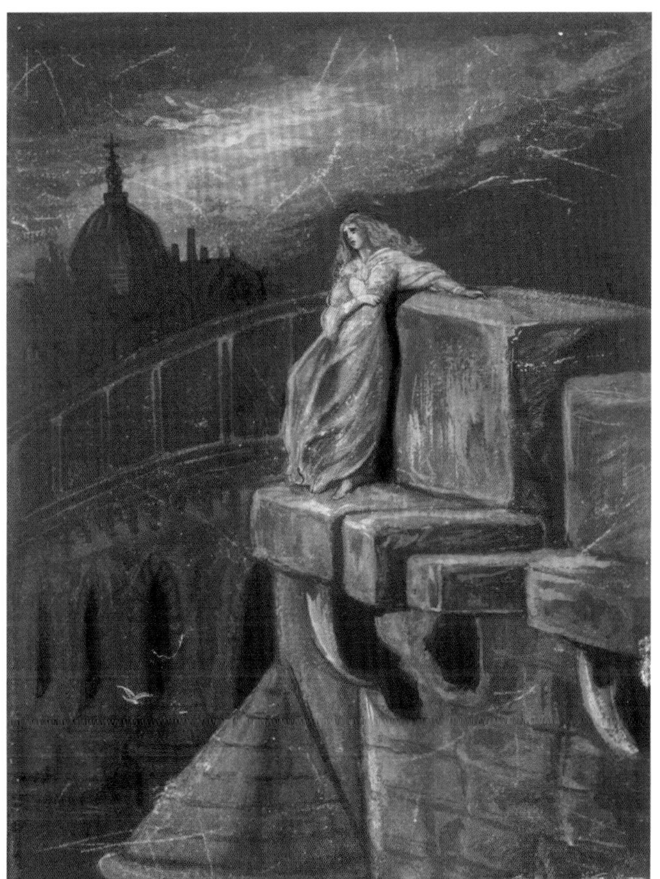

Fig. 53. Gustave Doré, 'Glad to death's mystery, swift to be hurl'd, Anywhere, anywhere out of the world!', title page illustration for *The Poetical Works of Thomas Hood*, London, 1871, drawing. © Victoria and Albert Museum

which contrasts with the woman, set apart from society, on the right, her singleness thrown into relief by the stark light off the water. There appear to be two mothers in the picture: the one who has just abandoned her child and the street seller whose child clings to her for protection. Another common Victorian narrative may lie in this juxtaposition: did the woman on the right fall prey to a seducer who promised to make her a 'lady', as did Little Em'ly in *David Copperfield*? If this is a possible trope here, then the contrast is with the street seller on the left, who, despite her poverty and attractiveness, has not yielded to similar temptations. Women street sellers were often enough branded with the suspicion of prostitution. Nancy Rose Marshall writes that the flower girl and the prostitute were commonly linked, as both were imagined to

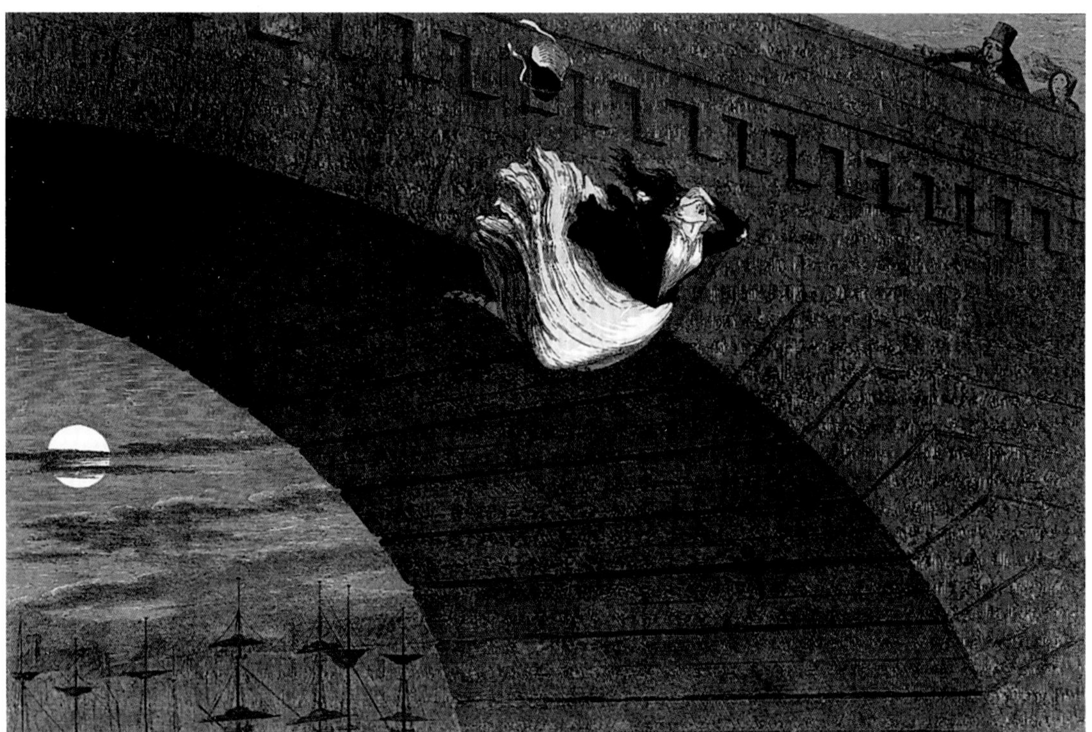

Fig. 54. George Cruikshank, 'The poor girl, homeless, friendless, deserted, and gin-mad, commits self-murder', from *The Drunkard's Children*, plate VIII, 1848, engraving. Watts Gallery Archive

have come from the freshness and innocence of the countryside, and 'both sold delicate, transitory beauty for money on the streets in urban public places'.[15] Henry Mayhew in *London Labour and the London Poor* classified one type of flower seller, for example, as 'immoral'. But Holl emphasizes the maternal nature of his street seller. Indeed, this woman and her daughter are the most attractive figures in the picture: the grace of the woman's stance and her classically flowing shawl and dress, and the pretty vulnerability of the child are meant to be aesthetically pleasing and to argue their case.

Frank Holl made at least two other illustrations of women street sellers in his years of working for *The Graphic* between 1871 and 1878. These are worth exploring partly for what they show of Holl's particular approach to social realism, but also because they reveal a disjunction between Holl's possible intentions in these pictures and the understanding of the pictures revealed in *The Graphic*'s commentary on them. Like 'The Foundling', Holl's 'A Flower Girl' is one of his 'Sketches in London' (fig. 57). It is a full front-page illustration for *The Graphic* issue of 22 June 1872 and, like 'The Foundling', it is divided into two by Holl's characteristic use of chiaroscuro. On the right of the picture the tall dark figures of well-dressed gentlemen buy flowers, most probably for their lady companions who wait at the back edge of the picture. The man who is foremost has his back turned to the viewer: with hands in pockets, his bearing displays something of a confident swagger. On the left the young flower seller's features and drapery are illuminated, as are the flowers that she is selling. Her unbonneted head, strong bare arms and feet, and the folds of her long shawl are almost classically statuesque, and this classicism is mirrored in the sculptured figure at the centre of the fountain behind her. Intent on choosing the flowers for her customers, she has turned her eyes away from them, giving her the appearance of modesty and honesty, but also emphasizing that she is a working woman, absorbed in her work, her means of survival. The lack of eye contact between the men and the street seller (neither man is looking

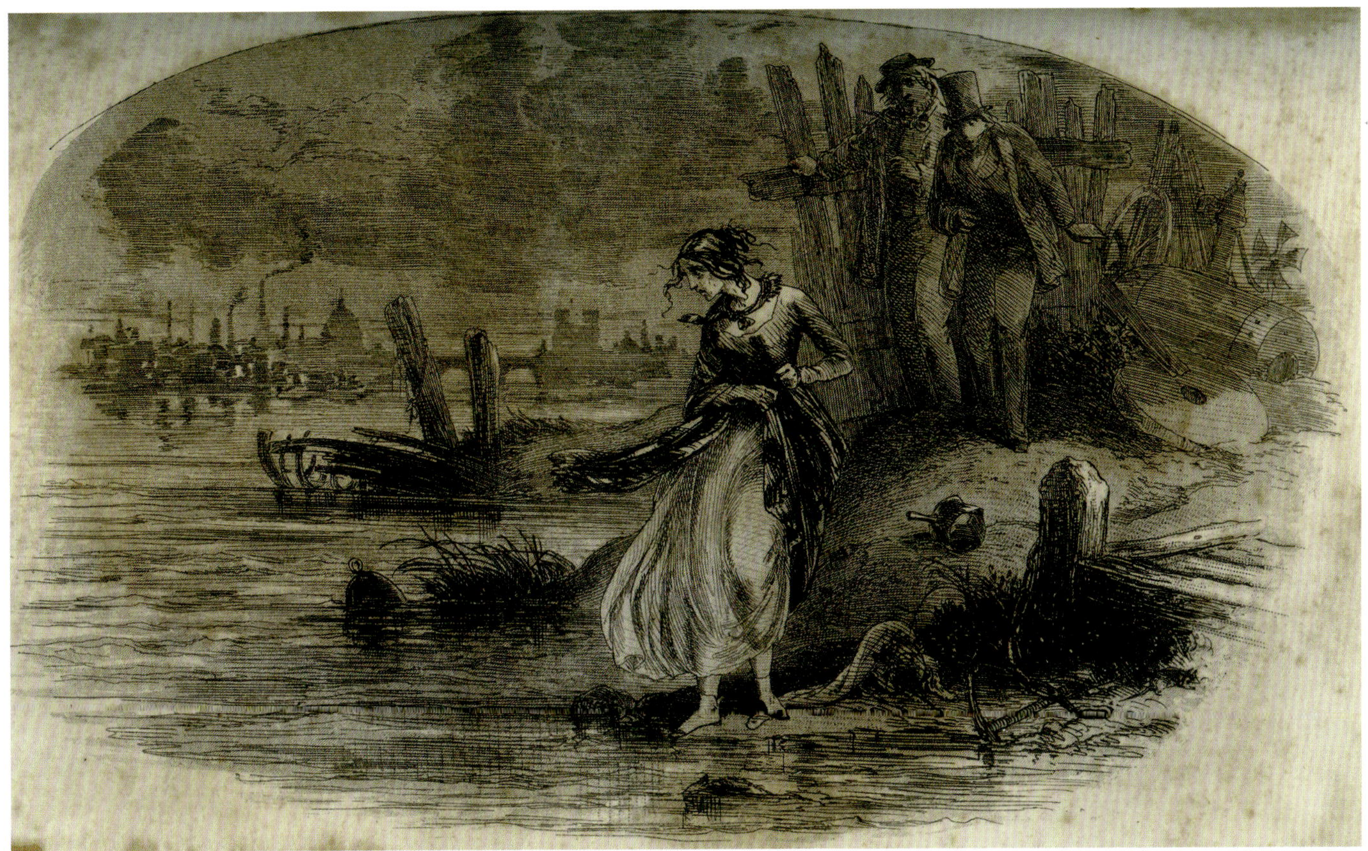

Fig. 55. Hablot K. Browne, 'The River', original illustration from *David Copperfield*, 1850, etching. Private collection

at her) further divides the picture in two halves, two worlds. The right side is marked by strong vertical lines and is dark, cluttered and confidently Victorian, peopled by well-to-do men and women at leisure. The left side of the picture is uncluttered, sparse and light: the flowers, the flowing classical lines of the statue and the working woman come together to create a very different world to that on the right. This separate sphere on the left is both mundane and of the moment, but also timeless and aestheticized. Holl depicts work here as beautiful, but does so without sentimentalization. There is a quiet and uncluttered dignity about this character and her scene of work, but the distinct division of the picture stresses that there is little contact (neither eye contact nor understanding) between the worlds of the rich and poor.

The subtleties of Holl's London sketch seem lost, however, on *The Graphic* columnist who wrote the regular commentary on 'Our Illustrations'. With a typically Victorian delight in categorizing, and therefore controlling his subject, he addresses the topic of the flower seller:

> One cannot define a flower girl off-hand. There are flower girls of various grades. There are well-dressed young ladies who abide in trim shops ... and there are ragged, miserable children who merely use the flowers which they carry as an excuse for beggary ... The flower girl in our picture belongs to neither of these extremes. She is a decent, honest girl ... Most likely she belongs to the Irish persuasion ... It is a hard life, but it is not unhealthy. Street vendors, it is said, rarely suffer from chest and throat complaints, and on a chilly winter's day, the fine lady, wrapped in her furs, with her feet on a hot-water tin, often feels far more shivery than old Nelly Flanagan, who for fifty years has braved the elements at the street corner, though, when the frost is very keen, she confesses that she does feel a bit envious of the baked potato man.[16]

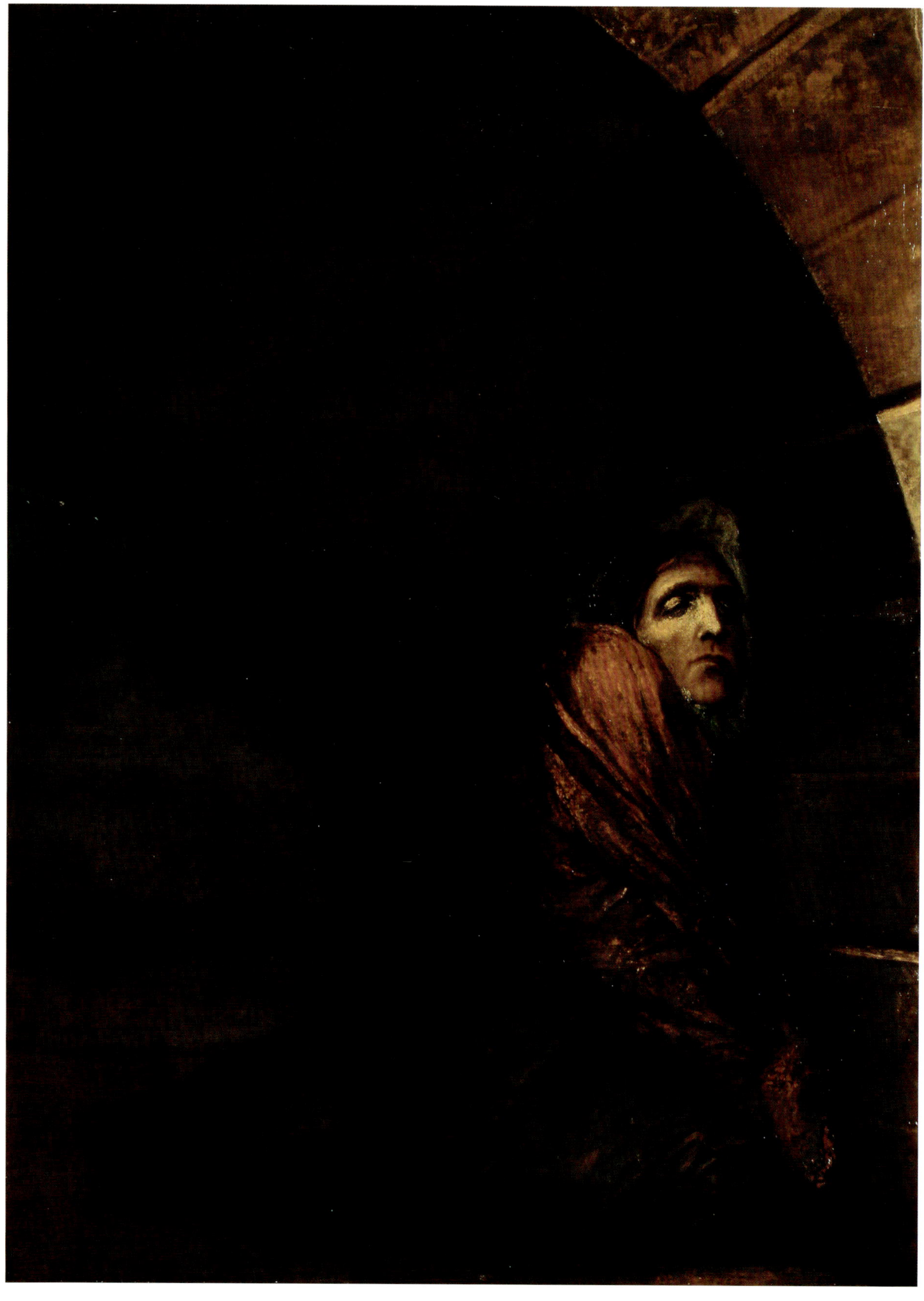

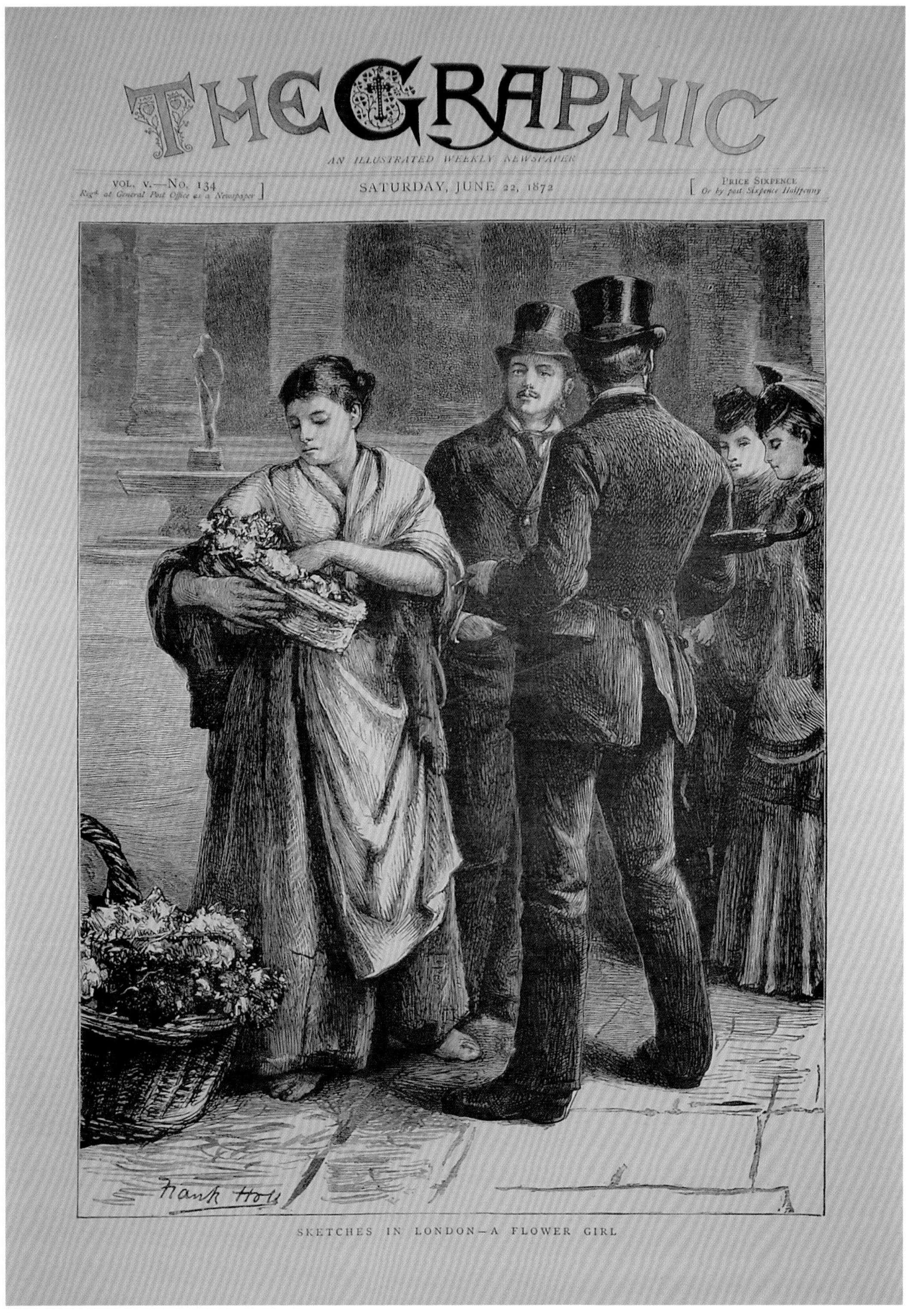

THE GRAPHIC

AN ILLUSTRATED WEEKLY NEWSPAPER

VOL. V.—No. 134 Regd. at General Post Office as a Newspaper

SATURDAY, JUNE 22, 1872

PRICE SIXPENCE Or by post Sixpence Halfpenny

Frank Holl

SKETCHES IN LONDON—A FLOWER GIRL

Fig. 56. George Frederic Watts, *Under a Dry Arch*, *c.*1848–50, oil on canvas. Watts Gallery

Fig. 57. Frank Holl, 'Sketches in London – A Flower Girl', *The Graphic*, 22 June, 1872, wood engraving. Private collection

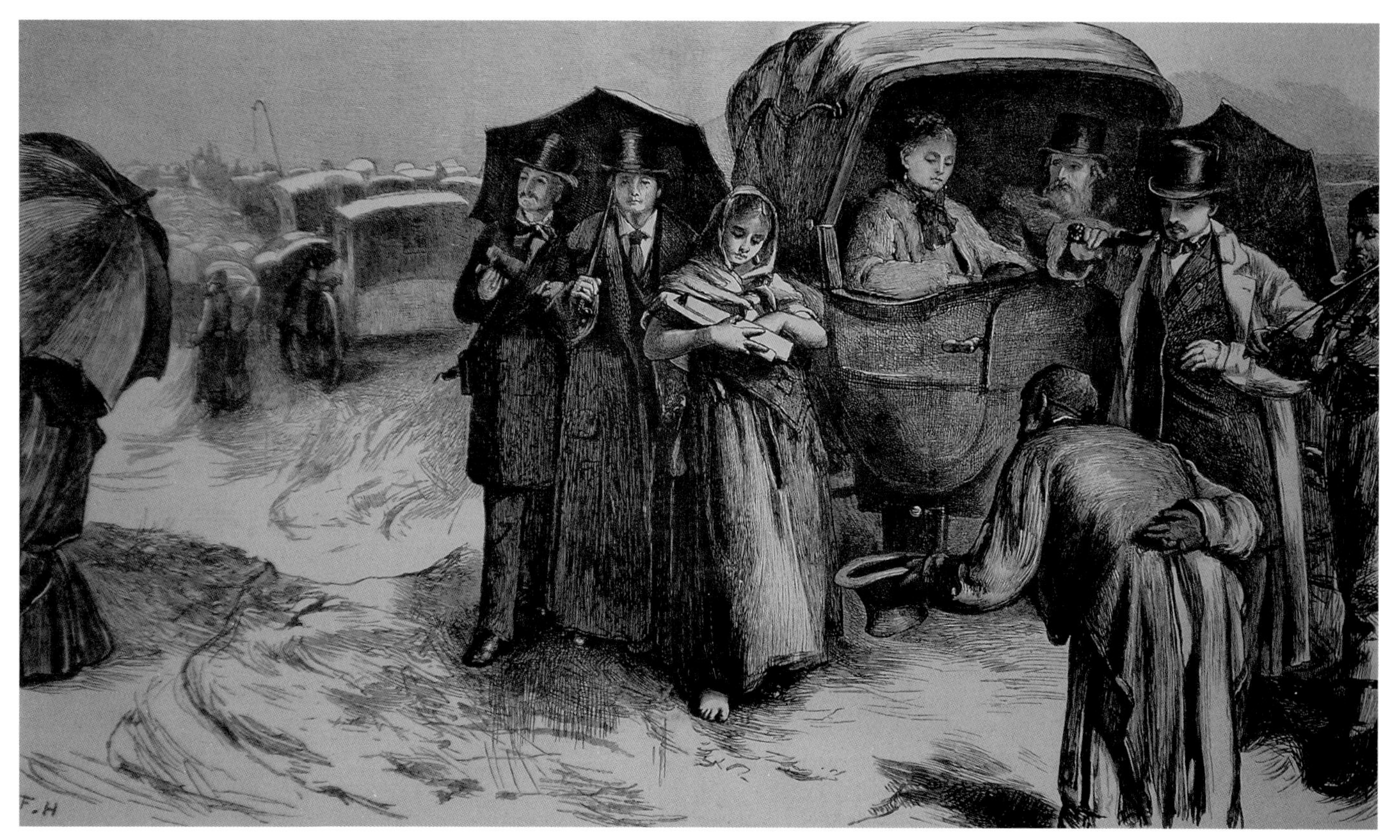

Fig. 58. Frank Holl, 'Sight-seeing – a Study from Nature at Mortlake', *The Graphic*, 20 April, 1872, wood engraving. Private collection

Presumably, as the writer implies, the bare feet and arms of Holl's flower girl will be just as impervious to the cold as she toils through another fifty years or so on the streets. The nuances by which Holl shows the separation between the worlds of the rich and poor in his London sketch are transformed by this columnist into reflections, not on two worlds but on two races, or species of human being: the poor, and especially those of 'Irish persuasion', are so physically different that they do not feel the cold, do not suffer in the same way.

Even an illustration of one of the sporting and social events of the season – the Oxford and Cambridge boat race – becomes in Holl's hands something other than a mere marking of the social calendar. His illustration's social realism is evident in his inclusion of a young barefoot street seller at the centre of this large picture, which covers two pages of the magazine (fig. 58). As the picture's commentator describes, the boat race coincided with a dramatic change in the weather, as suddenly winter came in 'utmost fury, and assailed us with volleys of sleet and snow'; he continues:

> British sightseers, however, especially those of the fair sex, will not be baulked of their amusement … and, so, what with sealskin jackets, and waterproofs, and Ulster coats, and umbrellas, thousands turned out to witness the great aquatic contest of the year, and, strange to say, the ladies seem to have enjoyed the buffeting they received from the elements.[17]

One representative of the 'fair sex' who may not have enjoyed the buffeting quite so much is the young girl selling flowers or food from her basket. She is standing barefoot in drifts of snow, and her arms are bare to well above her elbows. The well- and warmly-dressed couple in the carriage to whom she sells her wares, and the lounging gentleman who leans against the carriage and gazes superciliously at the street musicians are reminiscent of a similar group in Frith's *Derby Day* (R.A. 1858; fig. 59), but the drifts of snow and the more sparsely populated scene direct our attention to the central figure of the young street seller. The facial features of the woman in the carriage and the young girl are caught by the light as they both gaze down at the same angle. The diagonal that runs through their features and line of gaze forces a comparison between the two women, rich and poor. *The Graphic* commentator on this picture seems just as oblivious to the freezing child as are the gentlemen and the lady who have come to see the end of the boat race. Once again there is a disjunction between Holl's social realism, and *The Graphic*'s column on the illustration.

Of course the blindness to the nuances of Holl's social realism, and even to his direct presentation of social injustice, was not always the case in *The Graphic*. Clearly the periodical wanted to create an awareness of social ills from its inception, or Luke Fildes's 'Houseless and Hungry' would not have been awarded a full page of the first issue. The magazine also frequently accompanied the illustrations of its social-realist artists with appeals to pertinent charities, as was the case with Holl's illustration 'Shoemaking at the Philanthropic Society's Farm School at Redhill' (18 May 1872; fig. 60), which depicted former delinquents and homeless men being trained in shoemaking. Nevertheless, there is at times a selective vision in the discussion of the pictures. The focus in *The Graphic* commentary on 'The Foundling' is naturally on the foundling and the mother. But there is no mention of the other vulnerable child, the little unshod girl who wraps her thin shawl around herself against the cold.

Fig. 59. William Powell Frith, *The Derby Day*, 1858, detail, oil on canvas. © Tate, London

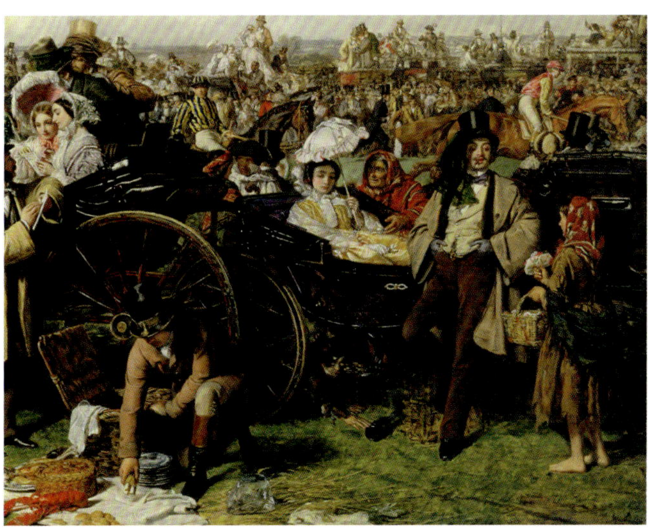

Holl often indicated the harsh impoverishment of street sellers, and particularly of children, by their footwear or lack of it. He was not alone in noticing this. Henry Mayhew time and again was fascinated by the shod or unshod state of the poor he spoke to on the streets, as when he interviewed two orphaned flower girls, aged fifteen and eleven: 'The older sister ... had a pair of old worn-out shoes on her feet, the younger was barefoot, but trotted along, in a gait at once quick and feeble – as if the soles of her little feet were impervious, like horn, to the roughness of the road.'[18] Charles Dickens, in his 'Night Walks' through London also seemed disturbed, even haunted, by the sound of destitute children's bare feet in Covent Garden:

> But one of the worst sights I know in London is to be found in the children who prowl about this place; who sleep in the baskets, fight for the offal ... dodge the constables, and are perpetually making a blunt, pattering on the pavement of the Piazza with the rain of their naked feet.[19]

Dickens is overwhelmed by the sheer number of these dispossessed children and the incessant noise of their unshod feet as they run, 'ever-hunted ... savages', pursued, like Oliver Twist, or hounded to move on, like Jo the crossing-sweeper in *Bleak House.*

In Frank Holl's long walks through the streets of London he observed those whose livelihoods and

Fig. 60. Frank Holl, 'Shoemaking at the Philanthropic Society's Farm School at Redhill', *The Graphic*, 18 May, 1872, wood engraving. © National Portrait Gallery, London

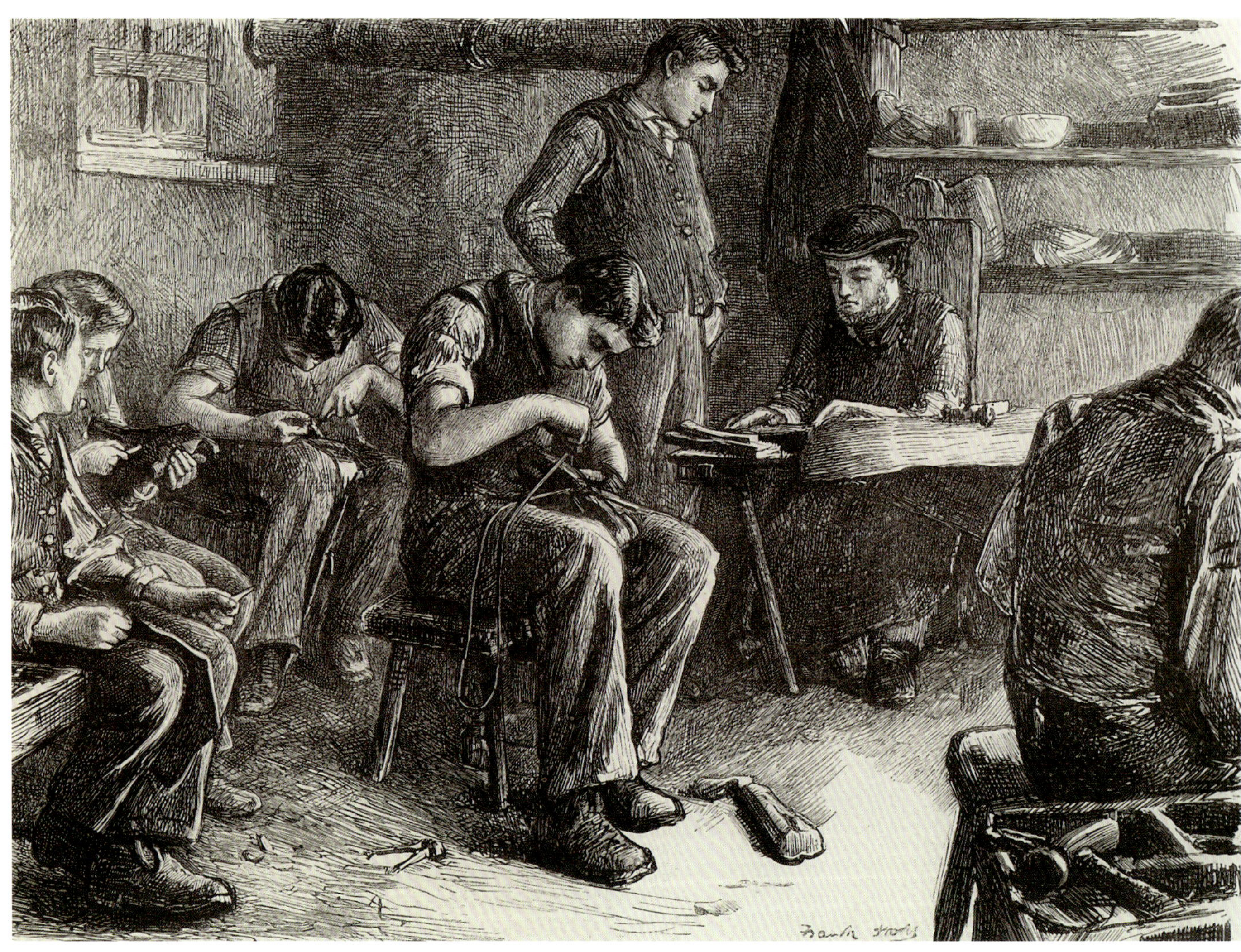

survival entailed walking, standing, running or prowling on those streets, day and night. Perhaps this accounts for his noticing the naked feet of children and street sellers, and also the heavy, worn boots of workers. Vincent van Gogh, who treasured his collection of copies of *The Graphic* and was an admirer of Holl's work, famously painted seven still lifes of workmen's boots and shoes in the 1880s. Peter Keating argues of these paintings: 'Their number alone shows how closely he identified with the honest life of the working man, which he saw symbolized in the boots.'[20] In Holl's work one notices the heavy, much worn boots of the generally down-at-heel old man on the bench in 'At a Railway Station – A Study', Holl's first *Graphic* illustration; the thick boots of the street seller in 'The Foundling'; the mother's boots in his painting *Hush!* of 1877 (cat. 12); and the foregrounding of a grieving woman's clogs, flung off as she enters, in *No Tidings from the Sea* (1870; cat. 6). Holl often pays tribute to the working woman and child. The marks of labour on their boots or on their naked feet draw attention to their direct and literal contact with the hard ground and life on the streets, unrelieved by the means to take a carriage or an omnibus. In the same year that he produced the two illustrations of the unshod street sellers discussed earlier, he also made 'Shoemaking at the Philanthropic Society's Farm School at Redhill'.

Holl also illustrated some works of fiction for *The Graphic*. He provided twenty-four fine illustrations for the serialization of Anthony Trollope's *Phineas Redux* in 1873–4 and a large illustration over two pages for W.S. Gilbert's short and sentimental story 'Little Mim' (fig. 61). This story was included in the Christmas number of the magazine for 1876, and is a mawkish

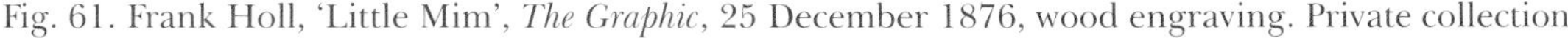

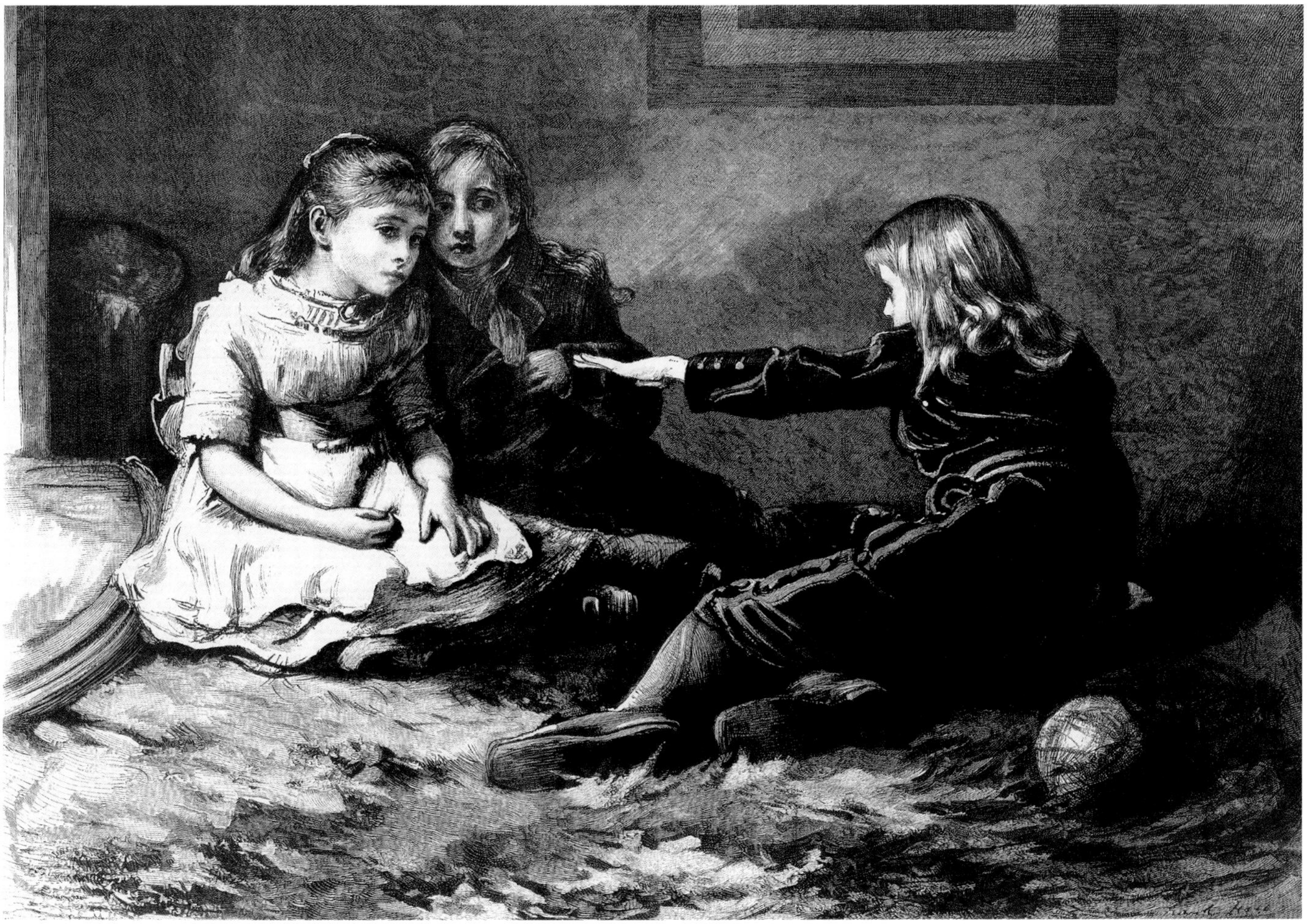

Fig. 61. Frank Holl, 'Little Mim', *The Graphic*, 25 December 1876, wood engraving. Private collection

tale of the death of an angelic orphan girl. Holl's model for the illustration of 'Little Mim' was the renowned child actress and model, Constance Gilchrist (1865–1946). She modelled for this picture when she was about ten years old, but had first sat for him when only four. She gained fame as a model for Leighton and Whistler, as well as for Holl and other artists. As Holl had a tight deadline to complete the wood block for 'Little Mim', Connie sat 'over five hours at a stretch without break ... so stiff and exhausted ... that she could hardly stand' and had to be held up by Holl and his wife at the end of the sitting. Holl's daughter recalls that Connie was much loved by herself and her sisters, and would sometimes come for a 'romp' in their nursery after a sitting. But, unlike the Holl children, Connie was a working Victorian child: she was celebrated as a child-actor, especially in the pantomime and for her skipping-rope dance. The strain on the child of a hectic working life on stage and in the studio comes through poignantly in Ada Reynolds's account:

> Poor little girl – she had a hard life of it! Sitting all day for one artist or another, then to be hurried home, washed, brushed and combed, and scurried off to the theatre, there to dance all the evening, until very late, then, tired to death, the poor child would go home, only to have to undergo the further torture of having her beautiful hair washed ready for the next day's performance. Once father went down to try and get Connie for a sitting the following day, and found the poor child in tears after a beating at the hands of her mother, because she refused to have her hair washed after eleven o'clock at night. The child was simply dead beat and utterly exhausted after a long day's sitting and the hard work at the theatre. Still her mother had no mercy, but whipped the little thing into submission.[21]

Holl's daughter does not say whether or not Connie Gilchrist did go to work for him the following day, but it is more than likely that she did. For all his sympathetic depictions of working people, and especially of children, and his reluctance to engage the exhausted child for more work, Holl's own deadlines and dedication to his art meant that his models had to work long hours, as he did. At least for Connie Gilchrist there was a fairy-tale ending that released her from this grinding work. Famous and celebrated, she caught the eye of the young Earl of Orkney, and at the age of twenty-seven she was married and entered the aristocracy.[22] For the working and dispossessed men, women and children depicted in his *Graphic* illustrations and genre paintings, a fairy-tale ending would have been a rare if not impossible outcome. So much of the power of Frank Holl's social-realist work lies in his conveying the dignity and endurance with which his subjects kept on, despite the small hope of a better life, let alone a fairy tale.

Notes

[1] Reynolds, p. 314.
[2] George Eliot, *Middlemarch* (1872), London 2000, p. 347.
[3] Reynolds, pp. 306, 321.
[4] Reynolds, p. 301.
[5] Reynolds, p. 98.
[6] Treuherz 1987, pp. 53–4.
[7] William Luson Thomas in a letter to Luke Fildes, 6 September 1869, quoted in Treuherz 1987, p. 53.
[8] Luke Fildes, quoted in Treuherz 1987, pp. 83–4.
[9] Reynolds, p. 109.
[10] Reynolds, p. 108.
[11] *Oxford English Dictionary*, entry for 'slumming', no. 2, cites the first usage of this meaning in 1884.
[12] Reynolds, p. 108.
[13] Hardy 2012, pp. 157–61.
[14] Hardy 2012, p. 161.
[15] Nancy Rose Marshall, *City of Gold and Mud: Painting Victorian London*, New Haven and London 2012, p. 208.
[16] 'Sketches in London – A Flower Girl', *Graphic*, 22 June 1872, p. 573.
[17] 'Sight seeing – A study from nature at Mortlake', *Graphic*, 20 April 1872, pp. 368–9.
[18] Henry Mayhew, 'Of Two Orphan Flower-Girls', in *London Labour and the London Poor*, London 1851, vol. 1, ch. 7.
[19] Charles Dickens, 'Night Walks', collected in David Pascoe, ed., *Charles Dickens: Selected Journalism* 1850–70, Harmondsworth 1997, pp. 78–9.
[20] Treuherz 1987, p. 125.
[21] Reynolds, pp. 95–6.
[22] Anne Varty, *Children and the Theatre in Victorian Britain: 'All Work, No Play'*, Basingstoke 2008, pp. 66–9.

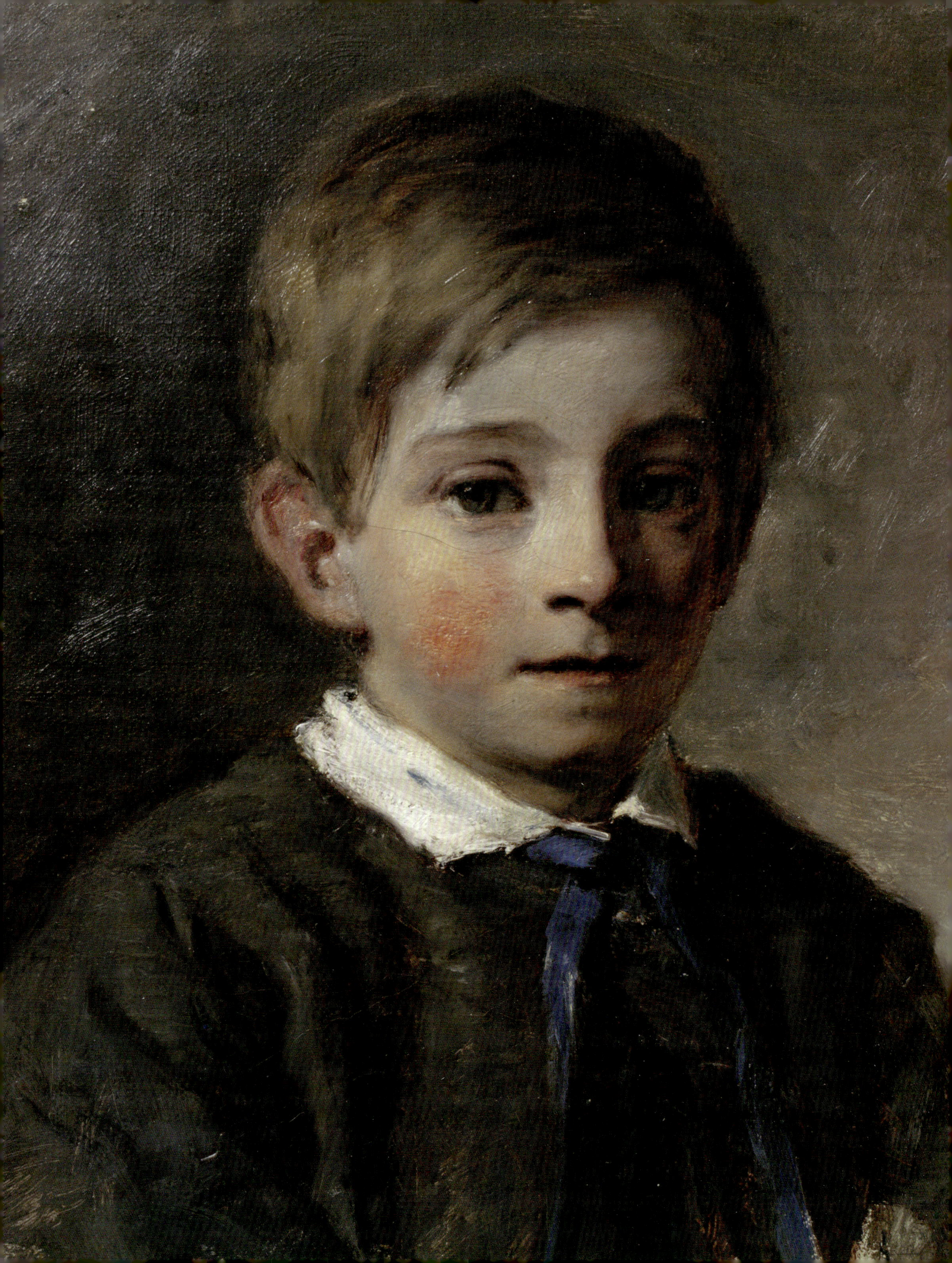

Catalogue

1. *Edgar Holl as a Small Boy*

*c.*1860–5
Oil on canvas, 26.4 x 21.3 cm
Provenance: Bequeathed by Mrs C.M. Baker (daughter of the sitter) through the Art Fund, 1958
Collection: Victoria and Albert Museum

This quarter-length study of the artist's younger brother Edgar is an early portrait, painted by Holl when in his late teens. Frank Holl was the son of the engraver Francis Holl (1815–84). At the age of fifteen Holl left the University Schools in London and entered himself as a probationer at the Royal Academy Schools, the following year becoming a student.[1] The portrait was produced at this point in his artistic career. The informality of the image, suggested by the identity of the sitter, would have provided Frank Holl with an opportunity to experiment in this genre.

The resultant image has a delicacy of style, with a muted palette. Despite the limited tonal range and loose brushwork, the image reflects a good sense of depth and figural modelling. The face has a soft finish, with the darker shadows bringing definition to the features. Large blue eyes and rosy cheeks highlight the innocence and youth of the sitter. There is an unfinished simplicity to the canvas, further accentuated by the positioning and clothing of the boy, with his grey jumper and blue ribbon or necktie. This blue echoes throughout the image, from the costume to the colour and pale tone of the child's face, most clearly visible in his eyes.

Later in life the sitter Edgar Holl married Ellen Sarah Gibbs. Both of Holl's portraits, *Edgar Holl as a Small Boy* and *Ellen Sarah Gibbs as a Little Girl* (cat. 2), were inherited by their daughter Mrs C.M. Baker, who bequeathed these items along with the *Head of a Welsh Fishergirl* to the Victoria and Albert Museum. MM

2. *Ellen Sarah Gibbs as a Little Girl* (ill. Page 110)

1863
Oil on millboard, 38.1 x 32.4 cm
Signed and dated bottom right: 'F Holl 1863'
Provenance: Bequeathed by Mrs C.M. Baker (daughter of the sitter) through the Art Fund, 1958
Collection: Victoria and Albert Museum

Ellen Sarah Gibbs was later in life to become Frank Holl's sister-in-law, marrying his younger brother Edgar (cat. 1). This image is significant not only because of the identity of the sitter but, painted when Holl was only eighteen years old, it provides an early example of his developing skill as a dynamic portrait painter. In 1863, the year this painting was produced, Holl received a silver medal for drawing from life and a gold medal for historical painting at the Royal Academy Schools. His work was beginning to stand out from that of his classmates.

The young girl Ellen appears distracted, her attention drawn by events beyond the frame. Her right hand sits in her lap, and in it she clutches an orange. This element of the composition is mirrored in a later image by Holl entitled *The Daughter of the House* (1878). The loose brushwork and dashes of vibrant colour bring life and vitality to the figure of the young subject. Unusually for Holl bright colours emerge in the details: the flash of red ribbon in the girl's blonde hair, her bright blue eyes and the embellishments of her costume. She sits on a large chair of shiny leather and polished wood, and the scale of the furniture accentuates her youth and size. Apart from the highly detailed and well-modelled face, the image appears sketch-like due to the loosely applied brushstrokes.

The millboard on which the image was painted had been used previously. On the reverse is an over-lifesize study of a hand with bent fingers, in grey and brown. This confirms the suggestion that the image was not commissioned but produced in a more informal context. MM

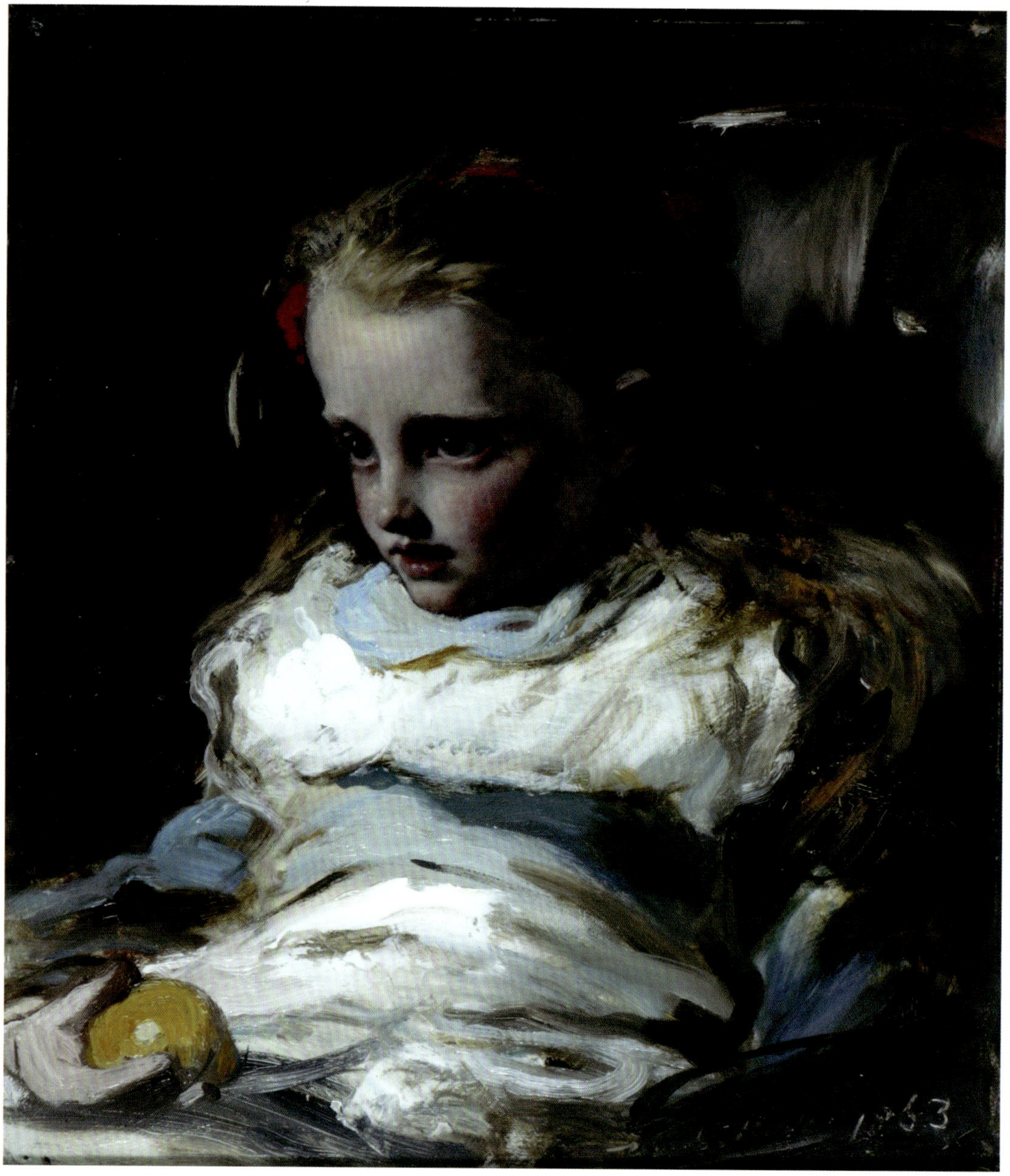

3. *Self-Portrait*

1863
Oil on canvas, 55 x 43 cm
Signed and dated lower left: 'novr.1863 / .F.H.'
Exhibitions: R.A., 1864 (145); R.A. Old Masters, 1889 (223); Victorian Exhibition, New Gallery, London, 1892 (192)
Literature: G. Aitchison, 'Holl, Francis Montague (1845–1888)', Dictionary of National Biography, London 1891; Reynolds, pp. 22–3; A. Ribeiro, The Gallery of Fashion, London 2000, p. 177
Provenance: The artist; by descent to his younger brother's widow, Mrs Edgar Holl, by whom given to the National Portrait Gallery, 1932
Collection: National Portrait Gallery, London

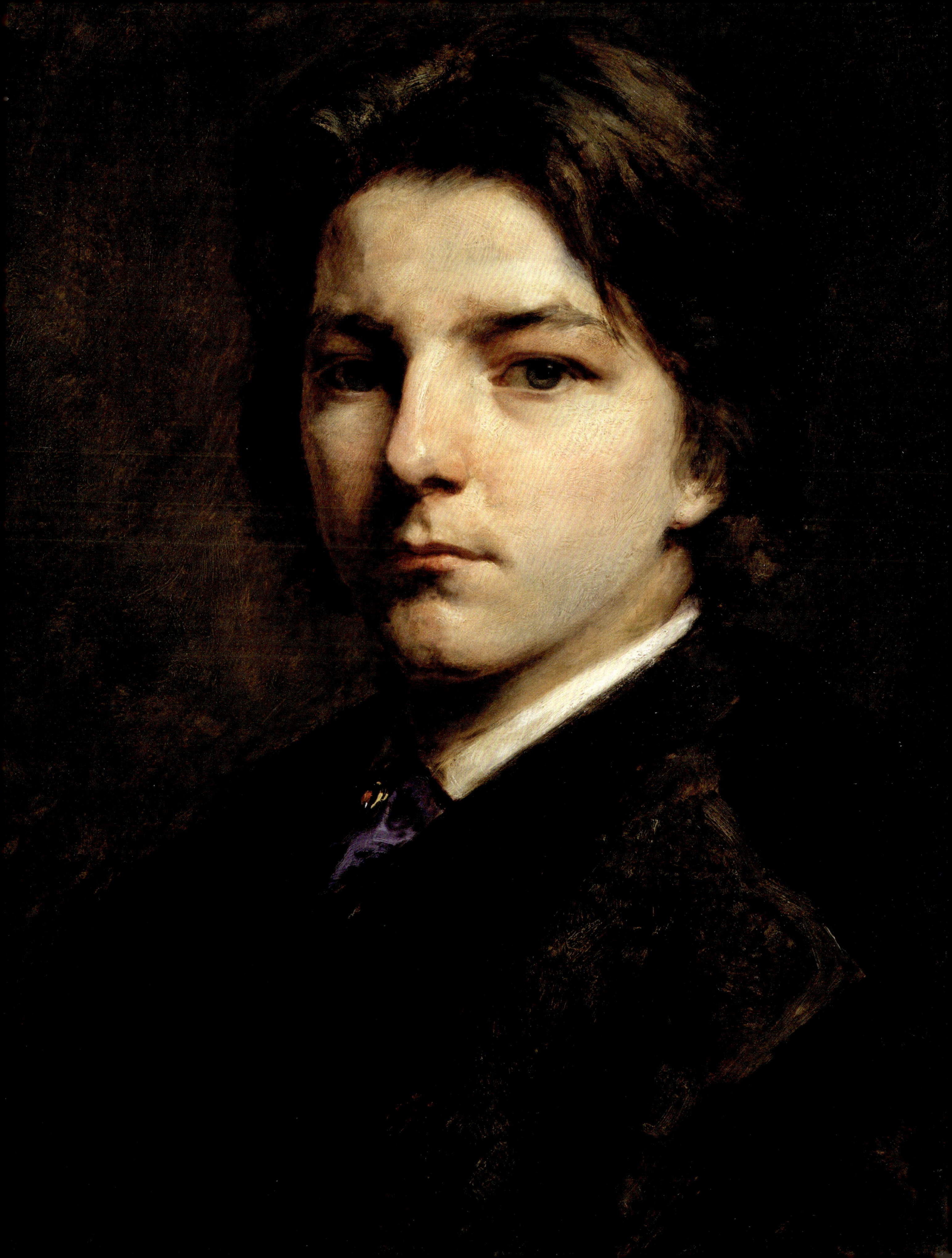

Frank Holl first exhibited at the Royal Academy in 1864 with a subject picture 'Turned out of church' (526) and 'A portrait' (145).[2] When it emerged that the head was a self-portrait by Francis Holl's gifted eldest son Frank, and supremely well painted at that, it excited a great deal of interest. Holl's daughter wrote:

> ['Turned out of church'] was well hung and favourably noticed but a head portrait of himself which he exhibited at the same time drew much attention to the young painter as being far above the ordinary level of students' work. The late John Pye, the then eminent engraver, being very much struck with the work, wrote to the boy's father, asking him to bring his son to see him ... Unfortunately, when the invitation was received, my father was ill in bed from the effects of a strain at cricket ... The crusty old gentleman, doubtless considering that his condescension had not been sufficiently appreciated, wrote retracting the offer, afterwards even refusing to see the boy when he called to explain and apologize.[3]

The portrait was painted in 1863, when Holl was eighteen and had already won R.A. Schools silver and gold medals.[4] It is a remarkably mature exercise in self-scrutiny; the brushwork is fluent and the artist's favoured, dark tonal palette is already in place. The scale is also significant: years later, in an address in 1888, Holl recommended that students experiment with painting heads large:

> I strongly advise you never to neglect the opportunity of painting heads life size. It is the greatest possible practice in your art that you can have ... I don't think I can impress upon you too strongly the great advantage you will find to taking every opportunity of painting these life-sized heads.[5]

It appears that Holl painted only one other self-portrait, in 1885, a rapidly executed profile for the collector Alexander Macdonald of Kepplestone (Aberdeen Art Gallery). For the harassed artist this may have represented little more than another commission to go with many others in hand. It is under life-size, thus complying with others in Macdonald's collection of self-portraits and, fluid brushwork aside, this later head presents little in common with the vivid one produced by the teenager.

The 1863 canvas had a sentimental value for the family. It passed to Holl's widow Annie Laura and later to his brother Edgar, whose widow Ellen offered it to the National Portrait Gallery in 1932.[6] It was exhibited soon after Holl's death, in 1889 and 1891, though apparently not reproduced. Nor was it illustrated in A.M. Reynolds's 1912 biography of her father, and so it remains to this day a marvellous, almost unknown gem of Victorian portrait painting.[7] CBO

4. *Faces in the Fire*

1867
Oil on canvas, 46.5 x 67.5 cm
Signed and dated: 'F. Holl 1867'
Exhibitions: R.A. 1867 (519); R.A. Winter 1889 (204)
Literature: *Art Journal*, 1867, p. 143; *Athenaeum*, 25 May 1867, p. 697; Reynolds, pp. 27–8, 34–5; Jon Whiteley, '"Faces in the Fire" by Frank Holl', *Ashmolean*, 21, 1991, p. 15
Provenance: Mr Herbert of Liverpool, 1867; Miss Gertrude Agnew, 1889; Sir David Piper; presented by the Friends of the Ashmolean, 1991
Collection: Ashmolean Museum of Art and Archaeology

In 1866 Frank Holl, aged twenty-two, painted the original version of *Faces in the Fire* and sold it to his friend, the artist Frank Topham.[8] Topham frequently purchased Holl's work in the early years of his career, and bought the initial *Faces* canvas 'for no small sum'.[9] The current painting, from the collections of the Ashmolean Museum, is the second version of *Faces in the Fire* that Holl replicated for the Royal Academy exhibition of 1867 (519), where it sold to a Mr Herbert of Liverpool.

The girl sits on the floor gazing absent-mindedly into the fire. The setting suggests a poverty-stricken household, dishevelled and dirty. The child leans back on a worn rug or cloth. The cage in the top right appears empty, perhaps indicating that the bird can no longer live in this environment. A small kitten is entering the room, where it stands beside the broken bowl with spilt milk on the floor. The tongs in the bottom-right corner of the image draw the attention of the viewer to the presence and location of the fireplace, which is not depicted in the scene itself. The composition of a young girl warming herself by the fireplace can also be seen in a later more ornate example by Holl entitled *By the Fireside*, painted in 1878.

Frank Holl exhibited two works in the 1867 Exhibition, the other being a 'little subject of an invalid child', entitled *Convalescent*.[10] Together the images received a warm reception with one reviewer remarking that Holl had made 'a debut of unusual success'.[11] *Faces in the Fire* was described as 'a picture which shadows forth a story, and moves to sympathy'. A criticism came from *The Athenaeum*'s commentator, who noted 'no sign of firelight on the figure', but then continued to deem the image 'good in all other respects'.[12] The view was expressed by many that 'Mr. Holl has only to continue as he begins, and his career is sure'.[13]

MM

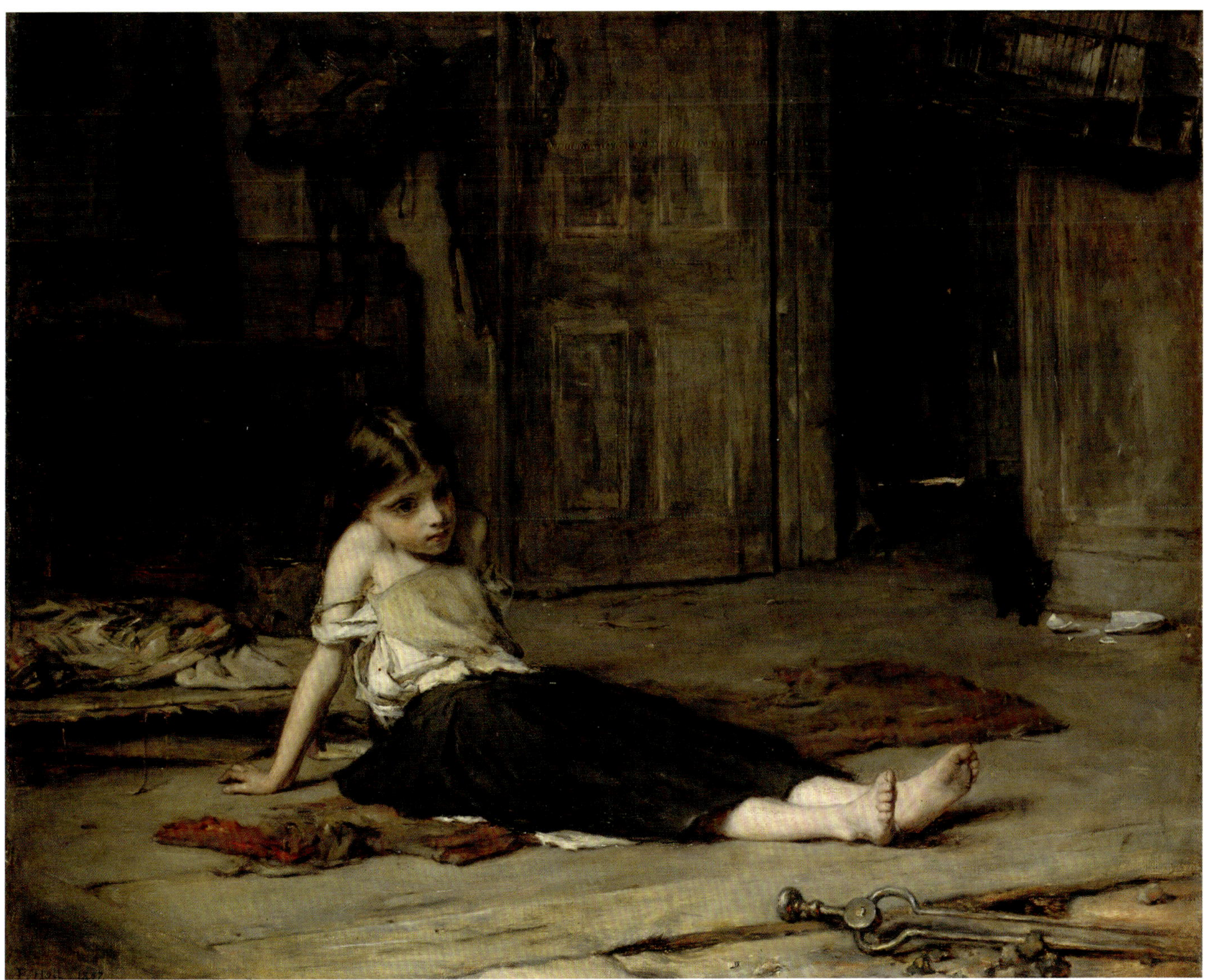

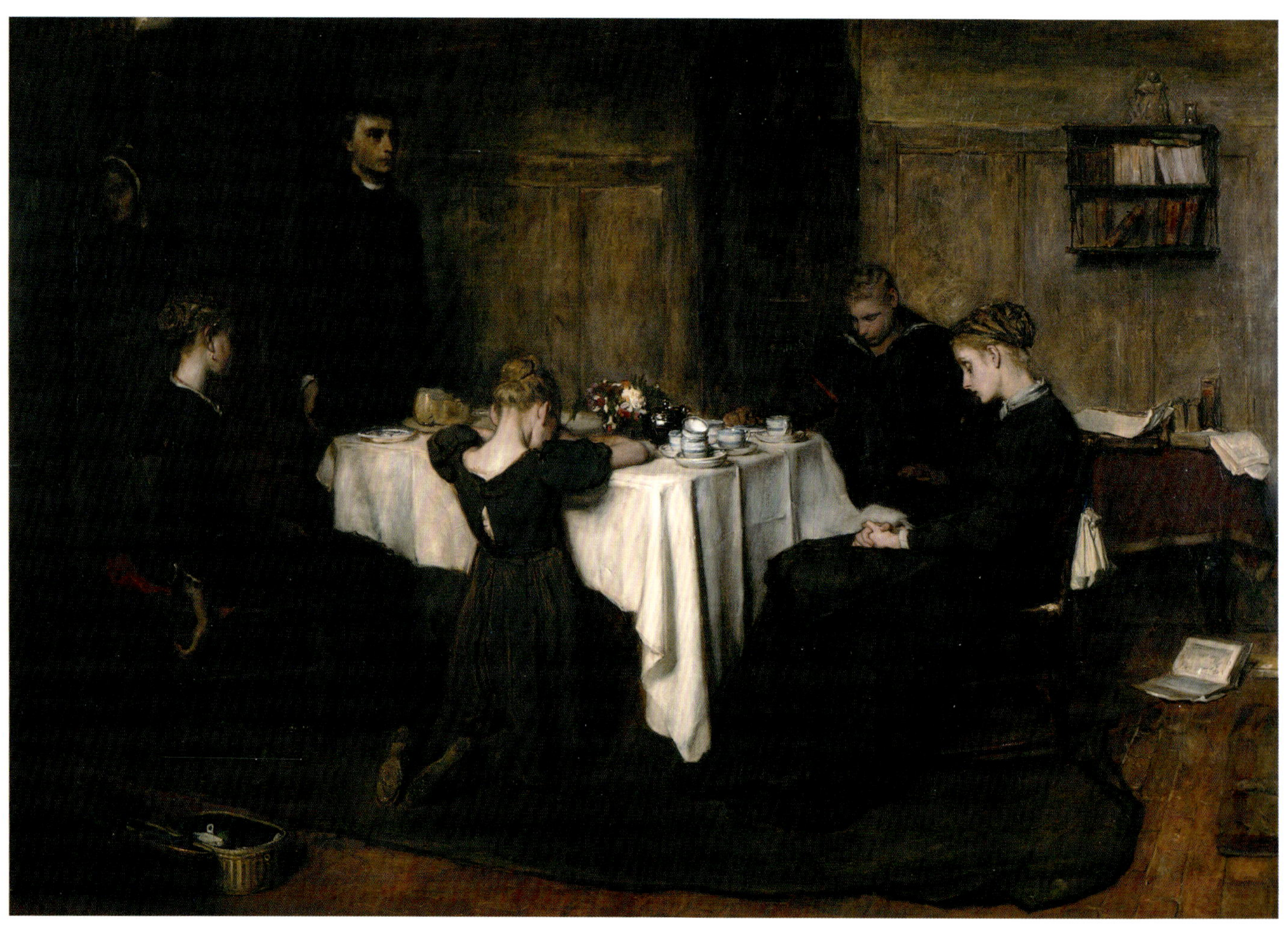

5. *'The Lord gave and the Lord hath taken away, Blessed be the Name of the Lord'*
1868
Oil on canvas, 91.5 x 124.5 cm
Signed and dated: 'Frank Holl 1868'
Exhibitions: R.A. 1869 (210); *Centennial International Exhibition*, Philadelphia, 1876; *Exposition Universelle*, Paris, 1878 (112); R.A. Winter 1889 (185); *The City's Pictures*, Barbican Art Gallery, London, 1984 (29); *Hard Times*, Manchester Art Gallery, 1987 (64)
Literature: *Art Journal* 1869, p. 169, 1876, p. 11, 1889, pp. 54–5; *Athenaeum*, 15 May 1869, p. 675; *Illustrated London News*, 22 May 1869, p. 527; *The Times*, 18 June 1869, p. 694; *Morning Post*, 11 December 1869, p. 5; James Dafforne, 'The Works of Frank Holl', *Art Journal*, XV (1876), p. 11 (ill.); Meynell 1880, pp. 188, 189 (ill.), p. 190; Quilter 1888, p. 307; Campbell 1889, p. 53 (ill), pp. 54–5; Alfred George Temple, *Painting in the Queen's Reign*, London 1897, pp. 339–40; Reynolds, pp. 44–9, 315; Temple 1918, p. 86
Provenance: Sold by the artist to F.C. Pawle for £262; bequeathed by Pawle to the City of London in 1915
Collection: Guildhall Art Gallery, City of London

'The Lord gave and the Lord hath taken away, Blessed be the Name of the Lord' was a significant painting for Holl. Painted at the age of twenty-three, the work brought him to prominence and won him the prestigious Royal Academy two years' Travelling Studentship in Painting in 1868 and led to a commission from the Queen.

Holl had begun the painting in his London studio before the family visited Whitby in 1867. While there, Holl was alerted by a letter from fellow artist Claude Calthrop (1845–93) to the travelling scholarship on offer at the Royal Academy. Entry involved the submission of a finished painting and 'the only picture my father had on hand then was the one from the "Head of the Family"', his daughter recalls.[14] As time to complete the painting was an issue, the Holls returned to London so that he could finish the painting in time for submission the following year.

The subject was based on the popular novel *The Head of the Family* (1852) by Dinah Maria Craik, née Mulock (1826–1887). The painting depicts the bleak scene in Chapter 1 where a mourning family are at the dinner table and the elder brother, a curate, assumes the duties of the head of the family:

> They gathered round the table – Lindsay sitting where she had presided for some years as mistress of her father's household. Opposite to her was that father's empty chair. Each glanced that way, and then all eyes were lowered. None looked up, and all kept silence as Ninian came in and took the vacant place. There was a pause – as if each waited for the voice that never would be heard more; and then Ninian, in his low, quiet voice, said the grace:
>
> '*Lord, we thank Thee for these and all Thy mercies; and forgive us our sins, for Christ's sake. Amen.*'
>
> And all felt this to be the token whereby their brother took upon himself the duties, responsibilities, and rights of eldership, and became henceforth the Head of the Family.
>
> It was a goodly sight – as indeed it always is – to see what may truly be termed a Family![15]

Holl shows how a family is brought together by their mutual grief. It is interesting to note that Holl chose not to name his work after the novel nor the words of grace being uttered, but instead the words of Job: *'The Lord gave and the Lord hath taken away, Blessed be the Name of the Lord.'* These words of comfort and acceptance appear much later in the novel, movingly uttered after the death of a baby; 'the sentiment of resignation', *The Times* wrote, 'softens the pain and suggests its consolations.'[16]

Unlike most of his subject paintings, this was based on a fictional account rather than an incident that he had observed. When he returned to London, he was keen to complete the work and both his wife and his brother acted as models for the mourning figures. Still early in his career, Holl struggled with the cost of producing such a large picture, and his wife, as well as acting as model, 'by dint of the utmost economy ... was able to get together enough cash to buy the dress' used in the painting.[17]

It was a big investment of time and money but immediately paid off, and on 10 December 1868 Holl was awarded the prestigious two-year travelling scholarship. The following May he exhibited at the Royal Academy Summer Exhibition. Its bleak subject and sombre tones concerned some critics: 'as well as much dextrous workmanship ...,' the *Illustrated London News* commented that 'its tone and effect are unnaturally sooty and excessively lugubrious.'[18] Despite this, it was recognized as both a masterly piece of painting and a truthful rendition of poignant emotion; *The Athenaeum* wrote: 'The pathos is profound and genuine. How rarely are we able to write thus!'[19] For another critic, who found its subject unsavoury, it is 'rendered with great delicacy and pathos. The expression of sorrow which pervades the figures, and fills the place where death has left a void as with an atmosphere oppressively sad, is wrought out with great power and truth.'[20]

The painting received great acclaim and Queen Victoria attempted to buy it. As the work was already sold, she commissioned Holl to paint another work for her collection, which became *No Tidings from the Sea* (cat. 6). MB

6. *No Tidings from the Sea* (ill. Page 116)

1870
Oil on canvas, 71.4 x 91.4 cm
Signed and dated: 'FRANK HOLL. 1870'; a damaged label on the back of the frame, probably in the artist's hand, reads: 'Frank Holl / painted November 1'
Exhibitions: R.A. 1871 (595); R.A. Winter 1889 (211) and 1901 (61); R.A. *Bicentenary* 1968 (312); *Hard Times*, Manchester Art Gallery, 1987 (65)
Literature: *Art Journal* 1871, p. 177, 1876, pp. 10–11, 1889, pp. 55–6; *The Times*, 22 May 1871, p. 6; *Athenaeum*, 10 June 1871, p. 726; *The Graphic*, 17 June 1871; *Magazine of Art*, 1883, p. 173; A.I. Durrant, *Catalogue of the Paintings, Sculpture & other Works of Art*, at Osborne, London 1876, p. 328; Reynolds, pp. 48–9, 83–7; K. Bendiner, *An Introduction to Victorian Painting*, New Haven 1985, p. 116; Treuherz 1987, pp. 75–6, 146; Oliver Millar, *The Victorian Pictures in the Collection of Her Majesty The Queen*, 2 vols, Cambridge 1992, pp. 122–3
Provenance: Commissioned by Queen Victoria from the artist
Collection: Her Majesty the Queen

6

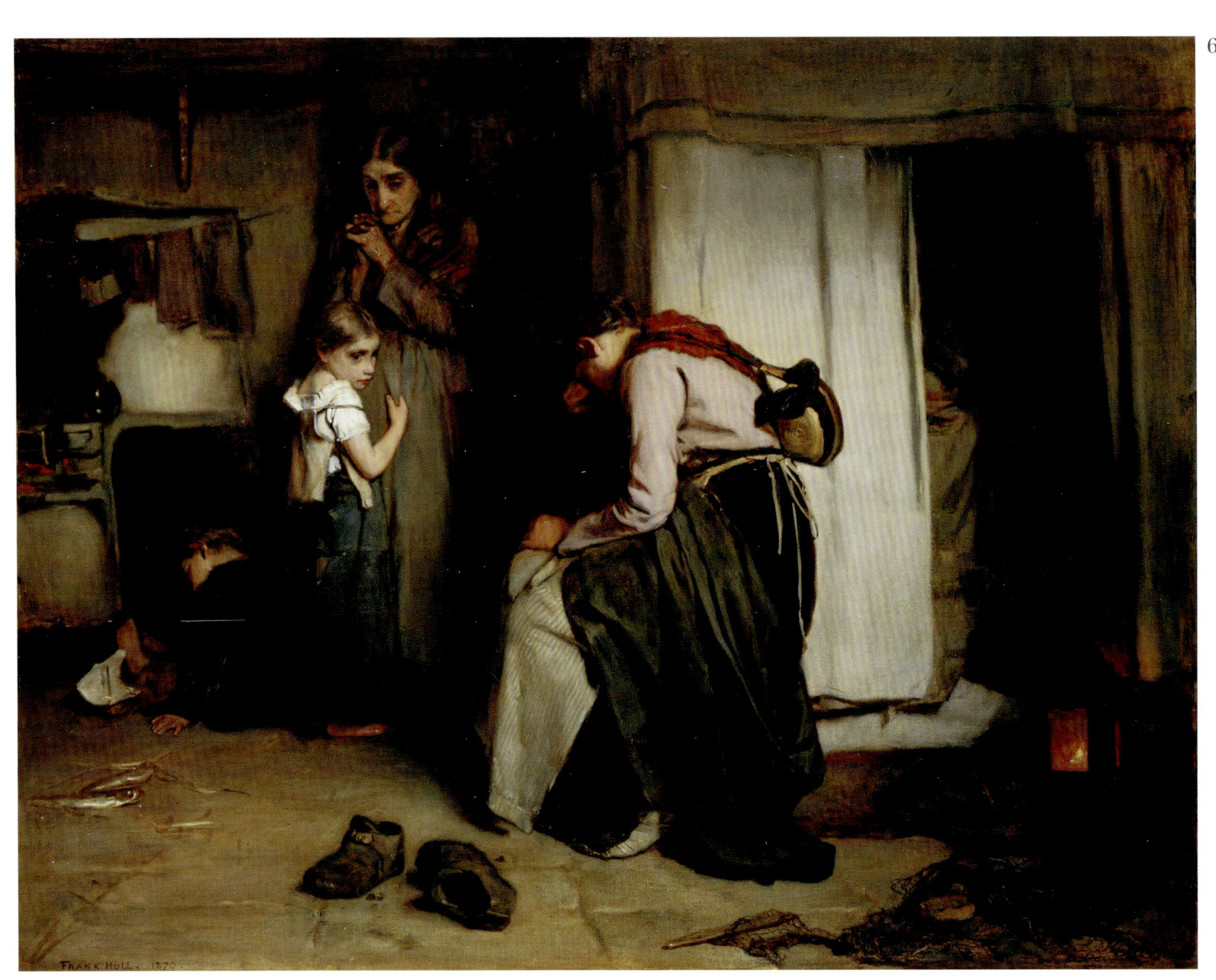

Queen Victoria had much admired Holl's '*The Lord gave* …' (cat. 5) when she saw it at the 1869 R.A. exhibition and attempted to buy the work, but it had already been sold to Fred Pawle. Pawle's refusal to sell the work led the Queen to commission Holl to paint her another picture, the subject of which would be the artist's choice. At the time he was just beginning his two-year travelling scholarship awarded by the Royal Academy, which made it difficult for him to begin this prestigious assignment. His early abandonment of the scholarship, however, meant that he was able to start thinking about the painting in 1870.

The search for a subject tied in with the Holl family summer holiday of 1870 when in June they travelled to Cullercoats on the Northumbrian coast. The choice of this rugged fishing village in contrast to their more usual visits to Wales was probably motivated by Holl's quest for a dramatic subject for the commission. While there, he lived close to the centre of the community and sketched in and among the fisherman's cottages. 'My father lived much amongst the village folk,' Reynolds recalled, 'going freely in and out of their cottages (his genial, sympathetic manner attracting them much), studying their ways and customs, and sketching incessantly.'[21]

The subject for the painting came from a dramatic experience described by the artist's daughter, who claimed that, while Holl was painting in a fisherman's cottage, the door was flung open by a woman 'half mad with suspense and misery'.[22] This was shortly followed by the dripping corpse of her husband being brought into the cottage. At the sight of her dead partner the agonized woman called for her own death. 'My father', Reynolds writes, 'was greatly moved and upset at the sight of her grief, terribly primitive in its intensity, which haunted him for days, finally resolving itself into a conception for a picture which he eventually painted, calling it "No tidings from the sea."'[23]

Holl began the work, but on 27 July sent a note to Sir Francis Grant apologizing for his tardiness in not completing the picture, blaming ill health and reporting that he was working on preparatory studies.[24] The painting was completed on 31 October 1870 and was sent to Windsor for the Queen to inspect; she accepted the work and paid him £105 for it in December that year.

The painting depicts the interior of a fisherman's cottage with the grief-stricken woman being fearfully observed by her own daughter clinging to the skirts of an old woman, 'the old mother of one of the neighbours'.[25] The mourning woman's young son is seated on the floor oblivious to the unfolding events. It is a dramatic and moving scene in which Holl fully utilizes the dim daylight of dawn and the still simple lives that emphasize the raw emotions.

The work was exhibited at the 1871 R.A. summer exhibition as the property of Her Majesty the Queen. The critics praised its pathos and narrative, but criticized it for being overly gloomy. In the same exhibition a painting entitled *How Bereft!* (1038) by Jozef Israëls, the Dutch artist whom Holl so admired, depicts a corpse being carried out of a fisherman's cottage. The similarity of the two and the influence of Israëls on Holl were not overlooked by the critics, and *The Athenaeum* declared that, although 'Mr Holl paints better than he used to', he still fell short of Israëls.[26]

In 1882 Holl made a replica of the painting for Arthur Tooth that was shown at his spring exhibition of 1883. MB

7. *The Wide, Wide World* (ill. Page 118)

Oil on canvas, 76.5 x 64 cm
Signed and dated lower right: 'FRANK HOLL 1873'
Private collection

This painting of a young woman dressed in black and seated on a bench on a railway station platform is a reworking of a single figure from Frank Holl's 1873 Royal Academy subject *Leaving Home*. Six years after appearing at the Royal Academy, the oil version in its complete form was reproduced as a line engraving in the *Art Journal* and written about in some detail in an accompanying article. This figure is described as 'a young and ladylike female, whose dress indicates, in some degree, her lonely condition … She has opened her purse, evidently not too plentifully furnished, and is counting out the money it contains after paying the cost of her ticket to her place of destination.'[27]

In the background Holl has included a billboard advertising an illustrated edition of Charles Dickens's *Nicholas Nickleby*. A.M. Reynolds wrote of her father's admiration for Dickens, explaining that, although he never made literal illustrations of themes from the novels, nonetheless, 'as one stands before certain of my father's earlier pictures … one seems to be looking backward at a dead tradition, the very life of the middle classes of the Victorian era'.[28] Some connection was perhaps intended between the sombre figure of the young woman in Holl's painting – whose garb indicates her insecure and lonely position in life – and Dickens's heroine Kate Nickleby. JS

7

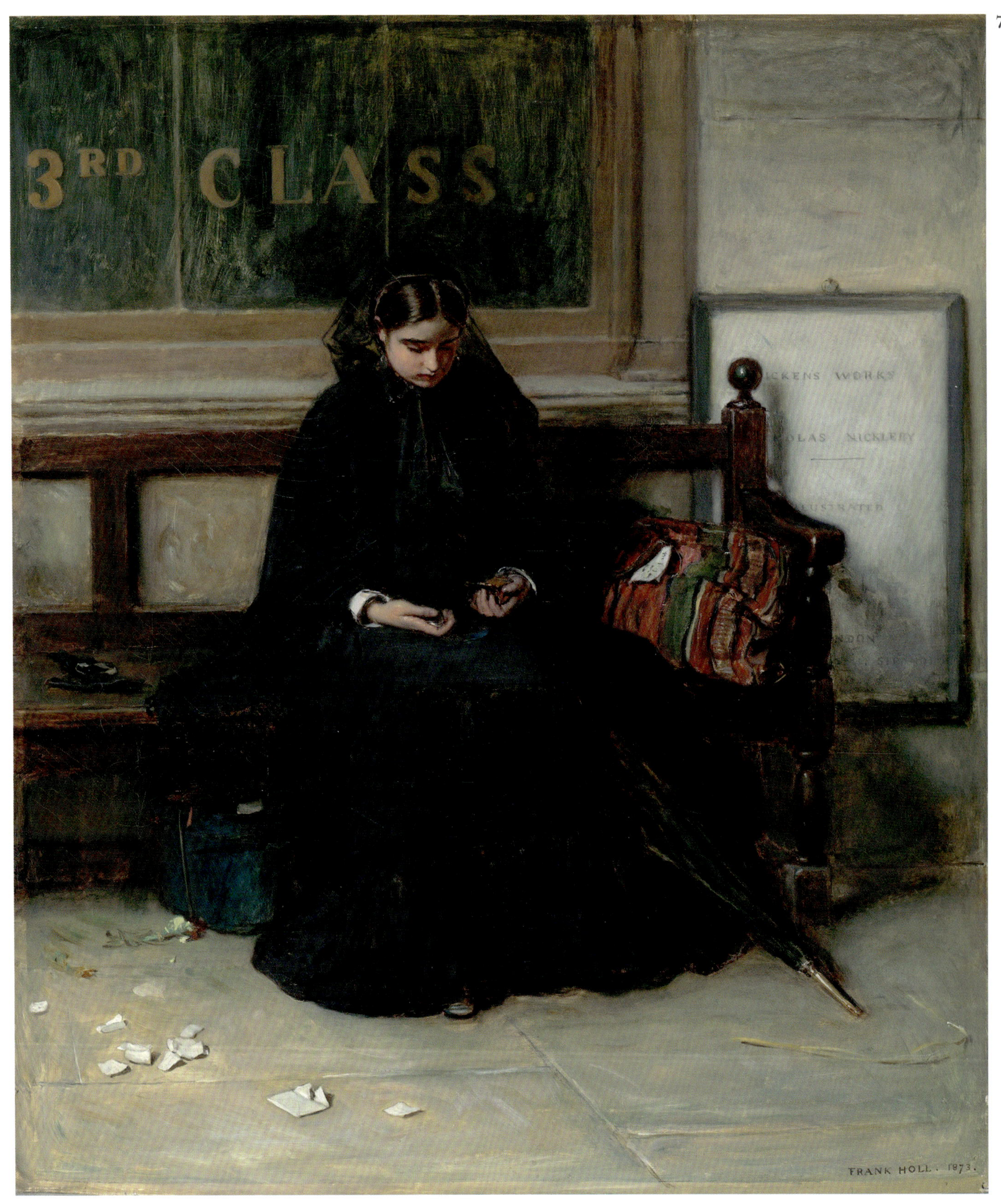

8. *Seamstresses*

*c.*1875
Oil on canvas, 48.3 x 66.2 cm
Signed: 'Frank Holl'
Exhibitions: Glasgow International Exhibition 1901 (181A); *Hard Times*, Manchester Art Gallery, 1987 (67), as *The Song of the Shirt*
Literature: William Roberts, *Memorials of Christie's; A Record of Sale from 1766 to 1896*, London 1897; Christopher Wood, *Victorian Panorama*, London 1976, p. 128; J. Baker, *Royal Albert Memorial Museum, Exeter: Catalogue of Oil Paintings, Watercolours, Drawings and Sculpture in the Permanent Collection*, Exeter 1978, p. 78; Treuherz 1987, p. 78.
Provenance: Probably commissioned by Captain Henry Hill of Brighton, 1874; Hill sale at Christie's, 25 May 1889 (135), for 285 guineas; bought Agnew; Sir Charles Tennant and by descent to Hon. Colin Tennant; Sotheby's Belgravia, 10 July 1973 (85), bought Agnew; sold to Exeter 1975
Collection: Royal Albert Memorial Museum, Exeter

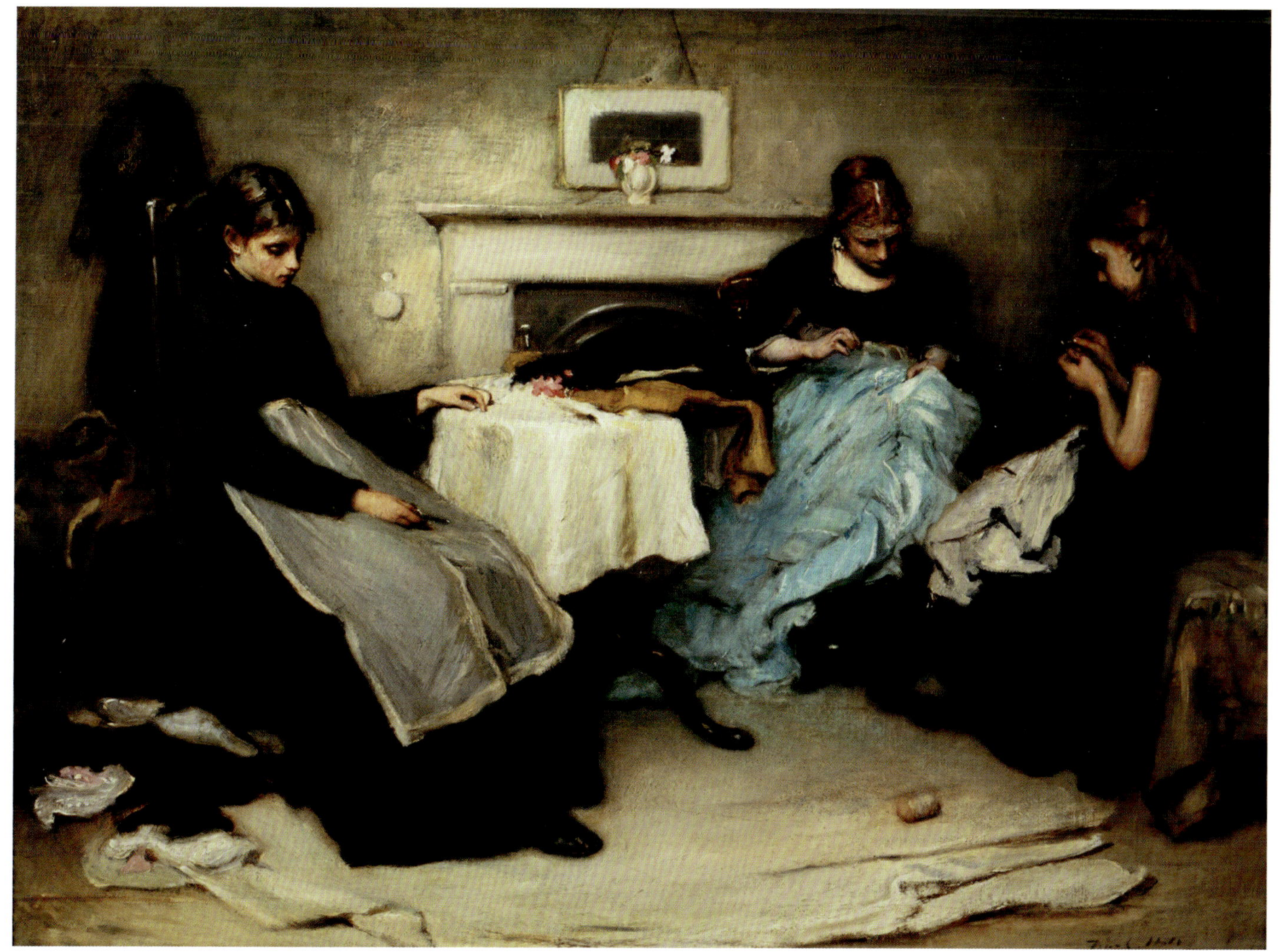

The exploitation of seamstresses came to prominence as a social issue in the 1840s. Their desperate plight was highlighted and epitomized by 'The Song of the Shirt', a hugely popular poem by Thomas Hood that was first published in the pages of the Christmas edition of Punch in 1843. It inspired a number of paintings, including G.F. Watts's painting of the same name (*c.*1848–50; Watts Gallery) and Richard Redgrave's *The Semptress* (1846; private collection). Undoubtedly, Holl was aware of the iconography of the subject when he first approached it around 1874 with a watercolour entitled *Song of the Shirt* (*c.*1874; private collection).[29] This oil version, entitled *Seamstresses*,[30] shows a significant departure from such images, characterized by their depiction of a lone seamstress in a sparse garret with its inherent drama.

Here Holl, taking the spirit of Hood's tragic outcome, gives the scene a refreshing naturalism, not present in earlier paintings of the subject. Instead of the lone figure, three are at work, not simply on shirts, but a variety of dress. They are working in a room that has a bed, a small table and two chairs and is decorated with a framed print and a small vase of flowers on the mantelpiece. One girl, seated on the bed, is threading a needle, another is sewing, while the one on the left, exhausted, appears to be grieving and reflecting Hood's lines:

> Oh! but for one short hour!
> A respite however brief!
> No blessed leisure for Love or Hope,
> But only time for Grief!
> A little weeping would ease my heart,
> But in their briny bed
> My tears must stop, for every drop
> Hinders needle and thread!

The sombre dress of the seamstresses and the darkness of the print above the mantelpiece are contrasted with the vibrant colour of the blue dress being stitched. Holl had seen the drudgery of printmakers' work through his father and grandfather, who were both engravers, and the dark image of the print in the centre of the painting is linked to the darkness of the seamstresses' dresses. The most significant figure is the seamstress on the left, who appears to be isolated from the other figures and lost in her tiredness and grief. MB

9. *Head of a Welsh Fishergirl*

Undated [mid-1870s]
Oil on millboard, 6.5 x 7.3 cm
Provenance: Mrs Constance Margaret Baker (Holl's niece) to the Art Fund, 1957; the Art Fund to the Victoria and Albert Museum in 1958
Collection: Victoria and Albert Museum

Holl was drawn to the north coast of Wales, where he sketched incessantly and was inspired to paint several of his finished works. According to his daughter, his diary, now lost, recorded that he first visited Wales in 1863, and it was somewhere he continued to visit for the rest of his life.[31] This makes dating the study difficult, although the model is very close to the central figure in *Waiting* (1876; private collection) and her appearance in his work probably dates from the mid-1870s. Holl met this

> most inspiring model ... [when] he took shelter from the rain in a little cottage, scarcely more than a hut, on the banks of a stream which flows through the marshy ground between Criccieth and Afonwen. This hut was tenanted by a widow with two young children ... The woman had scarcely any English, but her magnificent build and presence at once inspired my father with the idea of a large composition. She was of a massive and almost savage type, living quite alone with her children, and seeing no one for weeks together.[32]

This spontaneous sketch of the head of a Welsh fisher girl is a survival of the numerous sketches we know Holl made on his visits to fishing communities. In the finished painting, *Waiting*, the traditional Welsh bonnet is replaced by a more familiar and generic sou'wester. MB

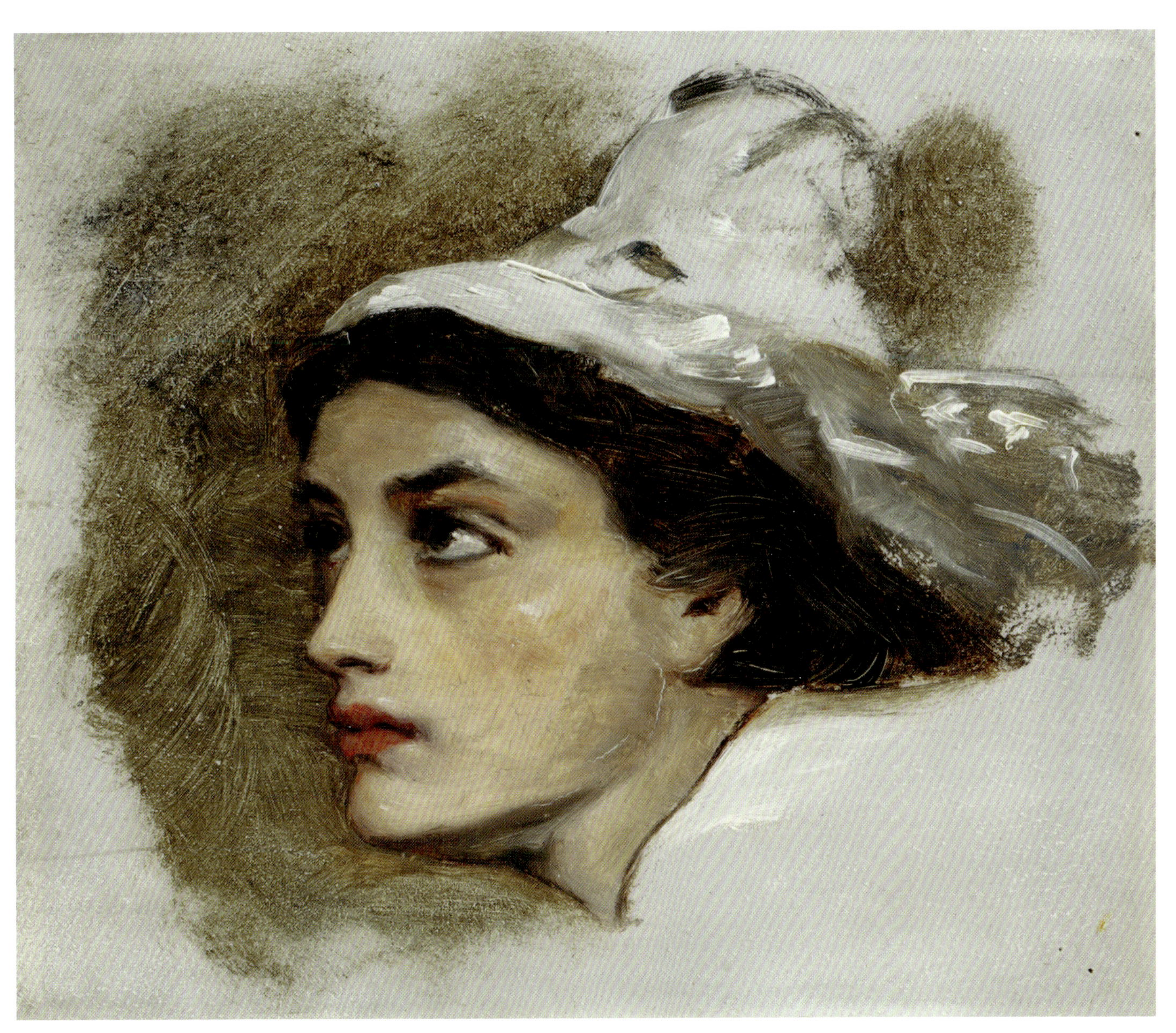

10. *Her Firstborn, Horsham Churchyard (Funeral of the First-Born/The First-Born)*

1876
Oil on canvas, 109.2 x 155.6 cm
Signed and dated: 'Frank Holl, 1876'
Exhibitions: R.A. 1876 (286); R.A. Winter 1889 (237); British Association, Dundee, 1912 (44)
Literature: *Illustrated London News*, 13 May 1876, p. 475; *The Times*, 18 May 1876, p. 8; *Graphic*, 20 May 1876, p. 491; *Art Journal*, 1876, p. 261, 1889, p. 56; Meynell 1880, p. 188; *Magazine of Art*, 1882, p. 3; Reynolds, pp. 128–9; *Dundee Art Gallery Catalogue*, 1926, as 'Funeral of the First-born'; *Dundee City Art Gallery Catalogue*, 1973, p. 63 (126/12); Treuherz 1987, pp. 79–80, 147
Provenance: Captain Henry Hill, 1876; Mrs Hill in 1889; presented to Dundee by anonymous donor in 1890
Collection: The McManus, Dundee's Art Gallery and Museum

When exhibited at the Royal Academy in 1876, Reynolds records that *Her Firstborn* was 'splendidly hung, and attracted a large amount of attention, [with] commissions pouring in on [her] father as a result'.[33] A 'quaint old churchyard at Shere' provided the backdrop for this scene, and a 'beautiful landscape study for it' remained in the possession of Frank Holl's wife, Annie.[34] The large subject picture was produced by Holl for one of his most reliable patrons, Captain Henry Hill, with a later replica made for a Mr Webster of Blackheath.[35]

The subject of *Her Firstborn* is outlined in a number of contemporary commentaries of the 1876 exhibition.[36] The painting depicts a small procession of mourners taking a young child to the grave. Four young girls of differing age

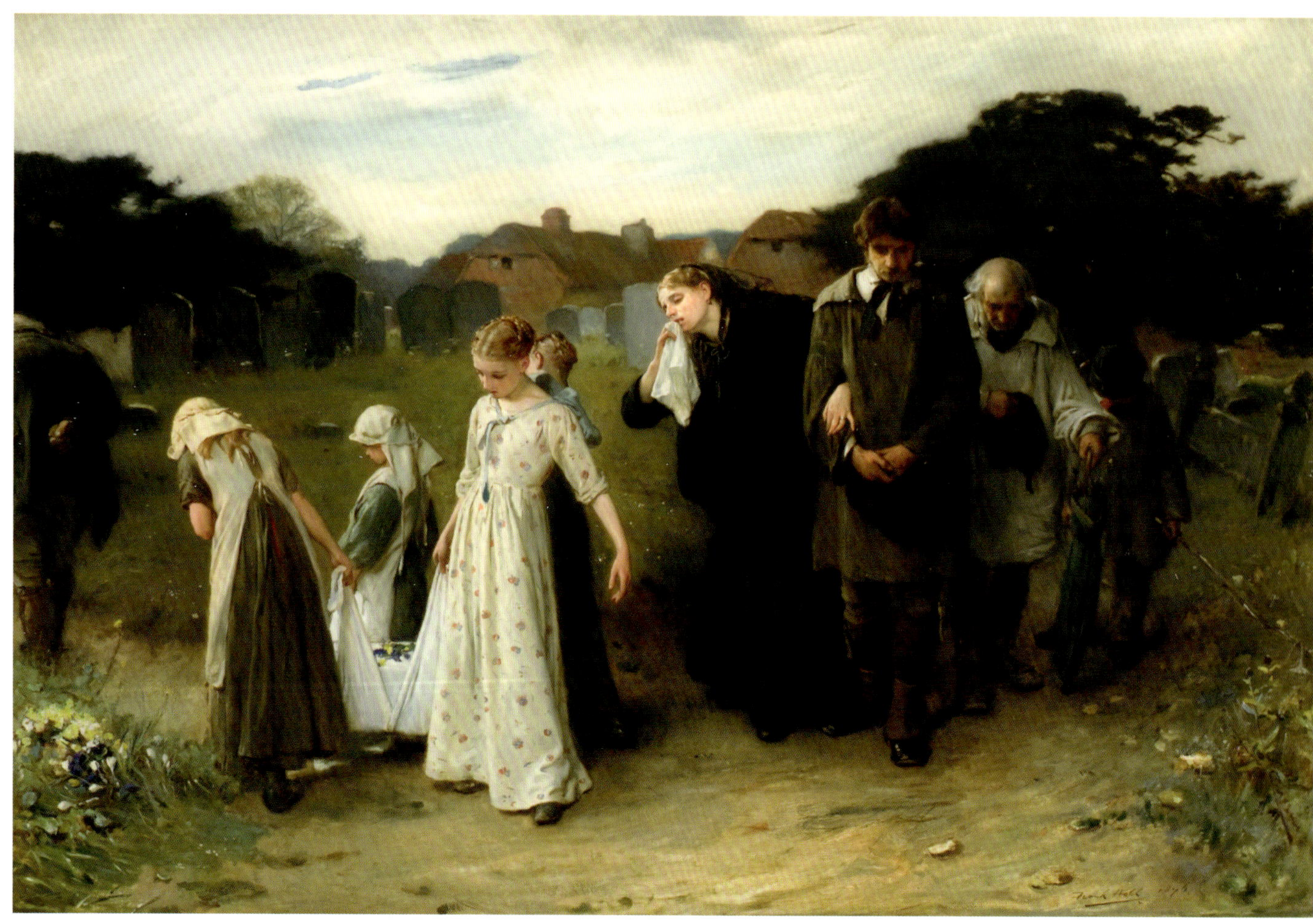

carry the small and humble coffin in pristine white cloths. The oldest of these girls stands with her body turned towards the viewer, her delicacy and youth highlighting the tragedy of the scene. The figure of the mother who follows behind is physically overwhelmed by her grief for the child, her body 'bowed forward with ... poignant anguish'.[37] She clutches in her right hand a white handkerchief and, with her other, the arm of the child's father, who proceeds stoically, appearing as if dazed by his grief. Two elderly gentlemen and a young boy complete the group. Both the father and grandfather clasp their hats in their hands. The clothing of all the figures suggests their social position to be lower class, and the natural setting further indicates that this is taken from rural country life, as Reynolds describes:

> The little group ... strike one in their simple, unaffected grief, with a sense of real sorrow for a real tragedy, as though one had happened upon it in life itself, not merely in art. The homely country folk with their bearing of quiet unostentatious grief, the simplicity of it all, its freedom from the theatricality which too often mars the treatment of such subjects in art, all help to intensify the pathos of the work. One can almost hear the hum of the bees, feel the warmth of the sunshine as the children bear all that remains of their little play-fellow to his resting-place under the flowery grass.[38]

Critical responses were mixed. In an 1882 article in the *Magazine of Art* the figure of the mother is described as 'true and impulsive', while the father's expression is too much 'a study of manly grief' to be an artistic truth. 'Great reserve' and 'great realism' were considered essential for such an 'acutely sentimental picture', but the continuity and realism of the scene were lost in the 'peasant-woman's delicate and high-bred hand, as it lies with the conscious pose of the little finger upon her husband's arm'.[39] The *Illustrated London News* further noted that 'the colouring partakes of the mournfulness of the theme, but we have had solider painting from the young artist'.[40] Conversely, the *Art Journal* stated: 'Mr Holl ... never painted better or made the onlooker sadder.'

The commentator from the *Graphic* noted that morose subject matter featured heavily in the 1876 Royal Academy exhibition, and considered the subject of 'agony' in art to be 'far too prevalent just now'.[41] This sentiment was echoed in the *Magazine of Art*'s reference to Holl's chosen subject of infant mortality as 'trite'.[42] High infant

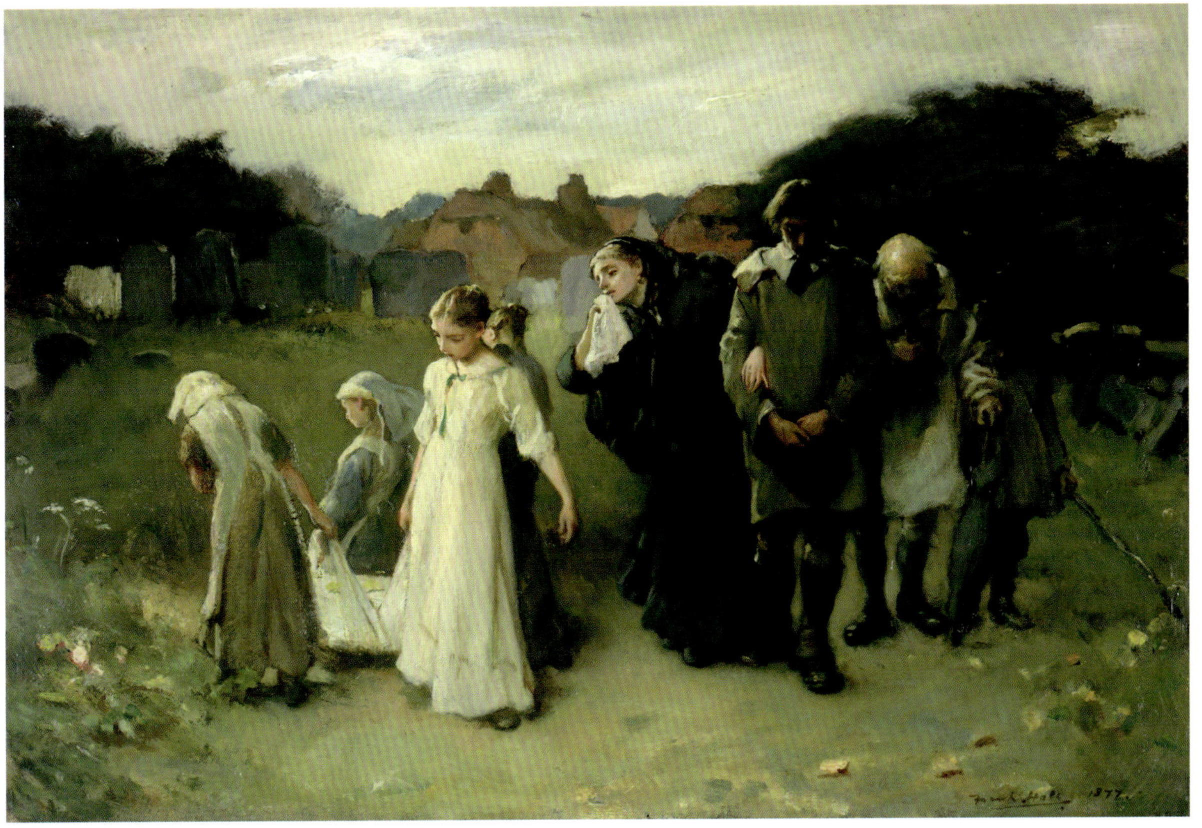

11

mortality was a present and visible truth of the Victorian age and often featured in the work of artists dedicated to portraying social realism. Holl regularly engaged with this subject in his work, but as Treuherz notes in *Hard Times*, he 'treated the subject of maternal grief as a universal one' and his pictures on this theme 'are not meant to be specifically modern' or radical in nature.[43] Despite this, a question suggested in many publications, and posed outright by *The Graphic*, was 'Who would choose to live in constant contemplation of such a domestic tragedy?'[44] MM

11. *Her Firstborn* (ill. Page 123)

1877
Oil on panel, 33.1 x 48.2 cm
Signed and dated bottom right: "Frank Holl 1877'
Exhibitions: *Recent Acquisitions*, Fine Art Society, 1969 (50); *The Art and Mind of Victorian England*, Minneapolis University Gallery, 1974 (21)
Literature: *Illustrated London News*, 13 May 1876, p. 475; *The Times*, 18 May 1876, p. 8; *Art Journal*, 1876, p. 261, 1889, p. 56; Meynell 1880, p. 188; *Magazine of Art*, 1882, p. 3; Reynolds, pp. 128–9; *Dundee City Art Gallery Catalogue*, 1973, p. 63 (126/12); Treuherz 1987, p. 147
Provenance: Mrs E.M. Dartford (artist's granddaughter); Fine Art Society; Sotheby's Belgravia, 12 June 1973 (138); bought by the Fine Art Society; Forbes Magazine Collection, New York; Sotheby's, 15 March 1983; bought by Museums Sheffield
Collection: Museums Sheffield

The smaller 1877 oil-on-panel sketch of *Her Firstborn* returns to Holl's scene of the graveyard at Shere, where the mournful figures process to lay the child to rest. This version passed from the artist's family to the Fine Art Society in 1969.

The variation of medium from the original oil on canvas to oil on panel in 1877 leaves a marked visual change, with a grainy texture to the finish of the painting. In this far smaller image Holl makes more extreme use of light and dark, heavily marking-in the shadows. This development is most notable in the figures of the weeping mother and stoic father in the group to the right of the panel.

This painting is referred to as a sketch for numerous reasons. The smaller scale, areas of blocked-in colour, less modelling and an extreme use of light and shade suggest an experimental purpose for the finished image. Additionally, there is less detail and pattern in elements such as the dress of the elder girl and the surrounding rural scenery. The mourner to the left in the 1876 painting has been removed entirely from this later work, perhaps due to the diminution in size.

Treuherz describes the smaller replica as 'beautifully and freely handled in dull subdued colours, with touches of pink, yellow and blue, but the faces of the three main figures are more highly finished'.[45] MM

12. *Hush!*

1877
Oil on canvas, 34.3 x 44.5 cm
Signed and dated: 'Frank Holl/ 77'
Exhibitions: Dudley Gallery, Winter 1877–8 (68); King Street Galleries of Mr E.F. White (18); R.A. Winter 1889 (200)
Literature: *The Times*, 1 December 1877, *Athenaum*, 1 December 1877, p. 705, 7 April 1883, p. 448; *Art Journal*, 1878, p. 54, 1893, pp. 197–8; Reynolds, pp. 146–7; Treuherz 1987, p. 147
Provenance: Bought by Fred C. Pawle of Reigate; Sir Henry Tate Collection by 1888; presented by Sir Henry Tate in 1894
Collection: Tate

Hush! and *Hushed* (cat. 13) were produced as a pair and nearly always exhibited as such. They are two of the earliest in a series of paintings by Holl that use as their setting a fisher cottage in Criccieth in North Wales, to which the artist returned over many subsequent years. This location was discovered by Holl in 1876 when he 'took shelter from the rain in a little hut owned by a young widow who lived there with two children, one still a baby'.[46] Both *Hush!* and *Hushed* were painted a year later in June 1877. The widow is the central figure of these and other scenes in Criccieth,

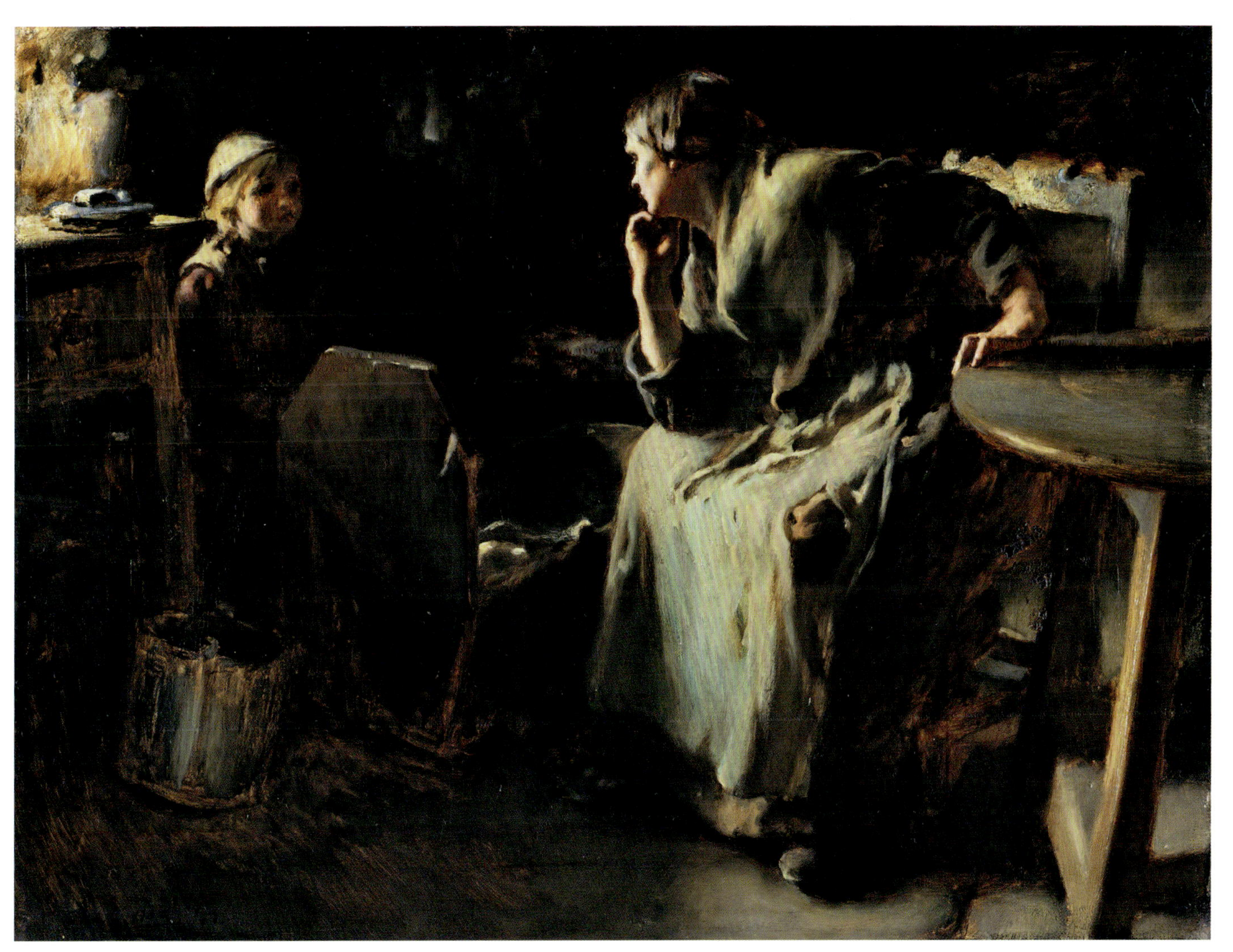

and Holl regularly found inspiration in her as a model and in her social predicament (see cat. 9).

Hush! depicts an intimate scene of a mother and baby. An older child stands on the other side of the crib and the mother is asking her to *Hush!* The only face visible is that of the child and the sorrow and confusion shown there informs the tone of the entire piece. The mother 'leans mournfully on her elbow' and supports herself with her other arm on the table.[47] The unhappy scene, when partnered with *Hushed*, suggests that the baby in the crib is gravely ill. The bleak and empty cottage, with its sparse decor and bare walls, indicates the poverty of its occupants, further accentuated by the outdated design of the wooden cradle in which the baby lies. The picture is almost stripped of colour, but the muted browns and soft modelling of Holl's technique create a dark yet tender image.

In an article in the *Art Journal* of 1893 concerning the Henry Tate Collection, *Hush!* and *Hushed* are considered once more:

> As arrangement of light and shadow, both pictures are excellent. The masses are well balanced; the daylight struggling in through the ungenerous window, is followed in its work with the utmost skill, so that, in the result, these two interiors seem to be modelled rather than painted. The peculiar blanket texture, which marked so much of Holl's work, is here very conspicuous, but in subjects such as these it has a certain fitness.[48]

The reviewer from the *Art Journal* singled out *Hush!* as the strongest image in its section of the Dudley Gallery's 1878 Winter Exhibition, and paid particular note to Holl's 'masterly chiaroscuro'.[49] MM

13. *Hushed*

1877
Oil on canvas, 34.3 x 44.5 cm
Signed and dated: 'Frank Holl/ 77'
Exhibitions: Dudley Gallery, Winter 1877–8 (100); R.A. Winter 1889 (203)
Literature: *Athenaeum*, 1 December 1877, p. 705; *The Times*, 1 December 1877; *Art Journal*, 1878, p. 54, 1893, p. 197; Reynolds, pp. 146–7; Treuherz 1987, p. 147
Provenance: Bought by Fred C. Pawle of Reigate; Sir Henry Tate Collection by 1888; presented by Sir Henry Tate 1894
Collection: Tate

It was in the fisher homes of Criccieth, North Wales, that Holl truly mastered the use of chiaroscuro with his depictions of the deprivation and fear that so blighted the life of a fisherman's wife. In the figure of a woman he sought to represent ideals of strength and depths of emotions such as hope and despair. These paintings, *Hush!* (cat. 12) and *Hushed*, did not receive positive feedback across the board. The commentator from *The Athenaeum* notes that the 'solemn ... grimy sorrowfulness' of these images failed to express the subtleties and the 'harmonies of tone and tint' of other paintings on display.[50]

The similarity of the scene and figures within indicate that the painting *Hushed* is intended to follow the image of *Hush!* and that the suffering baby has now died. The devastated mother gazes sorrowfully into 'the terrible vacancy in the cradle', her hand covering her face in a sign of grief.[51] The figure of the child appears bemused by the event, and unsure what to do for her mother, she has moved closer.[52] In *Hushed* the changed position of the mother places her figure largely in darkness. This reflects the mood of the piece.

When describing these works, the reviewer from the *Art Journal* believed that 'Mr Holl never did anything more touchingly idyllic'.[53] The reviewer also refers to a third painting 'Waiting' as the final phase of the story. This image is most likely the third painting, according to Reynolds, that her father made in Criccieth in 1877.[54] However, Reynolds clearly describes *Hush!* and *Hushed* as a pair, bought together by Fred C. Pawle, indicating that this third picture was not intended to be a part of the same narrative.

It was in these images that Treuherz in *Hard Times* saw the similarities of subject and execution between Holl and the Dutch master Jozef Israëls. He believed that Holl reused elements derived from Israëls, such as 'the cottage interior, the deep window sill, the cradle, the statuesque figure of the woman, [and] the half-hidden weeping face'.[55] MM

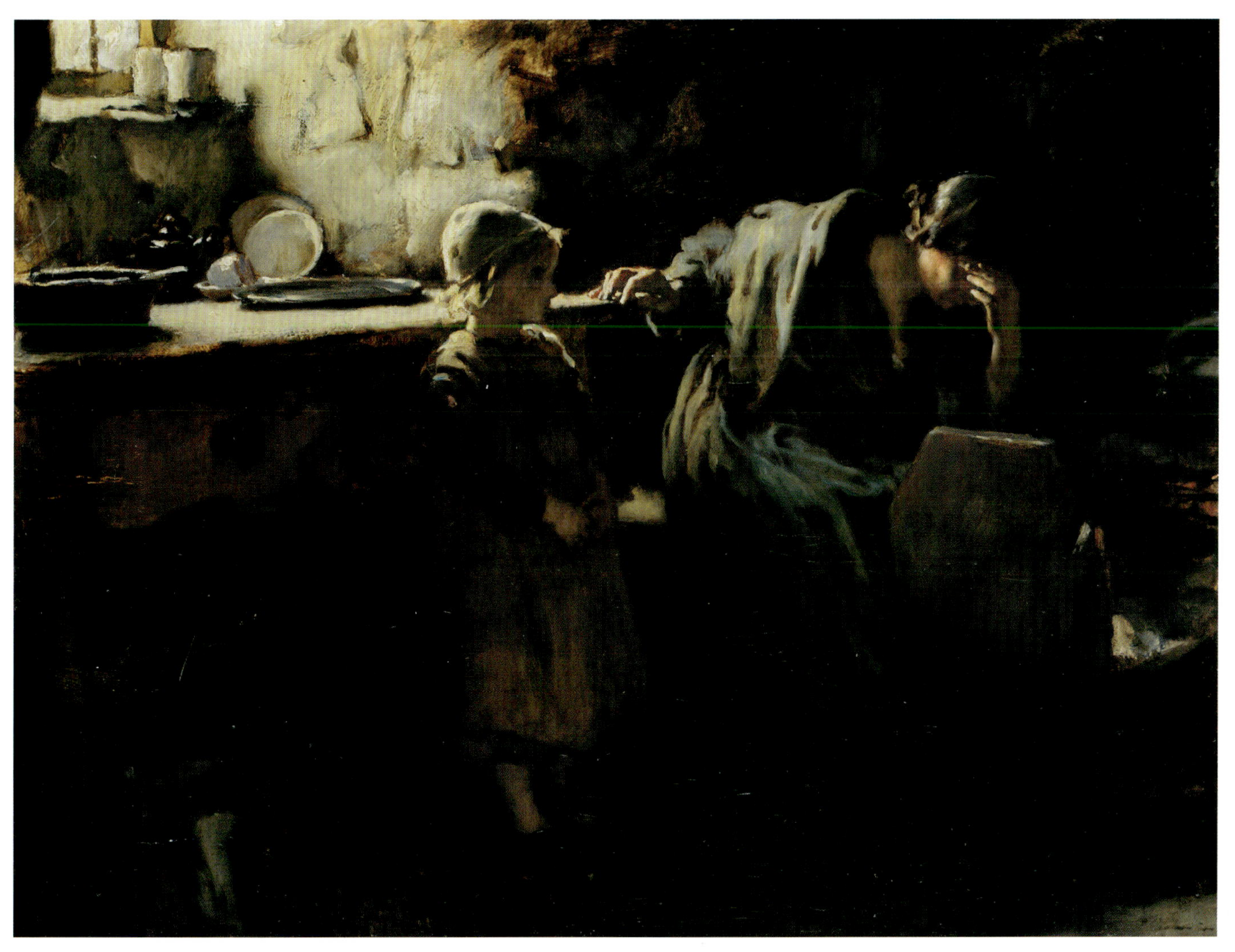

14. *Gone*

*c.*1877
Oil on canvas, 78.1 x 55.9 cm
Signed lower left: 'Frank Holl'
A reduced version of the prime version (56 x 43 in/142.2 x 109.2 cm, untraced), exhibited at Tooth's Winter Exhibition in 1877 (102) and R.A. Winter 1889 (235)
Exhibitions: *Autumn Anthology*, Pyms Gallery, London, 1983 (1); *Train Spotting*, Nottingham Art Gallery, 1985; *Hard Times*, Manchester Art Gallery, 1987 (69)
Literature: *Graphic* (engraving), 19 February 1876, pp. 176, 180–1; Reynolds, 147–8, 155; Treuherz 1987, pp. 78–9; [prime version reviews] *The Times*, 29 October 1877, p. 11, 1 December 1877, p. 4; *Morning Post*, 9 November 1877, p. 3; *Graphic*, 10 November 1877, p. 447; *Era*, 18 November, 1877, p. 3; *Art Journal*, 1878, p. 16, 1889, p. 57; Meynell 1880, pp. 188–9
Provenance: Sold to Tooth's, 1877, for £50; Pyms Gallery, 1983, sold to Geffrye Museum in 1984
Collection: Geffrye Museum, London

Gone was first conceived by Holl as a drawing for a print in *The Graphic* that appeared on 19 February 1876 as '"Gone" – Euston Station'. The wood engraving, subtitled 'Departure of emigrants, 9.15 pm. Train for Liverpool, September, 1875', emphasizes that although this is a familiar and generic scene at London's many termini, it is a real event taking place at a specific time and place. The commentary that accompanies the print highlights the poverty of those saying goodbye and notes that they were unlikely to see their loved ones again: 'The comparatively well-to-do classes who go to India or the Colonies generally hope and intend to return home again, but, to the poor the parting is generally for ever – as far as this life is concerned.'[56]

It is a powerful and emotive image, and one that particularly struck Vincent van Gogh, who referred to the wood engraving in four of his letters. He was particularly fascinated by the central female figure looking at the child she holds in her arms.[57] Van Gogh referred to the image consistently as 'Irish emigrants', and in the exhibition *Hard Times* it was assumed that the emigrants were Ireland bound, although neither *The Graphic* commentary nor the artist's daughter makes this link. Such emigration would be highly unlikely, as most emigrants travelled to Liverpool for an Atlantic crossing to find employment and a new life. Most contemporary commentaries agree that this was the subject, including the *Morning Post* who interpreted the narrative as showing the effects of 'the father of a poor English family,' who 'has "gone" to a distant colony in the hope of finding there the property he has sought in vain at home'.[58]

The scene depicts a platform on Euston Station just after the 9.15 pm to Liverpool has departed, where the remaining members of the family are grieving the departure of their father and son. The effects of loss, a consistent theme in Holl's work, is here played out at Euston station in the central figures: 'Death and absence', noted the *Morning Post*, 'differ but in name.'[59] The setting is all the more real and dramatic for being at a railway station at night. 'We may observe in conclusion', commented *The Graphic* in its commentary about the print, 'that our artist has endeavoured, and has, we think, succeeded in his endeavour, to represent, the misty steamy appearance which railway platforms present, particularly at night, when trains go out.'[60]

Holl had spent the summer of 1877 at Criccieth in Wales and on his return to London he worked on a painting from his drawing of 'Gone' that had appeared in *The Graphic*. It was sold to the dealers Messrs Arthur Tooth for £400 and was shown at their winter exhibition for that year.[61] Despite its appearance at this exhibition, rather than the Royal Academy, the work was widely and well reviewed, most critics seeing it as the picture of the show. 'There is one work,' wrote a review, 'which for gravity of intention and thoroughness of working-out deserves a place apart from its companions.'[62] Although Holl was often criticized for his sombre palette, all critics agreed that in this case the subdued colour and 'no unnecessary accessories' made the work powerful and evocative of the place and the sentiment expressed. *The Era* found 'great vigour and boldness' in Holl's handling of the painting, 'while the story is told with much clearness'.[63] MB

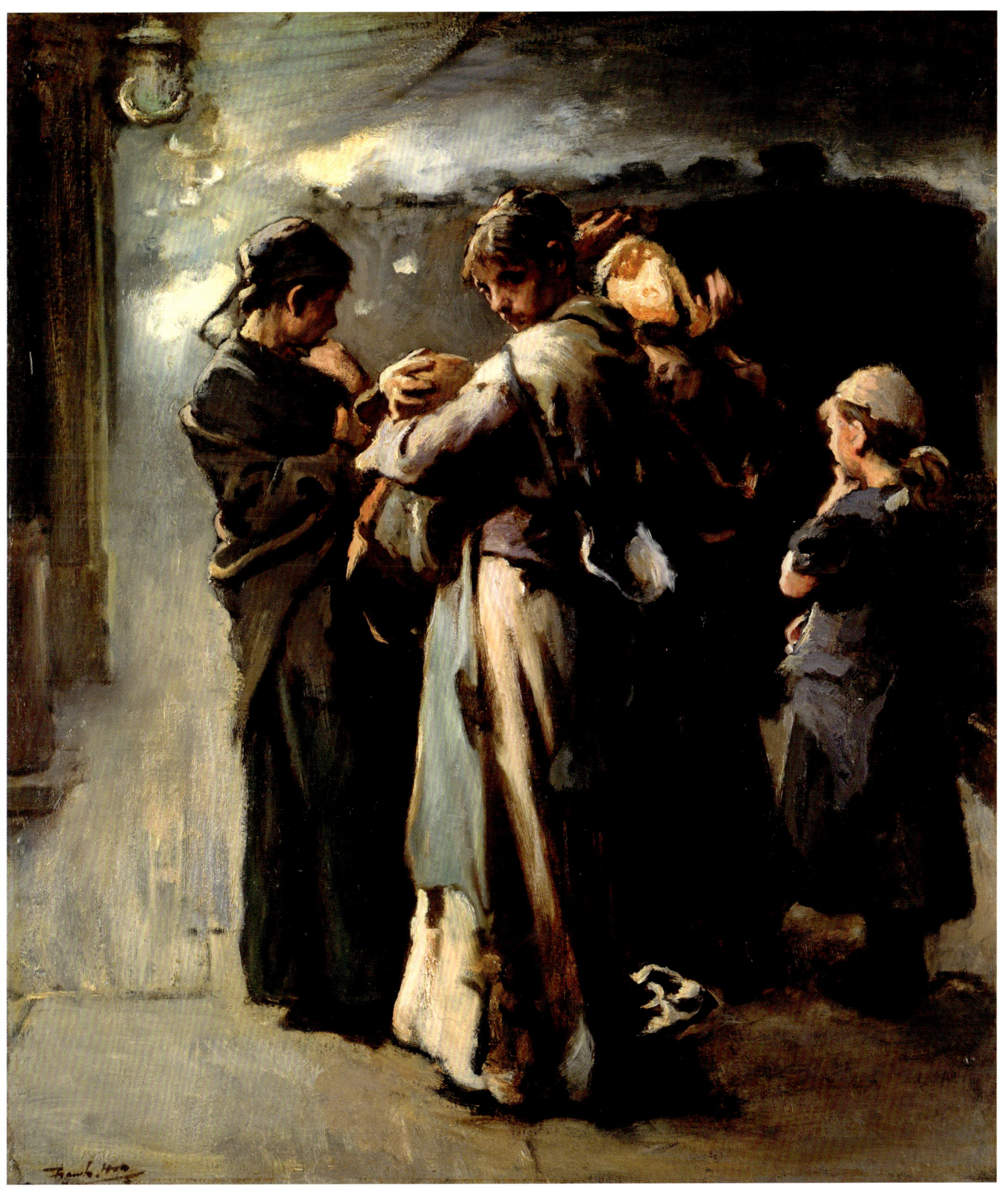

15. *Newgate, Committed for Trial*

1878
Oil on canvas, 152.3 x 210.7 cm
Signed and dated; 'Frank Holl 1878'
Exhibitions: R.A. 1878 (423); R.A. Winter 1889 (221); R.A. Bicentenary 1968 (317); *Thomas Holloway: The Benevolent Millionaire*, Agnews, London 1981 (17); *Hard Times*, Manchester Art Gallery, 1987 (73); *Paintings from the Reign of Queen Victoria*, US tour, 2008–9 (5)
Literature: *Examiner*, 4 May 1878, p. 568; *The Leeds Mercury*, 4 May, 1878, p. 12; *Reynolds's Newspaper*, 5 May, 1878, p. 1; *Saturday Review*, 11 May 1878, p. 592; *Academy*, 25 May 1878, p. 470; *Spectator*, 8 June 1878, p. 730; *Art Journal*, 1878, p. 168; *Illustrated London News*, 1878, p. 459; *Magazine of Art*, 1883, pp. 100 (illus. opp), 172–3; Reynolds, pp. 144–6; Chapel 1982, pp. 96–7; Mary Cowling, *Paintings from the Reign of Queen Victoria*, Alexandria, Virginia 2008, pp. 66–7
Provenance: Bought from the artist by Edward Hermon MP, Wyfold Court, Henley on Thames; his sale Christie's, 13 May 1882 (60); bought Martin for Thomas Holloway for £808 10s
Collection: Royal Holloway, University of London

Newgate, Committed for Trial, was considered one of Holl's greatest achievements and certainly in scale and execution it is the most ambitious and arguably most successful of his metropolitan paintings, depicting the unfortunate lives of those incarcerated in one of London's most infamous institutions, Newgate Prison. Standing where the Old Bailey now is, Newgate was a well-known sight in London, where executions took place and infamous prisoners lodged. It inspired writing and painting and the 'Newgate novel' was a whole genre of underworld fiction. Dickens had famously written about it in his *Sketches by Boz*, and Henrietta Ward's painting *Newgate, 1818*, depicting Elizabeth Fry visiting female prisoners there and exhibited at the 1876 Royal Academy Exhibition, must have been known to Holl.

Holl had an introduction to Newgate through his association with Mr Sidney Robert Smith, who was governor of the prison. He appears to have visited in the mid-1870s, but it is not clear exactly when or how many times he went there. The idea for the painting was in gestation for a few years and, according to his fellow artist, Charles Edward Johnson (1832–1913), he made several visits and actually gained permission to paint in the prison. Johnson, a neighbour of Holl, had made regular trips with Holl to the East End of London in search of subjects for his metropolitan paintings and drawings for *The Graphic*. He recalled that 'when he was intending to paint the Newgate picture, he managed to obtain all the materials at the prison itself, where, through influence at headquarters, he was allowed to paint. Once I went with him, and were shown all over the place, even to the condemned cell.'[64]

Holl also later wrote in detail about the painting, the place within the prison that the painting is set, 'the cage', and the vivid impression that it made on his mind:

> the part of Newgate prison, called the cage – in which prisoners whilst on trial are permitted at certain hours & on certain days, to see their friends – on the inner side the prisoners are placed, & in the passage – their friends are conducted to them when their relations or friends are at once brought out – A warden walks between the 2 gratings, who can hear and see everything that takes place between the friend & prisoner – It is particularly impressive for scenes of such pathos & agony of mind on both sides took place ... I witnessed this scene some years before I painted the picture – visiting the prison through the interest of the then Governor & I shall never forget the impression made upon me ... Prisoners of all sorts of crime were there – the lowest brutal criminal – swindlers, forgers, & boy thieves – all caged together, awaiting the results of their separate trials, & in one or two cases, the misery of their friends in seeing them in this hopeless condition, fell but lightly on their brains dulled by incessant crime.[65]

Like most of his major subject paintings, *Newgate* was inspired by a real incident, and Holl's daughter recalls in her biography of her father that he observed the meeting between the wife and her imprisoned husband. He is described as

> a young man of good family ... who had filled a trusted position in one of the largest and most important banking houses ... He had been tempted to misappropriate a very large sum of money ... was arrested, tried, and sentenced to five years' penal servitude.[66]

The incident sparked the idea for the painting although it evolved over a few years and

> he altered the main idea somewhat, and instead of the scene which had suggested the painting of the picture, feeling dissatisfied with it as being too melodramatic, it ended by degrees in making the principal group a poor woman with her baby and little girl, leaning against the railing dividing her from the brute who had probably half killed her

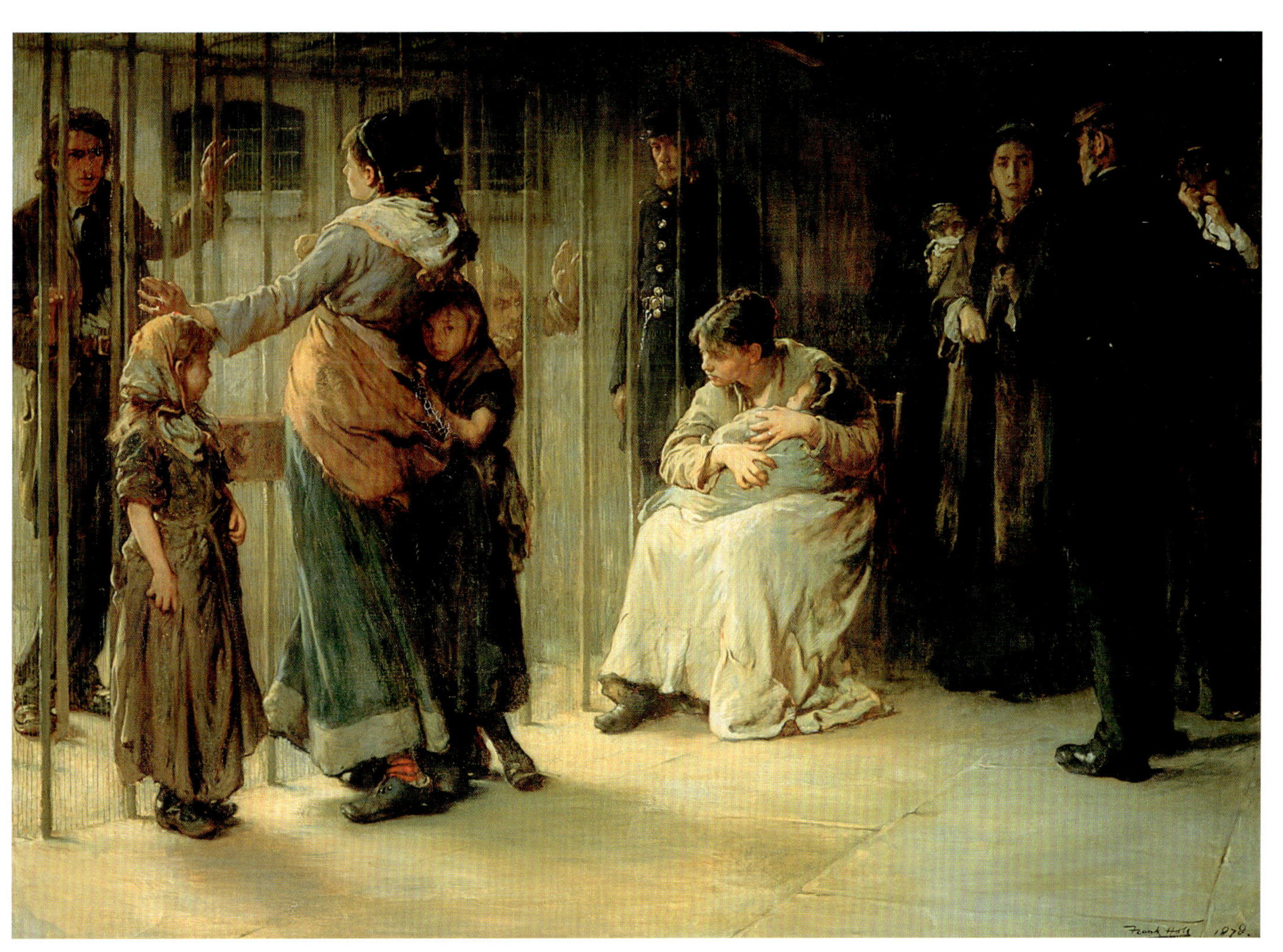
Frank Holl 1878.

before doing the deed which took him to a safeguarded asylum between the walls of Newgate, and released his wife from a life of martyrdom at the hands of the big, burly bully.[67]

If the creation of the painting followed that of his other major works, Johnson's account that he would have painted within the prison is likely to be true. What he would not have been allowed to do is capture the likenesses of prisoners, which was banned because they may have been recognized when the painting was finished and exhibited. Holl very often made sketches of the background, such as in his fishing cottage interiors and his funeral scenes, so it is likely that he sketched 'the cage' for this painting. The painting – even if most likely done using his favoured models – succeeds in showing the variety of criminal character that he observed, from white-collar crime to brutal domestic violence, although our sympathy, as with most of Holl's paintings, is with the women left behind.

The painting was an enormous success and secured his election as an Associate of the Royal Academy. Like most of Holl's subject paintings, critics praised with reservation: 'a most powerful and pathetic but irrepressibly dismal picture', wrote the *Illustrated London News*, although it went on to remark that 'Mr Holl's picture is so technically excellent as to deserve the honours of either engraving on steel or on wood ... the very highest praise that is within our power to bestow for the fidelity and assiduity which he displayed'.[68] In contrast, *the Examiner* was openly against both such a realistic approach to the subject as well as the subject itself: 'Unless a painter can satisfy the eyes with beauty, we know of no reason why he should be a painter at all, or why he should not relate his story in another way.'[69]

Undoubtedly, it was seen as an important work but divided critics who asked if such paintings, which often opened a window into tragic lives, treated subjects fit for art. As a work of social realism, it is one of the most significant painted in Britain.

There is a larger version in Rochdale Art Gallery, and a smaller version, painted for his friend and patron Henry Hill (private collection). MB

16. *Paul Falconer Poole, R.A.* (1807–1879)

1879
Oil on canvas, 61 x 50.8 cm
Inscribed lower right: 'Portrait of P.F. Poole R.A. / 2 hours sketch / F.H. 1879'
Exhibitions: R.A. Winter 1884 (299)
Literature: Ormond 1973, p. 382
Provenance: The artist; by descent to his younger brother's widow, Mrs Edgar Holl, by whom given to the National Portrait Gallery, 1932
Collection: National Portrait Gallery, London. Given by Mrs Edgar Holl, 1932

The painter Paul Falconer Poole was born the son of a Bristol coal merchant and appears to have been largely self-taught. His father sent him to Italy in the winter of 1828–9, when he was able to visit the Louvre en route and study paintings in Genoa, Milan, Florence, Rome and Naples. Returning to Bristol, Poole formed a relationship with the wife of the artist Francis Danby, Hannah, thirteen years his senior. The two were to marry after Danby's death in 1861. The original staple of Poole's practice as a painter comprised scenes of peasant girls and their children posed in landscape settings. But with his history painting of *Solomon Eagle Exhorting the people to Repentance during the Plague of the Year 1665* (Museums Sheffield), exhibited at the 1843 Royal Academy, Poole struck out in new and more ambitious ways. He continued to paint and exhibit similar historical works up to the mid-1870s, each characterized by dramatic compositions, exaggerated bodily forms and an idiosyncratic use of colour. *The Death of Cordelia* of 1858 in the V&A is an example of the latter. Poole became an A.R.A. in 1846 and full Academician in 1861.

Although settled in London from at least 1837, Poole also had a country home next door to Holl's father's in Elstead Surrey. Reynolds recalled Paul and Hannah Poole and how they and her grandparents 'were very devoted to each other, incessantly in and out of each other's houses, with evenings spent together over bézique or backgammon, or occasionally chess.[70] Painted in 1879, the year of Poole's death, Holl's sketch portrait is clearly the result of this close family friendship. The year 1879 was also when Holl first moved into portraiture, and this can be seen as an experimental work using a close associate as his subject. Its interest further stems from its unfinished appearance with its unusual combination of blues and yellows in the flesh tones, something that is less apparent but still present in later, finished works.

Holl's inscription that it was a '2 hours sketch' also

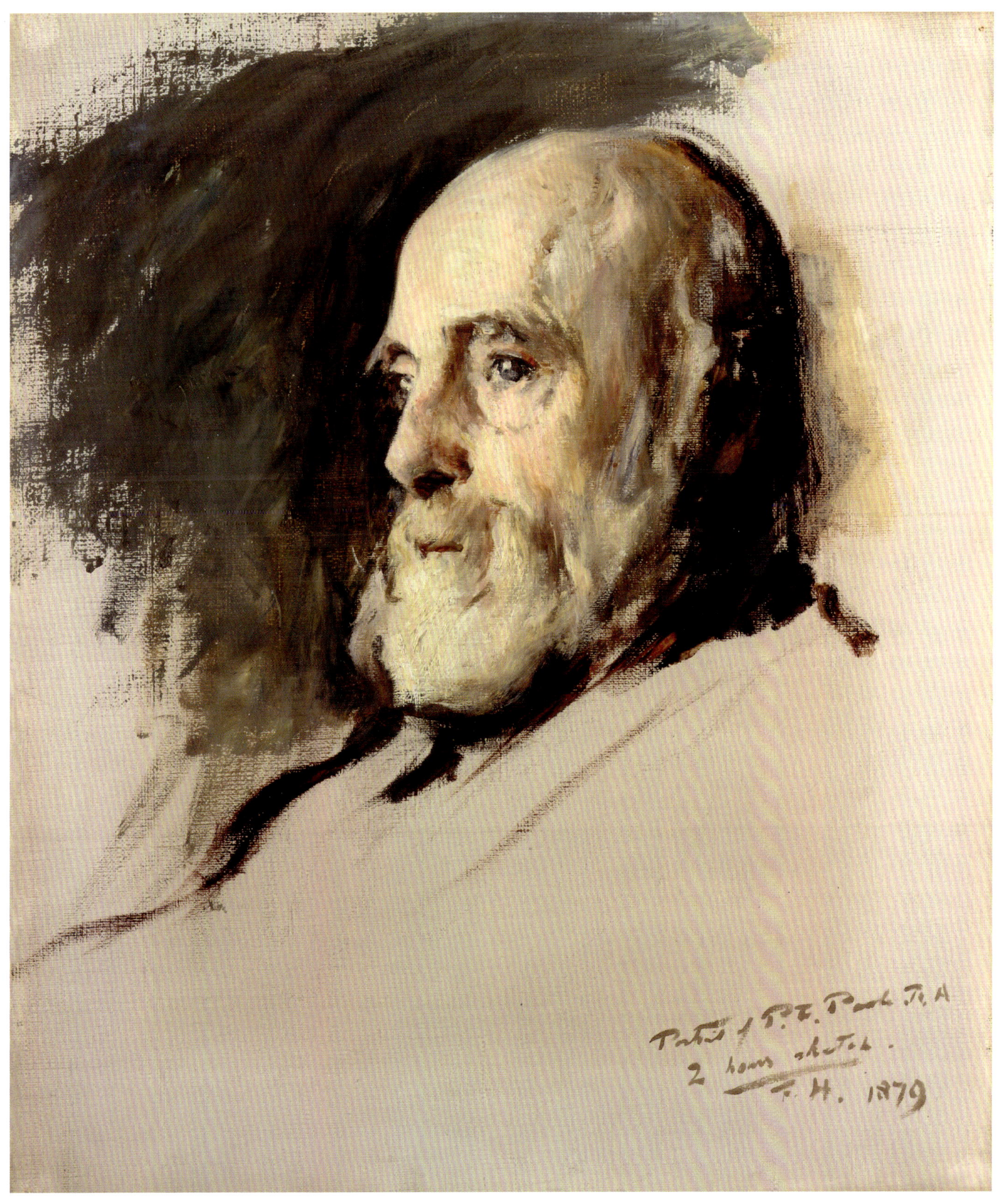
2 hours sketch.
F.H. 1879

indicates its experimental nature and that Holl was engaged in a practice fashionable at the time of rapidly painting portraits. A portrait of his mother of 1882 (Tate) is also recorded as having been done in two hours. The most direct influence would have been the French-born artist Alphonse Legros (1837–1911), who had been Professor at the Slade School of Fine Art since 1876. Among Legros's innovations in the teaching at the Slade were his 'demonstration heads', portrait heads painted with great panache in under two hours. So popular were Legros's performances making these portraits that he went on two tours in 1879–80 giving demonstrations before invited audiences in Sunderland, Manchester, Aberdeen and Liverpool, precisely at the time that Holl did his two-hour sketch of Poole. Similar exercises in painting portraits quickly are also recorded around this time in the work of Holl's future neighbour, John Pettie.[71]

Holl's sketch of Poole was exhibited at Poole's Memorial exhibition at the 1884 Winter R.A.. It is one of three portraits given to the National Portrait Gallery by Mrs Edgar Holl in 1932: the others are Holl's early self-portrait (cat. 3) and his portrait of his father (cat. 25). PF

17. *Samuel Cousins, R.A.* (1801–1887)

1879
Oil on canvas, 127 x 101 cm
Signed and dated bottom right: 'Frank Holl 1879'
Exhibitions: R.A. 1879 (189); Edinburgh, Royal Scottish Academy 1882 (116); Manchester Jubilee, 1887 (413); R.A. Old Masters, 1901 (64); Royal Society of Portrait Painters, London, 1907 (32) and 1925 (56)
Literature: *Art Journal*, 1879, p. 128; *World*, 1879, p. 442; *Athenaeum*, 7 June 1879, p. 734; Meynell 1880, p. 190; *Art Journal*, 1882, p. 93; *The Times*, 8 March 1882, p. 56; Spielmann 1888a, p. 693; *The Times*, 1 August 1888, p. 10; Campbell 1889, p. 57; Alfred Whitman, *Samuel Cousins*, London 1904, frontispiece and p. 26 (NPG drawing); Reynolds, pp. 155–9, 191; Ormond 1973, p. 118 (NPG drawing)
Engraved: C. Waltner (etching), pub. T. Agnew & Sons, 1881
Provenance: The artist; presented by his widow to Tate, 1925
Collection: Tate

Painted and exhibited in 1879, Holl's portrait of the engraver Samuel Cousins is regarded as marking his decisive move into portrait painting. According to Reynolds, the Cousins portrait was suggested by Holl's father, Francis, while Spielmann records that it was the idea of the veteran Academician, John Prescott Knight.[72] Holl's earliest portraits were all of those he knew well: the sketch of Paul Falconer Poole (cat. 16) and a portrait of the cellist Alfredo Piatti, which he exhibited with the Cousins portrait at the 1879 Royal Academy. The choice of Cousins was in many ways an obvious one. He was, Reynolds says, 'a very old friend' of Holl's father – the most distinguished engraver of the period, who would have been extremely well known to and respected by the Holl family of engravers going back to Frank Holl's great-grandfather, William Holl. They also resided near to each other in Regent's Park and Camden Town in north London. Reynolds says that Holl initially resisted the suggestion of painting Cousins but, having resolved to do so, tackled Cousins on the subject – and he was 'by no means an easy character' she says – on a visit to his house in Camden Square. After half an hour Holl emerged 'with the reluctant consent of "the old bear" ... to give him a few sittings for what he called "his ugly old mug"'.[73]

Born in Exeter, Cousins showed early ability at drawing and an example of his work when not yet ten years old received the award of a silver palette at the Society of Arts in London in 1811. A further drawing the following year was noticed by the leading mezzotint engraver, Samuel William Reynolds, who in autumn 1814 took Cousins on as an apprentice. Cousins subsequently worked for four years as Reynolds's assistant, contributing to his great series of prints after Sir Joshua Reynolds produced between 1820 and 1825. In 1826 Cousins set up on his own and his career was settled when he became the principal engraver after Sir Thomas Lawrence, producing a total of thirty-three plates after Lawrence's portraits in the following years. These included such popular engravings as *Master Lampton* published in 1827. But it was the commercial success of his engravings after Victorian artists such as Edwin Landseer and John Everett Millais that secured his prominent place in the art world and led to honours and wealth. He was, exceptionally for an engraver, made a full Royal Academician in 1855, while in 1879 he was able to command a fee of no less than 1,600 guineas for engraving Millais's *Princes in the Tower*.[74] Cousins was conscious of his significance as a reproductive engraver and gave to the British Museum, in January and March 1872, an almost

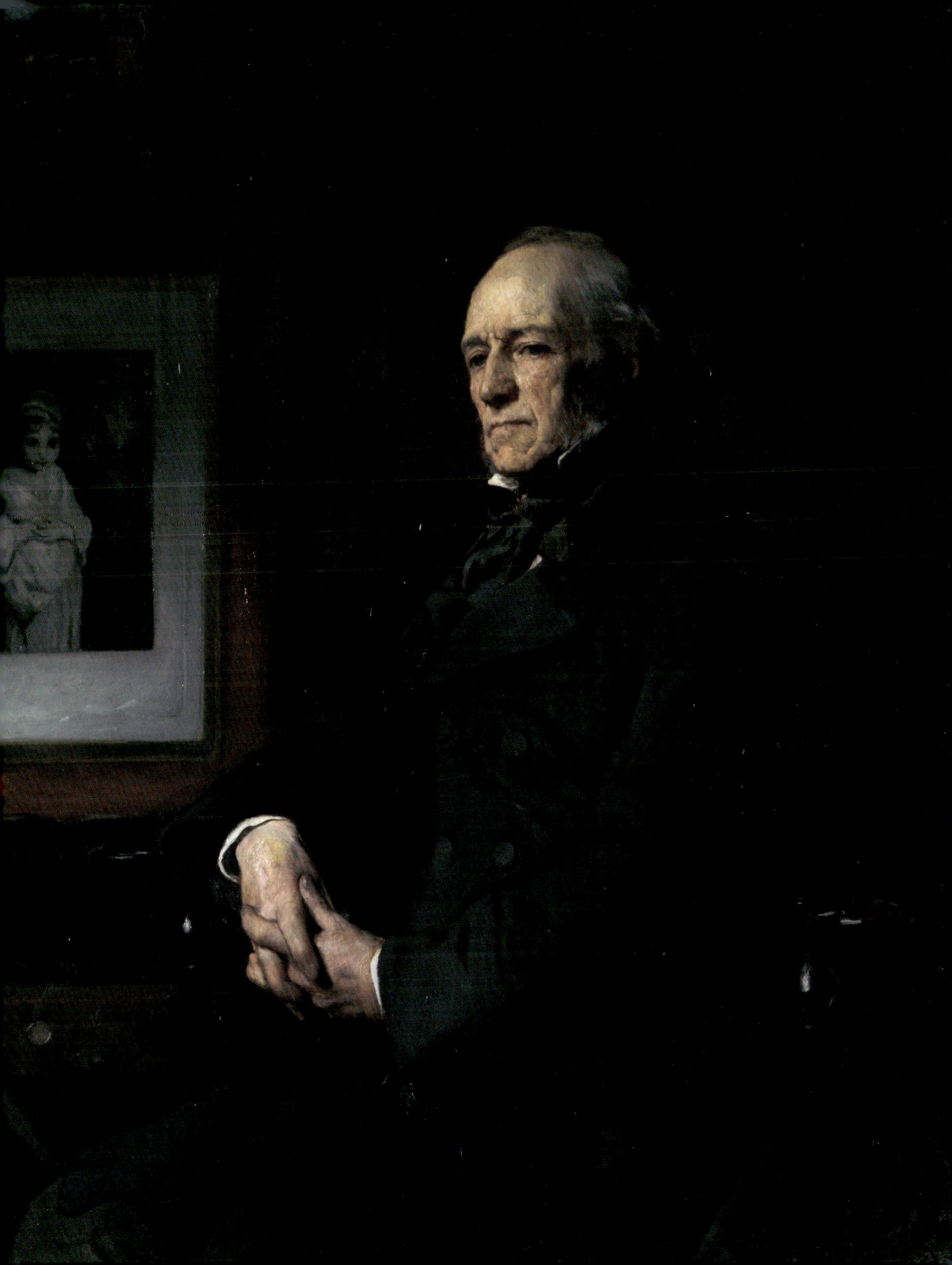

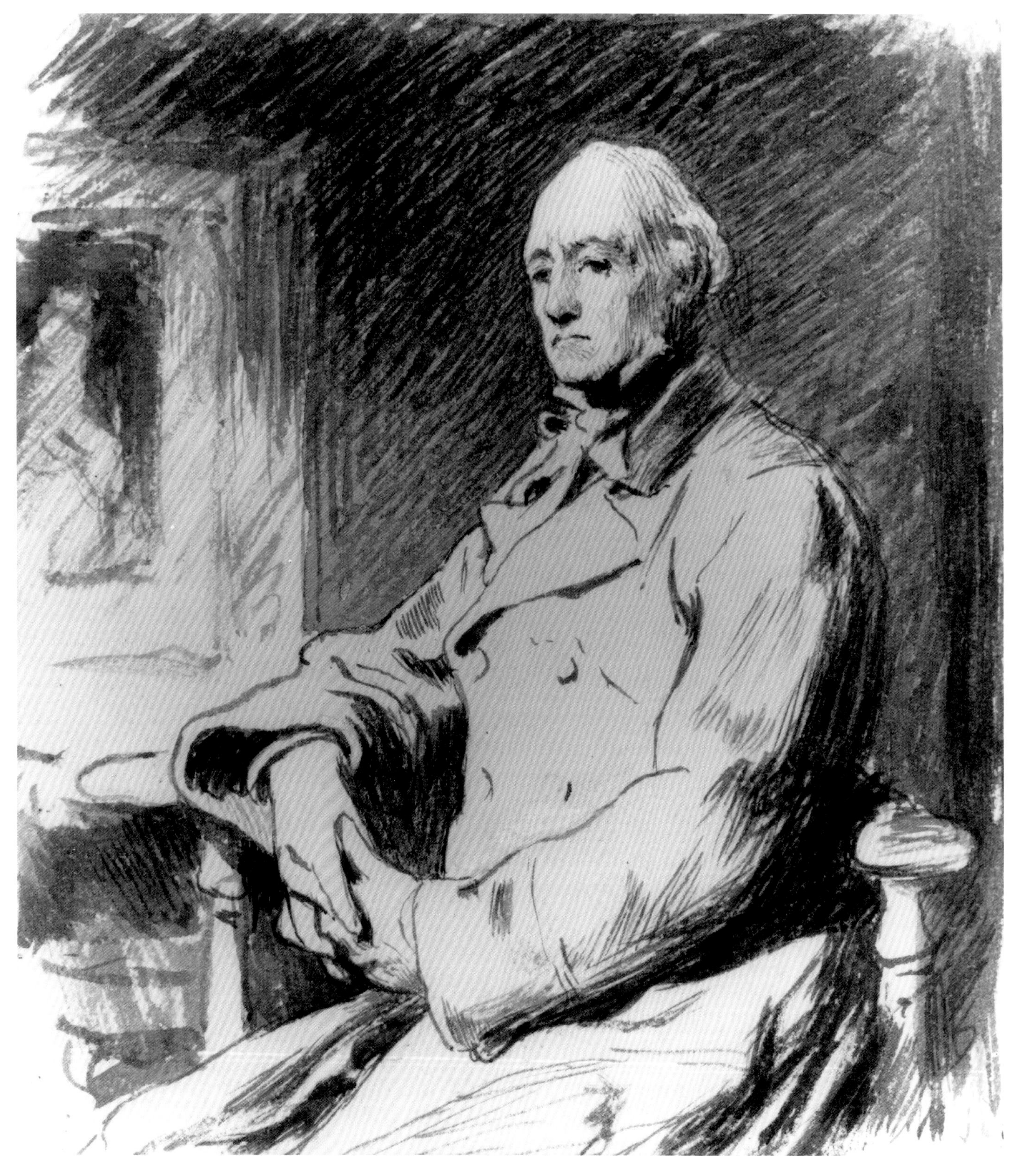

Fig. 62. Frank Holl, *Samuel Cousins*, 1879, pen and wash.

complete set of his works with the intention of retiring. But the revival of interest in Sir Joshua Reynolds's portraits after the R.A. Winter Exhibition of 1870 led to a secondary career producing prints after Reynolds's works. One of the most celebrated of these engravings, after Reynolds's *The Strawberry Girl*, published by Agnews on 1 May 1873, can be seen in the background of Holl's portrait.

Reviews of Holl's portrait were highly favourable. The *Art Journal* called it 'one of his finest portraits' when exhibited at the 1879 Academy and, when it was shown in 1882 at the Royal Scottish Academy, asserted that the painting 'firmly and distinctively exerts its power'.[75] *The Athenaeum* thought it 'a grave piece of work, full of character, an admirable likeness',[76] while Reynolds cites other reviews of high praise. It is variously called 'a superb work, glowing, for all the austerity of its execution, with animation and intelligence' and, elsewhere, 'extremely powerful in effect'. The critic Tom Taylor likewise thought it 'an admirable portrait, true as a likeness, full of individual character'.[77] Wilfrid Meynell in his 1880 profile of Holl noted that 'in the head of the venerable engraver he produced indeed what all must acknowledge as vital work; technically it was a masterpiece of handling'.[78] The portrait continued to be praised after Holl's death. His *Times* obituary noted that 'the impression which that portrait made is still fresh in the recollection of many', while Gertrude E. Campbell, reviewing Holl's 1889 Winter Academy retrospective, commented that it was one of Holl's 'very finest works' and regretted that, oddly, it had not been included in the memorial exhibition.[79]

A drawing in the National Portrait Gallery's collection (fig. 62) is usually thought to have been a preparatory study for the Tate's oil portrait.[80] But Cousins's biographer, Alfred Whitman, who reproduces the drawing as his frontispiece, is unambivalent as to why it was made, writing that it was 'from' the portrait and that 'it was executed as an illustration to Henry Blackburn's "Academy Notes"'.[81] Comparison of the drawing with the engraving in Blackburn's *Notes* – popular illustrated records of the annual exhibition – suggests that this was the case and it would have been supplied by Holl for this purpose. Like others, Blackburn noted that the Cousins's portrait was 'one of the finest in the exhibition'.[82] PF

18. *Major George Graham* (1801–1888) (ill. Page 138)

1880
Oil on canvas, 138.5 x 112.5 cm
Signed and dated bottom right: 'Frank Holl / 1880'
Exhibitions: R.A. 1880 (302)
Literature: *Graphic*, 22 May 1880, p. 518; *Newcastle Courant*, 23 December 1887; Reynolds, p. 174
Provenance: The sitter; ?by descent to Mrs Patrick Poer O'Shee by whom sold at Christies 20 December 1957 (lot 22) when purchased by H.M. Government
Collection: Government Art Collection

George Graham was Registrar General for England and Wales. Born into a leading landed family in Cumberland, Graham was a younger brother of the Peelite Home Secretary, Sir James Graham (1792–1861). Having served in the East India Company, George acted as his brother's private secretary and was appointed by him to the post of Registrar General in 1842. Although an example of nepotism common at the time, George proved himself to be an exceptionally able administrator during a term in office that lasted until 1879.

The General Register Office had been established in 1837 to administer the civil registration of births, marriages and deaths and, from 1841, was responsible for the censuses undertaken every ten years. The GRO became a key organization in the apparatus of Victorian public life partly through the work of Graham's colleague, William Farr (1807–1883), whose analyses of the cause of death among the population were crucial for the development of public health administration. But although Farr's achievements have tended to eclipse Graham's, current opinion has judged Graham's work to be crucial in turning around the fortunes of the GRO in its early days and making it a highly successful body within government.[83] It was Graham who attended to the day-to-day administration of the GRO, managing staff and budgets and liaising with central and local government departments. Graham was also responsible for the detailed organization of the censuses from 1851 to 1871, and the prospect of again undertaking this arduous task is said to have made him step down in advance of the 1881 census.

As recorded on its frame, Holl's portrait was made for presentation to Graham 'on his retirement from office

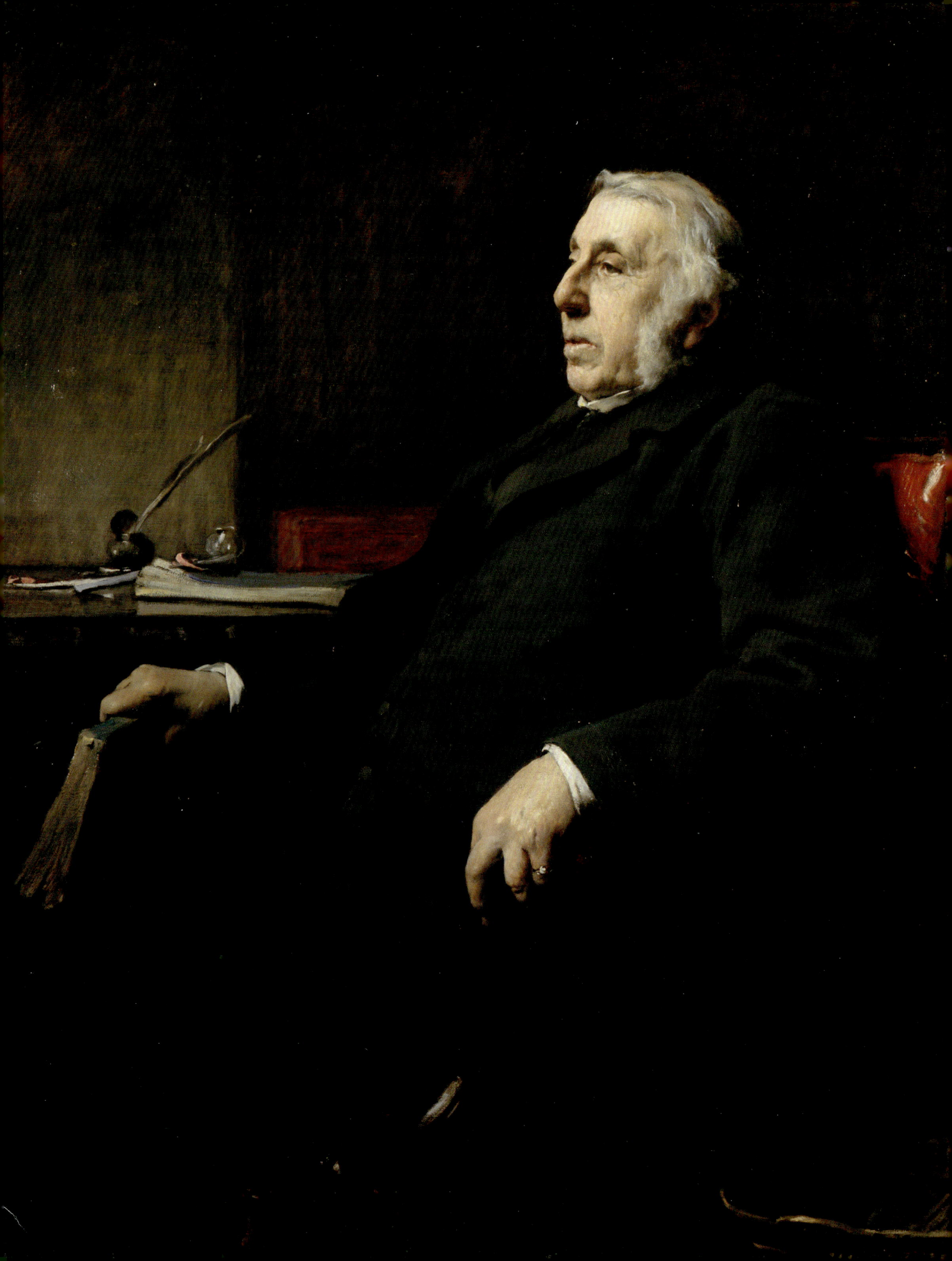

by the Central and Local Officers of the Registration Department, as a token of their respect and esteem'. Reynolds recalled that Graham 'proved to be a most charming and entertaining old man, and an excellent sitter, who could while away the time most delightfully with his numerous interesting reminiscences.[84] As was often the case with Holl's subjects, sittings appear to have engendered friendship and Graham is recorded to have given him an engraving of 'The Royal Academy of 1787' that hung in the vestibule of his Hampstead house.[85] The *Graphic* praised the portrait at the 1880 R.A. along with that of the lawyer and gas industrialist, Simon Adams Beck, as displaying 'a rare power, not only of seizing the salient traits of his sitters, but of realising their essential character as far as it is impressed on their outward features', though it also criticizes the portraits for being 'unnecessarily cold in tone'.[86]

Like Holl's portrait of Samuel Cousins of the previous year (cat. 17), that of Graham is a remarkable study of old age. It is also shows a similar attention to detail in evoking an office setting and a life that was particularly burdened with paperwork. Pen, ink and papers are on the table behind Graham and there is a waste-paper basket in the bottom-right corner. Also on the table and grasped in Graham's right hand are copies of the 'Blue Books', or the GRO's Annual Reports. This is appropriate since it would have been through his commentaries on the state of society based on the data in the reports that Graham would have been best known. As Muriel Nissel has written, 'George Graham's Annual Reports, particularly during the 1870s, included social comments on a wide variety of topics such as the prices of meat and cereals, the number of cattle and sheep, the supply of gold and the number of paupers receiving poor relief.'[87] Other subjects Graham ranged over included recommendations on the national diet, weather reports, the number of wills, the amount of property exchanged and, in 1873, a table recording road accidents in London.

Holl's portrait remained in Graham's family until it was purchased by the government at Christie's on 20 December 1957 on the recommendation of Richard Walker and David Piper to hang in Graham's old place of work, Somerset House.[88] PF

19. *Ordered to the Front* (ill. Page 140)

1880
Oil on canvas, 75 x 64 cm
Signed and dated: 'Frank Holl 1880'
A reduced replica of the 1880 Royal Academy-exhibited painting, 1880 (52½ x 42½ in/133.4 x 108 cm, untraced), bought by the dealer Thomas McLean for 500 guineas and sold to Sir Thomas Lucas (1822–1902), who commissioned the sequel, *Home Again*[89]
Exhibitions (prime version): R.A. 1880 (366); R.A. Winter 1889 (195)
Literature: *The Graphic* (engraving 'Summoned for Active Service') 11 January, 1879, pp. 32–3, 36 (article); [prime version reviews] *Art Journal* 1880, p. 187, p. 219; *Athenaeum*, 1 May 1880, p. 573; *Era*, 9 May 1880, p. 3; *Fun*, 12 May 1880, p. 188; *Magazine of Art*, 1880, p. 348; *Morning Post*, 1 May 1880, p. 6, and 7 May, p. 5; William Gilbert, *The Royal Cornwall Gazette Falmouth Packet, Cornish Weekly News, & General Advertiser*, 4 June 1880, p. 6; Reynolds, p. 173
Provenance: Possibly the Bradford collector Mark Stainsby; Walsall Art Gallery
Collection: Walsall Art Gallery

Ordered to the Front began as an illustration in *The Graphic* entitled 'Summoned for Active Service' in 1879.[90] Its subject is war or, more specifically, the everyday impact of war on troops and their families. It depicts a detachment of Highland solders saying goodbye to their loved ones. 'Here is the real tragedy of war,' wrote *The Era*, 'more, perhaps, than on the battlefield itself.'[91] Mothers, wives, sweethearts and children are in various states of anxiety, in contrast to the Highlanders who are putting on a brave face. The accompanying text that appeared beside it in the magazine reiterates Holl's depiction:

> He [the soldier] is aware that every bullet has its billet, but 'Hope springs eternal in the human breast,' and he somehow feels that whatever may happen to others he will be spared.
>
> But with the soldiers' womankind – with his wife, his sweetheart, his poor old mother – it is far otherwise. In their ears the blare of the war-trumpet reverberates with the dismal clang of a funeral knell. Not for them the excitement of the fight; they must stay at home and weep in silence for their departed warrior.[92]

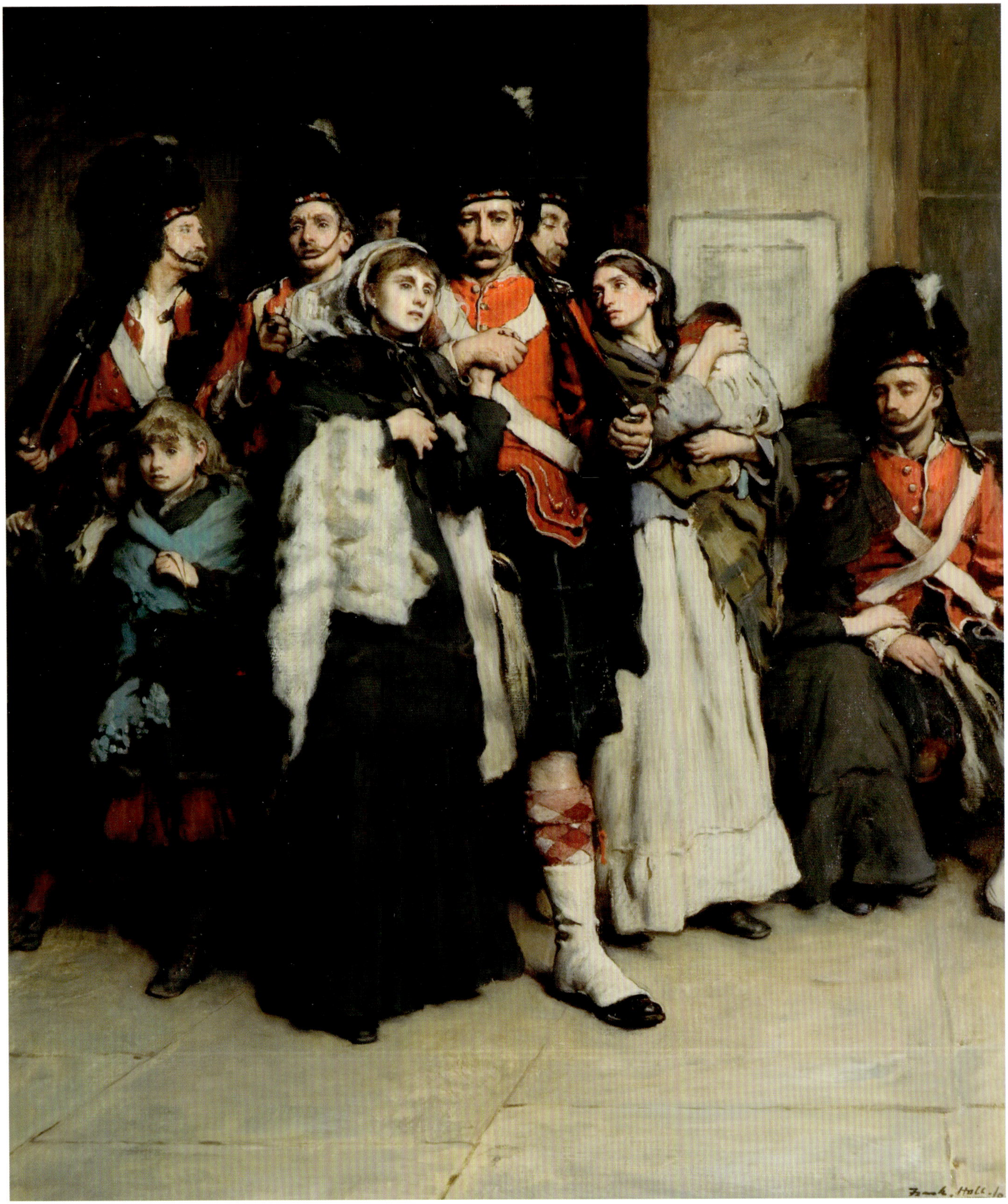

19

Characteristically, *The Graphic* illustration shows legible text on the wall, not visible in the painting, which reads, 'Daily Telegraph The Afghan War', revealing that these are the 72nd Seaforth Highlanders going to fight in the Second Anglo-Afghan War, which was fought between the United Kingdom and Afghanistan from 1878 to 1880.[93]

Holl painted the subject for the 1880 R.A. exhibition, making a few changes to the composition: the young girls to the left have been altered, as have the positions of the mothers and the notice about the Afghan War. The patriotic subject and picturesque dress of the Highlanders were enormously appealing to his audience, and although the painting focuses on Holl's characteristic depiction of the tragedy of loss and parting, the bright colour and brave stoicism of the troops made it a far less bleak image. As William Gilbert observed, it 'still contains a certain element of sadness, but this is kept judiciously in the background, and it detracts but in a very slight degree from the general spirit and vigour of the incident represented'.[94]

As a result the painting was well received at its exhibition, *The Athenaeum* calling it 'a capital specimen' and the *Morning Post* 'one of the greatest in the gallery'. The emotional content, rather than being seen as mawkish or gloomy, was considered touching and worthy: the *Art Journal* wrote that it was as 'touchingly emotional as anything in the exhibition', and the *Morning Post* that 'pathos has seldom been displayed with such touching effect'. The only dissenting voice was that of the *Magazine of Art* which found it 'a little too sentimental and the colour is somewhat black'.

This is a reduced replica of the Royal Academy-exhibited work and was painted in the same year. MB

20. *A Fisherman's Home* (ill. Page 142)

1881
Oil on canvas, 101.6 x 128.3 cm
Signed and dated: 'Frank Holl 1881'
Exhibitions: McLean's Gallery in Haymarket, 1881
Literature: *Art Journal*, 1881, p. 190; *Magazine of Art*, 1881, p. xxvi; Reynolds, p. 191
Provenance: Sold to McLean for £350; gift to the Walker Art Gallery from George Audley, 1925
Collection: Walker Art Gallery

A Fisherman's Home was first exhibited in Thomas McLean's Gallery in Haymarket in 1881. The *Magazine of Art* reviewer considered Holl's painting to be 'the lion of the gallery', sharing this honour with *The Launch* by Jozef Israëls, to whose style of work Holl's is sometimes compared.[95] McLean bought his painting for £350.[96]

The painting was developed from a sketch made during the family's visit to Criccieth in the previous year.[97] In this example, while using the same fisherman's cottage as in other images, Holl makes the fisherman himself the central figure. This change affects the feel of the image. The strong female figural model previously used features as a wife preparing the meal. Although her role appears more incidental, she is also more active in this scene, in comparison to her other images of quiet grief. Here the woman is defined less by the strength of her emotion and more by her practical activity as a wife and mother preparing the meal. She holds in her hands a knife and bread. Her head inclines towards the commanding, rough male figure who gazes beyond the picture's frame. The table is laid and set for one, and the male figure sits beside it fully dressed in his fisherman's attire. A cloak or coat is loosely placed on the seat of the chair to the right of the image. These details suggest that he has just returned from his work, as if following a burst of activity. The young child in the background who directly meets the gaze of the viewer further adds to this sense of energy. The reviewer from the *Magazine of Art* draws particular attention to the presence of the 'child whose bright and delicate expression plays well against the bearded and weather-beaten face of the mariner'.[98]

The light and shade that so often play their own role in Holl's work highlight the diverse elements within the setting: the variety of materials in the fisherman's costume, the metallic shine of the knife, and the light on the rim of the bucket in the bottom-left corner draw the eye of the viewer around the scene. MM

20

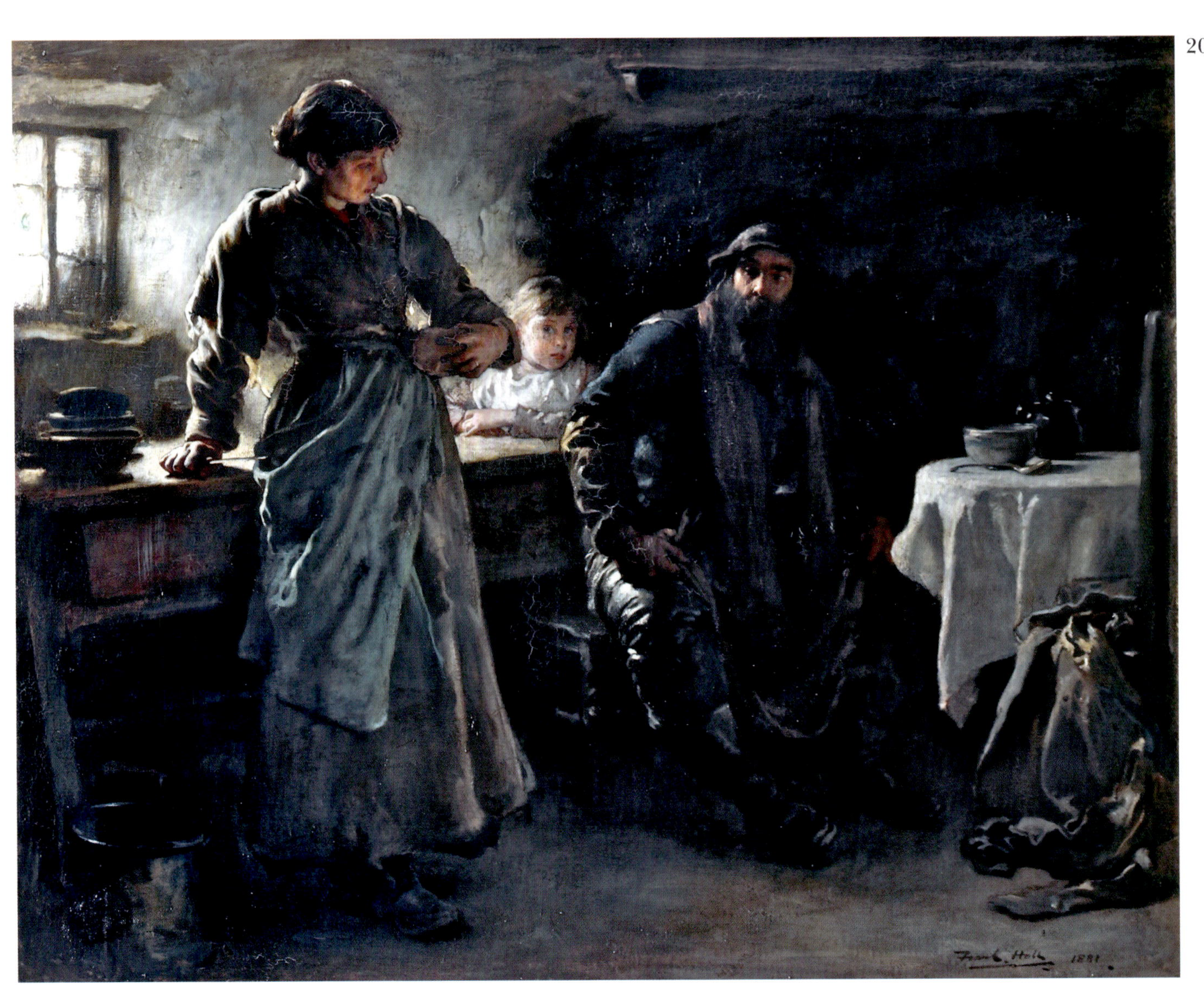

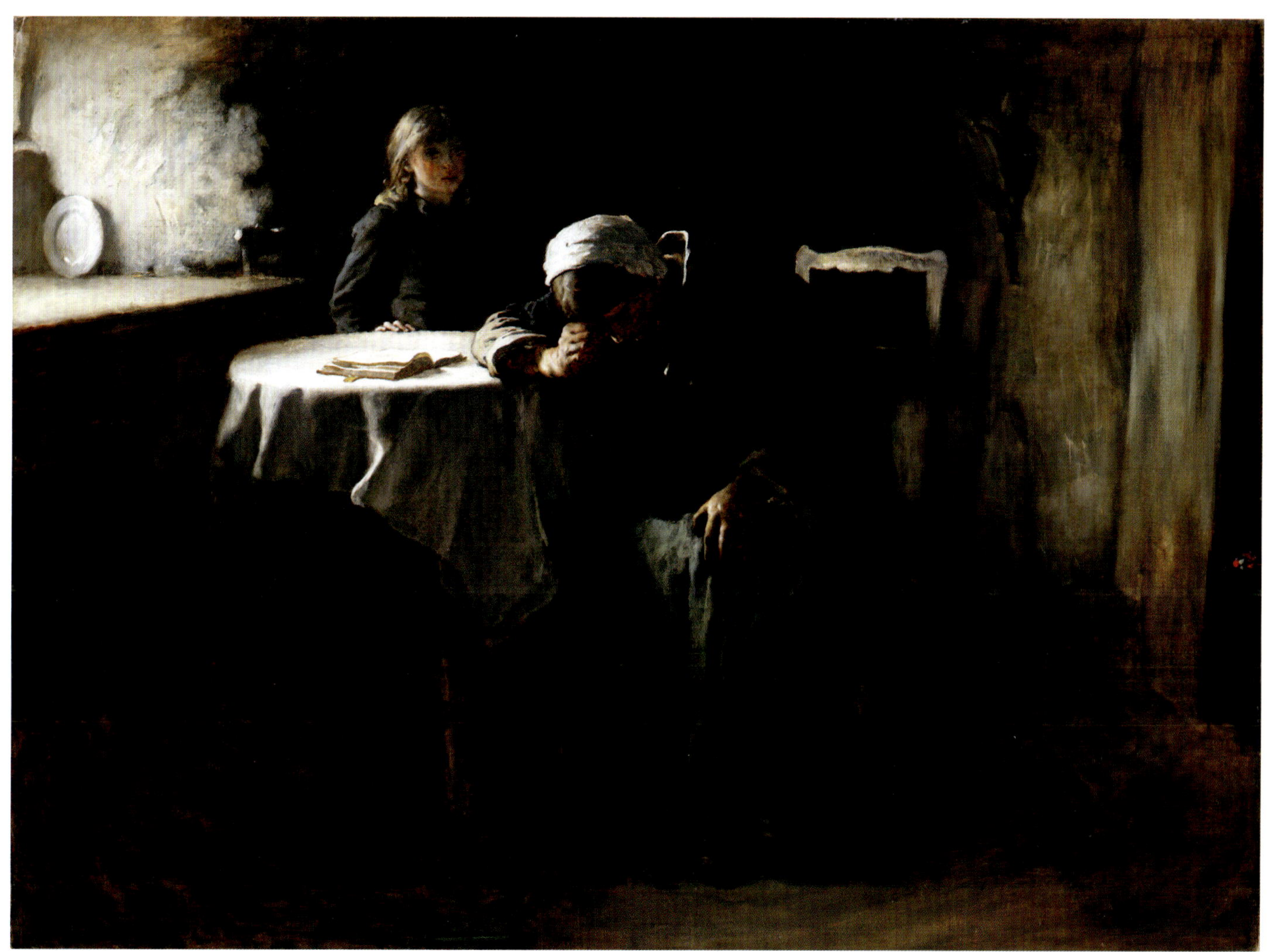

21. *Despair*

1881
Oil on canvas, 84 x 112 cm
Signed and dated bottom left: 'Frank Holl 1881'
Exhibitions: Gallery of Messrs Tooth, 1881
Literature: *Art Journal*, 1881, p. 377; *Athenaeum*, 5 November 1881, p. 603; *Graphic*, 29 April 1882, pp. 418, 436–7
Provenance: F.W. Amsden, Esq., of Lawrie Park, Sydenham, 1882; purchased by Southampton City Art Gallery with the assistance of the Frederick William Smith Bequest Fund, 1936
Collection: Southampton City Art Gallery

In the painting of *Despair* Holl makes heavy use of dark and light, creating a gloomy scene for this depiction of loss. It is bleak and minimalistic and has a figural focus. The details of the room, however, bring the picture to life. A book lies open on the table in front of the woman. The bellows hanging on the wall draw attention to the fire that has gone out, the emptiness of a plate on which the light falls highlighting the lack of food. Holl's painting speaks of the realities of the loss of a husband, the breadwinner of the family, to a fisherman's wife, with the resultant concerns regarding money and food. In the dangerous waters around Criccieth wives would often not know if their husbands would return for days, weeks or at all. This painting considers the implications if they did not return, and is another example of the social realities for a fisherwoman that had so struck Holl during his time in Criccieth.

This image can be linked to *Hushed* (cat. 13) by Holl, though here the scene represents the loss of a husband rather than a child. The misery and tension are reflected in the figure of the child who looks on unsure of what can be done. The child is more aware of the gravity of the situation than in *Hushed*, though there is still a level of confusion. Her hand rests on the table in a move towards her mother. She appears to wish to comfort her and is distressed by the depths of her sorrow. The child is older than the one in the previous work, reflecting the passing of years from Holl's first visit to the cottage.

When first created, the picture was exhibited under the title *Bereaved*, then engraved and used the following year in *The Graphic* on 29 April 1882. The following verse accompanies the image:

By hope unsoothed, by comfort unbeguiled
The widowed mother mourneth o'er her child
Talk not of joys the world may yet confer
That tiny baby was all the world to her.[99]

Critics' assessments ranged from 'lugubrious' and 'pathetic' to the review in the *Art Journal* that described *Bereaved* as 'one of those powerful realisations to which Frank Holl, A.R.A., can lend such pathos'.[100] MM

22. *Captain Alexander Mitchell Sim* (*c.*1787–1882)

1881
Oil on canvas, 125.7 x 100.3 cm
Signed and dated bottom left: 'Frank Holl 1881'
Exhibitions: R.A. 1882 (260); R.A. 1889 (220); Royal Society of Portrait Painters, London, 1907 (28) and 1925 (54)
Literature: *Art Journal*, 1882, p. 210, 1889 p. 58; *Graphic*, 27 May 1882, p. 527; *Athenaeum*, 3 June 1882, p. 705; Reynolds, pp. 193–6, 209; Bertram Stuart, *The Library and Picture Collection of the Port of London Authority*, London 1955, pp. 29–30
Provenance: Commercial Dock Company; Port of London Authority; on long term loan to the Museum of London since 1988

Regarded by contemporaries as a consummate study of great old age, *Captain Alexander Mitchell Sim* was one of Holl's most celebrated portraits. Sim rose from cabin boy in the navy to become a captain and, in later years, director of the Commercial Dock Company. He recorded his start in maritime life in a verse that he directed to be put on this portrait's frame:

The wind blew hard,
The sea was rough, far distant every joy
When forced by fortune to embark
I went a cabin boy.

Sim's eventful early career included being captured in the Napoleonic wars and following Nelson's body up the Thames in 1805. He held his directorship of the Commercial Dock Company from June 1847 until his death aged ninety-four on 9 January 1882. The portrait was commissioned by the company for their boardroom at a cost of 400 guineas.[101]

Unsurprisingly, given his age and connections to a distant era, Sim made a considerable impact on the Holl household when he came to sit for his portrait. Reynolds recalls him as being

hale and hearty, with a cheery laugh and a twinkling eye, and with quite an extraordinary personality ... At this great age, with a step as light and an eye almost as clear as any young man in his twenties, he used to come up from the City, where he lived ... He would have a short sitting, with a long talk after it, generally stopping to lunch, and another short sitting to follow, and then back home again.[102]

He would regale the company with stories from his life, often repeating the verse that appears on the portrait's frame. A letter from Sim to Holl suggests that the first sitting was on 22 June 1881.[103] Such was the success of the portrait that a second was commissioned by Sim's nephew. But only one sitting took place and, according to Reynolds, Sim caught a chill when driving back to the City in thick fog and died shortly afterwards. Holl attended Sim's funeral in January 1882.

The portrait was a noted critical success at the 1882 Academy. Although F.G. Stephens in the *Athenaeum* found it 'a little harsh and over-defined', he conceded that it was 'full of character, and exhibits pathos in the set lips'.[104] The *Art Journal* was less equivocal in its praise: 'In its complete

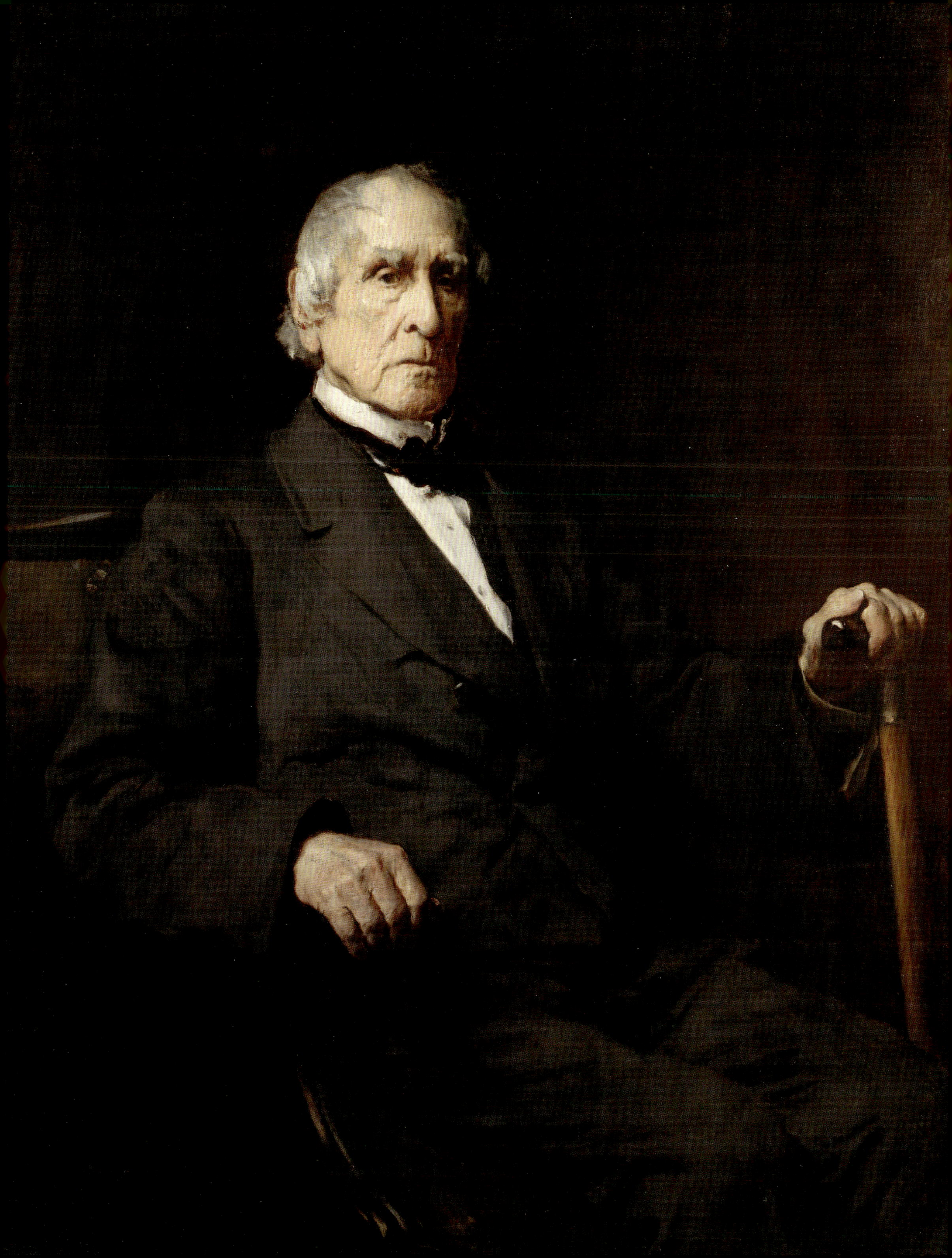

rendering of the aged face, and thin, but still upright frame, it is a masterpiece.'[105] For *The Graphic* it was 'the most striking of the artist's works' in what it considered a strong year of portraits for Holl.[106] The portrait was included in Holl's memorial exhibition in 1889 when it was singled out by Gertrude E. Campbell, also writing in the *Art Journal*, as one of Holl's great achievements. 'It would indeed be hard to find', she wrote, 'a truer or more unexaggerated rendering of a stately old gentleman', and she went on to praise 'the admirably painted' head – 'quiet, dignified, self-contained in expression' – and the way Holl has suggested Sim's defiance of old age through his upright bearing and the telling way in which 'he clutches the crutch-handled stick which has helped the old sea-dog so long to stand as erect as of yore.'[107] PF

23. *Hope*

1883
Oil on canvas, 79.7 x 110 cm
Signed and dated bottom left: 'Frank Holl 1883'
Provenance: Purchased by Southampton City Art Gallery with the assistance of the Frederick William Smith Bequest Fund, 1936
Collection: Southampton City Art Gallery

Frank Holl returned once again to the fisher cottage in Criccieth, the setting of many of his social-realist images. Holl's long-standing links with the family in Criccieth gave him the opportunity to use the same setting and space to investigate and develop his themes. This is one of his last images painted at this location.

In *Hope* the family wait in anticipation for the return of their father from a fishing trip. Reynolds notes that the coastline near Criccieth was renowned for its treacherous seas, and it was similarly commonplace for fishermen in Cullercoats to lose their lives.[108] The balance of fear and hope for the family of the fisherman is the subject of this image. The figure of the mother gazes out of the window, tightly clutching a cloth in her left hand. This small detail works as a signifier for the anxiety of the moment. The scene contains more figures than most of Holl's others set in Criccieth, with a mother figure and four children. Cumulatively, the children intensify the feeling of tension, as they gaze despondently around the room. They seem to mimic their mother's example, as they feel her fear.

The light that streams through the window draws the viewer's attention outside the building. This creates a division between the busy, almost claustrophobic interior, short of space with clothes densely hung by the fireplace and upset crockery by the window, and an exterior unknown world in which the fate of the fisherman is decided. Compositionally, this image can be closely linked with an earlier painting of 1882 by Holl called *No Tidings*. In this later version the addition of warm browns, yellows and moments of bright colour on the canvas creates a warmer and more active inner space. Arguably, this strengthens the image of nervous apprehension by creating a family scene threatened by as yet unknown external events. MM

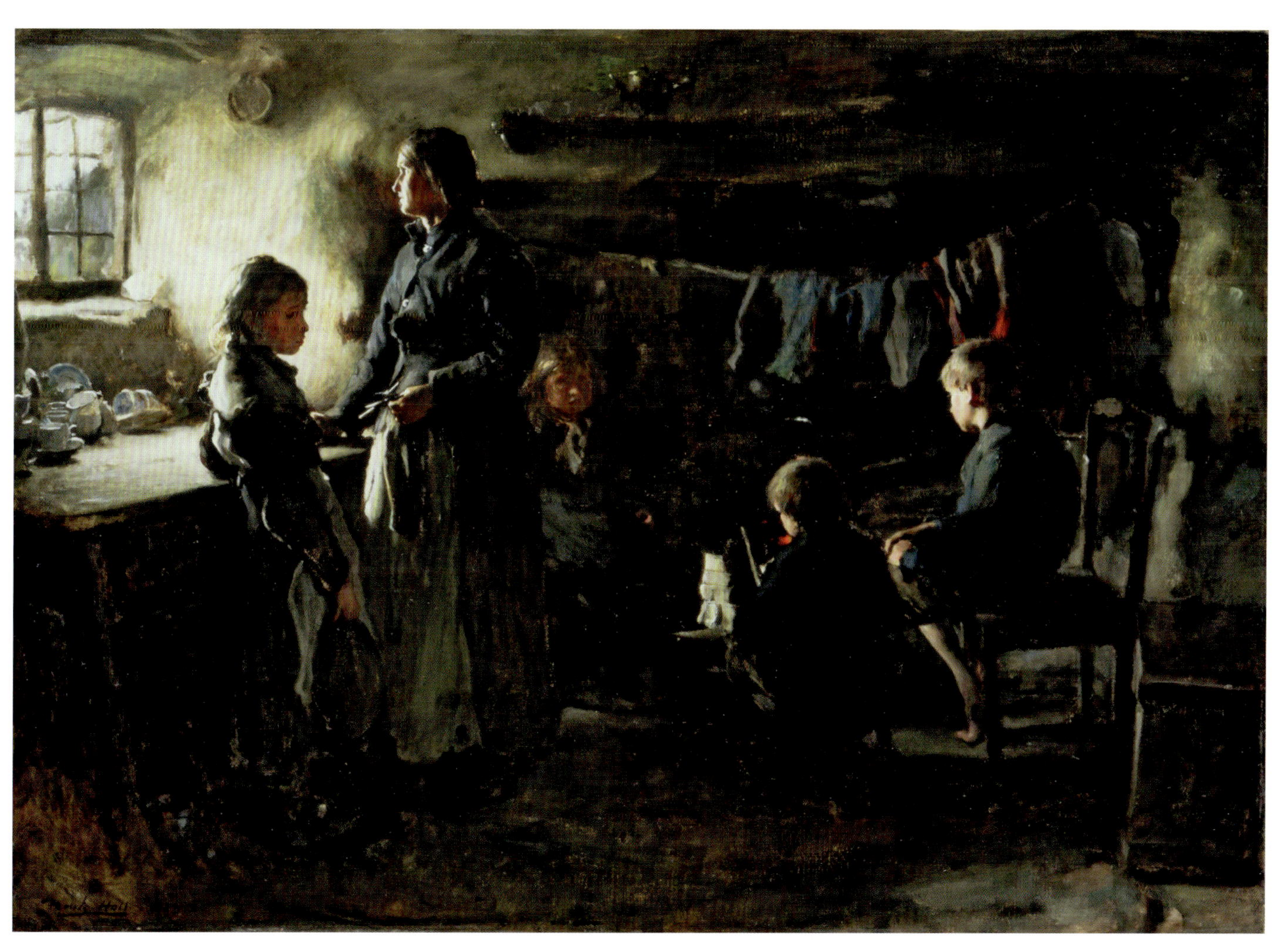

24. *Sir John Tenniel* (1820–1914)

*c.*1883
Oil on canvas, 60.3 x 47.6 cm
Exhibitions: Summer Exhibition, Grosvenor Gallery, London, 1883 (89); Royal Jubilee Exhibition, Manchester, 1887 (409); R.A. Old Masters, 1889 (187); Chicago Exhibition, British Section, 1893 (342)
Literature: Reynolds, p. 227; F. Morris, *Artist of Wonderland: The Life, Political Cartoons, and Illustrations of Tenniel*, Charlottesville, VA, 2005, p. 84
Provenance: Sir William Agnew, 1st Bt., by whom bequeathed to the National Portrait Gallery, 1911
Collection: National Portrait Gallery, London

John Tenniel, artist and cartoonist, was born in London in 1820. Fame came through his association with the magazine *Punch*, which he joined in 1850, rising to become Chief Cartoonist in 1864. It was also due to the illustrations he created for Lewis Carroll's *Alice's Adventures in Wonderland* (pub. 1865) and *Through the Looking Glass, and What Alice Found There* (1872); and his cryptic 'JT' monogram came to be the hallmark of fine wit and draughtsmanship. He was knighted by Gladstone in 1893.

Modesty was a trait, as was a quaintly conservative appearance. His dress style was fixed in the mid-century, and he maintained the bearing of a cavalryman well into old age, holding himself 'straight as a dart', while allowing his curled moustaches to trail over a stiff upright collar. The journalist Thomas Anstey Guthrie recalled him 'tall, slim, and upright, clean-shaven, except for long and drooping moustaches, quietly courteous and dignified, with a peculiarly distinguished voice'.[109] As a young man, Tenniel was blinded in his right eye in a fencing accident. Remarkably, this did not prevent him from excelling as a graphic artist, nor inhibit him from presenting his right side in two self-portraits of the 1880s and again here, when sitting for Frank Holl.

William Agnew (1825–1910), picture dealer and part-proprietor of *Punch*, was an early promoter of Holl's work, and A.M. Reynolds described him as one of her father's 'dearest friends and staunchest admirers.'[110] Agnew sat to him for a portrait that was exhibited at the Royal Academy in 1883 (Agnew's). Seemingly about this time, he commissioned a portrait of Tenniel by Holl and this portrait was also shown in 1883, at the rival venue of the Grosvenor Gallery.[111]

The 'double bill' of Tenniel and Holl provoked interest and reviews in the press. The *Art Journal* thought it 'very vigorous, but wanting in the sense of humour which twinkles in the eye and softens the mouth of the original';[112] the *Academy* commented that it was the 'most striking' of the portraits by Holl that year at the Grosvenor,[113] and the *Magazine of Art* agreed that it was the 'best', calling it 'simple and vigorous'.[114] Although often critical of Holl's work, the *Athenaeum* allowed that the portrayal was 'charged with character, and therefore extremely welcome'.[115] As Tenniel was a household name, at least until his retirement from *Punch* in 1901, the portrait was lent by Agnew to exhibitions across the country, and it travelled to Chicago in 1893.[116]

Agnew died in 1910. He bequeathed the Tenniel portrait to the National Portrait Gallery in his will and, unusually, the Trustees waived the rules to accept it without delay, an honour the aged sitter cannot have failed to appreciate. The painting entered the Gallery's collection in March 1911. Tenniel outlived Agnew, and of course Holl by many more years, dying on 25 February 1914, just three days short of his ninety-fourth birthday. CBO

25. *Francis Holl, A.R.A.* (1815–1884)

Undated [*c.*1883]
Oil on canvas, 83.8 x 71.1 cm
Exhibitions: R.A. 1884 (659); R.A. Winter 1889 (217)
Literature: *Art Journal*, 1884, p. 241; *Athenaeum*, 24 May 1884, p. 667
Provenance: The sitter; his widow; by descent to Mrs Edgar Holl, the widow of Frank Holl's younger brother; given by her and her daughter, Mrs Constance M. Baker, to the National Portrait Gallery, 1932
Collection: National Portrait Gallery, London. Given by Mrs Edgar Holl and Mrs Constance M. Baker, 1932

Holl exhibited this portrait of his father at the 1884 Royal Academy just a few months after the older man's death on 14 January 1884. Not surprisingly, critics were touched by the work, the *Art Journal* commenting that it was 'painted with dignity and pathos, and in Mr Holl's best manner' and F.G. Stephens, who could be critical of Holl, praising it highly. None of Holl's portraits that year was 'better', Stephens wrote, 'than the pathetic *Late Francis Holl, Esq., A.R.A.* (659)', since it had 'a touch of Van Dyck, with something of the true gentlemanliness of Velasquez in it'.[117]

Francis Holl was born into a family of engravers established by his father William Holl the elder (1771–1838). All four of William's sons, of whom Francis was the youngest, were apprenticed to him and practiced as engravers. Of them, Francis was the most successful, producing engravings for book as well as print publishers. He collaborated with his brother, William Holl the younger (1807–1871), on four plates after John Hayter for Finden's *Gallery of Beauty* (1841) and for twenty-five years worked on engravings of the Queen's Pictures as well as executing private plates for her and other members of the royal family. Two of his most important and popular engravings were after W.P. Frith's *Coming of Age in the Olden Time* (1854) and *The Railway Station* (1862). Frith described Holl in his *Autobiography* as 'an admirable engraver and most worthy man.'[118] Holl exhibited seventeen engravings at the Royal Academy between 1856 and 1879 and tried unsuccessfully to become an Associate Engraver in 1874. He was finally made one in January 1883, a year before his death.

A well-known amateur actor and an accomplished singer and cellist, Francis Holl comes across as an attractive personality and is remembered with affection by his granddaughter, A.M. Reynolds. 'I can see the old man now,' she writes, 'sitting at his raised desk on a high stool, burin in hand, monocle in eye, with the sloped white reflector above him, his old brown velveteen coat and large baggy trousers and skull cap, a quaint and characteristic figure.'[119] 'He was a wonderful old man', she continues, and goes on to recall how he would entertain the children by telling 'goblin tales' and, 'if he happened to be in a particularly good humour, he would wind up with a sort of fantastic dance, which he called the goblins' "shadow-dance."'[120]

Although Holl's portrait of his father is undated, the age of the sitter and date of execution suggest that it was made towards the end of his life, perhaps prompted by his final recognition by the Academy in his 1883 Associateship. Holl had earlier made a chalk portrait of him, which he exhibited at the 1868 Royal Academy (767) and which is reproduced in Reynolds.[121] PF

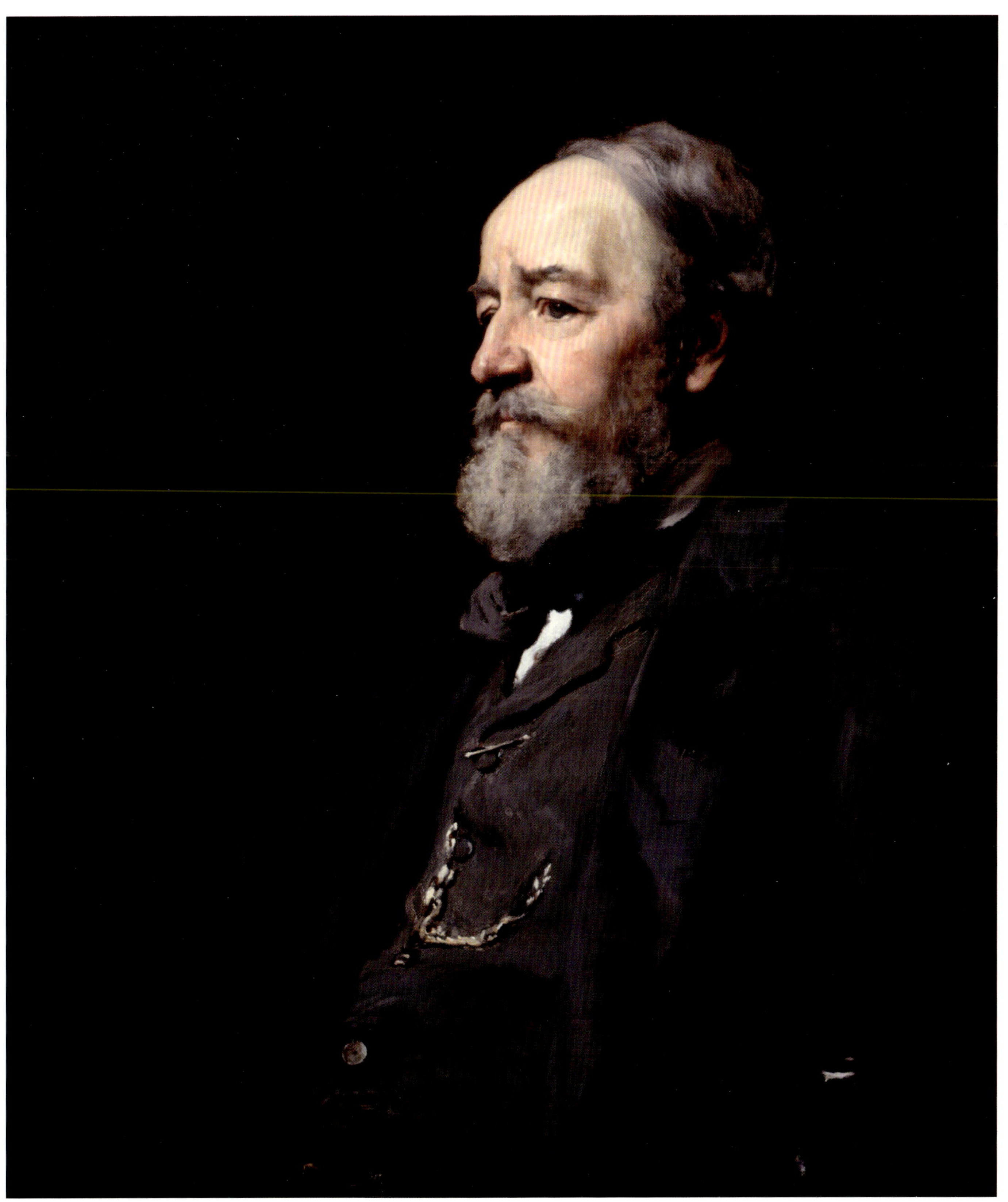

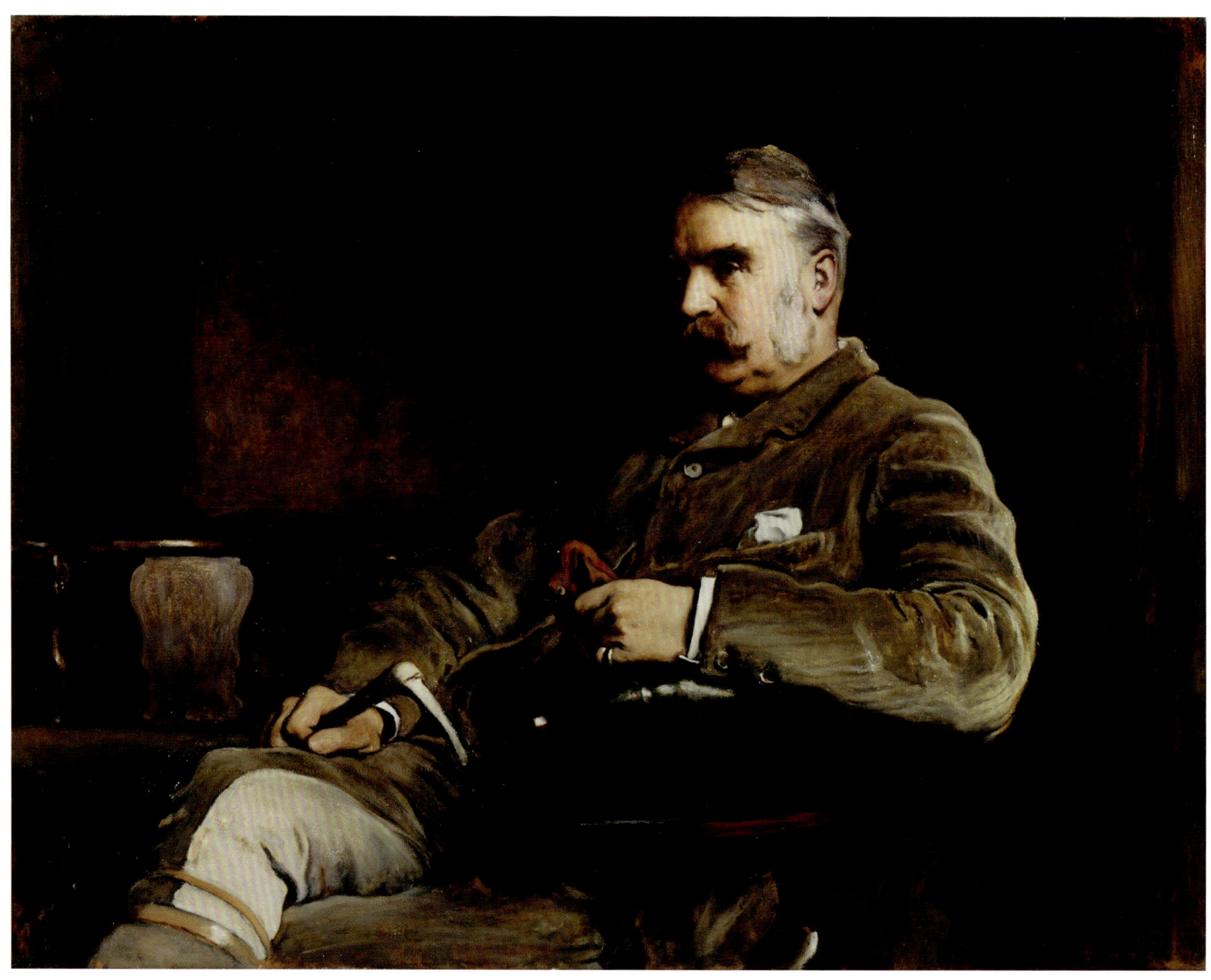

26. *Sir William Schwenck Gilbert* (1836–1911)

1886
Oil on canvas, 100.3 x 125.7 cm
Signed and dated bottom right: 'Frank Holl 1886'
Exhibitions: R.A. 1887 (300); *Victorian Era Exhibition*, London, 1897 (Music and Drama Section, 209); Centenary D'Oyly Carte Season, Riverside Promenade, Royal Festival Hall, 1975
Literature: Reynolds, p. 263
Provenance: The sitter, by whom bequeathed to the National Portrait Gallery subject to the life interest of his wife
Collection: National Portrait Gallery, London. Bequeathed by the sitter, 1937

Holl and his wife had spent time with Gilbert's father, the author and surgeon William Gilbert, in Verona during their 1869 visit to Italy. She described him as 'a most delightful conversationalist … who talked to us with much pride of his amazing son, who was just then taking his very first steps in the way to the fame which afterwards awaited him'.[122] By 1869 W.S. Gilbert had established himself as a prolific author in periodicals, in particular *Fun*, the rival to *Punch*, and had already written a number of pieces for the stage. But it was his collaboration with Arthur Sullivan and the 'Savoy' operas for which he wrote the librettos that were Gilbert's greatest successes, and he was at the height of the fame that these brought him when painted by Holl.

From Reynolds it seems clear that artist and sitter were well acquainted. She writes of childrens' parties at the Gilberts' London home in Harrington Gardens in South Kensington and recounts an anecdote of Gilbert and her mother at a dinner party. That this acquaintance made Holl the obvious choice to paint his portrait is clear from the first of a series of letters from Gilbert to Holl. On 2 November 1886 Gilbert writes that 'my wife insists that I shall have my portrait painted, & that being so, my thoughts naturally turned towards you.[123] Further letters detail arrangements for sittings, making this one of the better documented of Holl's portraits. Gilbert next wrote again on 22 November to arrange two morning sittings and raised the question of what he should be shown wearing:

> My usual writing dress would hardly do for exhibition – consisting, as it does, of a nightshirt & dressing gown – for I only write after 11. pm when everyone has gone to bed. As I am obliged to ride for two hours every day (to drive away gout) I shall generally get to Fitzjohns Avenue on a horse. Would an easy-going riding dress do? Say broad cords – with a velveteen character?[124]

It is thus that he is shown, holding a riding crop in his right hand, in an unusual landscape format. Other letters of 27 and 30 December concern times for sittings, and on 2 January 1887 Gilbert wrote with a cheque for £525 and his 'sincere thanks for having exercised your magnificent art on so unworthy a subject'.[125] The sequence ends with two letters, on 15 and 20 March 1887, concerning arrangements for the portrait to be taken from Harrington Gardens to go into that year's Royal Academy exhibition.

The portrait was bequeathed to the National Portrait Gallery by Gilbert, subject to the life interest of his wife. PF

27. *William Ewart Gladstone* (1809–1898) (ill. Page 154)

1887–8
Oil on canvas, 127 x 102 cm
Signed and dated bottom left: 'Frank Holl 1888'
Exhibitions: R.A. 1888 (499); Whitechapel Art Gallery, Winter Exhibition, 1901 (91); Palace of Arts, British Empire Exhibition, Wembley, 1925 (N23)
Literature: *Magazine of Art*, 1888, pp. 267–8; *Art Journal*, 1888, p. 218; *Athenaeum*, 23 June 1888, p. 800; Reynolds, pp. 265–6, 271–91, 299; John Steegman, *A Survey of Portraits in Welsh Houses*, Cardiff 1957, vol. 1, p. 178; Matthew 1994, pp. 22, 74–5, 108, 136; Funnell and Warner, pp. 30–1
Provenance: Presented to the sitter, 1888; by descent
Private collection

Holl's *Gladstone* is of outstanding importance in his portrait output and was among the greatest challenges of his career. 'It was into the "Gladstone" that I put all I knew and threw my whole self', he is reported to have said.[126] Four times Prime Minister, who had first held office in 1834 and only left office for the last time in 1894, Gladstone was one of the commanding political, intellectual and moral presences of the Victorian period. The pressure to successfully paint a figure of his stature was compounded by the strength of the competition. As an 1889 article on 'Mr Gladstone and his Portraits' declared, 'For thirty years past no face in England has more frequently engaged the attention of the portrait-painter than that of Mr. Gladstone.'[127] The circumstances of the portrait further demanded that it be successful, since it was commissioned on subscription by the 5th Earl Spencer (1835–1910) and other Gladstone supporters, along with a portrait by Herkomer of Gladstone's wife, to mark the couple's golden wedding anniversary. Travelling to the Gladstones' home at Hawarden to begin work on the portrait in October 1887, Holl recorded:

> I felt like a man about to walk the slack wire before the world, and I feared failure ... I had worked myself up into a state of semi-exaltation, for I had determined to paint the picture in a 'do-or-die' fashion, feeling that if I hesitated I was lost.[128]

The beginning of the project seems to have been on 2 April 1887 when, perhaps prompted by its promoters, Gladstone recorded in his *Diaries* a visit to Holl's studio. He recounts seeing 'the fine portraits at Mr Holl's'.[129] Gladstone's meticulous *Diaries*, combined with a detailed journal and letters Holl wrote describing his visit to Hawarden, make his portrait of Gladstone his best documented. Holl's journal begins with his arrival there on Saturday 29 October 1887, when he dined with Gladstone and his

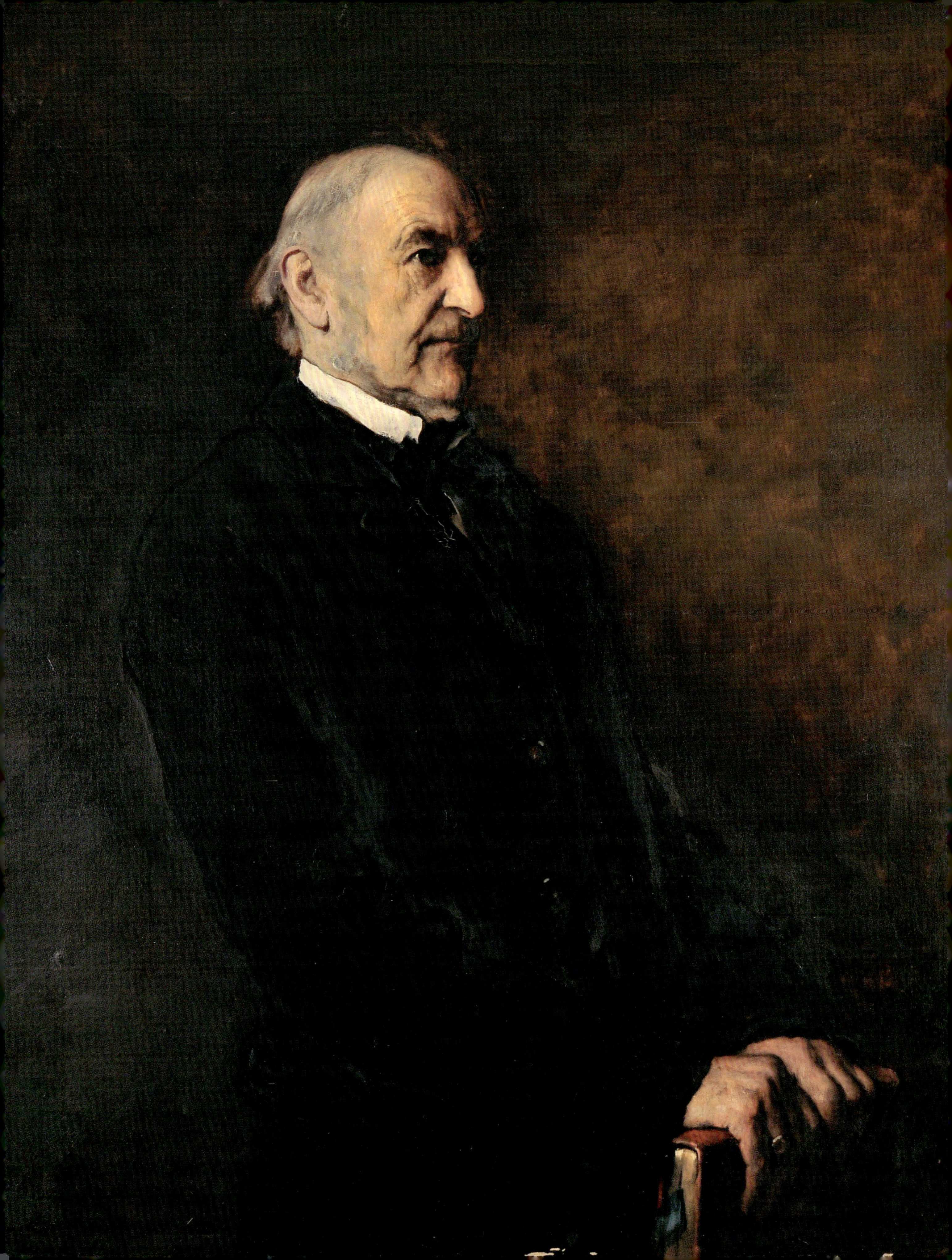

family and the following morning accompanied them to the local church. That afternoon he 'determined that the best, in fact the only good light available was in his [Gladstone's] own library' and that the portrait should be painted there.[130]

Work on the painting began on Monday 31 October, Holl deciding that Gladstone's personality meant that he should be shown in a standing, as opposed to a seated, pose (as discussed on p. 47). 'Sat to Mr Holl (or rather stood)', Gladstone recorded, 'nearly all the forenoon.'[131] Later Holl joined Gladstone and his son in the famous pastime at Hawarden of tree-felling, beginning on a large walnut tree. A further sitting, of two and a half hours according to Gladstone, took place the following morning: 'again a good sitting', Holl noted, with Gladstone agreeing to another half- hour after lunch. The next sitting took place on Wednesday 2 November, though the standing pose was evidently beginning to take its toll on the elderly man. 'Stood 2½ hours', Gladstone wrote, '(with the aid of supports) to Mr Holl, whom it is a pleasure to assist even to *extremity.*'[132] He nevertheless offered Holl another half-hour session in the afternoon, which Holl was 'glad to accept, especially as my work was proceeding well'.[133] 'Again stood 2½–3 hours,' Gladstone wrote on Thursday 3rd, 'sleep comes on in afternoon & keeps me. But I delight to render all the aid I can to a great painter.'[134] That afternoon Holl assisted Gladstone in completing the felling of the walnut tree, though he questioned in his journal the advisability of 'such hard labour at his time of life'.[135] The final Hawarden sitting, of nearly three hours, took place on Friday 4 November with Gladstone reflecting that 'the operation for me has been most exhausting: but the work is of a very high order indeed.'[136]

As work progressed on the portrait other guests arrived at Hawarden, including the grandees who had been instrumental in the commission – Lord and Lady Spencer and Lord and Lady Granville – and Holl's friend, the dealer Sir William Agnew (1825–1910). Holl's letters to his wife during his stay repeatedly refer to the 'anxiety' and 'strain' that painting the portrait had caused him and of how it had 'weighed upon me and cost me more sleepless nights than from what Mr Gladstone told me he had ever passed'.[137] But, as is evident from Gladstone's *Diaries*, he had clearly helped and encouraged Holl. 'Mr Gladstone is extremely good, in *every way* with his sittings', Holl himself wrote, conceding that his week at Hawarden was also 'one to be remembered for its pleasures'.[138] Moreover he was able to report on the Friday that 'the portrait is a great success', Agnew being in 'the most wild state of enthusiasm over it', Mrs Gladstone 'almost embracing' Holl and calling it '*Simply Magnificent*', and Gladstone himself calling it 'such a grand work'.[139]

Holl returned with the portrait on Saturday 5 November to London where it was completed, Gladstone giving him a one and three-quarter hour sitting on Saturday 24 March 1888. It can be seen on an easel in an engraving of Holl's studio that illustrated M.H. Spielmann's *Graphic* profile of Holl published in June 1888.[140] The portrait, along with Herkomer's of Mrs Gladstone, was presented to them at Spencer House on 25 July 1888, though curiously there had been a misapprehension about the date of the Gladstones' golden wedding anniversary, which was not until 25 July 1889.[141] The frame bears the 1889 date as opposed to that of the portrait's execution.

The painting was generally well received when exhibited at Holl's last, 1888, Royal Academy show, with reviewers recognizing its importance though not being completely uncritical. F.G. Stephens considered it 'perhaps the finest piece of vigorous prose in art of which the ex-Premier has been the subject' and compared it to the 'poetry' to be found in Millais's 1879 portrait. While admiring its force, Stephens nonetheless thought it over-dramatized.[142] The *Magazine of Art* was of a similar view saying that 'the painter has lavished all his knowledge and skill' on the picture, which showed 'the highest point of Mr Holl's power', but it also felt he had 'brought a little too much force into his canvas'.[143] The *Art Journal* too found it a striking portrait but criticized it for being 'somewhat coarse and brutal in colour'.[144] PF

28. *Sir Andrew Clark, Bt.* (1826–1893)

1888
Oil on canvas, 127.6 x 101.6 cm
Signed and dated bottom left: 'Frank Holl 1888'
Exhibitions: R.A. 1888 (22)
Literature: *Art Journal*, 1888, p. 181; *Magazine of Art*, 1888, p. 268; *Graphic*, 5 May 1888, p. 483; *Athenaeum*, 23 June 1888, p. 800; Reynolds, p. 270; Gordon Wolstenholme (ed.) and David Piper, *The Royal College of Physicians: Portraits*, London 1964, pp. 120–2
Provenance: The sitter; bequeathed by his widow to the Royal College of Physicians, 1922
Collection: Royal College of Physicians

Clark was London's leading practising consultant physician and had just become President of the Royal College of Physicians when Holl exhibited this portrait at the 1888 Royal Academy exhibition. Clark had studied medicine in his native Scotland before joining the Royal Navy in 1846, in which he served as a pathologist at the Haslar Royal Naval Hospital, Hampshire, until 1853 when he was appointed to the London Hospital. He was physician there from 1866 to 1886. By the 1870s he had become one of the principal society physicians in London with a busy practice conducted from his house and consulting rooms at 16 Cavendish Square.

Famous patients included Thomas Henry Huxley but, most notably, William Ewart Gladstone (cat. 27), to whom he was personal physician from about 1868. Colin Matthew, in his *Oxford Dictionary of National Biography* entry, has emphasized how Clark 'soon played an important part in the prime minister's life'.[145] Gladstone, Matthew tells us, was quite often incapacitated by the strains of office and it was Clark's job to see him through bouts of illness at times of political crisis. Equally, the Gladstone connection was advantageous to Clark's practice and he was made a baronet by him in 1883. Clark played an active role in medical politics in the later years of his life, though his performance at meetings also gave him a reputation for garrulousness. As a personal physician, however, he was regarded as tolerant and hard working with an ability to explain illnesses to his patients precisely and effectively. His *Times* obituary praised him for 'rendering the unfamiliar intelligible by the lucidity of his words; insomuch that a consultation with him even over the simplest case, was an intellectual treat to which all looked forward in pleasure' (see also p. 45).[146]

The portrait was a private commission and was bequeathed to the Royal College of Physicians by Clark's widow in 1922. It received praise as part of Holl's strong submission to his final Royal Academy summer exhibition, which also included his portrait of Gladstone. Indeed, in the view of *The Graphic* there was a danger that it was overshadowed by such works.[147] Nonetheless, the *Art Journal* praised it as an example of 'robust and natural portraiture' and the *Athenaeum* thought it to be 'painted with firmness and mastery'.[148] PF

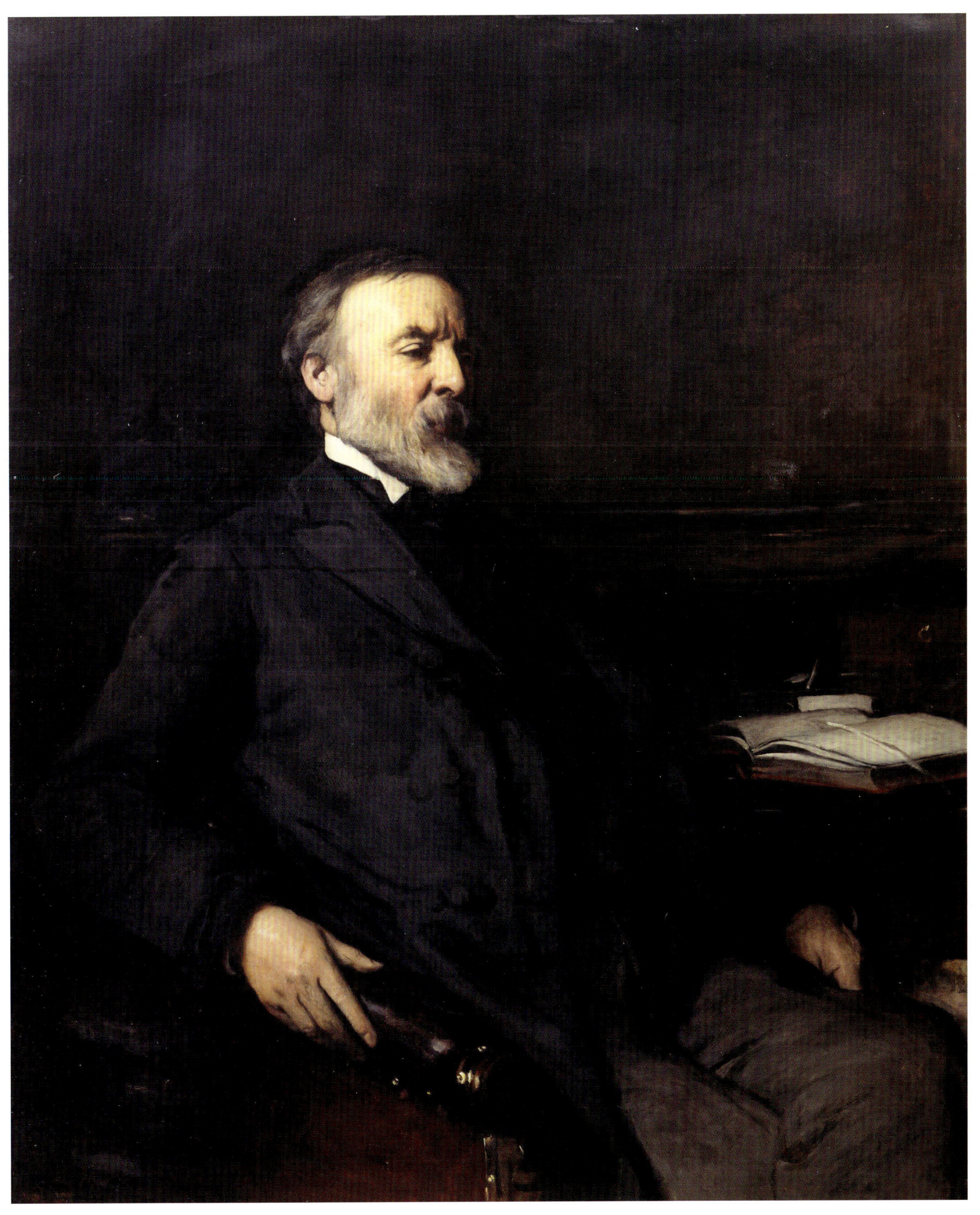

Catalogue Notes

[1] Reynolds, p. 18.

[2] 'Holl first exhibited at the Royal Academy in 1864, when he sent "Turned out of Church" and a portrait of himself' (G. Aitchison, 'Holl, Francis Montague (1845–1888)', *Dictionary of National Biography*, London 1891, p. 135).

[3] Reynolds, pp. 22–3.

[4] See the inscription on the back of the stretcher, lower bar: 'Painted in the year 1863'. In the twentieth century and until 2006 the inscription was read as 'Painted in August 1863'.

[5] Address to Sutton Coldfield Art Classes, 14 January 1888, cited Reynolds, pp. 335–6.

[6] Ellen Holl offered two other portraits in 1932: see *Francis Holl* (cat. 25) and *Paul Falconer Poole* (cat. 16).

[7] The portrait has been displayed at Bodelwyddan Castle, Denbighshire, since 1988.

[8] Previous version of 1866 signed and dated 'F.H. 6/66'.

[9] Reynolds, p. 28.

[10] Reynolds, pp. 34–5, sold to Messrs Agnew.

[11] *Art Journal*, 1867, p. 143.

[12] *Athenaeum*, 25 May 1867, p. 697.

[13] *Art Journal*, 1867, p. 143.

[14] Reynolds, p. 45.

[15] Dinah Maria Craik, *The Head of the Family*, 3 vols, London 1852, vol. 1, pp. 12–13.

[16] *The Times*, 18 June 1869, p. 694.

[17] Reynolds, p. 46.

[18] *Illustrated London News*, 22 May 1869, p. 527.

[19] *Athenaeum*, 15 May 1869, p. 675.

[20] Professor Weir quoted in Meynell 1880, p. 190.

[21] Reynolds, pp. 83–4.

[22] Reynolds, p. 84.

[23] Ibid.

[24] Millar 1992, p. 122.

[25] Reynolds, p. 85.

[26] *Athenaeum*, 10 June 1871, p. 726.

[27] *Art Journal*, 1879, p. 16.

[28] Reynolds, p. 315.

[29] T.J. Edelstein, 'They sang the "Song of the Shirt": The Visual Iconology of the Seamstress', *Victorian Studies*, 23 (1980), pp. 183–210.

[30] Henry Hill sale in 1889 and the Glasgow International Exhibition of 1901 (181A).

[31] Reynolds, p. 23.

[32] Reynolds, p. 133.

[33] Reynolds, pp. 128–9.

[34] Reynolds, p. 261.

[35] Reynolds, pp. 128–9.

[36] *Graphic*, 20 May 1876; *Illustrated London News*, 13 May 1876, p. 475; *Art Journal*, 1876, p. 261; *Hard Times*, pp. 79–80.

[37] *Illustrated London News*, 13 May 1876, p. 475.

[38] Reynolds, pp. 128–9.

[39] *Magazine of Art*, 1882, p. 3.

[40] *Illustrated London News*, 13 May 1876, p. 475.

[41] *Graphic*, 20 May 1876, p. 491.

[42] *Magazine of Art*, 1882.

[43] Treuherz 1987, pp. 79–80.

[44] *Graphic*, 20 May 1876, p. 491.

[45] Treuherz 1987, p. 147.

[46] Ibid.

[47] *Art Journal*, 1878, p. 54.

[48] *Art Journal*, 1893, pp. 197–8.

[49] *Art Journal*, 1878, p. 54.

[50] *Athenaeum*, 1 December 1877, p. 705.

[51] *Art Journal*, 1893, p. 197.

[52] Treuherz 1987, p. 147.

[53] *Art Journal*, 1878, p. 54.

[54] Reynolds, pp. 146–7.

[55] Treuherz 1987, p. 147.

[56] *Graphic*, 19 February 1876, p. 176.

[57] Vincent van Gogh, Letter 311, 'To Anthon van Rappard. The Hague, on or about Saturday, 10 February 1883'.

[58] *Morning Post*, 9 November 1877, p. 3.

[59] Ibid.

[60] *Graphic*, 19 February 1876, p. 176.

[61] This version was also painted for Tooth and is not a preliminary sketch but painted after the prime version: 'My father also agreed to paint for them a sketch of the same picture, for which he was to receive £50, the copyright being sold to them for £50' (Reynolds, p. 148).

[62] *Graphic*, 10 November 1877, p. 447.

[63] *Era*, 18 November, 1877, p. 3.
[64] Charles Edward Johnson, quoted in Reynolds, pp. 145–6.
[65] Holl to Carey, 1 September 1887, Royal Holloway Archive, quoted in Chapel 1982, p. 96.
[66] Reynolds, pp. 144–5.
[67] Reynolds, p. 145.
[68] *Illustrated London News*, 1878 p. 459.
[69] *Examiner*, 4 May 1878, p. 568.
[70] Reynolds, p. 75.
[71] Martin Hardie, *John Pettie R.A., H.R.S.A*, London 1908, pp. 158 ff.
[72] Reynolds, p. 155; Spielmann 1888a, p. 693.
[73] Reynolds, p. 157.
[74] Whitman 1904, p. 129.
[75] *Art Journal*, 1879, p. 128, 1882, p. 93.
[76] *Athenaeum*, 7 June 1879, p. 734.
[77] Reynolds, p. 158–9.
[78] Meynell 1880, p. 190.
[79] *The Times*, 1 August 1888, p. 10; Campbell 1889, p. 57.
[80] Ormond 1973, p. 118.
[81] Whitman 1904, p. 26.
[82] Henry Blackburn, ed., *Academy Notes*, London 1879, p. 25.
[83] See Edward Higgs, 'Graham, George (1801–1888), *Oxford Dictionary of National Biography*, Oxford 2004.
[84] Reynolds, p. 174.
[85] *Newcastle Courant*, 23 December 1887.
[86] *Graphic*, 22 May 1880, p. 518.
[87] Muriel Nissel, *People Count: A History of the General Register Office*, London 1987, p. 39.
[88] Government Art Collection records.
[89] Frank Holl, *Home Again*, 1881 (50 x 40 in/127 x 101.6 cm), is in the National Gallery of Victoria, Melbourne. A study for this, *c.*1881 (16¾ x 13¼ in /42.5 x 33.7 cm), is in a private collection.
[90] *Graphic*, 11 January 1879, pp. 32–3, 36 (article).
[91] *Era*, 9 May 1880, p. 3.
[92] *Graphic*, 11 January 1879, p. 36.
[93] Van Gogh admired the print and sent one as a gift to Anthon van Rappard. See Letter 275, 'To Anthon van Rappard. The Hague, between about Tuesday, 24 and about Friday, 27 October 1882.'
[94] William Gilbert, *The Royal Cornwall Gazette Falmouth Packet, Cornish Weekly News, & General Advertiser*, 4 June 1880, p. 6.
[95] *Magazine of Art*, 1881, p. xxvi; Treuherz 1987, p. 147.
[96] Reynolds, p. 191.
[97] Ibid.
[98] *Magazine of Art*, 1881, p. xxvi.
[99] *Graphic*, 29 April 1882, pp. 436–7.
[100] *Athenaeum*, 5 November 1881, p. 603; *Art Journal*, 1881, p. 377.
[101] Bertram Stuart, *The Library and Picture Collection of the Port of London Authority*, London 1955, p. 29.
[102] Reynolds, pp. 193–4.
[103] Reynolds, p. 196.
[104] *Athenaeum*, 3 June 1882, p. 705.
[105] *Art Journal*, 1882, p. 210.
[106] *Graphic*, 27 May 1882, p. 527.
[107] Campbell 1889, p. 58.
[108] Reynolds, p. 84.
[109] F. Anstey, *A Long Retrospect*, London 1936, p. 59.
[110] Reynolds, p. 226.
[111] There is evidence of a second portrait by Holl though this is presently untraced. See the letter from John Tenniel to the dealer Ernest G. Brown, Maida Vale, undated but *c.*1906–7, concerning two portraits of himself by Frank Holl, both commissioned by Sir William Agnew, the first of which, full face, Tenniel thinks must be the one that Brown has acquired and that was in the possession of Mrs Tom Agnew. Letter in the collection of Roy Davids, 30 November 2012: see www.roydavids.com/details.asp?item=82
[112] *Art Journal*, 1883, p. 203.
[113] *Academy*, 5 May 1883, p. 316.
[114] *Magazine of Art*, 1883, p. 352.
[115] *Athenaeum*, 12 May 1883, pp. 608–9.
[116] It remained of interest: see the application by H. Allan (copyist or student) to copy this portrait, 8 October–21 December 1921, NPG Register of applications to copy portraits, NPG 77/5.
[117] *Art Journal*, 1884, p. 241; *Athenaeum*, 24 May 1884, p. 667.
[118] W.P. Frith, *My Autobiography and Reminiscences*, London 1887, vol. 1, p. 219.

[119] Reynolds, p. 2.
[120] Reynolds, p. 4.
[121] Reynolds, facing p. 72.
[122] Reynolds, p. 66.
[123] W.S. Gilbert to Frank Holl, 2 November 1886, copy of manuscript letter in National Portrait Gallery Archive, London.
[124] W.S. Gilbert to Frank Holl, 22 November 1886, copy of manuscript letter in National Portrait Gallery Archive, London. This is also quoted by Reynolds (p. 263), who evidently had the letter when she was writing her father's biography.
[125] W.S. Gilbert to Frank Holl, 2 January 1887, National Portrait Gallery Archive, London.
[126] Reynolds, p. 271.
[127] Wemyss Reid 1889, p. 82.
[128] Reynolds, pp. 271–2.
[129] Matthew 1994, p. 22.
[130] Reynolds, p. 277.
[131] Matthew 1994, p. 74.
[132] Matthew 1994, p. 75.
[133] Reynolds, p. 282.
[134] Matthew 1994, p. 75.
[135] Reynolds, p. 283.
[136] Matthew 1994, p. 75.
[137] Reynolds, p. 284.
[138] Reynolds, pp. 287, 289.
[139] Reynolds, pp. 289–90.
[140] Spielmann 1888a, p. 693.
[141] Matthew 1994, p. 136. Matthew records that there were 116 subscribers to the two portraits.
[142] *Athenaeum*, 23 June 1888, p. 800.
[143] *Magazine of Art*, 1888, pp. 267–8.
[144] *Art Journal*, 1888, p. 218.
[145] H.C.G. Matthew, 'Clark, Sir Andrew, first baronet (1826–1893)', *Oxford Dictionary of National Biography*, Oxford 2004.
[146] *The Times*, 7 November 1893, p. 5.
[147] *Graphic*, 1888, p. 483.
[148] *Art Journal*, 1888, p. 181; *Athenaeum*, 23 June 1888, p. 800.

References

Anon. 1888a
Anon., 'By one who knew him, "Personal Reminiscences of the Late Mr. Frank Holl, R.A. –I"', *Pall Mall Gazette*, 1 Aug. 1888a, p. 8

Anon. 1888b
Anon., 'By one who knew him, 'Personal Reminiscences of the Late Mr. Frank Holl, R.A. –II"', *Pall Mall Gazette*, 2 Aug. 1888b, p. 6

Bills 1998
Mark Bills, *Edwin Longsden Long, R.A.*, London 1998

Campbell 1889
Gertrude E. Campbell, 'Frank Holl and his Works', *Art Journal*, 1889, pp. 53–9

Chapel 1982
Jeannie Chapel, *Victorian Taste*, Egham 1982

Funnell and Warner 1999
Peter Funnell and Malcolm Warner, *Millais: Portraits*, London 1999

Garrard and Parrott 1998
John Garrard and Vivienne Parrott, 'Craft, Professional and Middle-Class Identity: Solicitors and Gas Engineers, *c.*1850–1914', in Alan Kidd and David Nicholls, eds, *The Making of the British Middle Class: Studies of Regional and Cultural Diversity since the Eighteenth Century*, Stroud 1998

Goodall 1902
Frederick Goodall, *The Reminiscences of Frederick Goodall*, London and Newcastle, 1902

Hardy 2012
Pat Hardy, 'Dickens and the Social Realists', in Mark Bills, ed., *Dickens and the Artists*, New Haven and London 2012

McEvansoneya 1998
Philip Daniel McEvansoneya, '"I am the Resurrection and the Life": Frank Holl and Victorian Images of Death', *Leeds Museums and Galleries Review*, No. 1, 1998, pp. 8–13

Mandler 2006
Peter Mandler, *The English National Character: The History of an Idea from Edmund Burke to Tony Blair*, New Haven and London 2006

Matthew 1994
H.C.G. Matthew, ed., *The Gladstone Diaries*, Oxford 1994, vol. 12

Meynell 1880
Wilfred Meynell, 'Our Living Artists. Frank Holl, A.R.A.', *Magazine of Art*, 1880, pp. 187–91

Millar 1992
Oliver Millar, *The Victorian Pictures in the Collection of Her Majesty The Queen*, 2 vols, Cambridge 1992

Ormond 1973
Richard Ormond, *Early Victorian Portraits*, 2 vols, London 1973, vol. 1

Quilter 1888
Harry Quilter, 'Frank Holl: In Memoriam', *Universal Review*, August 1888, pp. 478–93

Reynolds
A.M. Reynolds, *The Life and Work of Frank Holl*, London 1912

Saint 2010
Andrew Saint, *Richard Norman Shaw*, New Haven and London 2010 (2nd edn)

Spielmann 1888a
M.H. Spielmann, 'Painters in their Studios IV. – Mr. Frank Holl, R.A.', *The Graphic*, 30 June 1888a, pp. 692–4

Spielmann 1888b
M.H. Spielmann, 'The Late Frank Holl, R.A.', *Magazine of Art*, 1888b, pp. 412–13

Temple 1918
Sir Alfred George Temple, *Guildhall Memories*, London 1918

Thane 2000
Pat Thane, *Old Age in English History: Past Experiences, Present Issues*, Oxford 2000

Treuherz 1987
Julian Treuherz, *Hard Times: Social Realism in Victorian Art*, London 1987

Vincent van Gogh
Letters of Vincent van Gogh: vangoghletters.org

Walkley 1994
Giles Walkley, *Artists' Houses in London 1764–1914*, Aldershot 1994

Wemyss Reid 1889
T. Wemyss Reid, 'Mr Gladstone and his Portraits', *Magazine of Art*, 1889

Whitman 1904
Alfred Whitman, *Samuel Cousins*, London 1904

Zimmern 1885
Helen Zimmern, 'Artists' Homes: Mr. Frank Holl's, in Fitzjohn's Avenue, *Magazine of Art*, 1885, pp. 144–50

Contributors

Mark Bills is Director of Gainsborough House, and was Curator of Watts Gallery 2005–2012. Prior to that he was Senior Curator of Paintings, Print and Drawings, Museum of London, and Visual Arts Officer at the Russell-Cotes Art Gallery and Museum. He has written widely including *An Artists' Village: G.F. Watts and Mary Watts at Compton* (editor and author, PWP, 2011), *G.F. Watts Victorian Visionary: Highlights from the Watts Gallery Collection* (2008), *The Art of Satire: London in Caricature* (PWP, 2006), and *William Powell Frith* (co-editor and author, 2006), as well as *Art in the Age of Queen Victoria: A Wealth of Depictions* (editor and author, 2001) and *A Victorian Salon* (editor and author, 1999). He has written numerous articles on eighteenth- and nineteenth-century British art for books and publications including *London: The Illustrated History*, *Burlington Magazine*, *Apollo* and *Print Quarterly*.

Peter Funnell is Curator of Nineteenth-Century Portraits and Head of Research Programmes at the National Portrait Gallery, London. Since joining the NPG in 1990 he has curated many exhibitions and led major projects ranging from the redevelopment of the Gallery's first-floor displays to directing the research of 10,000 portrait illustrations for the *Oxford Dictionary of National Biography* of which he is a Consultant Editor.

Barbara Bryant is an art historian, writer, and consultant specializing in the work of G.F. Watts. She wrote the exhibition catalogue *G.F. Watts Portraits: Fame & Beauty in Victorian Society* (2004) and *G.F. Watts Victorian Visionary: Highlights from the Watts Gallery Collection* (co-editor and author, 2008). She was a major contributor to the exhibition *The Age of Rossetti, Burne-Jones & Watts: Symbolism in Britain 1860–1910* at Tate Britain in 1997, and she is the author of the forthcoming Oxford Dictionary of National Biography's entry on Watts, as well as other articles and essays on the artist and on eighteenth- and nineteenth-century British art.

Jane Sellars is Curator of Art at the Mercer Art Gallery, Harrogate, and was formerly Education Officer at National Museums Liverpool and Director of the Brontë Parsonage Museum. She has written widely about women and art and is author of several books on the Brontës, including *The Art of the Brontës*, (with Christine Alexander, 1995), and *Writers' Lives: Charlotte Brontë* (1997). For *William Powell Frith: Painting the Victorian Age* (2007) she looked at the role of women in Frith's personal and professional lives. Jane Sellars was the main contributor and editor for *Atkinson Grimshaw: Painter of Moonlight* (2011), published by Harrogate Borough Council to accompany the award winning exhibition of the same name.

Sophie Gilmartin is Reader in Nineteenth-Century Literature at Royal Holloway, University of London. She has written on blood relations and nation in *Ancestry and Narrative in Nineteenth-Century British Literature* (CUP), and co-authored with Rod Mengham the book *Thomas Hardy's Shorter Fiction: A Study* (EUP). She lectures widely on Victorian literature, and has a special interest in Victorian painting. Currently she is writing a book on Cape Horn, women and navigation.

Mary McMahon is Curatorial Fellow at Watts Gallery. She has an MA in Design History from the Royal College of Art, and a BA in Art History from University College London. She has spent two and a half years studying at the V&A, one and a half working at the National Art Library and completed internships at the National Portrait Gallery and the V&A.

Philip McEvansoneya is Lecturer in the History of Painting at Trinity College, Dublin. His research interests are in aspects of the history of art in Ireland and Britain with particular reference to the history of collections and the history of institutions. His PhD concerned the work of Frank Holl and Luke Fildes. He has published widely including articles in *Burlington Magazine* and *Journal of the History of Collections*.

Carol Blackett-Ord is a researcher at the National Portrait Gallery, and has worked on Frank Holl's iconography for the gallery's online catalogue of Later Victorian Portraits. She is researching the life of M.H. Spielmann (1858–1948), critic, biographer and editor of the *Magazine of Art*.

Index

Notes:
1. All references are to Frank Holl unless otherwise specified
2. Paintings without attribution are by Frank Holl
3. **Emboldened entries** indicate extents of essays
4. Italicised references are to illustrations, paintings, or titles of books, journals etc